CITIES AND LABOUR IMMIGRATION

Research in Migration and Ethnic Relations Series

Series Editor:
Maykel Verkuyten, ERCOMER
Utrecht University

The Research in Migration and Ethnic Relations series has been at the forefront of research in the field for ten years. The series has built an international reputation for cutting edge theoretical work, for comparative research especially on Europe and for nationally-based studies with broader relevance to international issues. Published in association with the European Research Centre on Migration and Ethnic Relations (ERCOMER), Utrecht University, it draws contributions from the best international scholars in the field, offering an interdisciplinary perspective on some of the key issues of the contemporary world.

Other titles in the series

Moving Lives
Kathy Burrell
ISBN 0 7546 4574 6

Globalizing Migration Regimes
Edited by Kristof Tamas and Joakim Palme
ISBN 0 7546 4692 0

Migration, Regional Integration and Human Security: The Formation and Maintenance of Transnational Spaces
Edited by Harald Kleinschmidt
ISBN 0 7546 4646 7

Cities and Labour Immigration
Comparing Policy Responses in Amsterdam, Paris, Rome and Tel Aviv

MICHAEL ALEXANDER
University of Haifa, Israel

Routledge
Taylor & Francis Group

LONDON AND NEW YORK

First published 2007 by Ashgate Publishing

Reissued 2018 by Routledge
2 Park Square, Milton Park, Abingdon, Oxon OX14 4RN
605 Third Avenue, New York, NY 10017

First issued in paperback 2021

Routledge is an imprint of the Taylor & Francis Group, an informa business

© Michael Alexander 2007

Michael Alexander has asserted his moral right under the Copyright, Designs and Patents Act, 1988, to be identified as the author of this work.

All rights reserved. No part of this book may be reprinted or reproduced or utilised in any form or by any electronic, mechanical, or other means, now known or hereafter invented, including photocopying and recording, or in any information storage or retrieval system, without permission in writing from the publishers.

A Library of Congress record exists under LC control number: 2006007243

Notice:
Product or corporate names may be trademarks or registered trademarks, and are used only for identification and explanation without intent to infringe.

Publisher's Note
The publisher has gone to great lengths to ensure the quality of this reprint but points out that some imperfections in the original copies may be apparent.

Disclaimer
The publisher has made every effort to trace copyright holders and welcomes correspondence from those they have been unable to contact.

ISBN 13: 978-0-815-38805-0 (hbk)
ISBN 13: 978-1-351-16172-5 (ebk)
ISBN 13: 978-1-138-35668-9 (pbk)

DOI: 10.4324/9781351161725

Contents

List of Figures		*vii*
List of Tables and Boxes		*ix*
Preface		*xi*

1 Strangers at the City Gates — 1
  1 Labour Immigration and Local Policy Responses — 1
  2 The Gap in Existing Theory — 7
  3 A Theoretical Framework for Understanding Local Policies toward Migrants — 12

2 Host-Stranger Relations in Theory and Practice — 25
  1 Different Types of Strangers, Different Host-Stranger Relations — 25
  2 Modern and Postmodern Attitudes toward Strangers — 27
  3 Linking Host-Stranger Relations and Local Policies toward Labour Migrants — 32

3 Local Policies Toward Migrants – a Typology — 37
  1 Defining 'Local Policies toward Migrants' — 37
  2 The Typology — 40

4 Rome: From Non-Policy to Delegation — 55
  1 Introduction — 55
  2 The National Context: Italian Responses to Labour Immigration — 56
  3 The Local Context — 59
  4 Local Migrant Policies in Rome — 67
  5 Summary: From Ignoring to NGO-ing? — 80

5 Tel Aviv: The Limits of Liberalism in a Guestworker Regime — 83
  1 Introduction — 83
  2 The National Context — 84
  3 The Local Context — 89
  4 Local Migrant Policies in Tel Aviv — 96
  5 Summary: 'As Long As They Are Here …' — 109

6 Paris: A Century of Assimilation — 115
  1 Introduction — 115
  2 The National Context — 116
  3 The Local Context — 121
  4 Urban Policy in Paris: 150 Years of Distancing the Other — 130

		5 Other Policy Domains	141
		6 The New Integration Policy, 2001 – ...	144
		7 Summary: '*Plus ça change, plus c'est la même chose*'?	149
7	**Amsterdam: Pluralism and its Discontents**		**153**
	1	Introduction	153
	2	The National Context	154
	3	The Local Context	165
	4	Migrant Policies in Amsterdam	172
	5	Summary	193
8	**Summary and Conclusions**		**197**
	1	Introduction	197
	2	Summarizing the Case Studies	198
	3	Comparison and Generalization	203
	4	Rethinking the Typology: A New Policy Phase?	209
	5	Implications for Research and Policy	214

Appendix: List of Interviews   *217*
Bibliography   *221*
Index   *235*

List of Figures

1.1	The analytical framework	14
1.2	City Halls of Amsterdam, Paris, Rome and Tel Aviv	21
2.1	Host-stranger relations as expressed in local authority attitudes toward labour migrants	35
4.1	Registered foreign residents in Rome, 1991–2004	61
4.2	Registered foreign residents in Rome, by content of origin (31 December 2004)	61
4.3	Distribution of registered foreign residents in Rome, by districts (2004)	63
5.1	Development of the secondary labour market in Israel, 1956–99	87
5.2	Population of Tel Aviv-Yafo, with estimated labour migrant population	90
5.3	Estimated labour migrant population in Tel Aviv, by continent of origin, 2001	91
5.4	Labour migrant concentrations in Tel Aviv-Yafo, 1999	94
6.1	Immigration to Paris and France, 1861-1990 (% foreign resident population)	121
6.2	Foreign resident population in Paris, 1954–99	123
6.3	Foreign resident population in Paris, by country of origin, 1999	124
6.4	The croissant populaire: working class quarters in east Paris, 1990	125
6.5	The *embourgeoisement* of Paris and its suburbs, 1982–90	126
6.6	Distribution of foreign population in Paris, 1975–99	128
6.7	Planned renovation areas in Paris, 1938 and 1987	133
7.1	Population of Amsterdam and 'ethnic minorities', 1947-2004	166
7.2	Resident population in Amsterdam, by country of origin (numbers)	167
7.3	Resident population in Amsterdam, by country of origin (%)	167
7.4	Amsterdam, city districts	170
7.5	Geographical distribution of migrant/minority population in Amsterdam	170

List of Tables and Boxes

Table 1.1	Migrants/ethnic minorities in survey cities	3
Table 1.2	The case study cities	19
Box 1.1	Four city halls, four styles of governance	22
Table 3.1	A typology space for classifying local migrant policies in terms of local authority attitudes and expectations	42
Table 3.2	Typology of local migrant policies, by domains and issue areas	43
Box 4.1	The Esquilino: Rome's 'multiethnic quarter'	64
Box 5.1	Neve Sha'anan: the 'foreign workers neighbourhood' of Israel	93
Box 6.1	Policies toward Algerians in Paris: the 'second front'	120
Box 6.2	Bringing order to the 'eastern crescent'	138
Box 6.3	The Goutte d'Or: the politics of renovation in a migrant neighbourhood	140
Box 7.1	The Bijlmer: Amsterdam's ethnic district	171
Box 7.2	The Aya Sofya Mosque conflict	184
Box 7.3	From a 'black school' to a 'Community School' in the Pijp	190
Box 7.4	'Links in the chain' of the inburgering process	192
Table 8.1	Revised typology of local policies toward migrants/minorities	211

Preface

In 1996 I was asked to prepare policy proposals on 'what we should do with the foreign worker problem' in Tel Aviv. During the time I worked in the Planning Division we began to realize that Tel Aviv had become home to tens of thousands of overseas labour immigrants (mostly undocumented, no one knew just how many). I began to suspect that Tel Aviv was passing through a phase that the 'veteran immigration' cities in Europe had undergone decades earlier. Might our 'new immigration' city learn a lesson from the European experience?

Clearly, local authorities in different countries have responded very differently to labour immigration, with very different results. Yet there also appear to be underlying similarities in their reactions over time, as the 'guestworkers' became permanent new minorities in city after city. Furthermore, the policy responses of municipal planners, administrators and politicians appear to reflect implicit, even unconscious, attitudes and expectations in the host society toward these newcomers, and toward strangers in general. Rather than comparing local policies in terms of 'how to respond to the arrival and settlement of labour migrants' (a 'best practices' approach), this book compares local responses to labour immigration as an expression of host-stranger relations. Following the theoretical writings of Georg Simmel, David Sibley and others, and especially Zygmunt Bauman, it sets out to uncover what Foucault called the 'hidden structures of knowledge' underlying the visible policy responses.

Nonetheless, this project was grounded from the start in personal experience and empirical research. My view from the municipal planner's desk was followed by a brief stint as a street-level bureaucrat, when I participated in the start-up of Tel Aviv's first municipal 'Aid and Information Center' for labour migrants, bringing me into contact with the foreign workers and their families on a daily basis. The empirical research for this book included a broad survey of local migrant policies, followed by four case studies carried out between 2000–2003 in Europe and Israel.

The survey owes much to the research network 'Multicultural Policies and Modes of Citizenship in European cities' (MPMC). Here I wish to thank my fellow MPMC researchers for sharing their findings and particularly Hassan Bousetta and Marco Martiniello for their later feedback. The case studies were made possible by generous funding provided by the University of Amsterdam's Study Centre for the Metropolitan Environment (AME), which served as my European base. I am especially grateful to both Sako Musterd at AME (then heading the Department of Geography and Planning) and Rinus Penninx, then MPMC coordinator and director of the Institute of Migration and Ethnic Studies (IMES), for their guidance, patience and support throughout.

In the period spent on this project I experienced (again) what Simmel described as the 'simultaneous nearness and distance' of the Stranger. In my wanderings between Amsterdam, Rome, Tel Aviv, Marseille and Paris, I was helped, hosted and housed by dozens of people who made it all an unforgettable experience.

In AMSTERDAM – Valuable commentary on the Amsterdam case study was provided by Leo de Klerk, Peter Terhorst, Virginie Mamadouh and others at the AME and by Jan Rath, Anja Heelsum, Jeroen Doomernik and others at IMES. Bedankt to AME's helpful staff and my trusty office-mate Martijn Arnoldus! Thanks also to Boris Slijper, Marcel Maussen, Floris Vermeulen and Maria Berger for their collegial feedback. Among those who made me feel *'t'huis'* away from home, special thanks to Yvon and Erik, and to Ines, Monica, Nadav, Ellen and Wieke, my companions in the magical city. Barbara Da Roit provided crucial help in the graphics and editing, feedback on the Rome case, and so much more.

In ROME – Marco Accorinti at Caritas di Roma's Centro Stranieri, and Franco Pittau and Antonio Ricci at Caritas' research department, were outstandingly helpful and provided invaluable information on the situation in Rome. Cinzia Conti at the Universita La Sapienza was similarly generous in responding to my repeated requests. The officials that I interviewed in the municipality of Rome, especially Claudio Rossi at the Ufficio Speciale Immigrazione, were without exception gracious and forthcoming. *Grazie mille* to Jonathan and Giovanna and to Filippo Rinaldi, *un vero Romano*, for his gracious hospitality and great cooking!

In MARSEILLE – I spent two weeks of intensive research during which I gained valuable insights from that city's exceptionally friendly research community, before transferring the case study to Paris. To my friend Alain Reboul, *'merci biengue' pour ton amitié et hospitalité Marseilleise*.

In PARIS – Patrick Simon arranged my stay at the Institut Nationale des Etudes Demographiques, which served as the logistical base of the Paris case study. I am indebted to him and the INED staff. Elise Palomares and Tania Vichnevskaya provided much needed intellectual and social interaction. In Paris, too, the local officials and activists that I interviewed were surprisingly forthcoming, and patient in regard to my imperfect French. Above all, I wish to thank Yankel Fijalkow at the Université de Paris for his help, important insights and feedback, as well as his amicable responses to all my queries on the Paris case.

In TEL AVIV – I wish to thank Tammy Gavriely and the staff at the Long Term Planning Department, and Edna Altar-Dembo, then director of MESILA, for the openness they displayed toward their former-colleague-turned-interviewer. I am indebted to Izhak Schnell of Tel Aviv University for his help on the Tel Aviv case study as well as the more theoretical aspects of the typology. Finally, *hamon todot* to Marcos and Shirley for their crucial assistance with the book graphics.

This book is lovingly dedicated to my father, Ernest Alexander. From the first sketches of the theoretical framework in 1999 through the final drafts of this book, he was always willing to discuss any and every point I raised. His intellectual support was invaluable to this project.

Chapter 1

Strangers at the City Gates

Any nostalgia for some by-gone time of ethnic homogeneity simply lacks sense, is indeed unrealistic: we cannot just stop the large migratory inflows. But we can, and we must, manage them with rigour, pragmatism and an open mind [...] by making the most of the opportunity and the richness that 'the other among us' has always provided.
Francesco Rutelli, Mayor of Rome, Oltre l'accoglienza

In essence, we have here a population that is isolated, a Fourth World within a modern city, disconnected from all the welfare systems, and they have to survive somehow....so they create their own networks, and we end up with a city within a city, a community within a community.
Zeev Friedman, Welfare Division director, Tel Aviv

All different. All Amsterdammers.
Amsterdam leeftsamen, municipal brochure

1 Labour Immigration and Local Policy Responses

This book explores the response of cities to one of the most potent aspects of globalization: the arrival and settlement of ever larger numbers of labour immigrants from ever more distant lands. In Europe (as elsewhere), more and more local authorities are facing what Patrick Ireland (1994) called 'the policy challenge of ethnic diversity'. This challenge is no longer limited to the traditional 'gateway cities'. In Europe alone, hundreds of towns and cities now host a significant proportion of foreign-born and second-generation immigrant populations.

The policy challenge posed by labour migrant settlement extends beyond the problems of adequate housing, education and so forth. Local authorities must deal with an increasingly diverse population, where ethnicity and religion often parallel socio-economic cleavages. Moreover, the presence of newcomers with a very different background, and local responses to this presence, reveal what I will term 'host-stranger relations'. In particular, local policies toward migrants reflect the (often implicit) expectations and attitudes of municipal policymakers toward 'foreign workers', 'ethnic minorities' and other Strangers. This book will focus on that often hidden dimension of local policy responses to labour immigration.

1.1 The Labour Migrant as Stranger in our Midst

In postwar western Europe the most common type of Stranger has arguably been the labour migrant. Between 1945 and 1973 all the industrialized European countries recruited temporary labourers from abroad, resulting in an influx of millions of 'guestworkers', mostly from southern Europe, the Balkans, Turkey and North Africa. In the 1980s-1990s the countries of southern Europe became themselves destinations for non-EU immigrants. Meanwhile, a process of family reunification resulted in a second generation of migrant children who arrived at a very young age or were born of migrant parents in their new country. Despite increasing restrictions imposed by the member states, economically motivated immigration to the European Union continues, with the newcomers arriving from ever farther corners of the globe.

Altogether, the number of labour migrants who have settled in western Europe in the last half century is estimated in the tens of millions.[1] By 'labour migrants' I mean those foreign workers recruited in the economic boom after the Second World War plus their families and offspring (second generation), as well as the economically motivated immigrants of the last two decades. For reasons elaborated below, I exclude from my analysis immigrants from OECD countries, who are not regarded as 'strangers' in the same sense as those above.[2]

As with previous migrations, most labour migrants arrived and eventually settled in cities. From Stockholm to Brussels to Athens, the presence of labour migrants and their families has changed the face of urban Europe. In 'veteran immigration' cities such as Frankfurt and Birmingham, between a tenth to a third or more of the residents are now of non-EU origin. In southern European cities that experienced labour immigration more recently, the figures are usually lower, but rising (**Table 1.1**). But even in 'new immigration' cities such as Barcelona, where labour migrants are still a small proportion, their presence has become a major issue due in part to their geographic concentration (White 1993).

Two characteristics that are particular (although not exclusive) to labour migrants have shaped the receiving societies' response to their arrival and settlement. The first was their transformation from temporary sojourners to permanent residents. 'Guestworkers', as the label implies, were expected to come for a while and then return home. But contrary to the 'myth of return' shared by hosts and immigrants alike, a significant proportion settled in the receiving countries.

---

[1] Castles and Miller (2003: 80–81) estimate the 'foreign resident population' in 15 European countries at just over 20 million, but this figure excludes naturalized immigrants (particularly significant in the UK, France and Sweden) and immigrants from colonies or former colonies holding citizenship of the 'mother country' (significant in France, the UK and the Netherlands). They also note (p. 5, citing Widgren 1994) that 'between 250,000 and 300,000 illegal entrants are estimated to arrive in Northern Europe each year.'

[2] My definition of 'labour migrants' is elaborated in Chapter 3.

Table 1.1 Migrants/ethnic minorities in survey cities

	State	City	Municipal population[1]	% 'migrants/ ethnic minorities'[2]	'Migrant/ethnic minority population'[3]	Main ethnic groups[4]
Veteran immigration cities	SWEDEN	Stockholm	704,000	17	118,000	Fin, Yu, ME, Tu
	GERMANY	Berlin	3,500,000	12	410,000	Tu,Yu, Pl, ME, EU
		Cologne	1,013,000	18	188,000	Tu, It,Yu, Gr, Pt
		Frankfurt	660,000	28	187,000	Yu, Tu, It, Mo,Gr, Sp
		Stuttgart	566,000	24	136,000	Tu, Yu, Gr, It
	ENGLAND	Birmingham	961,000	22	207,000	Pk, CA, India
		Bradford	457,000	20	91,000	Pk,India,CA,Bangl
		Sheffield	501,000	5	25,000	Pk, CA, Ch
	NETHER.	Amsterdam	739,000	49	+360,000	CA,Mo,Tu,EU,SE,AF
		Rotterdam	591,000	32	191,000	CA, Tu, Mo, SE
		Utrecht	230,000	11	26,000	Mor (>50%)
	BELGIUM	Brussels	953,000	29	280,000	Mo, EU
		Antwerp	453,000	13	59,000	Mo,Tu, EE
		Liege	189,000	18	33,000	It, Mo, Tu, Sp
	FRANCE	Paris	2,126,000	22–41	++465–872,000	EU, EA, Al, Mo, Tu
		Marseille	800,000	11	88,000	MA (mostly Alg)
		Lille	170,000	15	26,000	Mo, Al
	SWITZ.	Zurich	336,000	28	94,000	It, Yu, Sp, Pt, EU
New immigration cities	ITALY	Rome	2,823,000	est. 8–11	est. 224–300,000	EA,EE, MA,AF, EU
		Milan	1,300,000	7	91,000	Eg, Fi, Ch, Mo, EU
		Turin	915,000	ca. 3	26–32,000	Mo, Peru, EE, AF
	SPAIN	Barcelona	1,509,000	2–3	30–45,000	Mo, Peru, EU, Gipsy
	PORTU.	Oeiras (Lisbon)	151,000	est. 5	est. 8,000	CapVerde, AF
	GREECE	Athens	772,000	est. 18–22	est. 139–170,000	Ab (> 50%), Pl , Eg
	ISRAEL	Tel Aviv	360,000	est. 8–15	est. 30–60,000	EE, EA, AF, SA

Notes

1   Data for most cities is from late 1990s/early 2000s. Municipal population rounded to nearest '000.
2   Definitions of 'migrant/ethnic minority' vary from city to city. Figures exclude irregular migrants, thus a large irregular population could significantly raise the figures for some of the cities. Estimates for Rome, Oeiras (Lisbon), Athens and Tel Aviv include irregular migrants.
3. The accuracy of data on migrants/ethnic minorities varies according to the source. + Amsterdam: includes residents with at least one foreign-born parent (see Chapter 7). ++ Paris: 465,000 refers to registered foreigners and self-declared naturalized French citizens. 870,000 is estimate of total foreigners/ethnic minorities (including 2nd generation) (see Chapter 6).

Notes (Table 1.1, cont'd)

4   Definitions vary by source. 'European Union' refers to the 15 member states prior to 2004.
    AF=Sub-Saharan Africa, CA=Caribbean, EA=E. Asia, EE=E.Europe, EU=Eur.Union, MA= Maghreb, ME=Mid.East, SA=S.America, SE=S.Europe, Ab=Albania, Al=Algeria, Ch=China, Eg=Egypt, Fi =Filippines, Fin=Finland, Gr=Greece, It=Italy, Mo=Morocco, Pk=Pakistan, Pl=Poland, Pt=Portugal, Sp=Spain, Tu=Turkey.

Sources: Alexander 2004: Table 4.1 (based largely on MPMC 'City Templates': www.unesco.org/most/p97.htm), updated to 2004 for Amsterdam and Rome.

The second characteristic regards the ethnic/racial and cultural/religious Otherness of Europe's postwar labour migrants. Foreign workers were and often remain outwardly different in appearance and behaviour from the host society. 'Selected according to rational economic criteria, notably willingness to work for very low wages and under harsh or dangerous conditions', labour migrants were 'usually drawn from some less developed country or region, which belongs to the world of "others" in opposition to which the hosts have elaborated their identity' (Zolberg 2000: xvi).

This distinctiveness is compounded by their low economic status, as 'the work they do in the country of immigration as well as the living conditions to which they are subjected ensures that the separation between the segments widens' (ibid.). In this sense, labour migrants have replaced Europe's traditional ethnic minorities and the urban proletariat in the role of the threatening-yet-exotic Other. In the eyes of the host society they are the new 'stranger *ante portas*', at the city gate (Bauman 1995b: 135).

1.2   Local Responses to Immigration

The concentration of labour immigrants in cities, and within cities in particular (usually poor) neighbourhoods, creates specifically local problems as well as opportunities. It affects the local housing and labour markets, places demands on a city's welfare services and schools, changes urban development patterns. But the presence of labour migrants is not just another 'problem to be solved' by the local authorities, on a par with crime or congestion: 'When foreigners enter a community, they bring with them an alternative conception of society, thereby representing competition over the definition of the local community' (Money 1999: 59). Local inhabitants may react to labour migrant settlement with acceptance, indifference, fear or hostility. Here the relative power (or powerlessness) that indigenous residents feel in relation to migrant settlement plays a crucial role, as we will see. Friendly reactions occur when residents do not feel threatened by the Otherness of the newcomers, for reasons elaborated below. Hostile reactions occur when residents perceive migrant settlement as an 'invasion of strangers'. Moral panic may be expressed in 'white flight', voting for anti-immigrant parties or acts of violence to 'defend the territory under siege' (Bauman 1995a: 11).

The migrants, too, do not remain passive as their stay extends. Over time, they assert themselves as residents in their own right, as entrepreneurs and as political participants (with or without voting rights). At first they mobilize on an ethnic basis, establishing their own cultural, religious and sometimes political frameworks. Over time they may be incorporated into existing structures of the host society. Conversely, if they are excluded for too long (economically, socially, politically) the result may be various forms of protest, often in the second generation. The dynamics of migrant settlement, local reaction and counter-reaction often involve positive as well as negative interactions between the local host society and the newcomers. Indeed, more and more European cities display a range of interactions, from various forms of pluralism (vibrant 'mixed' or 'ethnic' neighbourhoods, interracial marriage, etc.) to various forms of xenophobia and ethnic tensions. The recent eruption of violence in cities across France is the most widespread and striking example of what can happen when second-generation immigrants remain excluded (socially, economically, geographically and politically) in their host cities. Indeed, extreme cases of ethnic tension have flared up periodically over the past 30 years, as in Marseille (1973), Birmingham (1981), Brussels (1991) and Bradford (2001).

More and more municipalities are coming to terms with the permanent presence of a large migrant population. Local authorities have responded in different ways to migrant settlement, applying traditional as well as innovative methods, often in the absence of a clear or effective national policy. These responses are not usually articulated within a clearly defined municipal migrant (or 'integration') policy. More often, they are scattered across various policy domains within local jurisdiction.

In the legal-political policy domain, municipal actions range from deliberately marginalizing ethnic-based political mobilization (e.g. Paris) to the establishment of ethnic 'advisory councils' (e.g. Amsterdam). In the socio-economic domain, municipalities may deliberately target specific migrant needs through local health, welfare and education services, or deliberately ignore them. Similarly, local authorities may disregard minority cultural and religious needs (e.g. places of worship), treat them on a par with the majority population, or allocate them specific resources. Spatial policies can range from 'dispersal policies' aimed at migrant enclaves (through housing quotas or gentrification) to urban renewal aimed at safeguarding 'ethnic neighbourhoods'. All these measures, whether inclusionary or exclusionary, migrant-targeted or general, can be considered as 'local migrant policies' if they significantly affect the migrant population.[3]

---

[3] Chapter 3 elaborates on the definition of 'local migrant policies' and the various policy domains and issue areas.

Until quite recently, local migrant policies were limited to those cities in northwestern Europe which had experienced labour migrant settlement for several decades. Since the 1980s, local migrant policies have spread to new immigration cities in southern Europe and elsewhere. Concurrently, most western European states have devolved migrant policy to the local level. Together with an upsurge in international migration, this has resulted in more and more cities developing their own policy responses to migrant settlement, so that today it is possible to discern a European-wide phenomenon of local migrant policies, with different cities at different stages of policy development.[4]

1.3 The Significance of Local Migrant Policies

Municipal migrant policies deserve our attention for several reasons. Originating in particular local circumstances, they often relate to and magnify issues going far beyond the local context. In France, one school's decision to ban Muslim pupils from wearing headscarves escalated in 1989 from a local pedagogical dispute into a nationwide debate on the relevance of the French republican model of integration and the place of Islam. In Rome, the municipality's failure to respond to the occupation of an abandoned building by irregular migrants in 1990 raised questions that went beyond the housing situation in that city (where squatting by indigenous residents is common), to Italy's role as a country of immigration.

The (mis)management of such localized incidents often begins (although it may not end) in local decisions. Thus, opposition to a proposed mosque building may remain localized in one case and become nationalized in another. Municipal policies that highlight the positive side of ethnic diversity (through 'multi-culti campaigns', ethnic festivals and the like) play a role in the broader discourse at the national and supra-national level, on the future of the European nation-state as a multicultural democracy. Often, however, negative incidents such as a fire in an overcrowded migrant hostel or a racially-motivated attack make a greater impact. Although such events may have more to do with local conditions (inadequate housing, unemployment), local policymaking may be overtaken by national policies. Britain's anti-racism policy and France's Politique de la ville were both (very different) national policy reactions to the urban riots of the 1980s.

Ultimately, national-level migrant policies are tried, tested and articulated at the local level, in the school and the neighbourhood, where local authority actions (or inaction) remain significant. Often the perceived success or failure of local initiatives, presenting alternative ways of dealing with ethnic diversity, serve as an example for further action at the national level. In the Netherlands, for example, the cities of Tilburg and The Hague developed a 'civic integration programme' for new immigrants that was later adopted as a compulsory national policy. In other cases municipal policies toward migrants develop as a reaction to national

---

[4] The upsurge in local policymaking toward migrants is not limited to Europe. See e.g. www.international.metropolis.net.

policies which have failed to solve local problems.[5] Focusing on policymaking toward migrants at the local level but within the context of national policy reveals in a more general sense the changing relationship between the city and the state. In Europe, the state's 'relegation of the treatment of complex social problems to the local sphere' (Body-Gendrot and Martiniello 2000: 4) has been especially noticeable in the area of migrant policy since the 1980s (Lahav 1998).

Looking beyond the framework of the nation-state, local migrant policies reflect the response of local actors (municipalities) to globalization in its most potent aspect: the arrival and settlement of people from far-away places. As cross-border flows become increasingly difficult to control despite national-level efforts, what happens after migrants settle in their new destinations (and these are almost always cities) becomes crucial. Local authorities thus play a vital role in the 'increasingly important interfaces of different scales of governance in the global order' (Keil 1998: 625). Decisions taken in city halls affect not only the receiving end of these global movements of people. They may also affect the points of origin, as chain migration links migrants from a particular village in Africa or Asia to a specific neighbourhood in Brussels or Berlin.[6]

Thus, local policy responses toward labour immigration articulate the interaction between local and global forces, in what has been termed 'glocalization'. At the same time, the national context remains crucial as a framework for understanding local migrant policy, as the case studies here show. What is needed, then, is more research that reduces the nation-state to 'one of several potential structuring variables' of migrant policy (Favell 2001: 350).

2   The Gap in Existing Theory

Despite the importance of local policymaking, most of the research and nearly all of the theorizing on immigration policies has focused on the national level (Neymark 1998). However, national-level models remain overly abstract, overlook differences between policies in different domains, and tend to ignore local variations within the same country. Local-level research, on the other hand, is often confined by the particular circumstances of the city under study. Many of these studies focus on local policies as an institutional-political context for migrant mobilization, disregarding other policy issue areas that are no less (and possibly more) important in their impact on migrants in cities, such as housing.

---

[5]   An example of the latter is Tel Aviv's policy since 1999 of providing local services to 'illegal' labour migrants, contravening national policy (see Chapter 5).

[6]   In some cases, cities are bypassing the national level in their attempts to affect migration flows at the source. For example, the French municipality of Montreuil invests in the development of a region in Mali where many of the city's residents originate, in the hope of minimizing immigration and encouraging return migration (Gaxie et al. 1998: 260–80).

Moreover, local-level comparisons are limited to a handful of cities. Broader, multi-city comparisons are scant and tend to focus on a single policy area and/or limit the comparison to a 'best practices' approach. This gap in the existing theory is discussed in the following sub-sections.

2.1 The Problem with National-level Theories

Most of the literature in this field focuses on various national (and sometimes supranational) factors that shape national immigration and immigrant policy.[7] Jeanette Money (1999: 26–7) distinguishes between theories that look to the interplay of economic and political interests and those 'emphasizing the primacy of cultural values', that is, national traits and identity, in explaining how different states respond to immigration. The latter approach (e.g. Brubaker 1992 on Germany, Weil 1991 and Hollifield 1994 on France) clearly connects between national immigration policies and host-stranger relations. This literature 'builds upon sociological and psychological theories and concepts such as national identity, nation building, prejudice, alienation and social closure' (Meyers 2000: 1251).

The best example is Stephen Castles' 'citizenship regimes' model (1995) which proposes three archetypal 'national responses to immigration' that derive, respectively, from three ways in which nation-states define membership. States that define themselves by ethnicity will have 'exclusionary' immigration regimes (e.g. Germany). States based on political and cultural community will be 'assimilationist' toward newcomers (e.g. France), while states defining themselves as multi-cultural societies (historically, settler states such as the US and Canada) will be 'pluralist' in regard to immigrants (ibid.: 303–5). Other comparative analyses of immigration regimes follow a similar reasoning and present the same countries as examples, with some variations. The basic distinctions between different national immigration regimes in this literature relate to different types of host-stranger relations, i.e. between settler states that define membership (citizenship) by place of birth (*ius soli*) and tend to be more open to immigration, and states where membership is ethnically defined (*ius sanguinis*) and tend toward exclusionary immigration policies.

Critics have exposed several weaknesses in the national-level analyses of immigration/immigrant policies (Vermeulen 1997, Money 1999, Meyers 2000, Favell 2001). The main objection is that the proposed models are based more on *a priori* explanations of 'national objectives' rather than actual policy differences. 'As elegant and convincing as these arguments are', writes Ireland (1994: 9), '... they remain far too theoretical and abstract. Their proponents have marshalled

---

[7] The distinction between 'immigration policy' (immigration control) and 'immigrant policy' (citizenship and integration) is elaborated in Chapter 3, below. On immigration control policies see Brochmann and Hammar 1999; Cornelius, Martin and Hollifield 1994.

surprisingly little evidence to support their conclusions'.[8] Hans Vermeulen (1997) has also questioned the assumption of cohesion in national immigration policy. Drawing from a comparative analysis of integration, language and religion policies toward migrants in five European countries, he shows that no country can be classified according to one model across all these policy areas. Thus, Great Britain is 'assimilationist' in its language and religion policies but 'multicultural' in its integration policies (ibid: 153).[9]

Finally, national-level explanations ignore local-level policy variations. Regarding migrants' places of worship, for example, Vermeulen notes that policy variations between cities in each country are 'considerable', while 'variation between countries seems smaller' (ibid: 151). Money arrives at a similar conclusion after comparing immigration policies and levels of immigration in different countries over time. Her explanation is that 'the use of national-level indicators overlooks one central feature of the immigration process: *immigrants are geographically concentrated in the host country*' (1999: 42–3, original italics).[10]

2.2   The Problem with Local-level Studies

Long overshadowed by national-level analyses, the city is nevertheless emerging as a distinct unit of study in the field of migrant policy (Brenner 1999). Research on local migrant policies can be grouped into three types. The first comprises descriptions or case studies of individual cities (e.g. Grillo 1985 on Lyon; Vertovec 1996 on Berlin; Friedman and Lehrer 1997 on Frankfurt; Jacobs 2000 on Brussels). Most of the single-city studies cover just one policy domain, and do not generalize beyond the city in question. The second type consists of comparative case studies that are limited to a small number of cities. Patrick Ireland's (1994) comparison of four towns in France and Switzerland was one of the first comprehensive attempts to analyze the political interaction between migrants and the host polity at the local level.[11]

---

[8]   Ireland refers here specifically to institutional channeling theories regarding the impact of citizenship policies on migrant integration, i.e. Brubaker 1989, Castles 1992 and Soysal 1994.

[9]   Vermeulen notes (p. 137) that the assumption of cohesion across policy areas results in the same countries being classified differently by different authors, depending on the policy focus of their analysis. Castles (1995: 306) also admits this point.

[10]   Money postulates that this geographical concentration creates an uneven distribution of the costs and benefits of immigration, resulting in 'the organization of political pressures for and against immigration' (ibid.: 206). It is the interplay between these localized pressures and national-level politics that better explains change as well as continuity in national immigration policies.

[11]   This groundbreaking work analyzes local-level variations in the political opportunity structure facing migrants in two French and two Swiss towns, using an institutional-political channelling approach. It does not, however, provide a systematic or comprehensive comparison of local migrant policies, using instead selected examples of migrant policies in the legal-political domain (Ireland 1994).

Other studies of this type follow Ireland's political-institutional channelling approach (e.g. Garbaye 2000, Bousetta 2001, Fenemma and Tillie 2004), limiting their comparison to policies that affect migrants' civic status and political participation.[12] Indeed, most local-level comparative research has focused on the legal-political domain with little or no mention of other local policies affecting migrants (e.g. Rex and Samad 1996 on Birmingham and Bradford; Blommaert and Martiniello 1996 on Antwerp and Liege). Only a handful have explored other policy areas affecting migrants (e.g. Body-Gendrot 2000, on policing policies in New York, Chicago, Paris, Marseille and Lyon; Rath et al. 2001, on local policies toward Islam in Utrecht and Rotterdam). Even Moore's (2001) revealing comparison of 'ethnic diversity management' in Marseille and Manchester remains limited to urban-social development policies.[13]

The third type consists of studies carried out within the framework of multi-city research projects.[14] Most of these focus on particular issue areas (e.g. evaluating migrant advisory councils in different cities) and involve relatively little theorizing, considering the amount of comparative data they produce.[15] The more

---

[12] Garbaye (2000) compared between Birmingham and Lille; Bousetta (2000, 2001) compared between Antwerp, Liege, Lille and Utrecht; Fenemma and Tillie (2004) compared between Amsterdam, Liege and Zurich. While Garbaye focused on the local authority more than the migrants, the focus of the others is on patterns of migrant mobilization (cf. the May 2004 issue of *Journal of Ethnic and Migration Studies* for an ongoing comparison of Amsterdam and Berlin).

[13] Moore (2001) shows how, despite ideological differences at the national level between the French *Politique de la Ville* and the British Inner Cities Policy, local-level practices in Marseille and Manchester are quite similar.

[14] Multi-city research networks/projects covering local migrant policies in Europe and beyond include: **DIECEC** – Development of Intercultural Education through Cooperation between European Cities, which compared language education policies for migrant/minority children in nine cities (DIECEC 1996); **ELAINE** – European Local Authorities Interactive Network for Ethnic Minority Policy, compared consultative structures (advisory councils) for migrants/minorities in 37 cities (ELAINE 1997a); **LIA** – Local Integration/Partnership Action, evaluated pilot projects for migrant/minority integration in 23 cities, with a 'best practices' approach (LIA 2000); **METROPOLIS** is an ongoing international forum for research and policy on migration and cities, combining theoretical and 'best practices' approaches (www.international.metropolis.net); **MPMC** – Multicultural Policies and Modes of Citizenship in European Cities, compared migrant/minority mobilization and local policy responses in 17 cities (Rogers and Tillie 2001, Penninx et al. 2004, www.unesco.org/most/p97htm); **Multi-Ethnic Metropolis** compared segregation patterns of immigrants and policy reactions at state and local level in nine cities (Musterd et al. 1998); **URBEX** – Spatial Dimensions of Urban Social Exclusion and Integration, compared the urban dimensions of social exclusion and integration in 11 cities (www2.fmg.uva.nl/urbex/menureps.htm).

[15] Many of the European multi-city research projects (e.g. LIA, ELAINE) were developed and funded with the aim of providing policy recommendations, and consequently limit their analysis to a 'best practices' approach. One exception is the DIECEC final report (1996), which proposes a model on intercultural education based on the project findings.

academically-oriented studies contain some comparative generalizations (e.g. Musterd et al. 1998, linking between welfare regimes and segregation patterns), but these are not translated into more universally applicable models or theories of local migrant policies.

2.3 Summary: the Gap between National-level Theorizing and Local-level Research

This brief overview of the literature suggests several observations. First, national-level theorizing suffers from several weaknesses, among them the tendency to ignore variations across policy areas and to overlook local variations within states. This is possible since national-level explanations rely not so much on a systematic comparison of actual policies, as on their own internal logic. In his overview of the European immigration policy literature, Adrian Favell notes (2001: 390) that this logic is '... often normatively biased in favour of state-centered policy approaches.' His conclusion:

> Too many studies have compared immigration politics or policies of integration using the general institutional features of national political systems. Although initially productive, this now leads to repetitive research that reproduces national stereotypes and assumptions about the nation-state (ibid).

Instead, he suggests,

> the city is a far better unit of comparison ... that enables both contextual specificity and structural comparisons, allowing for the fact that immigrant integration might be influenced simultaneously by local, national and transnational factors (ibid.).

However, most research at the local level has been limited in several ways. Single- as well as multi-city studies have tended to look at only one policy domain (usually policies affecting migrant civic status and political participation). But focusing on the local 'political opportunity structure' may present a distorted picture, since different cities may emphasize different dimensions in their policy response to migrants. For example, German cities tend to focus on migrant integration in the labour market, French cities respond through territorially-based policies, etc. Multi-city comparisons of the 'management of ethnic diversity' should therefore be carried out across different policy domains. Until now, none of the local-level studies have attempted a *systematic, multi-policy area comparison*. Above all, none have developed their findings into a general explanation or model of local migrant policies, that is, an analytical framework that could be applied to other cities.

Such an analytical framework should enable researchers and policymakers to compare local responses to immigration across a wide spectrum of cities and policy domains, and to make some sense of it all despite the local peculiarities of each city. I propose doing this by using the concept of *host-stranger relations* (until now, applied only in national-level models) to construct a *typology of local policy responses toward migrants*. The host-stranger relations model and typology are briefly sketched below, and developed in Chapters 2 and 3.

3 A Theoretical Framework for Understanding Local Policies toward Migrants

3.1 The Host-Stranger Relations Model

As shown below, municipal governments reflect to varying degrees the local host society in their response to the arrival and settlement of newcomers. In regard to labour migrants, the local authority may regard them as a passing phenomenon best ignored, as a threat to stability, as a positive potential for the city, and so on. Using concepts developed in the host-stranger relations literature, it is possible to distinguish between several general assumptions made by local authorities in this situation. By 'host-stranger relations literature' I mean various writings about how we define and relate to otherness. These range from theories of interpersonal relations and ethics regarding the Other, to historical or sociological analyses on how host societies (or their elites) define belonging, membership and alterity, to writings on the political, spatial and urban aspects of the host-stranger relationship (see Chapter 2).

Writers who invoke historic national characteristics to explain differences in national immigrant policies base their models on the theme of host-stranger relations without necessarily using those terms. Castles' citizenship regimes model (above) is based on how the host society defines who is 'one of us' and who is an outsider, a Stranger. However, economic and political explanations also touch on this theme. For example, Faist (1996:228) describes the 'fundamental symmetry' between welfare state regimes and immigration/integration regimes. But welfare regimes differ not only in distributive terms; they also offer different definitions of membership, rights, and 'a sense of belonging' (ibid.: 243). Koser and Lutz (1998: 8) point out that recent restrictions in welfare regimes are linked 'with notions of defending home, space and territory against "the other"'. Even writers who emphasize the importance of supra-national variables in determining migrant policy (Sassen 1998, Soysal 1994) often tie their explanations to host-stranger relations at the national level.[16]

In the case of local migrant policies, I refer to 'host-stranger relations' in a more specific sense, as the assumptions, expectations and attitudes of the local

---

[16] For example, Yasemin Soysal focuses on the effect of international human rights discourse on national migrant policies. Her typology of four 'membership models' or 'incorporation regimes' is partly based on different types of host-stranger relations, as '[d]ifferences in incorporation regimes reflect the different *collective modes of understanding and organizing membership in host polities*' (Soysal 1994: 35, my italics).

host society, represented here by the local authority, toward one type of Stranger, represented here by labour migrants.[17] The local authority's assumptions and expectations relate to the temporariness or permanence of the migrant presence and to their spatial segregation. Certain attitudes also shape local assumptions regarding the labour migrants' Otherness. Thus, City Hall may assume their cultural differences will disappear through assimilation, or it may expect them to remain as distinct minorities. These assumptions often reflect general attitudes in the local host society toward Strangers, based on past experience with indigenous Others as well as with previous newcomers, as shown in the case studies below.[18]

Local authority attitudes and assumptions are expressed in seemingly disconnected policies such as the municipality's relation to migrant organizations, access to local services, and urban renewal. I do not propose here that these attitudes and assumptions are the only variable explaining local policies toward migrants. Other factors, such as the political-institutional context, clearly play a role (see Chapter 3). Nevertheless, I posit that *local host-stranger relations – specifically the attitudes and expectations of the local authority regarding the permanence, spatial separateness and Otherness of the migrant population – are an important factor shaping local migrant policies.*

3.2 The Typology

To operationalize the link between host-stranger relations and local migrant policies, I propose a typology that classifies policies *in specific issue areas* according to local authority attitudes toward labour migrants. This requires a classification system with two dimensions. The first dimension distinguishes between several types of host-stranger relations, expressed in several general archetypes or phases of local policy responses, which I term 'Non-policy', 'Guestworker', 'Assimilationist' and 'Pluralist' responses. These policy types are based on a set of universal criteria (local authority assumptions toward the migrants in terms of their expected temporality, spatial separation and Otherness) that can be applied across different cities and periods. To some extent this resembles the deductive method used in Castles' citizenship regimes models.

However the typology presented here is also inductive, being based on a large number of actual policies gathered from a survey of literature covering some 25 European cities (below). To put some order into the findings from this survey, the typology divides local migrant policies into *domains* (Legal-political, Socio-

---

[17] The terms 'local authority' and 'labour migrants' are defined in Chapter 3.

[18] While most governments try to distinguish between policies toward different migrant categories, attitudes and policies toward one type of newcomer clearly affect those toward other newcomers. Thus, attitudes toward labour migrants that evolved in the 1960s–70s later affected host attitudes and policies toward asylum seekers and refugees in the 1980s–90s (see Robinson et al. 2003).

economic, Cultural-religious and Spatial) and *issue areas* (housing, education, etc.). This second dimension of the typology makes it possible to compare local policy responses to immigration *across* different policy domains – something previous models have failed to do systematically.

The analytical framework thus consists of a model linking host-stranger relations to local policies toward migrants, and a typology elaborating this across several response types (or phases) and policy domains (**Figure 1.1**). While the model proposes a universal explanation (host-stranger relations), the typology links this to actual policies in specific issue areas. This connection makes it possible to test the model against actual policies observed in one or more cities, and to use the typology as a tool for comparison. Although I propose that a relation exists between host-stranger relations and observed policies, I do *not* suggest that this is a strict cause-effect relationship, nor that this is the only variable affecting policymaking toward migrants. Rather, I suggest that host-stranger relations should be taken into account when we come to analyze local policymaking toward migrants (in one city, or comparatively), and I propose a framework for carrying this out.

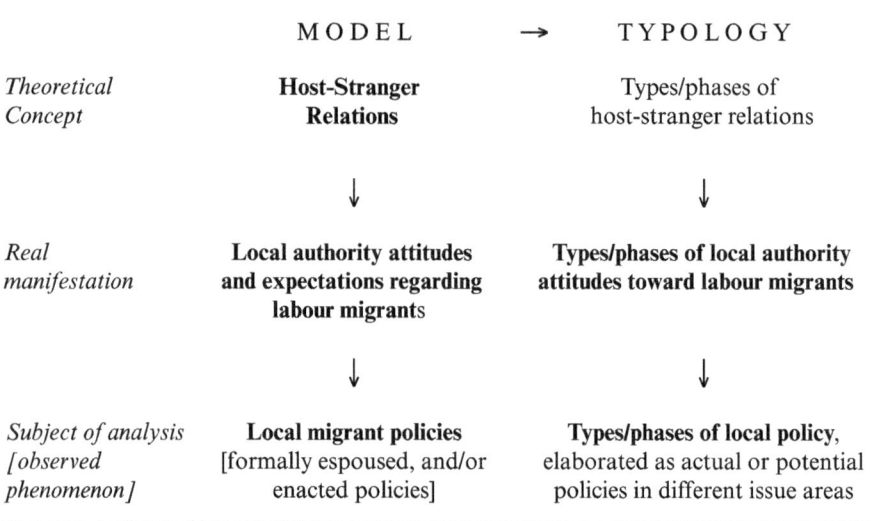

Figure 1.1 The analytical framework

Note: Arrows indicate corresponding to/associated with.

3.3 Research Aims and Questions

This study is meant to fill a gap in the existing literature on migrant policy between national-level theorizing and local-level research. My primary aim is to propose an analytical framework for analyzing and comparing local policy responses to labour migrant settlement. Such a framework should allow us to generalize beyond any particular city at any particular time, while remaining grounded in empirical findings. Using this framework, it should be possible to follow the development of actual policies toward migrants in one or more cities over time, and to relate the findings to a broader theme, namely host-stranger relations. This is tested in the four case studies below.

A second aim of this book is to test the validity of host-stranger relations as an explanatory variable, without dismissing other explanations. The following chapters reveal this implicit aspect of policymaking and explore its theoretical and practical implications. Through the four case studies, the host-stranger relations dimension will be tested as a factor accounting for, and relating between, empirically observed migrant policies in different cities and periods. Third, this book should contribute to the pool of empirical knowledge on local migrant policies. Three of the case studies provide insights into relatively unknown cities in this area (Rome, Tel Aviv and Paris). Local migrant policies in Amsterdam have been fairly well studied, but the Amsterdam chapter presents the first multi-domain analysis of these policies over a 50 year period.

Beyond the case studies, the typology proposed in this book is meant to serve as a *first step toward organizing* the extant knowledge on local migrant policies. To date, the available information is scattered among various sources with no attempt to provide a comprehensive comparative overview. The typology presented below, illustrated with local policies from a variety of cities, serves as an example of how findings from different sources may be organized. Far from exhaustive, this is a modest first attempt to create a multi-city, multi-domain data base for further theorizing on local migrant policies.

The above aims can be formulated in two sets of research questions. First, how do local authorities respond to the settlement of labour migrants? More specifically, can we identify general *archetypes*, or *phases*, of local policy responses to labour migrants? Can we identify certain *trajectories* of local policymaking, evolving from one response type to another over time? Do these trajectories repeat in different cities? In which policy domains and issue areas are local responses articulated, and which appear to be the most significant?

Second, how are local migrant policies shaped by what we define as local host-stranger relations? Specifically, what is the role of local authority *attitudes* and *expectations* regarding the labour migrant presence, in the development of local migrant policies? How do previous host-stranger relations (relating to previous newcomers or indigenous Strangers) affect the local policy response to labour migrants?

A third set of questions does not directly relate to the focus of this study but runs as a thread throughout the book, namely: what does the relation between local and national migrant policies reveal about city-state relations? Is there a clear top-down relationship (from national to local levels) in policymaking toward migrants, as is often assumed? Or, do policy responses to immigration and ethnic diversity develop from the bottom up?

3.4   Research Process and Methods

The questions raised above, and the answers proposed in the following pages, are the result of a learning process that I began as a municipal planner in Tel Aviv, and culminated in doctoral research at the University of Amsterdam (see Preface, above). This involved several stages and different research methods which are summarized below.

3.4.1   From participant observation to model-building
Between 1994 to 2000 I participated in the awakening of the local authorities in Tel Aviv to the city's 'foreign worker problem', and in the steps that followed in implementing a local migrant policy (Chapter 5, below). In my role at the municipal Planning Division I looked at the experience of European cities in dealing with labour immigration, and was surprised by the variety of different policies. While this research was guided by a clear 'best practices' approach, I began to think about the different attitudes toward immigrants that appeared to be behind these various policy responses. A subsequent survey of more theoretical literature led to development of a preliminary model linking 'host-stranger relations' to local policies toward labour migrants. As noted above, this model was partly based on deductive reasoning, borrowing from Castles' citizenship regimes model, and partly inductive, based on my observations from Tel Aviv and the findings on municipal policies in Europe.

Next, I conducted a survey of secondary sources on local policies toward migrants and ethnic minorities that eventually covered over 25 cities in Europe, plus Tel Aviv (**Table 1.1,** above). The core of the survey was based on a multinational research project 'Multicultural Policies and Modes of Citizenship in European Cities'.[19] I supplemented the MPMC project findings with a questionnaire sent to the project research teams, as well as secondary literature on local policies in those and other cities. Based on this, I assembled a data base of local migrant policies per city which served as the raw material for development of the typology (for a summary of the survey data see Alexander 2004: 74–8).

While superficial, this data base established the range of actual policies with which cities have responded to the presence of migrants and ethnic minorities. It

---

[19] The MPMC project involved research teams from 17 different cities (I was responsible for Tel Aviv), coordinated by the Institute of Migration and Ethnic Studies at the University of Amsterdam. The findings appeared in 'city templates' and 'progress reports' on Amsterdam, Antwerp, Athens, Barcelona, Birmingham, Brussels, Cologne, Liege, Marseille, Milan, Oeiras (Lisbon), Paris, Rome, Stockholm, Tel Aviv, Turin and Zurich (www.unesco.org/most/p97city). See Rogers and Tillie 2001 for final results by city; see Penninx et al. 2004 for results by topic.

also served to define what constitutes 'local migrant policies'. I then elaborated the host-stranger relations model and constructed a typology of local migrant policies. Based on my observations from the Tel Aviv case and survey findings, I added a 'Non-policy' category to the three response types (exclusionary, assimilationist and pluralist) usually proposed in the literature on national immigration policies. Unlike the national-level models, my typology included a second dimension (policy domains and issue areas), putting some order in the numerous local policies that the literature survey produced.

3.4.2 Testing the analytical framework: four cases

Between June 2001 and March 2003 I conducted field research in four case study cities, to test the robustness of the typology as an analytical tool for understanding policymaking toward migrants in a given city, as well as its usefulness as a framework for comparing between cities. The case studies provided a more in-depth, qualitative analysis of local policy development over time, as well as throwing light on the relation between host-stranger relations and local policymaking. They cover two cities with long but very different experiences in this field (Paris and Amsterdam), and two cities that underwent significant labour immigration only recently (Rome and Tel Aviv).

Despite the differences, as will be shown, the case studies are comparable and their findings can be generalized to other cities with the help of the typology. The inclusion of Tel Aviv demonstrates that the typology can also be applied to cities outside Europe. The case studies do not provide an exhaustive description or evaluation of each city's policy responses toward labour migrants. Instead, the city chapters illustrate and highlight the *links* between host-stranger relations and local policymaking that are proposed in a more abstract form in the model and the typology.

The choice of cities Four cities were chosen to test the typology, one case to illustrate each policy type: Rome (Non-policy), Tel Aviv (Guestworker policy), Paris (Assimilationist policy) and Amsterdam (Pluralist policy).[20] These cities were

---

[20] Time constraints limited the sample to one case for each archetype identified in the typology. Rome was chosen after an exploratory visit (May 2001) confirmed its feasibility as a case study for Non-policy. Tel Aviv and Amsterdam were chosen to represent the Guestworker and Pluralist policy types, respectively, based on the survey findings as well as my preliminary knowledge regarding their policies. Amsterdam's Minorities Policy (1980–94), for example, offers a particularly robust version of a Pluralist-type response to ethnic diversity for which Dutch cities were famous in the 1980s–90s. For the Assimilationist type, the choice of a French city was obvious, as France represents the prototypical Assimilationist-style immigration regime (Brubaker 1992, Castles 1995). Only Paris, Marseille and Lyon were comparable to the other case study cities in terms of size and national ranking. Lyon was not chosen due to the scarcity of material on its migrant policies. Preliminary research in Marseille (May 2002) revealed two main problems: first, its tradition of ethnically-oriented clientalist politics is atypical for a French city; second,

chosen out of the larger sample of the survey (above), which served to identify which cities could represent which policy types. The case study cities had to be sufficiently different in terms of representing one of the four types, yet sufficiently similar in other respects to make them comparable (see **Table 1.2**).

Regarding their comparability, two considerations were foremost. First, the nature of migrant settlement in the city: all the cities must have experienced a minimal period of settlement *by labour migrants*. A city that experienced immigration of another type (e.g. repatriates who are defined by the host society as a different kind of newcomer) would not fit the purpose of this study, since we would be comparing between two different types of stranger (and therefore, of host-stranger relations), rather than different responses to the same type of stranger (see Chapter 2). For example, Tel Aviv could not have served as a case study in this book prior to the arrival of labour migrants in the 1990s, despite its previous decades of Jewish immigration. This has less to do with any objective differences between the previous Jewish immigration (some of it economically motivated) and the labour migrants who arrived in the 1990s. Rather, the former are regarded by the host society as repatriates to be incorporated into their old-new 'homeland' (for which a comprehensive 'immigrant absorption' system exists), while the latter are regarded as temporary foreign workers. This makes Tel Aviv's response to the arrival of the labour immigrants comparable to other cities' reactions. Similarly, Amsterdam's policies toward 'repatriated' immigrants from Indonesia in the 1950s is only a contextual variable in that case study; the focus is on policy responses from the 1960s to the arrival of 'guestworkers'.

All four cities now host a significant labour migrant population, consisting largely of newcomers from non-industrialized countries. The current size of the migrant population varies, reflecting the different city sizes and immigration phases. In Rome and Tel Aviv, it is estimated at around 10 per cent of the total population. Its ethnic composition and other characteristics are similar in both the cities: extreme diversity with substantial representation of new labour emigration regions such as south-east Asia and the former Soviet bloc, together with migrants from Africa and Latin America. In the 'veteran immigration' cities of Paris and Amsterdam, the total migrant/minority population is estimated at around forty percent of the total population. Here the lines blur between classic labour migrants (including second- and third-generation children of foreign workers from the 1950s–60s from southern Europe, Turkey and the southern Mediterranean basin), post-colonial migrants, and the new labour migrants of the 1980s–90s. What makes these cities comparable for our purpose is that in all four cases the labour migrant presence became at some point *significant in the eyes of the local authority*.

Marseille's local migrant policies have already been extensively researched (see Moore 2001). Paris, *au contraire*, is a surprisingly un-researched city in this field and presented an interesting challenge.

Table 1.2 The case study cities

	Rome	Tel Aviv	Paris	Amsterdam
Municipal population (metropolitan pop.)	2,823,000 (ca. 4 mill)	360,000 (2.54 mill)	2,126,000 (ca. 10 mill)	739,000 (1.3 mill)
Rank in national urban hierarchy	1–2	1	1	1
Type of local government	Mayor-led	Mayor-led	Mayor-led since 1977	Council-led
Registered foreign residents (% of municipal pop.)	223,879 (7.9%)	n.a.	308,266 (14.5%)	n.a.
Total migrant/ethnic minority population	Estimated 298,000	Estimated between 30,000–60,000	Estimated 872,000	Official 359,632
% of total population	Estimated 10.6%	Estimated 8–15%	Estimated 41%	48.7%
Migrants/minorities from non-OECD countries	Over 80%	Over 95%	Over 80%	80%
Main countries of origin (descending order)	Philippines, Romania, Poland, Peru, Bangladesh, Albania	Philippines, Romania, Thailand, Poland, Ukraine, Ghana, Nigeria, Colombia	Portugal, Algeria, Morocco, Tunisia, Spain, China	Surinam, Morocco, Turkey, Indonesia, Germany, Antilles, Ghana, U.K.
Beginnings of main labour immigration	1980s	Late 1980s	1950s	1960s

Notes: Rome data for 2004 (see Chapter 4 for elaboration); Tel Aviv data for 2001 (see Chapter 5); Paris data for 1999 (see Chapter 6); Amsterdam data for 2004 (see Chapter 7).

The second dimension of comparability relates to the cities as autonomous and unitary players. All four cases involve major metropolises governed by one municipal authority. While their absolute size differs, all four cities top their national urban hierarchy.[21] The cities are also comparable in administrative and financial autonomy, i.e. in their capability and will to enact local migrant policy.[22] While the national context differs in each case, all four municipalities operate within some form of advanced capitalist, European-style democratic regime. In the case of Tel Aviv, that city is comparable to European cities in terms of city-state relations and specifically *in regard to local policy responses toward labour migrants*, despite the non-European circumstances of the Israeli context (see Chapter 5). Finally, all four cities display in varying degrees secondary world city characteristics in terms of their connections to larger international economic systems, including their function in global labour flows (Friedmann 1986, Keil 1998). An analogy to the different-yet-comparable features of these four municipalities may be found in their City Halls, which present very different architectural styles and building histories, yet perform the same basic functions of local policymaking and administration (**Figure 1.2 and Box 1.1**).

Conduct and structure of the case studies The field research (4–5 months in each city) included the following steps in more or less the same order in each case: analyzing secondary material on migrant policies and the local and national context; interviews with local scholars; interviews with municipal officials at the professional level; collecting and analyzing primary material (policy papers, draft reports, memos, etc.); interviews with municipal officials at the political level; interviews with representatives of civic organizations, migrant activists, and others (see **Appendix**). The interviews themselves were of a semi-open structure, between one to two hours.

The case study chapters follow a similar structure (see below) to maximize their comparative value, although the particularities of each city led to variations between chapters as well.[23] All the chapters also devote significant attention to

---

[21] Regarding the smaller cities: Amsterdam's relatively small size is offset by its function as the centre of a metropolitan region of 1.3 million inhabitants, and its leading role in the Randstad region, which contains over six million inhabitants (about 45 per cent of the Netherlands' total population). Similarly, Tel Aviv's resident population belies its real size as Israel's economic and demographic centre. The city is the core of the Tel Aviv Metropolitan Area, containing 2.54 million people (42 per cent of Israel's population).

[22] In the case of Rome, the limited capabilities of the municipality are one of the characteristics that make this a case study for Non-policy. In the case of Paris, the limited autonomy of the municipality before 1977 did not prevent the development of *Parisian* migrant policies, as will be argued in Chapter 6.

[23] In Chapter 4 (Rome), the Non-policy phase is described in relative brevity due to the scarcity of material on that period (which in itself characterizes Non-policy), while the following phase (1993–2002) receives more attention. Chapter 5 (Tel Aviv) devotes more attention to the policymaking process. Chapter 6 (Paris) begins, rather than ends,

Figure 1.2   City Halls of Amsterdam, Paris, Rome and Tel Aviv

Sources: Amsterdam – Nadav Haran; Paris – n.a.; Rome – Carstem Clasohm, www.classohm.com. Tel Aviv – Michael Alexander.

the city's latest phase in local policymaking toward migrants. These new policy phases (initiated in Rome in 1993, Amsterdam in 1994, Tel Aviv in 1999 and Paris in 2001) point to future developments that are discussed in the final chapter.

3.4.3   Rethinking the model, revising the typology
In light of the findings from the case studies, the relevancy of the host-stranger relations model and the typology was reviewed. In particular, the research on Amsterdam revealed another policy phase, in reaction to the Pluralist-type policies of the 1980s–90s. This possibility was strengthened by findings from other 'veteran immigration cities' in the policies survey. As a result, I revised the original typology, adding a fifth policy type/phase (see Chapter 8). Since then, the dramatic events of 2004–05 (terror attacks carried out by first- and second-generation Muslim migrants in Amsterdam, Madrid and London, and the riots by Muslim and African-origin second-generation migrants in the suburbs of

---

with the Spatial domain due to the predominance of urban/territorial policies. Chapter 7 (Amsterdam) is the most comprehensive because Amsterdam's migrant policy has gone through more phases and included the most issue areas. The Paris and Amsterdam chapters also go back farther in time, to present the local policies of these two veteran immigration cities as part of a history of host-stranger relations that are not limited to labour migrants.

Box 1.1   Four city halls, four styles of governance

While the architectural analogy should not be taken too far, the buildings housing the seats of local government in Amsterdam, Paris, Tel Aviv and Rome, do reflect something fundamental about the *style* of governance in each of these cities.

Amsterdam's postmodernist *Stadhuis* was planned as a 'city hall for the people', with a skylit passageway in the middle designed as a public thoroughfare. The ground-level conference rooms at one end have glass walls facing Waterlooplein (the city's flea-market), so that passers-by can see committee meetings as they scavenge for old clothes or bicycle parts. From inside, local policymakers are confronted with a background of real people from all walks of life just beyond the glass – unlike policymakers in the city halls of Rome, Tel Aviv and Paris, who sit in the top floors with god-like views of their city.

Paris's *Hôtel de Ville*, an enormous nineteenth-century construction in neo-Renaissance style, expresses centralized power and inaccessible grandeur in the best French fashion. Paris's *Hôtel de Ville* has localized the history of its country as perhaps no other city hall in the world. The previous city hall on this site witnessed the effective dethroning of Louis XVI, the capture of Robespierre (ending the Terror) and the establishment of modern municipal administration in France by Napoleon in 1808. The current building was constructed under Baron Haussmann on the site and in the style of the city hall which was burnt down by the Communards in 1871. Mayor Chirac used it as his base to run for the Presidency in 1995.

Tel Aviv's *Iria* is a modernist, concrete 12-story block towering over an equally ugly modernist plaza. The building appears to radiate bureaucratic invincibility, but at closer look its somewhat deteriorated condition reflects a more mundane reality. In 1995 Prime Minister Yizhak Rabin was assassinated on its steps after a peace rally. In the following months the *Iria* acquired a refreshingly democratic appearance, as the grey concrete base was covered by pro-democracy graffiti and candles. A year later the grafitti was painted over and replaced by an official memorial commemorating the event, reminding the public that they are not the final arbiters of what goes on in the building.

Rome's *Palazzo Senatorio* on the Capitoline Hill is perhaps the most architecturally prestigious City Hall in the world. With its foundations in the Temple of Jupiter Maximus, the current building dates from the 12th century, was given a Renaissance facelift by della Porta and Rainaldi, and overlooks the piazza designed by Michelangelo! But all this is largely symbolic: the real administration of the city takes place in more banal settings, in various municipal buildings scattered haphazardly throughout the city.

Paris and other French cities) have exposed the failings of the pluralist as well as the assimilationist approaches. It appears that the local management of ethnic diversity is entering a new phase, beyond multiculturalism.

3.5 Structure of the Book

This book is divided into three parts. The theoretical basis is presented in Chapters 1–3. This first chapter has introduced the phenomenon of labour migrant settlement and local policy responses, discussed the gap in existing research on migrant policy, and sketched a proposed analytical framework for comparison. Chapter 2 explores the meaning of host-stranger relations, clarifying key terms including the different types of strangers and different reactions to Otherness. Here I explore the links between interpersonal (I-Other) relations, social (host-stranger) relations, their urban and spatial manifestations, and local authority attitudes toward labour migrants. Chapter 3 first defines 'local policies toward labour migrants', and then presents the typology in two dimensions: the policy 'types/phases', and the policy 'domains/issue areas'. The last section presents the integrated typology and its elaboration based on actual policies.

The second part of the book presents the case studies in the order suggested by the typology: Rome (Chapter 4), Tel Aviv (Chapter 5), Paris (Chapter 6) and Amsterdam (Chapter 7). Each city chapter is organized in the same way, with some local variations: an overview of the national context (host-stranger relations, immigration cycles and the national immigration regime) is followed by a section on the local context (local host-stranger relations, a summary of immigration to the city, characteristics of the migrant/minority population). The following sections describe the evolution of the city's responses to labour migrant settlement, i.e. the policy phases identified in each city, elaborated according to the domains and issue areas relevant in each phase. The last section in each chapter summarizes that city's policy trajectory.

The third part (Chapter 8) summarizes the findings and conclusions from each of the case studies, relating the policy trajectories identified in each city to the evolution of local host-stranger relations. This serves as the basis for a more general comparative analysis that addresses the research questions raised in the first chapter. The typology is then re-evaluated in light of the findings, and a revised version is presented with a fifth policy type/phase. The final section discusses the theoretical implications of the study results and some directions for future research, as well as the relevance of the analytical framework to policymakers.

Chapter 2

Host-Stranger Relations in Theory and Practice

All societies produce strangers; but each kind of society produces its own kind of strangers, and produces them in its own inimitable way.
                    Zygmunt Bauman, 'Making and Unmaking of Strangers', 1995

1   Different Types of Strangers, Different Host-Stranger Relations

The arrival and presence of immigrants has always raised fears as well as expectations in the receiving society. But the human response to strangers goes beyond the 'fight-or-flight' instinct that is common to many animals when facing the unfamiliar. We ascribe meaning to the Other. At the societal level, the label of 'Stranger' is applied to foreign as well as indigenous individuals, and can brand entire populations on the basis of real or perceived differences from the host society. Social perceptions of Strangers can endure for centuries but they also evolve over time, for example in longstanding as well as changing European attitudes toward Gypsies or Jews. Often the label has been applied to newcomers, in a continual process of re-definition by the host society of itself and its Strangers.

Indeed, how societies have defined and related to Others remains one of the great themes of social science. 'Few issues have exercised as powerful a hold over the thought of this century as that of 'the Other' notes Theunissen (1984: 1). 'It is difficult to think of a second theme, even one that might be of more substantial significance, that has provoked as widespread an interest as this one' (ibid.). Georg Simmel (1908), who introduced the concept of 'the Stranger' in the sociological literature, noted that Strangerhood actually concerns a type of *relationship* – indeed, the concept of Stranger has no meaning without a Self which defines what and who is 'strange'.[1] In defining the Other, Hegel noted, we in effect define ourselves.[2] Simmel also observed that host-stranger relations are necessarily power relations. As Foucault (1965) and others have shown, the

---

[1]   On Simmel's 1908 essay 'The Stranger' and its implications in the sociological discussion and research, see McClemore 1970, Bochner 1982, Gudykunst 1983.

[2]   Hegel argued that the Other is the basic category of human thought, for the I can only posit itself in opposition to the Other, to that which is different from itself.

dominant group or class defines what is normal and what is deviant at the societal level, creating its Strangers through time-honoured exclusionary practices such as social stigma, economic and political exclusion, and physical segregation. In this chapter and the next I propose to link explicitly between the concept of host-stranger relations and local policies toward labour migrants. Below, I elaborate on what I mean by 'host-stranger relations', focusing on host definitions of, and attitudes toward, strangers.[3]

The delineation of Otherness creates several (often overlapping) types of Strangers, including indigenous marginal individuals and groups (e.g. homeless), subcultures (e.g. adolescent gangs), ethnic minorities (e.g. gypsies) and newcomers (e.g. immigrants). While this book focuses on labour migrants as 'newcomers' or 'ethnic minorities', the relation of the host society toward these 'exterior Others' is often shaped by previous or ongoing interactions with other types of Strangers. The latter may be newcomers from other regions in the country (Sicilians in Rome), 'repatriated' immigrants (Dutch-Indonesians in Amsterdam), indigenous minorities (Palestinians in Tel Aviv) or other 'interior Others' (the urban proletariat in Paris). One aim of this book is to differentiate these various types of host-stranger relations and show how they affect local responses to the arrival and settlement of labour immigrants.

Different writers have distinguished between various types of Strangers, including individual 'outsiders', marginalized groups and 'ethnic minorities'. All of these may be of immigrant origin but can also be indigenous ('Exterior Others' and 'Interior Others', see Miles 1993, Rath 1999). In the city Strangerhood is not necessarily associated with a marginalized group in relation to a dominant culture; indeed, an urban subculture may itself be a part of the host society (e.g. the Dutch gay community in Amsterdam). Urban sociologists, in particular, have analyzed host-stranger relations in the city, some focusing on relations between members of different urban communities, others defining Strangerhood in terms of interpersonal relations of anonymity in the 'City of Strangers'.[4] However, the most common type of Stranger is probably the newcomer, as Simmel described:[5]

---

[3] A narrower definition of 'host' is provided in Chapter 3.

[4] Pioneering works in the urban sociological literature on host-stranger relations include Park and Burgess 1921, Wirth 1938, Meyer 1950, Jacobs 1961, Lofland 1973. Notable examples of theorizing on host-stranger relations in terms of marginality and Insider/Outsider relations include Stonequist 1937, Elias and Scotson 1994, Foucault 1965, Boal 1978, Miles 1993, Sibley 1995. For summaries of this literature see Krupat 1985, Bochner 1982.

[5] Simmel's prototypical Stranger is the Wandering Jew, but his analysis of host-stranger relations goes beyond the circumstances of the immigrant. Following Simmel, Wood (1934) and Schuetz (1944) pioneered the sociological research on newcomers. Gudykunst (1983) proposed a 'typology of stranger-host relations' building on a previous typology by Levine (1979). See McLemore 1970, Gudykunst 1983, Tabboni 1995.

> The Stranger is the person who comes today and stays tomorrow. He is, so to speak, the potential wanderer: although he has not moved on, he has not quite overcome the freedom of coming and going. (Simmel 1909, translated in Wolff 1950: 402)

In the following pages I analyze the concept of host-stranger relations according to host expectations and attitudes regarding the *temporality*, the *Otherness* and the *spatial separateness* of Strangers. The first dimension relates to the host's expectations regarding how long the stranger will remain (or will remain 'strange'). The second relates to attitudes regarding the stranger's Otherness, i.e. difference from host society norms. From these two, as well as from changing perceptions of space, follow host society attitudes toward the spatial separation of strangers, i.e. physical segregation. In analyzing these three aspects, I borrow from Zygmunt Bauman's distinction between modern and postmodern attitudes toward Strangers. This chapter ends with a theoretical model of host-stranger relations that links these to local policies toward labour migrants (**Figure 2.1**).

2 Modern and Postmodern Attitudes toward Strangers

While the modern/postmodern distinction remains controversial for some as an analytical tool, I find Bauman's analysis of host-stranger relations in these terms useful in highlighting some fundamental differences in local policy responses to migration.[6] Bauman (1988, 1995a, 1995b) distinguishes between 'modern' and 'postmodern' expectations in the host society, regarding the relative transience or permanence, and the relative separateness or pervasiveness, of the Stranger. In a nutshell, Bauman's thesis is that the modernist worldview regards Strangerhood as a temporary phenomenon – either the strangers will disappear or their Otherness will disappear – and as spatially separable. In contrast, postmodern attitudes regard Strangers as a permanent and pervasive (spatially inseparable) phenomenon.

2.1 The Temporality of Strangers

According to Bauman (1988: 13), the modernist worldview in both its liberal and nationalist/racist versions assumed that heterogeneity would one day be replaced by homogeneity and Order, 'the omnipotence of design and achievement'. Strangers, by their 'mere being around', disturb the universalism that modernist

---

[6] For our purpose, 'modernity' refers to an historical period which has unfolded over the past several hundred years through the development of capitalism; 'modernism' is 'the cultural expression of the experience of modernity' (Cooke 1998: 476). 'Postmodernity' corresponds to the stage of global (or late) capitalism commencing with the end of the Cold War and 'the new world disorder', a period characterized by economic uncertainty from the global to the personal level (Bauman 1995a: 5). 'Postmodernism' is the cultural expression of this era.

values aspire to (Bauman 1995a: 2). Indeed, the definition of Strangers is based just on their *ambivalence* – on that quality which makes them so disturbing to the modernist project of order-building:

> What makes certain people 'strangers' and therefore vexing, unnerving, off-putting and otherwise a 'problem', is their capacity to befog and eclipse the boundary lines which ought to be clearly seen. (Bauman 1988: 8)

Accordingly, the basic modernist assumption was that '[t]he strangers were, by definition, an anomaly to be rectified. Their presence was defined a priori as temporary ...'. Bauman notes two strategies employed in the modernist 'war of attrition waged against the strangers and the strange'. The first is the liberal option of assimilation, that is, the possibility and necessity of 'making the different similar'. The second is 'the strategy of exclusion', by social exclusion, physical segregation or in extreme cases, physical annihilation. Both strategies assume the eventual disappearance of Otherness, either through assimilation into, or physical separation from, the host society (Bauman 1995a: 2–3, 8).

In the postmodern era, constant change and bewildering diversity have become the norm, leading to a change in attitudes toward Otherness. The belief that Strangers can disappear through assimilation has been abandoned, and geographical separation is increasingly difficult. The presence of Strangers is now regarded as permanent and pervasive, an inherent characteristic of the postmodern disorder:

> The essential difference between the socially-produced modality of modern and postmodern strangers is that while modern strangers were earmarked for annihilation [....] the postmodern ones are by common consent or resignation, whether joyful or grudging, here to stay. (Bauman 1995a: 12)

'The question', he summarizes, 'is no longer how to get rid of strangers and the strange, but how to live with them, daily and permanently' (ibid.).

2.2 The Otherness of Strangers

The 'joyful or grudging' acceptance of strangers relates to the second dimension of host-stranger relations: how to live with Otherness. At the individual level this dimension touches on the most basic human emotions. Sartre (1943), for example, describes the dialectics of I-Other relations as a mutually threatening relationship: either I objectify the Other, or am objectified by it. Levinas (1961) is more optimistic, proposing two possible relationships toward others, one objectifying and the other non-objectifying. In the objectifying relation, the Self uses the Other to create its own identity and in doing so, the Self lives from other people, objects, ideas. The 'process by which the subject makes itself at home in an environment where otherness is not a threat to be overcome, but a pleasure to be experienced' (Davis 1996: 43) can be recognized in what is sometimes termed the 'embrace of strangers' (below).

The non-objectifying relationship, according to Levinas, occurs when we recognize the total *separateness* of the Other (*l'autre*). This can only happen in a direct encounter with another human being, when I recognize Otherness in the face (*visage*) of another person. This confronts me with a choice of responses (therefore Levinas sees it above all as an ethical encounter):

> The Other makes me realize that I share the world ... and I do not like this realization. My power and freedom are put into question . ... I am confronted with real choices between responsibility and obligation toward the Other, or hatred and violent repudiation. (Davis 1996: 48–9)

The first option, to safeguard the stranger's Otherness, is the normative basis for what I will term 'Pluralist' approaches toward migrants (and other minorities). At its most genuine, this response is based on respect and empathy for Otherness, regardless of one's own interests. The second option is to repudiate the Other – the xenophobic response. Between these two extremes lies the possibility of regarding the Other as an exotic presence to be enjoyed and used (an exploitative rather than genuine 'embrace of strangers').

Here, perceptions of relative power or powerlessness become crucial in understanding individual as well as communal responses to strangers (including local policies toward migrants). The loss of control we feel when confronted with some other person or thing that threatens to overwhelm us (in Sartre's terms, '*le visqueux*', i.e. the slimy Other that cannot be rid of) can explain phenomena such as 'moral panic' and 'white flight' among some local inhabitants in the face of immigration (see following chapters). As Bauman (1995a: 11) notes, xenophobic responses tend to originate in neighbourhoods 'populated by people not able to choose whom they meet and for how long ... powerless people, experiencing the world as a trap, not an adventure park ...'.

For those powerful enough to *not* feel threatened by Otherness, the presence of Strangers can elicit a positive response, ranging from genuine empathy to the exploitative enjoyment of strangers: 'What seems slimy to some, may be fresh, pleasant, exhilarating to others ...' (ibid: 10). Thus, while local inhabitants may complain of 'too many foreigners', wealthier residents coming from outside will regard 'ethnic neighbourhoods' (the Goutte d'Or in Paris, the Esquilino in Rome) as exotic locales for eating and going out. Others will deliberately choose to live there and defend their new neighbourhood's cultural diversity against further attempts at gentrification.[7] Local authorities may also respond to ethnic diversity

---

[7] See Boxes 4.1, 5.1 and 6.3 in the chapters below. The term coined for this type of gentrifier, attracted by the ethnic 'color' of migrant neighborhoods, is 'bourgeois-bohemians', or Bobos (Brooks 2002).

as a threat to urban order, as a springboard for urban renewal, or as a genuine expression of the city's character.

2.3 The Spatial Separation of Strangers

Regarding the spatial dimension of host-stranger relations, Bauman's distinction between modern and postmodern perceptions is again useful for understanding local urban policies, e.g. regarding migrant enclaves. Briefly, the modernist approach assumed that social distance could be equated with the spatial distance between different communities. In the postmodern context where Otherness is pervasive, spatial distancing becomes less important and socio-spatial exclusion becomes more complex.

This is due not only to the increasing ethnic diversity characterizing large cities, but also to changes in the perceived character of urban space. Following the Chicago School, the modern city was described during most of the twentieth century as 'neatly parcelled up into distinctive "niches" occupied by distinctive human "communities"', or as 'fractured into "suburb-slum" patterns reflecting a straightforward capital-labour "class" divide' (Cloke et al. 1991: 177). This modernist paradigm, in which space was conceived 'essentially as a neutral medium for the operation of social and economic processes' (Sibley 1995: 73), envisaged a continuum of relatively homogenous territories (downtown, black ghetto, white suburb, etc.) with objectively measurable boundaries. Strangerhood was measured, both socially and geographically, in relation to a relatively stable Order, characterized by a dominant host culture.[8] The implication was that slums or ethnic enclaves were temporary, or potentially so under the right conditions.

The postmodern city, in contrast, is characterized by the openness and fragmentation of spaces, with an unprecedented flow and mix of people, lifestyles, architectural forms and functions. Spaces and places are now perceived as multi-layered, their boundaries fluid, their character changing, their identity multi-dimensional (Harvey 1989, Soja 1989).[9] In this context, Otherness is pervasive: strange people and unfamiliar forms are not as clearly located within well-defined areas; the homeless rub shoulders with the newly urbanized rich and gentrified inner city blocks sit within old immigrant neighbourhoods. Davis (1985: 110) describes 'the burgeoning city of third-world immigrants that totally surrounds

---

[8] The original concentric zones model of urban development, developed by Burgess (1925), was based on the growth patterns of early twentieth century Chicago, a city undergoing massive immigration. The assumptions of this 'consensualist view of society' were later criticized by Behavioural and Structuralist/Marxist geographers, however, they too remained within the modernist view of host-stranger relations (see Jackson and Smith 1984: 167–83).

[9] See also Schnell and Benjamini (2001) on the fragmentation of postmodern spaces; Racine and Mager (1997) on subjective rather than objective definitions of ethnic neighbourhoods, citing studies from Montreal, Toronto and Paris.

and lays siege to the sumptuous towers of the speculators' in Los Angeles, while Van Amersfoort (1992: 452) describes Amsterdam as a postindustrial city in which 'all kinds of subcultures centred around a "lifestyle" (the singles, the traditional families, the gay scene, etc.) exist side by side with little social contact and in different residential patterns'.

In this juxtaposition of differences in close proximity, spatial segregation is still possible, but not as simple as before. One response to the perceived pervasiveness (and expected permanence) of Strangers is the development of complex forms of exclusion. These rely on architecture and technology rather than geographical distance to limit the contact with unwanted Strangers. This strategy of co-existing with Otherness is expressed in urban developments which are planned in close yet unbridgeable proximity to marginal populations. These include 'skyscraper fortress enclaves' and 'gated communities' (Davis 1985, 1992) as well as indoor shopping centres which have come to replace the open street as the primary public social area, excluding unwanted Strangers from more and more public spaces (Sibley 1995).[10] At the same time, more traditional forms of segregation survive as well.[11] All are spatial manifestations of different types of host-stranger relations.

Another response to the pervasiveness of Strangeness, as noted above, is to enjoy it. After decades of homogenous suburbanization, the rediscovery of urban Otherness is expressed in the gentrification of inner city 'ethnic neighbourhoods', municipally-sponsored 'ethnic festivals' and the development of 'heritage landscapes' in peripheral or marginal areas whose otherworldly character is recreated according to postmodern tastes.[12] The presence of migrants and ethnic minorities can play a central role in such policies. In the following chapters we will come across several examples, including planning proposals in Tel Aviv to upgrade the labour migrant 'core area' into a 'touristic-ethnic magnet' (Chapter 5) and an 'Oriental market' of ethnic-minority vendors initiated by the municipality of Amsterdam in the mid-1980s (Chapter 7).

Such projects raise questions not only regarding the authenticity of the Otherness carefully displayed for consumption, but also as to the intentions of the policymakers toward the migrant/minority communities. But how to distinguish between exploitative policies toward minorities and those that are genuinely sensitive to Otherness? What lay behind Amsterdam's policy of ignoring

---

[10] See also Short 1988 on the 'bunker architecture' of the London Docklands, Soja 1989 on the 'urban citadels' of Los Angeles, and Cooke 1988.

[11] Boal (1978) suggests three traditional forms of segregation in the city: the 'colony' (an immigrant community characterized by temporary segregation prior to their assimilation), the 'enclave' (an ethnic community characterized by a certain degree of segregation which is in part voluntary), and the 'ghetto' (a stabilized socio-spatial form characterized by a high degree of segregation forced on it by the host society).

[12] Citing Harvey (1989), Cloke et al. (1991: 182–3) note 'an "aestheticising" of poverty that renders the poor, the homeless and the oppressed more objects of cultural interest than objects for radical political action'. For examples of residential and commercial gentrification of inner city areas, see Short 1988, Hall 1991, Breen and Rigby 1994.

unauthorized mosques in the 1960s, a similarly negligent policy toward mosques in Paris of the 1980s, and Tel Aviv's policy of ignoring 'underground churches' of irregular immigrants today? Which response expresses religious intolerance, which demonstrates tolerance, and why? Part of the answer can be found by examining the assumptions and attitudes of the local authority in each case: is the newcomers' presence expected to be short-term or permanent, should their Otherness be tolerated, gradually eliminated, exploited or genuinely accepted?

3 Linking Host-Stranger Relations and Local Policies toward Labour Migrants

The concept of host-stranger relations provides several insights into why and how local residents, as well as local authorities, respond to the arrival and settlement of newcomers. Below, I summarize these observations and offer a model linking them with local policies toward migrants. This model will be elaborated in a typology of municipal policy responses in the following chapter.

3.1 Migrant Settlement as the 'Stranger Within the City Walls'

The most basic insight provided by the host-stranger literature is that the arrival and eventual settlement of migrants in the city is not just another 'practical' problem to be addressed by the local authority. If the arrival of migrants is first perceived as the 'stranger at the city gates', then by the time migrant settlement is noticed, they are perceived as the 'stranger within the city walls'. The presence of newcomers with a very different background from the local population touches on deep-seated fears (as well as desires) in the host society. Local residents, especially in poor neighbourhoods where labour migrants tend to settle, may feel their territory has been invaded. For those who feel 'trapped' (in Sartre's terms: those who perceive Strangerhood as viscuous), the reaction may be to 'defend the territory under siege' (Bauman 1995a: 10–11). This may express itself in local acts of violence or support for xenophobic parties. Residents who can afford it may opt for exit ('white flight'), while others may respond by empathizing with the newcomers, or welcoming ethnic/cultural diversity as enriching their city. Often these perceptions depend on one's relative feelings of power (or powerlessness) vis-à-vis the presence of strangers.

Another insight is the importance of distinguishing between different types of strangers *as defined by the host society*, i.e. between different types of host-stranger relations. Local responses to labour migrants are shaped in part by other host-stranger relations (with indigenous Others, previous newcomers, etc.). Often, the response to a certain migration will depend less on the characteristics of the newcomers and more on the host society's definitions of itself. As we shall see, criteria for membership in the host society may emphasize ethnicity in one place, religion in another and political/cultural assimilation in a third, resulting in different definitions of Otherness. The latter will determine which newcomers are defined as members upon arrival ('repatriates' returning to their historic homeland), which are potential members, which are defined as 'foreign workers' and which will always remain Outsiders.

3.2 Modern and Postmodern Responses to the Presence of Strangers

Bauman's distinction between modern and postmodern perceptions of strangers can put some order into the variety of host responses. The modernist worldview assumes a stable, dominant host society which serves as the ground against which the figure of the Stranger is drawn. According to this view, Strangerhood always contains the seeds of its potential disappearance, whether through physical disappearance (the Stranger moves on) or assimilation into the host society (to paraphrase Levinas: the Stranger loses his Otherness and becomes part of the Same). Until this happens, marginalization and exclusion will be the Stranger's lot. Another modernist assumption is that Strangers are spatially separate (or separable) from the host society. The changing position of the Stranger, from marginalization to assimilation, will be expressed in decreasing spatial distance.

Assuming the temporary nature of Strangerhood, modernist responses to the presence of migrants may be inclusionary or exclusionary. Inclusionary strategies will aim to assimilate migrants, i.e. erase their Otherness. In this case, spatial segregation will be seen as an obstacle to integration. In cases where the newcomers are perceived as transient or temporary (e.g. guestworkers), spatial segregation may be considered tolerable or even desirable (see Chapter 3, below).

In the postmodernist worldview, Strangerhood is conceived as permanent in a double sense: not only will strangers physically remain, but their Otherness will also remain. Due to their increasing numbers (the local effects of globalization) and the changing nature of urban space (open, fragmented, multi-use), strangers are no longer as easily segregated, i.e. spatially separate. This is the perceived *pervasiveness of strangers* characterizing the postmodern city. Again, this can lead to inclusionary or exclusionary responses, again depending on subjective feelings of power(lessness), as well as different worldviews toward Otherness, from multiculturalism to neo-racism.

Multiculturalist/pluralist attitudes will include a responsibility to protect and preserve the Stranger's right to remain different. As immigrants and ethnic minorities represent the most visible strangers, host-stranger relations have become increasingly ethnicized, revolving around the proper relationship of the host society toward ethnic minorities, especially toward minorities holding values that clash with the host society (Tabboni 1995, Tamir 1995). Here two approaches are apparent. The first defines Strangers in terms of their communal, ethnically-based identity. Communitarian strategies espouse the acceptance or even promotion of a certain degree of separation (e.g. in schools) in the name of respecting the collective rights of Strangers. However, this can imply an acceptance of living *next to* instead of *with* Strangers (Kymlicka 1995).

The communitarian approach to ethnic diversity has been criticized on several grounds, for example, that it fosters sectarianism. In response, a second approach focuses on the need to protect individual rather than communal Otherness, and emphasizes the diversity *within* migrant/minority populations.[13] This emphasis of individual over communal Otherness finds expression, as we will see, in a relatively new type of policy response to ethnic diversity that has emerged in some cities. This may be seen as a reaction to previous ethnic-based pluralist policies that advocated communitarian solutions (see Chapters 7 and 8).

3.3 Local Migrant Policies as One Aspect of Host-Stranger Relations

We can now view local policies toward labour migrants as one aspect of host-stranger relations (other aspects include the relation of local residents toward the migrants, and the migrants' relation toward the host society). These policies may be seen as a response by the local authority to the reactions of local residents noted above. City Hall will normally be aware of the relative power/powerlessness of different constituencies vis-à-vis the migrant presence when it formulates its urban renewal policies. Thus, gentrification policies in neighbourhoods of migrant settlement may be seen as an attempt by the local authority to pre-empt xenophobia, or minimize 'white flight'. The same policies may also play to the desire of potential gentrifiers, those for whom the presence of a migrant population is viewed as an attraction. Outwardly multicultural policies may in fact be limited to symbolic actions that ignore the real problems of ethnic minorities, or an exploitation of Otherness. These aspects of policymaking will normally not appear in official documents or statements, which speak instead of 'neighbourhood upgrading', 'diversity' and so on.

However, local migrant policies are often pre-emptive and pro-active, as the local authority attempts to set its own agenda in shaping the city's relation to the presence of migrants/minorities. The model below (**Figure 2.1**) presents four possible archetypes of host-stranger relations, defined by local authority assumptions and attitudes toward labour migrants, in the three dimensions described above. Regarding the temporal dimension, the municipality may view the labour migrants as a *transient* phenomenon. Rome in the 1980s, for example, assumed that labour migrants were 'just passing through' the city. In this case, City Hall may choose to ignore labour migrant needs as well as manifestations of their Otherness (e.g. ad hoc places of worship). Similarly, manifestations of (self-) segregation can be ignored as a passing problem. In terms of host-stranger relations, I label this a *Transient attitude*.

The local authority may assume the labour migrant presence is more than transient, but still limited to a certain period. This expectation usually occurs in the

---

[13] Bauman (1995a: 14–5) argues that empowerment of migrant/minority communities through 'communal self-determination' can lead to oppression of individuals (particularly women) within their communities.

HOST-STRANGER RELATIONS	MODERNIST worldview			POSTMODERNIST
	Stranger as temporary, spatially separable			Stranger as permanent and pervasive
Local authority attitudes towards labour migrants	**Migrants as TRANSIENT**	**Migrants as TEMPORARY**	**Migrants as PERMANENT, but their OTHERNESS is TEMPORARY**	**Migrants as PERMANENT and their OTHERNESS will REMAIN**
Assumptions re: temporal presence	Just passing through	Short-term stay (few years)	Permanent	Permanent
Attitudes re: Otherness	Otherness ignored	Otherness tolerated	Otherness discouraged/ignored: assimilation or marginalization	Otherness accepted; genuine or exploitative 'embrace of strangers'. Support for communal/ethnic-based difference
Attitudes re: spatial segregation	Segregation ignored	Segregation tolerated, perhaps formalized	Assimilation leads to spatial integration ('melting pot')	Some degree of segregation understandable/acceptable ('salad bowl')
POLICY TYPE/PHASE	*NON-POLICY*	*GUESTWORKER*	*ASSIMILATIONIST*	*PLURALIST*

Figure 2.1 Host-stranger relations as expressed in local authority attitudes toward labour migrants

context of a national guestworker policy, in which labour migrants are regarded as temporary sojourners in the country. Municipal attitudes will tend to accept their 'temporary' marginality, and ignore or treat leniently any manifestations of their Otherness – rather as the peculiar behaviour of tourists is tolerated. Similarly, spatial segregation will be tolerated as a temporary phenomenon or even formalized (separate guestworker housing) as a preferred short-term solution.

At some stage, most local authorities realize that the labour migrant presence in their city has (or will) become *permanent*. At this point two attitudes are possible, expressing different worldviews and value systems. The assimilationist-minded municipality will assume that its newcomers will remain, but their Otherness will eventually disappear (or be reduced to a minimum). In this case City Hall may ignore some manifestations of difference and discourage others. In effect, migrants will be presented with the choice: assimilate or remain marginalized. The overall expectation, however, is for eventual assimilation into the urban 'melting pot'. Spatial segregation, too, will be treated as a temporary phenomenon, with attitudes varying from laissez faire to pro-active assimilation.

The above attitudes can all be characterized as 'modernist' in the sense that labour migrants are expected to disappear, if not physically (by moving on to other cities or returning home), then as a distinct population of Strangers (by assimilating within the dominant host culture and polity).

However, the local authority may assume that labour migrants will not only remain physically, but will also remain distinctly different, even in the second generation and beyond. This postmodernist worldview expresses a different attitude not only regarding these Strangers but also in regard to how the city perceives itself. A local authority that defines the city as a complex of minorities, subcultures and lifestyles, in which Otherness is a permanent feature, will relate to labour migrants and their offspring as one more element in the local 'salad bowl'. This may be expressed in policies that not only recognize ethnic differences, but support minorities' right to remain different. In the latter case the city may adopt policies that seek to protect communitarian (rather than individual) rights to Otherness. Strong ethnic identity will then be regarded as supporting, rather than delaying, migrant integration. Different attitudes toward Otherness will also be expressed in different policies regarding spatial segregation. Ethnic enclaves, for example, may be regarded in a positive light rather than as a threat.

Up to now I have hinted through various examples at the ways in which the varying attitudes and expectations toward labour migrants may find expression in specific policies toward migrants. In the following chapter we will see how this can be systematically elaborated, resulting in a typology of local migrant policies as an expression of host-stranger relations.

Chapter 3

Local Policies Toward Migrants – a Typology

In the previous chapter I outlined a theoretical basis for understanding local policy responses to immigration, using a model of host-stranger relations. In this chapter I propose a typology that links the host-stranger relations model to the data collected on actual policies observed in cities (based largely on the cities survey). In this chapter I propose a typology that classifies local policies toward migrants in terms of host-stranger relations, linking the above model to the data collected on actual policies observed in cities (Section 2, below).[1] The typology is presented as an analytical framework for summarizing a city's policy reactions to labour migrant settlement, as well as allowing structured comparison with other cities. Below, Section 1 sets the parameters of this study, defining 'local policies toward migrants' in general, and 'labour migrants' in particular. Section 2 elaborates on the typology, its potential uses and limitations.

1 Defining 'Local Policies toward Migrants'

1.1 Defining 'Local Policies'

In this study I adopt the narrow definition of policymaking (i.e. limited to governmental agencies, see Keil 1998), and focus specifically on the municipality. What makes certain policies 'local' is the exercise by the local authority of its own discretion, e.g. in initiating a project, distributing funds according to municipal criteria, or affecting the implementation of a national policy in some significant way.[2] When the local authority has no discretion (or does not exercise it) in the implementation of a national policy, e.g. it simply channels government funding for local actions according to predetermined criteria, this will not be considered 'local policy'. This means that the actions of other players in this policy area, such as local civic organizations (whether indigenous or migrant-based), as well

---

[1]   An earlier version of this chapter appears in Alexander 2004.
[2]   This is based on Waste's definition of local policies as 'actions, commitments and decisions taken by persons in authority in local government, and involving the allocation of the symbolic and/or substantive resources of government' (Waste 1989: 10).

as national agencies, are regarded in this study as contextual variables affecting local (municipal) policymaking.

Since this study focuses on cities, 'local authority' here is synonymous with municipal government.[3] However, even in highly centralized local authorities the municipality is not a monolithic body. One finds differing attitudes and assumptions between the political level (councillors, aldermen, mayor) and the professional level (municipal officials, department directors), between different municipal departments, and between councillors representing differing ideological views. Thus, a strong mayor, an influential alderman or an independent municipal bureaucracy may all determine local policies in different issue areas. Nevertheless, while these policies may be divergent and even contradictory, we can usually identify *prevailing* municipal policies in a given area during a given period.

In the case of local policy responses to immigration, several clarifications are in order. First, limiting the study to espoused policy (formal declarations, published documents) would mean missing much of the picture. Second, understanding 'non-policy' is a crucial part of policy analysis especially in regard to immigrants (Hammar 1985: 277–8). My definition of 'local migrant policies' thus includes both espoused and enacted policies (the latter including informal but systematic practices by 'street-level bureaucrats', see Lipsky 1980), as well as inaction and non-commitments in response to migrants, *when these are relevant to our understanding of local policy as an expression of host-stranger relations.*

1.2 Defining Policies 'Toward Labour Migrants'

A second clarification regards the distinction made by Hammar (1985: 7–9) between national *immigration* policy, which deals with the 'regulation of flows of immigration and control of aliens' and *immigrant* policy, which 'refers to the conditions provided to the resident immigrants', e.g. work and housing conditions, welfare provisions, etc. At the local level, nearly all policies toward migrants can be classified as 'immigrant policy' although there are some examples of what might be called 'local immigration policy', for example when the municipality plays a significant role in naturalization or deportation procedures. To simplify matters, this book drops the im- prefix in most cases.

The term 'local policies toward migrants' as used in this book is flexible, encompassing those policy areas that significantly affect a given city's labour migrant population. It includes 'specific' (or 'direct') policies that target particular groups or population categories using criteria based on ethnicity or civic status (e.g. 'Turkish women','alien residents'), as well as 'general' ('indirect') policies, i.e. measures for the general public – *as long as these significantly affect migrants* (Vermeulen 1997: 9; cf. Hammar 1985). More specifically, the case studies in the book cover those policy areas that reveal something about local authority attitudes

---

[3] In some municipalities, city districts represent another tier of local government that may also promote its own policies toward migrants (see Chapter 7).

toward migrants. Thus, transport policies are excluded while urban renovation (both indirect) are included.

While the focus of this book is on local policies toward *labour* migrants,[4] it is not always possible to differentiate between policies toward 'foreign workers' and other types of migrants. Indeed, this distinction itself is a policy matter, as the case studies demonstrate. Most cities in the industrialized countries have several types of migrant and ethnic minority populations, including unskilled 'guestworkers' and their families originating from developing countries, skilled economic migrants from wealthy countries (e.g. staff of multinationals), postcolonial migrants, and asylum seekers and refugees. Official categorization of migrants and ethnic minorities is a notoriously fluid business which depends as much on the labeller as on the labelled. Governments can reverse a migrant's status almost overnight, from national (citizen/subject) to non-national, from legal to illegal and vice versa.[5] Migrant categories are to a large extent social and legal constructs determined by the host society, varying from place to place as well as over time, depending on administrative and legal changes as well as social perceptions.

Nevertheless, a general definition of 'labour migrants' in this book is possible at this point. In Europe, this term usually refers to foreign workers recruited from poorer countries largely in the 1960s and 1970s, as well as other economically-motivated immigrants who arrived in northern Europe on their own, sometimes illegally ('undocumented' or 'irregular' labour migrants). Family members who joined them, as well as children born in the destination country (hereafter: 'second-generation') are often included as well. In the southern European cities, 'labour migrant' refers primarily to immigrants arriving since the 1980s, constituting one element of the so-called 'new migration' of the last two decades (Koser and Lutz 1998).[6]

The social construct of 'labour migrant' in a given city does not always correspond to the above categories, just as it may not correspond to the migrant's nationally-defined status. In some cities, the perception of this type of migrant may include people of postcolonial and/or refugee origin (including second-generation), while excluding economic migrants from wealthy countries (other Europeans,

---

[4] The focus on labour migrants is explained in Chapter 1.

[5] Migrants may be legalized through regularization legislation or illegalized due to changes in government policy (e.g. requiring migrants to give up dual nationality). The same applies to changes in national or non-national status, when a government redefines the dimensions of the nation-state, e.g. when the Kingdom of the Netherlands or France redefined themselves to exclude, respectively, Surinamese and Algerian migrants from the category of nationals.

[6] The 'new migration' refers to the global movement of people since 1989, characterized by an increasingly wide variety of countries of origin, feminization of migrant flows and polarity of migrant types, from highly skilled workers to transit migrants, clandestine migrants and asylum seekers, with the lines blurring between economically- and politically-motivated immigration (Koser and Lutz 1998).

Americans, Japanese), as in Amsterdam from 1980.[7] Rather than deciding on a precise definition *a priori*, I will critically follow the process of defining 'labour migrants' according to the distinctions made by the local authority in its policies. As we shall see, the relevant parameters for local definitions of 'labour migrants' are usually the *perceived foreignness* of these newcomers (specifically, those from less developed countries) and the *assumed temporariness of their stay*.

This skirts a problem characterizing much of the literature on migrant policies, namely the automatic adoption of nationally-defined migrant categories, such as 'guestworkers'. As Adrian Favell (2001: 350) points out, the increasing relevancy of local-level policymaking means that the 'reproduction of nation-state-centered and nation-society-centered reasoning ... increasingly fail to represent the evolving relation between new migrants or ethnic minorities and their host societies.' To avoid this pitfall, I follow the local definition of 'labour migrants' and regard it as an integral element in the policymaking process.

Thus, postcolonial migrants are excluded as an object of 'local migrant policies' in this book (although they may not differ significantly from labour migrants in demographic characteristics, economic status, etc.) *if local authority attitudes and policies effectively treat them as a different category of Strangers*. Instead, they may appear as part of the context explaining policies toward labour migrants, for example, in the case of Dutch-Indonesian migrants in Amsterdam, or Algerian migrants in Paris (Chapters 7 and 8). When a city's policies do *not* distinguish between labour migrants and, say, postcolonial migrants (e.g. in determining eligibility or access to services), then the focus of this study will encompass those migrant types as well (for example, in Amsterdam's 'ethnic minorities policy' of the 1980s–90s).

In sum, this book encompasses under the heading of 'local policies toward migrants' (or 'local migrant policies') all policies determined exclusively or to a significant degree by the local authority, which are aimed explicitly or implicitly at those migrants (specific/targeted policies), or in the case of general policies, which significantly affect them. Inaction (non-policy) may also be a variant of local migrant policy. The criterion determining which groups are included in the 'labour migrant' population which is the subject of these policies, is the *de jure* or *de facto* distinction made by the local authority at the time.

2   The Typology[8]

The typology consists of two dimensions. The first dimension proposes several *general types* of local policy reactions toward labour migrants, based on the host-stranger relations model described in Chapter 2. These should be seen as ideal archetypes rather than exact descriptions of alternative policy reactions.

---

[7]   See Chapter 7, section 4.
[8]   See Alexander 2004, 2003a.

When several types are identified in a given city over time, we may call them local policy *phases* regarding labour migration (section 2.1, below). The second dimension defines four policy *domains* subdivided into *issue areas*, in which the alternative policy types may be expressed. The policy domains (Legal-political, Socio-economic, Cultural-religious and Spatial) are elaborated in section 2.2, below. Together the two dimensions form a matrix (**Table 3.1**), with the columns representing policy types or phases, the rows expressing issue areas, and the cells representing potential policy alternatives in specific issue areas (section 2.3, below). In this way, the typology translates the concept of host-stranger relations into possible or potential policies in all the domains and issue areas, facilitating the identification of actual policies observed in a given city (**Table 3.2**).

2.1 Local Authority Attitudes and Policy Types/Phases

The first dimension identifies four general types (or phases) of local authority attitudes and assumptions toward labour migrants, and their expression in four ideal types of local policy responses: Non-policy, Guestworker policy, Assimilationist policy and Pluralist policy (**Table 3.1**). These are described below and illustrated with examples.[9]

The 'Transient attitude' is typical of local authorities in the first years of labour immigration, when labour migrants make up a small and often undocumented population. In this phase the local authority is either unaware of, or chooses to ignore, their presence. In the latter case the municipality regards labour migrants as a transient phenomenon: the expectation is that they will soon return home or move on to other cities (many may indeed be just passing through). Avoidance of responsibility characterizes the Transient attitude. Within the municipality, however, especially among street-level bureaucrats confronted daily with the migrant presence, opinions may differ from the view from City Hall. Indeed, different attitudes between the lower and higher levels of the municipality characterize this phase.

The Transient attitude toward labour migrants is expressed in what can be termed **Non-policy** in which the municipality turns a blind eye to the problem. In effect, it passes the responsibility to others: employers, civic society, government agencies. This may be due to (wilful) ignorance or to policy prioritization that leaves no resources for dealing with this issue, as in Rome during the 1980s. However, lower-level bureaucrats in individual departments may adopt informal policies to meet pressing needs, as in Athens in the 1990s.[10] City Hall will also react to specific problems when they can no longer be ignored, such as migrant squatting that must be cleared if it becomes too great a nuisance. Non-policy

---

[9] The examples are taken from the survey of local policies (see Chapter 1), unless otherwise indicated. Examples from Amsterdam, Paris, Rome and Tel Aviv are taken from the case study findings (see Chapters 4–7).

[10] See also Chapter 5.

Table 3.1 A typology space for classifying local migrant policies in terms of local authority attitudes and expectations

Local authority ATTITUDES toward labour migrants		TRANSIENT	GUESTWORKER	ASSIMILATIONIST	PLURALIST
POLICY TYPES/PHASES		NON-POLICY	GUESTWORKER POLICY	ASSIMILATIONIST POLICY	PLURALIST POLICY
Policy aims		De facto: ignore migrants	Meet guestworkers' basic needs; ignore irregular migrants	Facilitate individual integration by assimilation into host society	Facilitate migrant integration while safeguarding ethnic/cultural identity
Measures		Avoidance of responsibility (rely on employers, NGOs) Ad-hoc reaction to crises	Formal division of responsibility (state, municipality, employers, NGOs) for specific limited tasks	Universalist (non-ethnic criteria); formal anti-discrimination mechanisms	Targeted (ethnic-based) measures; pro-active minority empowerment; affirmative action
POLICY DOMAINS/	Issue areas				
LEGAL-POLITICAL	Civic status				
	Consultative structures				
	Migrant associations				
SOCIO-ECONOMIC	Social services				
	Labour market				
	Schools				
	Policing				
CULTURAL-RELIGIOUS	Religious institutions/public practices				
	Public awareness				
SPATIAL	Housing				
	Urban development				
	Symbolic use of space				

Table 3.2 Typology of local migrant policies, by domains and issue areas

Local authority attitudes toward labour migrants	Migrants as TRANSIENT	Migrants as TEMPORARY 'guestworkers'	Migrants PERMANENT but their OTHERNESS is TEMPORARY	Migrants PERMANENT, their OTHERNESS will and should REMAIN
POLICY TYPES:	NON-POLICY	GUESTWORKER POLICY	ASSIMILATIONIST POLICY	PLURALIST POLICY
DOMAINS/Issue areas				
LEGAL-POLITICAL Civic status	—	Lobby the government to regularize illegals (*Tel Aviv*)	Facilitate naturalization (*Berlin, Cologne*)	Support regularization (*Oeiras*) Extend local enfranchisement (*Turin, Bologna*). Lobby government to regularize illegals (*Paris '01*)
Consultative structures	—	—	Reject, or mixed (non-ethnic) advisory councils (*Paris, Lille, Liege*)	Initiate/support ethnic-based advisory councils (*Frankfurt, Amsterdam '80s, Birmingham '80s*)
Migrant associations	Ignore migrant associations (*Rome '80s, Athens*)	Informal cooperation with migrant associations on limited issues (*Barcelona, Tel Aviv*)	Co-opt or exclude migrant associations; delegation to migrant associations is implicit (*Paris, Lille*)	Support migrant associations as agents of empowerment (*Amsterdam '80s, Birmingham*). Delegate services to associations (*Amsterdam, Birmingham*)
SOCIO-ECONOMIC Social services (health, welfare, etc.)	Ad-hoc access to some services (*Athens*)	Formalize access to selected local services (*Tel Aviv mid-'90s*)	Equal access to all services (ignore ethnic-based needs) (*Brussels, Barcelona*)	Reception/orientation service (*Rome '90s, Tel Aviv '00s*). Ethnically-targeted specific services (*Amsterdam, Birmingham, Stuttgart*)

Table 3.2 cont'd

POLICY TYPES:	NON-POLICY	GUESTWORKER POLICY	ASSIMILATIONIST POLICY	PLURALIST POLICY
DOMAINS/issue areas				
Labour market	Ignore black market activity (*Rome '90s, Tel Aviv*)	Minimal regulation of legal work conditions. Limited vocational assistance	Anti-discrimination policy. General vocational training (non-ethnic criteria) (*Lille*)	Affirmative hiring policy (*Antwerp*) Ethnic-based vocational training and entrepreneurs policy (*Amsterdam '80s*)
Schools	Ad hoc access for migrant children (*Rome '80s, Tel Aviv '90s*)	Possible home-language classes (*Berlin '70s*)	Spatial dispersal (school desegregation) (*Berlin*). Support national-language tutoring (*Zurich*)	Extra support to schools based on ethnic pupil ratio (*Turin, Amsterdam*). Home-language classes (*Berlin*), religion/culture classes (*Birmingham*)
Policing/Conflict resolution	Ad hoc reaction to conflict situations	Municipal police as agents of migrant regulation	Area-based policing (possible implicit targeting of migrants)	Police as social agents with migrant-targeted projects (*Rotterdam*). Pro-active anti-racism enforcement (*Leicester*)
CULTURAL-RELIGIOUS				
Minority cultural/religious practices and institutions	Ignore ad hoc places of worship	Informal acknowledgement of ad hoc places of worship (*Amsterdam '70s, Tel Aviv '90s*)	Discourage institutions (e.g. mosques, religious schools) (*Utrecht '80s, Marseille*)	Support religious institutions as agents of integration and empowerment (*Amsterdam, Birmingham*)
Minority religion in school	—	—	Ignore/discourage religious practices (*Paris*)	Support religious practices (*Birmingham*)

POLICY TYPES:	NON-POLICY	GUESTWORKER POLICY	ASSIMILATIONIST POLICY	PLURALIST POLICY
DOMAINS/issue areas				
Public awareness/ Communication policies	—	—	Anti-racism/anti-discrimination campaigns	Multicultural manifestations, projects 'celebrate diversity' (*Berlin, Frankfurt*)
SPATIAL Housing	Ignore housing problems, ad hoc reaction to crises (*Rome '80s*)	Possible short-term solutions (guestworker lodging (*Berlin '60s, Amsterdam early '70s*)	Equal access to social housing (universal criteria). Ignore ethnic-based discrimination in housing market (*Marseille*)	Anti-discrimination policy including ethnic monitoring (*Bradford, Birmingham*)
Urban development, relation to ethnic enclaves	Ignore ethnic enclaves, disperse if crisis arises. (*Rome '80s*)	Ethnic enclaves considered temporary (*Amsterdam '70s, Tel Aviv '90s*)	Ethnic enclaves seen as urban problem. Dispersal policy (*Berlin, Frankfurt '70s*). Gentrification policy (*Cologne, Brussels, Paris*)	Recognize potential of ethnic enclaves (*Tel Aviv*). Renewal with residents policy (*Frankfurt*)
Symbolic uses of space, public spaces	Ignore in peripheral locations, discourage in central locations (*Rome*)	Ignore in peripheral locations, discourage in central locations (*Tel Aviv*)	Oppose physical manifestation of Otherness ('mosques w/out minarets') (*Utrecht, Paris*)	Support physical manifestations of Otherness (minarets, monuments, museums) (*Amsterdam, Cologne*)

Note: Selected policies and cities are given as examples, based on survey of local policies and case studies (see Chapter 1).

implies ad-hoc solutions to such crises – it is figuratively and sometimes literally a matter of 'putting out fires'.

The 'Guestworker attitude' differs from the above in that City Hall acknowledges the presence of its labour migrant population, but considers this to be temporary, requiring limited solutions to short-term problems. This change usually (but not always) occurs when a national guestworker policy is initiated. The expectation, often shared by hosts and migrants, is that the newcomers' stay will only last a few years (the 'myth of return'). Furthermore, the municipality expects the 'guestworkers' to have only minimal needs, assuming this population consists of young single men and women willing to live frugally in very basic conditions. If the presence of families is recognized, they too are considered temporary. Meanwhile, the municipality expects its share of responsibility to be minimal, with employers or national government expected to address most migrant needs. The assumption of *controlled temporariness* that characterizes this phase means that spatial segregation is not necessarily considered problematic, and may even be formalized, for example in 'guestworker housing'. The beginnings of ethnic enclaves, informal markets and so on are ignored or tolerated, unless they lead to conflict with local residents. Similarly, the municipality displays a tolerant attitude toward *ad hoc* places of worship and other manifestations of Otherness, based on the expected temporary nature of these phenomena.

Guestworker policy is meant to meet the basic needs of labour migrants during their (presumably temporary) stay in the city. The municipality then assumes certain responsibilities, often as part of a division of tasks formulated in the national guestworker policy. Within this framework, local policies may range from minimalistic to generous, but Guestworker-type policies remain short- or medium-term solutions. Preventing (and not just reacting to) crises is the guiding line. Undocumented labour migrants falling outside the guestworker system are generally ignored, leaving civic organizations (unofficially) responsible for their welfare and holding the government responsible for their eventual repatriation or regularization.

Guestworker policies assume no need for representation and will thus ignore migrant mobilization, although informal cooperation with migrant organizations may occur (e.g. Tel Aviv, 1990s, Amsterdam early 1970s). The municipality will allow limited access to certain basic services, e.g. local welfare and health services, as well as education for 'guestworker children'. The latter may include home-language teaching to encourage return (Berlin). Housing policies are minimal, on the assumption that employers are taking care of their workers' lodging. In some cases the municipality may provide short-term solutions such as guestworker barracks or lodging migrants in housing scheduled for demolition, as Amsterdam did until the mid-1970s.

The 'Assimilationist' attitude marks a fundamental shift, in that labour migrants are now perceived as a permanent phenomenon (this may even extend to undocumented migrants whose eventual regularization is expected through government amnesties). However, the Assimilationist attitude assumes that the migrants' Otherness will eventually disappear as they gradually but inevitably assimilate into the host society. This process is considered one-sided: the migrant is expected to shed his/her strange ways and integrate into the dominant culture – if not in the first generation, then in the second. Conversely, public expressions of the migrant's cultural Otherness (e.g. ethnic-based associations) are frowned upon, serving as an obstacle to integration. Spatial manifestations of difference and segregation in general are regarded as problems that must be overcome.

Assimilationist policy is meant to help the individual migrant integrate into the dominant host society while minimizing the ethnic dimension. Needs are calculated and services provided (scholastic aid, public housing, neighbourhood renewal) according to universal criteria (e.g. income) that disregard ethnic background and ignore any special problems (or opportunities) stemming from the migrants' Otherness. Often it is difficult to identify Assimiliationist-type policies toward migrants/minorities, since one characteristic of such policies is to deliberately ignore the ethnic factor. Indeed, the *absence* of any ethnically-based definition of the target population (which is considered to be stigmatizing) is a characteristic mechanism of Assimilationist policy (Paris).

Assimilationist policies will encourage the civic incorporation of migrants while discouraging their mobilization on an ethnic basis (Lille, Paris). Socio-economic policies encourage integration into the labour market (e.g. vocational training projects) but tend to ignore the ethnic factors involved, such as particular migrant entrepreneurial skills. The exception to the rule of general rather than specific policies are migrant-targeted language education policies (Paris, Barcelona). This follows from the view that language fluency is a key to successful assimilation. In the Spatial domain the municipality will try to minimize physical manifestations of Otherness, such as mosques.[11] Assimilationist urban policies will discourage ethnic concentration through planned dispersal or quota policies (Antwerp, Berlin, Brussels) or more implicitly, through policies encouraging redevelopment and gentrification in areas of ethnic concentration (Brussels, Paris). Often couched in universalist planning terms, such actions may be identified as *de facto* 'migrant policies', based on the policymakers' intentions and on the impact on the migrant/minority population in those areas. Paris provides a good example of this (Chapter 6).

The 'Pluralist attitude' assumes not only the permanence of the migrant presence, but also accepts their Otherness as a permanent feature in the city. Integration of ethnic minorities is now considered a process of mutual adjustment involving the host society as well as the newcomers. Indeed, the municipality may try to play down the dominant national culture and emphasize instead a local culture of urban cosmopolitanism. Sensitivity to particular needs and problems arising from the migrants' cultural Otherness characterizes the Pluralist attitude. In addition, the positive potential of this Otherness is recognized, and is expected

---

[11] See Gale and Naylor 2002 on policies toward mosques in England; see Rath et al. 2001 for a comparative analysis of policies in Rotterdam and Utrecht.

to enrich the local host culture and economy in the long term. Thus, the 'salad bowl' metaphor replaces the assimilationist 'melting pot', with labour migrants and their descendants becoming another colourful ingredient in the multicultural mix.

Pluralist policies deliberately focus on ethnicity as a vital factor in the integration process. From support for minority religious and cultural practices, to promotion of ethnic entrepreneurship, to pro-active encouragement of ethnic organizations, Pluralist policies often apply a community-based approach, regarding communal, ethnic-based empowerment as a vehicle rather than an obstacle in the integration process. But while stressing sensitivity to Otherness, these policies tend to overlook individual differences within the same 'ethnic category', e.g. gender and educational background. Pluralist communication policies also target the host society, propagating the acceptance of difference and 'selling' ethnic Otherness as a positive potential for the city.[12]

In the Legal-political domain, pluralist policies promoting migrant participation are explicitly communitarian, as in the case of Amsterdam, which established no less than five advisory councils along ethnic lines. Socio-economic policies may also be set up on an ethnic basis, e.g. Sheffield's literacy programmes, and Birmingham's 'Employment and Resource Centres' run by and for different ethnic communities. Within the municipality, special programmes or units promote 'cultural sensitivity' in the provision of local services while ethnic monitoring measures the effectiveness of policies aimed at increasing the proportion of municipal employees of ethnic origin (Birmingham, Amsterdam). In the Cultural-religious domain, the municipality will support religious institutions which are regarded as instruments of integration (Rotterdam's subsidization of mosque organizations, 1980s–90s). In the Spatial domain, urban renewal policies will be sensitive to preserving the ethnic character of neighbourhoods.[13]

2.2 Policy Domains and Issue Areas

The second dimension of the typology arranges all the (potential and actual) local migrant policies into four policy domains, which are subdivided into issue areas **(Table 3.1)**. Policies regarding migrant representation and mobilization are grouped in the Legal-political domain. The Socio-economic domain includes newcomer/reception services, labour market policies, education and welfare policies, etc. The Cultural-religious domain includes policies relating to minority religious and cultural practices as well as policies aimed at changing attitudes toward ethnic/cultural diversity in the host society. Housing, urban renovation

---

[12] Vertovec (1996) describes Berlin's promotional 'multikulti' policy in the 1990s for 'changing public mentality'; Friedmann and Lehrer (1997) describe such an attempt in Frankfurt in the early 1990s.

[13] For example, Utrecht's development scheme for the Lombok district deliberately involved the area's ethnic entrepreneurs to prevent their dispersion (ELAINE 1996).

and other policies with a strong spatial dimension are grouped under the heading of the Spatial domain. This is one possible format for dividing local migrant policies into domains and issue areas. It is not meant to be exhaustive, nor is it the only way in which local migrant policies can be ordered.[14]

The use of policy domains not only puts some order into the potentially huge number of policies; such a modular format also allows us to identify if a city has, say, Assimilationist-type spatial policies but Pluralist-type cultural-religious policies. This is important when following the changes in one city over time, and vital in multi-city comparisons, since different cities may focus on different policy domains in their response to migration, as noted above.

The **Legal-Political domain** addresses the civic incorporation of migrants/ethnic minorities in the host polity. Local migrant policies in this domain can be divided into three issue areas. The first relates to migrant civic status. Although acquisition of legal residency and citizenship status (naturalization and regularization) is usually a prerogative of national agencies, this can become a local policy matter when it is partly delegated to local authorities (as in Switzerland, the Netherlands and Germany), who can speed up or slow down procedures. Thus, Berlin adopted a liberal policy which accounts for nearly a quarter of all discretionary naturalizations in Germany (Haussermann 1998). The right to participate in local referenda, etc. may also be left to municipal discretion.[15] Other policies in this area range from providing information to migrants on their civic rights (Rome, Tel Aviv), to actively encouraging them to vote (Amsterdam, Stockholm).

The second issue area regards consultative structures, which often substitute or supplement formal voting rights. In the 1980s-90s, dozens of local authorities across Europe experimented with migrant 'advisory councils' and other consultative forms, with varying degrees of success.[16] Another crucial area is the local authority's relation toward migrant mobilization. Policies can range from support for migrant organizations as a means of empowerment, to cooptation or exclusion of these organizations as a means of control.[17]

---

[14] The issue areas are based on the findings of the literature survey. For clarity, each issue area is assigned to only one domain, although some could be placed in more than one domain. For example, 'school policies' appears in the Socio-economic domain but could also appear in the Cultural-religious domain (e.g. Birmingham's school policies relating to religious practices) or the Spatial domain (e.g. school desegregation policy).

[15] For example, some cities in Italy (Turin, Bologna) have extended this right to non-citizen migrants while others have not. Since the European Commission Directive of 1994 local voting rights in EU member states have been extended to all foreign residents with EU citizenship.

[16] See Anderson 1990 for a classification of consultative structures for migrants. For a (not very positive) evaluation of migrant advisory councils in various cities, see ELAINE 1997b.

[17] Delegating the provision of local services to migrant organizations is another policy option with political implications. For comparative analyses of local policies toward migrant political mobilization, see Penninx et al. 2004 and the May 2004 issue (Jacobs and

The ***Socio-Economic domain*** comprises a large number of issue areas, including newcomer reception services, education, welfare services, labour market policies, etc. German cities, for example, have focused on labour market integration, while Dutch cities have focused on political participation and social services. Many cities with a significant migrant population provide reception and orientation services. These may be part of a national reception policy (Paris) or a local initiative (Tel Aviv), and may range from minimal 'office hours' services to comprehensive programmes that include short-term lodging (Rome).

Social (welfare) services are an issue area where the local authority has a wide choice of policies. These may include developing specific services or programmes for migrants (projects for migrant youth or women, etc.), or adapting general (health, welfare) services to migrant needs. Adaptation of local services ranges from translating municipal brochures to providing 'cultural mediators' to help newcomers (Rome).[18] Providing services to migrants as part of the general population rather than preferentially is also a policy option (Brussels, Oeiras), as is delegation of some services to civic (including migrant) organizations (Amsterdam, Rome). Policies to strengthen migrant participation in the labour market may include vocational training, language instruction, support for migrant entrepreneurs, monitoring discrimination in the labour market, and affirmative hiring policies within the municipality.

A crucial issue area in cities with second-generation migrants is education.[19] While this policy area is often dominated by the state, local authorities still have considerable leverage (even where school directors and teachers are not formally municipal employees). Local policies may include allocating extra resources to schools with a high proportion of migrant pupils, attempts at school desegregation, support for extra-curricular projects (e.g. tutoring in the home-language), etc. Conversely, local education policies may disregard the ethnic element, 'treating all children equally'.

Finally, policing and security may be considered an area of local migrant policy in cities with a municipal police force (in the four case studies in this book, policing was not a significant local policy area in regard to migrants).[20] Municipal police may then serve as agents of social change (Stuttgart, Leicester) or as agents of control toward migrant residents (see Body-Gendrot 2001).

Tillie, eds) of the *Journal of Ethnic and Migration Studies*, 30 (3). See also: Blommaert and Martiniello 1996, Bousetta 2001, Garbaye 2000, Ireland 1994.

[18] Cultural mediators are persons of the same ethnic origin as the target population, but with veterancy in the host society that allows them to act as translators and cultural interpreters. Cultural mediators may be formally trained and accredited (see Chapter 4).

[19] See DIECEC 1996 for a comparison of national and local policies on intercultural education; Schnapper 1994 on the role of the school in the integration process; Mazzella (1996: chapter 5) for an analysis of school policy in a migrant/minority neighbourhood in Marseille.

[20] On policing policies in Amsterdam, see Diijkink 1990.

The **Cultural-Religious domain** includes those policies specifically relating to the cultural Otherness of the migrants. Local authorities' relations toward religious institutions and practices (mosques, *halal* butchers, ethnic festivals), as well as their relation to religious schools, range from neglect to support to discouragement.[21] Religious instruction/practices in local schools may play an important role in this domain. For example, Birmingham's city council established a joint working committee with religious organizations to settle matters such as prayer facilities, Muslim dress and diet, and curriculum changes in schools. Another issue area involves sensitizing the public to cultural differences. Communication policies use media campaigns, employee seminars, cultural manifestations and permanent 'multicultural centres' to sensitize the local host society to ethnic diversity. Such policies can emphasize anti-discrimination, anti-racism, multiculturalism or assimilation.

Lastly, the **Spatial domain** groups certain issue areas with strong spatial implications. This includes housing policies, whether migrant-targeted (e.g. guestworker hostels) or general (social housing or renovation policies, when they significantly affect migrants). Local housing policies are especially influential where a significant percentage of the housing stock is controlled by the municipality, either directly (e.g. in the UK) or indirectly (e.g. in the Netherlands). An overlapping policy area is urban development and renewal which, like housing policy, may not target migrants explicitly, but can significantly affect them. This includes explicit or implicit policies to disperse migrant enclaves (housing quotas in Berlin until 1990, urban renewal policies in Brussels), as well as urban renewal that protects local residents (Amsterdam, Stockholm).[22]

The Spatial domain also includes the issue of symbolic uses of space. In Europe the outstanding example is mosques. Here again cities have adopted very different policies, from discouraging or limiting these physical manifestations of Otherness (withholding building permits, limiting minaret height, etc.), to providing financial support (see Rath et al. 2001). Even the use of public parks or shopping malls by migrants, if perceived by native residents as an 'invasion

---

[21] In their comparative study on policies toward Islam (focusing on Rotterdam, Utrecht, Bradford and Brussels), Rath et al. (1999: 10) observe: '[i]nstitutions can react in three different ways to the presence of Islam, its adherents and their claims: they can actively promote or support the formation of new Muslim institutions; they can be passive and adopt a more or less neutral attitude; or they can actively oppose the development of new institutions, for instance by the literal application of regulations, and by delays in putting them into force, or by laying down new restrictions.'

[22] For example, Kesteloot & Cortie (1998) compare urban development policies in Amsterdam and Brussels. The former aimed for a population mix through subsidized public and private rentals in the central city as well as outlying neighbourhoods, while the latter favoured home ownership over tenants and office development in the central city. This created very different situations for migrants in these cities, not only in housing but also in terms of social, economic and spatial segregation.

of strangers', may turn into a policy matter that the municipality can address in various ways (Sibley 1995).[23]

2.3   Using the Typology: Potentials and Limitations

Combining these two dimensions produces a typology space or classification system of actual or potential local migrant policies. The cells of this matrix can now be filled in, with each cell representing how a specific policy phase is expressed in a specific issue area (**Table 3.2**). Some of the policies in Table 3.2 are based on actual policies found in the survey (see Chapter 1) and classified according to the scheme; others were deduced directly from the typology as potential policies that may or may not actually exist. Following one policy type (column), we can see how it is expressed across different issue areas. Following one issue area (row), we can see how policies will change according to the different types (or phases).

The typology can be used as an analytical framework for in-depth research of a city's migrant policies. This framework allows us to identify the various local migrant policies in a city, arrange them by domains and issue areas, and classify them according to the ideal types described above. We can then follow changes over time from one type to another (e.g. from Non-policy to Assimilationist to Pluralist policy), identifying a trajectory of phases in the city. A policy response trajectory may be identified across several domains or only in certain policy areas.

If we identify the phases of actual migrant settlement (e.g. when family reunification occurs in a significant proportion of the migrant population this signals a shift from a guestworker phase to permanent settlement), we can then follow the degree of fit between the trajectory of migrant settlement and the trajectory of policy responses in the city (as shown in the case studies, below). This can be repeated for different cities to determine if there are typical or common trajectories of local policy responses to migrant settlement, and to compare the degree of fit between migrant settlement phases and policy responses in different cities (see Chapter 8).

As with every classification system, this typology is subject to various qualifications. First, it does not present an accurate description of a particular situation, but an analytical framework that can be applied to different cities and policies, to better understand them as a whole. The policy types proposed here are ideals, and no city is expected to conform to one type across all the issue areas. As noted above, local authorities are not unitary agents and may (indeed, often do) pursue different types of policies concurrently. Nevertheless, as the case studies demonstrate, it is possible to identify *prevailing* municipal attitudes and policy types in a city over a given period (another city may be characterized by a mix

---

[23] See Chapter 4, Box 4.1, on Rome's response in this area. See also Body-Gendrot (2001) on Marseille's policy aimed at preventing vandalism, by involving ethnic-origin youth in the planning and construction of a new shopping mall in an overwhelmingly minority-inhabited area.

of policy types across different domains). Such a framework may also suggest which domains or policy areas tend to dominate in municipal responses to the presence of labour migrants in a given period.

It is also important to note that the order of the policy types in Table 3.2 does not represent a fixed trajectory of policy responses. Although the policy types can represent a development over time (i.e. phases), they do not necessarily represent a development from exclusionary to inclusionary responses. In other words, this typology is not meant as a normative framework. However, the typology can be useful in judging actual policies responses based on the fit between the policy type and the actual phase of migration. Thus, Guestworker-type policies may be appropriate when the migrant presence is indeed of a temporary, guestworker character. If this develops into a phase of permanent settlement but local policies remain 'stuck' in the Guestworker phase, then they are problematic.

This classification scheme can be used as a framework to follow one city's policy reactions over time, or to compare the policy reactions of different cities across various domains and issue areas. It is not meant as a formula into which we can 'plug in' a policy or city and summarily draw conclusions. Instead, the typology can be used to reach *preliminary* conclusions about the prevailing attitudes and policy aims in the city (or cities) under study, by identifying what policy types appeared, at what time, and in what domains. Having mapped out the 'what and when', we can then focus on the 'hows and whys' using a case study approach. The typology is thus meant to complement, and not replace, the in-depth approach that has characterized much of the local-level research up to now. This method will be tested in the following four chapters.

Chapter 4

Rome: From Non-Policy to Delegation

> In these [past] years we have definitely understood that a correct and efficacious integration passes necessarily through the acknowledgement on equal conditions of the values of the 'other'.
> (*Oltre l'accoglienza*, USI 2000, p. 6, my translation)
>
> *Nu me po' frega de meno.*
> Traditional expression in Roman dialect: 'I couldn't care less'.

1   Introduction

Rome presents an interesting example of a 'new immigration' city's transition, from Non-policy to an espoused Pluralist policy – that, at least, is the first impression. For nearly two decades (from the mid-1970s to 1990) City Hall largely ignored the presence of overseas immigrants, most of whom stayed temporarily before moving on to seek work in northern Italy and beyond. In the 1980s as the migrant presence increased, local civic organizations tended to their growing needs. It was only in the wake of the Pantanella crisis (the 1990 takeover of a vacant building by some two thousand homeless migrants) that the municipality faced up to its migrant presence. The change was dramatic: in 1993 the newly elected mayor Francesco Rutelli proclaimed Rome to be a multicultural city and adopted a long-term, avowedly Pluralist-type policy that aims to permanently integrate migrants in the capital.

A closer look, however, raises doubts about the depth of change in this new phase. Rome's strategy is based on the outsourcing of nearly all integration services to the civic organizations that had developed these services since the 1980s. Rome's migrant policy since 1993 has thus been largely a matter of delegation and coordination, channelling public funding to local NGOs that operate the services for migrants. Is this the correct strategy for a city where civic organizations are more experienced and efficient than the public sector? Or is it simply a variation of Rome's previous Non-policy, when City Hall avoided taking responsibility for its migrant population?

In the following pages I will address this question, as well as proposing an explanation for the previous two decades of Non-policy. I first describe the national and local contexts (Sections 2 and 3). Section 4 follows the evolution of Rome's policy toward migrants since the 1970s, identifying two main phases of host-stranger relations and policy responses. In Section 5, I propose several explanations for Rome's lengthy Non-policy phase as well as the gap between espoused and actual policy in the current phase.

2   The National Context: Italian Responses to Labour Immigration

Charles Richards notes (1994: 256) that Italians 'pride themselves on their racial tolerance' but adds:

> ... Italians had no reason to harbour racial prejudice or show it because they had with the exception of the small Jewish communities no long history of distinct racial groups living among them. Rapid immigration and growing economic strains could test quite how deep the much vaunted tolerance of the Italians really is, and how ready society is to welcome strangers in its midst. (ibid.)

Indeed, the presence of non-Italian labour migrants as a new type of Stranger dates back to the mid-1970s (in 1970 there were only 144,000 immigrants in the country). Until then, host-stranger relations in Italy were primarily a matter of regional differences, and these were significant. Thus, the most common Strangers in northern Italy were labour migrants from southern Italy. In Milan, construction workers from the *mezzogiorno* needed a middleman (today he would be termed a cultural mediator) who could bridge between their Calabrian or Sicilian dialects and the Milanese dialect. In the 1970s the national budget included an item for the integration of these '*immigrati*'. Conversely, the most common Outsiders in southern Italy were 'northerners' representing business interests or the government.[1]

After 1973, when other European countries suspended their guestworker policies, Italy became the primary backdoor entry for irregular immigration to the EU, and by the beginning of the 1980s had itself become a net labour importer. In the second half of the 1980s immigration to Italy reached record levels and the organized smuggling of illegal immigrants became 'endemic' (Sciortino 1999: 237). In the 1990s the migrant presence took on permanent features: family reunification, rising school enrolment, etc. By 2001 there were an estimated 1.69 million legally resident foreigners in Italy; by 2005 the estimate was 2.8 million foreigners (including second-generation), or 4.8 per cent of the population.[2]

Most of the foreign residents in Italy today can be characterized as labour migrants with the vast majority being of non-EU origin, including a large

---

[1]   Host-stranger relations between northern and southern Italians remains a favourite theme in Italian cinema, from Latouada's 1948 comedy *Verano* to Scola's (1989) *Splendor*, Visconti's (1993) *Il Gatopardo*, Calias' (2002) *Respiro*, etc.

[2]   The number of irregular migrants is unknown, see below (Caritas 2001, 2005).

ex-Soviet and Balkan contingent.[3] The common term for these newcomers, *extracomunitari* (which technically refers to immigrants from outside the EU) has 'strong overtones of exclusion, of describing those who lay outside of the national community' (Ginsborg 2001: 62). Indeed, the reception of the *extracomunitari* has been on the whole negative. As Ginsborg notes in his latest history (ibid.: 64), 'the Italian population ... was quite unprepared for, and hostile to, the idea of a multi-ethnic Italy.'

The 1990s was the decade in which immigration became 'visible', and politicized (Caritas 2000). The 1990 Pantanella crisis was succeeded by the highly publicized arrival of boatloads of Albanian refugees (1991) followed by 'waves' of refugees from Somalia, Rwanda and Yugoslavia and a 'second Albanian crisis' in 1997. Although relatively small in numbers, the unexpected arrival of these immigrants and the total inadequacy of official responses, as well as media exaggeration, created an atmosphere of 'moral alarm' and 'moral panic' (Sciortino 1999).

Italy's 'immigration crisis' of the 1990s coincided with a general destabilization of the political system and the rise of two anti-immigrant parties, the neo-fascist *Aleanza Nazionale* and the populist *Lega Nord*. An economic recession in the mid-1990s made it easy to turn foreign workers into scapegoats for rising unemployment levels. Furthermore, the geographic concentration of the immigrants (nearly half now reside in six major cities) highlighted the competition between immigrants and working-class Italians over low-cost housing and overloaded public services.

But while the 'war between the poor' remains a key feature of host-stranger relations in Italy, it is the image of migrants as a source and a symptom of *disorder* that has come to dominate public discourse (Pallida 1998, Calavita 1994). Indeed, a fundamental feature of labour migrants in Italy is their irregular status: an estimated three out of four migrants have been irregular at one time or another, due to unauthorized residency and/or irregular employment.[4] This is a result of Italy's restrictive immigration regime on one hand, and its large underground economy (estimated to employ up to 17 per cent of the labour force) on the other.[5] Estimates of the number of migrants employed in the underground economy range from 350–400,000 and up to 40 to 60 per cent of the migrant population, or a sixth of Italy's total informal labour sector (Calavita 1994, Caritas 2001).

Many researchers have pointed to the link between the exclusionary nature in which Italy absorbs labour migrants (into the informal economy, without

---

[3] Over 60 per cent of the legal migrants in 2001 had residency permits for work reasons (Caritas 2001). Italy's ratio of foreign residents to natives (1:35) remains low in comparison with veteran immigration countries (France 1:15, Germany and Belgium 1:10), but for Italians the change over the past decade appears momentous.

[4] See Reyneri 2001. Frequent regularizations (which are often temporary) confuse the picture between the status of regular and irregular migrants.

[5] See Sciortino 1999.

civic status, no provisions for housing) and their image in the host society.[6] The migrants' irregular status is easily connected to criminality, as the *extracomunitari* are associated with the shadow economy, street peddling, petty crime, homelessness and squatting. Work in Italy's underground economy, in itself 'quite legitimized by soical consensus', is stigmatizing when connected to migrants (Reyneri 2001: 26).

A turning point in Italy's redefinition of migrants as a public order problem occurred in July 1990, when more than 2,000 migrants of various nationalities occupied the former Pantanella bread factory, an abandoned building near Rome's Central Station. Most were homeless and undocumented migrants awaiting an amnesty. After months of frantic negotiations they were evicted in January 1991 (some were resettled, see below). The Pantanella occupation attracted national attention, highlighting the desperate situation of migrants in Italy, their irregular status and lack of housing, and the government's inability to deal with these problems. One result was the staging of Italy's first large pro-immigrant rallies. Since then, anti- and pro-immigrant sentiment have become embedded in the Right-Left divide of Italian politics, ensuring that immigration remains high on the political agenda.

National immigration policy has only added to the sense of disorder. After ignoring the phenomenon for almost a decade, a series of largely reactive, ad-hoc decrees and laws were enacted in the 1980s and 1990s. Their aim was to limit labour immigration through stricter border controls and restrictions on the legal employment of foreigners, while regularizing irregular migrants already residing in the country through 'amnesties'. Instead, national legislation has resulted in the exclusion of most labour migrants from the legal framework by dint of unlawful entry, residence, and/or employment. The Italian immigration regime, while theoretically controlling residency and work conditions, in fact allows migrants to live for years without supervision. This is periodically corrected through large amnesty programmes which have resulted in over 1.3 million applications for regularization (!) over the past 20 years.[7]

---

[6] For example, Quassoli (2001: 13) analyzes the 'criminalization of certain types of immigrant ... who have become in the political context a kind of highly-productive scapegoat for social problems in the metropolitan areas of the north and centre of Italy...'.

[7] In 1982 the first decree prohibited the issuing of work permits for importation of workers from outside the EC, and offered amnesty to irregular migrants. The amnesty failed and the permit restrictions led to an increase in illegal entry and employment. In 1986, Act 943 further restricted legal immigration and offered another amnesty to irregular migrants in the country (118,000 regularized). In 1990, Act 39 (the Martelli law) further restricted legal immigration and included another amnesty (235,000 regularized). In 1995–96 another amnesty programme (nearly 250,000 regularized) highlighted the huge number of illegal migrants inside the country. In 1998, Act 40 attempted to unify the various decrees and laws. In 2002, the Bossi-Fini law further restricted legal entry and employment of foreigners, while proposing another massive regularization. This latest amnesty (Italy's fifth) was the largest: some 700,000 regularized (Caritas 1998 and 2005, Pallida 1998, Sciortino 1999, Reyneri 2001).

In 1998, Act 40 attempted to unify immigration legislation, with the aim of regulating flows and establishing a comprehensive national integration policy. In principle, Act 40 declares Italy to be a country of immigration and welcomes multiculturalism. However, the law is full of lacunae regarding rights of entry and residence (i.e. in its definition of legal migrants), while responsibility for the integration of these migrants is delegated to local authorities and the civic sector (Caritas 1998). It is in this confusing setting that the civic sector in Rome, as well as the municipality, developed local responses to migrant settlement.

3 The Local Context

Although cities in northern Italy experienced foreign migrant settlement several years earlier, Rome today has the country's largest concentration of *stranieri*. Of the city's 2.8 million residents, an estimated 220,000 to 298,000 are foreign, most of them labour migrants (see below). In relative terms, too, the proportion of foreigners in Rome's population (around eight per cent) is the highest in Italy.[8]

3.1 The Roads Leading to Rome

As capital of the world's first truly multi-ethnic empire, and later in its role as seat of the Catholic church, Rome has always had its share of Strangers. Modern Rome is no longer the *caput mundi*, but today's Romans are used to rubbing shoulders with a constant stream of foreigners, whether pilgrims, clergy, diplomats or tourists – some of whom stay on. But it is only in the last two decades that these traditionally 'welcome guests' have been supplemented by a new kind of newcomer: overseas labour migrants. The latter are attracted to Rome as a gateway into the EU, as a religious capital (for Christian migrants), and above all as a busy metropolis with a large informal economy. Rome offers labour migrants a relatively tolerant atmosphere and a network of services run by church and other civic organizations.

Postwar labour immigration to Rome can be roughly divided into two periods: the transient or 'invisible' phase from the mid-1970s to 1990, and the stable or 'visible' phase after 1990 (Accorinti 1998).[9] Excepting a few small established communities (Filipinos, Egyptians), most of the migrants in the first phase stayed in Rome for a period of several months before moving northward in search of better work opportunities. The 1980s saw an increase in predominantly irregular migrants, especially from Africa. Often the change from irregular to regular status (through amnesties) was followed by migration to another city. The transient

---

[8] The second city is Milan (124,000 foreign residents); the third Turin (under 50,000).

[9] Before the 1970s there was a small but steady arrival of mostly female migrants from Cap Verde, Philippines and the Horn of Africa, hired as domestic helpers.

nature of the city's migrant population remains significant today: in a survey of 29,537 migrants registered at the Caritas Foreigners Centre, 60 per cent said their final destination was outside Italy (Caritas 2000: 1488).

Between 1991 and 2004 the number of registered foreign residents in Rome nearly tripled (**Figure 4.1**). In this second phase, significant signs of migrant settlement appeared in the city, as many re-assessed their migratory projects. The nature and composition of Rome's migrant population also changed, with more immigrants from East Europe, the Balkans and South America, and a relative decline in the proportion of Africans and Asians (Collicelli et al. 1998).

By the end of 2004 there were 223,879 foreign residents officially registered in Rome (7.9 per cent of the city population). The overall foreign-origin population including second-generation children was estimated at 298,000, or 10.6 per cent of the population (Caritas 2005), however the overall number of foreigners, including undocumented migrants residing in Rome, may be higher.[10] In 2001, the number of *labour migrants* (excluding gypsies and residents from OECD countries) was estimated at around 200,000, of which some 15 per cent were irregular (interview F. Pittau).

Rome's foreign population is extremely heterogeneous in ethnic origin, as characteristic of a 'new immigration' city (**Figure 4.2**). Among well over a hundred countries represented, the city's four largest ethnic communities (Filipinos, Romanians, Poles and Peruvians) accounted in 2004 for just 32.6 per cent of the total migrant population (Caritas-CCR 2005b).

In their migratory projects, too, Rome's migrant population is heterogeneous. The city's large submerged economy (estimated to employ about a quarter of the local labour force) makes it attractive as a first stage for labour migrants; they and their families make up the majority of the city's migrant population.[11] Paolo Accorinti identified four general types in Rome (in addition to transit migrants awaiting decisions on their refugee status): legal, stable communities, often self-employed (Filipinos, Chinese, Egyptians, Palestinians); irregular but stable (settled) migrants working in low-skill informal jobs such as street peddling (Bangladeshis, Pakistanis, Albanians, etc.); legal but temporary residents with work permits employed as domestics and in other low-skill jobs (East Europeans, Latin Americans); and illegal, temporary migrants, some moving back and

---

[10] Caritas' annual *Dossier Immigrazione* is the most reliable source in Italy for data regarding immigrants. Caritas' estimate for Rome is based on registered foreign residents plus 96,000 regularized but not yet appearing on the city registrar. Various estimates of the number of *undocumented* foreigners range from 30,000 to over 150,000. The upper estimate brings the total (regular and irregular) migrant/minority population in Rome to 320,000 (see Alexander 2003: 84).

[11] Of *registered* migrants in Rome Province (of which 90 per cent reside in Rome), work was the primary motive for residence (55 per cent) with another 15 per cent for family reasons, 19.6 per cent reside in Rome for religious reasons and only 0.8 per cent are asylum seekers (ibid.).

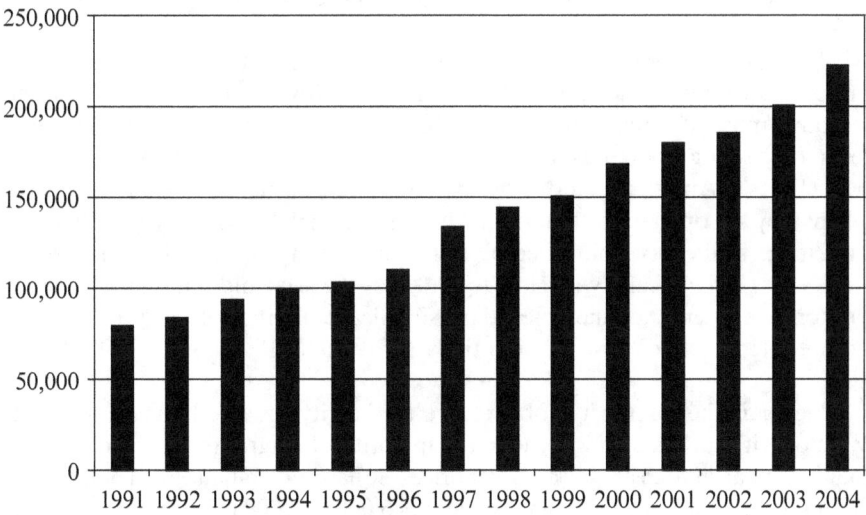

Figure 4.1   Registered foreign residents in Rome, 1991–2004

Source: Data compiled from Municipality of Rome 2001, Caritas 2005 and Camera di Commercio di Roma 2005a.

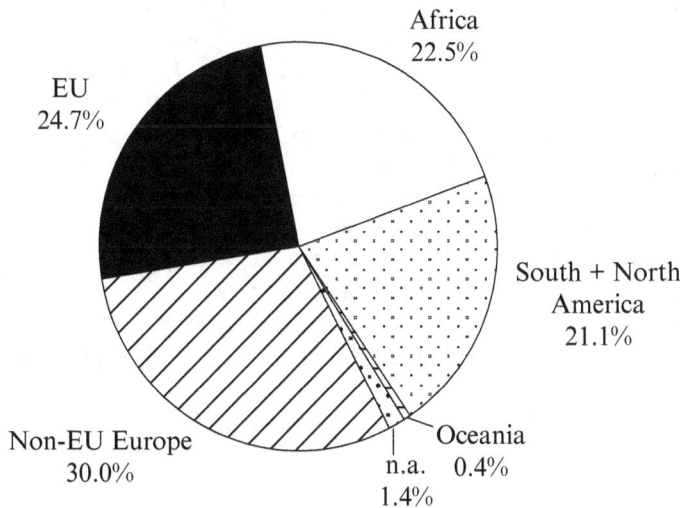

Figure 4.2   Registered foreign residents in Rome, by content of origin (31 December 2004)

Source: Data compiled from Caritas and Camera di Commercio de Roma 2005a.

forth between Italy and their country of origin (Poles) (Accorinti 1998, Caritas 2000).

Within this diversity, however, the unifying characteristic of labour migrants in Rome is their precarious situation. As the state provides little to no protection, migrants must rely on voluntary organizations for bed and board in the short-term. In the long term, they have to survive through self-help networks and their own efforts.[12] An estimated two out of three work in the 'submerged economy' where they are open to exploitation. An estimated 2500 migrant women work as prostitutes in the city, controlled by Italian and foreign criminal organizations. Joblessness is significant, with close to 20,000 of the legal migrants in the Province of Rome registered as unemployed. A significant number of migrant children do not attend school, in part or entirely (Caritas 2001, Accorinti 1998, Pittau 2001).

Shelter is the foremost problem, due to the city's severe housing shortage. With or without residency permits, the majority of migrants are forced to find lodging in flats rented at black market prices. Squatting of abandoned buildings is common, and on any given night as many as 6,000 to 7,000 migrants are 'sleeping on the streets' (interview E. Serpieri). These conditions were first highlighted in 1990 by the Pantanella occupation. A decade later, Caritas (2001: 401) reported on dozens of 'mini Pantanellas' with hundreds of migrants living in extremely precarious conditions, mainly in the centre of the city.

Rome's migrant population (10.4 per cent of the city population in 2004) is fairly evenly distributed between the central, intermediate and outer areas of the city, however in a few districts migrants account for only 5–7 per cent, while in others that proportion rises to 15 per cent and more (**Figure 4.3**). District I, encompassing the historic city centre, is home to over 33,000 foreigners or 27.4 per cent of that city district. This includes residents from OECD countries as well many migrants engaged in domestic services, especially Filipinos. Two general settlement directions can be discerned. The first is in the city centre, especially south of Termini central train station, containing the neighbourhoods with the highest proportion of foreigners in the city. The other is a large zone extending to the north of the city (Districts II and XX, with 15.7 per cent and 18.7 per cent, respectively). Due to the heterogeneity of the migrant population, one cannot speak of ethnic 'ghettos' in Rome (Caritas 2005: 23); instead, the nearest approximation to a 'migrant neighbourhood' is the Esquilino in District I (**Box 4.1**).

---

[12] See Korac 2003 on the comparative situation of refugees in Rome and Amsterdam.

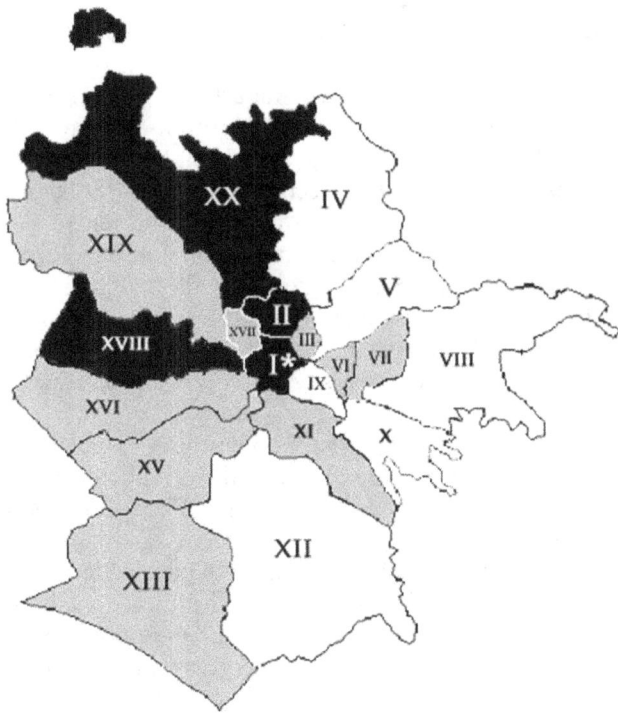

■ Over 13% of total population
▨ 9 - 13% of total population
☐ Less than 9% of total population

* - The Esquilino

Figure 4.3 Distribution of registered foreign residents in Rome, by districts (2004)

3.2 Local Host-stranger Relations: From Nonchalance to Polarization

Misiani notes (1999: 12) that Romans are known for their traditional tolerance-cum-indifference toward Strangers. However, this 'nu me po' frega de meno' attitude is conditional:

> If there are too many on the bus, the slogan is quickly forgotten and if one is not ready for cultural change, the first consideration one makes is that there are too many 'others'. In sum 'I couldn't care less' as long as there is no competition (ibid., my translation).

In fact, Rome has experienced some violent anti-immigrant incidents, mostly in the peripheral areas where competition for cheap housing between migrants

> **Box 4.1 The Esquilino: Rome's 'multiethnic quarter'**
>
> If Rome has an 'ethnic neighbourhood' it is the Esquilino, a once-elegant neighbourhood just south of Termini Station. Like many central city neighbourhoods, it suffered significant loss of population in the 1970s and 1980s. Its proximity to the central station and the large number of abandoned houses and shops attracted migrants who rented or squatted apartments during the 1990s. Ethnic entrepreneurship transformed the Esquilino into Rome's first 'international quarter' with 'side-by-side shops of Filipinos and Bengalese, Eritrean cafes, Chinese restaurants, Indian and Pakistani video stores, small African import-exports and various other businesses of East European and EC citizens' (Accorinti 1998: 36). By 2004, one in six Esquilino inhabitants was foreign.
>
> As the area gentrified, local opposition grew to the open-air market located in Piazza Vittorio, the centre of the neighbourhood. With a large number of unlicensed stalls run by migrants, Piazza Vittorio became Rome's main 'ethnic market'. A number of residents committees campaigned against this irregular market. One newspaper reported that 'some residents use such language as "inclusion" and "multicultural", while others complain about "the attempt to occupy the territory." In response the leaders of the migrant communities claim that when they arrived 90 per cent of these shops were abandoned' (Wolferstan 2001).
>
> It is difficult to gauge the extent to which the controversy over Piazza Vittorio contained a xenophobic element, beyond the obvious NIMBY (Not In My Back Yard) reaction to the unlicensed market. City Hall avoided the issue for several years until local residents threatened to withhold their city taxes. Finally, in 2002 the municipality relocated the market stalls to new facilities near Termini station. It appears that City Hall has tried to accommodate all the sides, including the migrants, after delaying for as long as possible.
>
> In recent years the municipality has organized a multicultural festival for children in Piazza Vittorio, highlighting foreign cultures. However, the municipal website admits that the area's 'concentration of multiple ethnic groups ... may slow down the process of integration' (my translation).
>
> *Sources*: Accorinti 1998, Wolferstan 2001, www.commune.roma.it 2001, Caritas 2005.

and poor Romans was strongest. Discrimination in the labour market is also commonplace, especially against darkskinned Muslims. A 2003 survey by the Small Houseowners Association found that 51 per cent of Roman houseowners opposed renting to migrants (Caritas 2000, 2005: 20).

But the city is also host to abundant, often organized, expressions of empathy toward its migrant population, from a variety of civic associations to the largest pro-migrant rallies in Italy. Paul Ginsborg (2001: 96) has analyzed the growth in Italy of 'an autonomous and active civil society' in the 1980s, partly in response to the weakness of the state. This is evident in Rome, which boasts a highly developed network of religious and lay organizations with thousands of volunteers. Religious associations (some commanding impressive resources) are active in providing assistance ranging from shelters to food kitchens to lobbying for migrant rights. This is supplemented by significant activism of left-wing, union and civil rights organizations in the capital. Since the 1980s much of this 'social solidarity' focuses on migrants, who occupy the bottom rung of the socio-economic ladder in Italy (see below). Although civic society activism in Rome created a supportive environment for pro-migrant municipal policies, it may also have resulted in a 'lumping together' of migrants with other types of Outsiders (indigenous homeless, gypsies) in the eyes of the local population.

Until 1990, there was little awareness in Rome of labour migrants *as a new type of newcomer*. Most migrants were assumed to be transient, and many in fact were 'passing through'. The Pantanella crisis awoke Romans to the possibility that their city was not just a gateway but a final destination for migrants. The dramatic occupation, negotiations and eventual eviction of the migrants, amply covered in the local media, raised feelings of solidarity but also strengthened their image as outsiders and lawbreakers. During the 1990s, as the migrant presence in the city doubled, the traditional Roman nonchalance gave way to increasingly polarized attitudes. A 1996 survey of residents showed an ambivalent response of 'compassion together with repulsion and a propensity to criminalize [migrants]' (Caritas 2000:1525). According to one official, the survey revealed that 'Romans were not xenophobic, but they were uncomfortable with the irregular situation and expected the municipality to do something' (interview C. Rossi).

3.3 Institutional and Political Context

The extent to which the municipality can 'do something' regarding the migrant presence is limited in part by the broader institutional context. The City of Rome is located within the Province of Rome, which is part of Lazio Region.[13] The division of authority between the various levels is confusing, with overlapping competencies. In the area of migrant policy, decentralization formally commenced in 1986[14] and was institutionalized in the 1990s. Act 39/1990

---

[13] The City and Province are virtually synonymous in area and population. Foreign residents in Rome constitute 90 per cent of the foreign population in Rome Province, which in turn makes up 90 per cent of the foreign population of Lazio Region.

[14] Act 943/1986 first delegated the implementation of integration policy from national government to local authorities and civic associations. In typically vague language, it mandated local authorities 'to facilitate, through the civic service [associations], any exigencies of [migrant] integration into the community, eventually including institutionalized consultation' (cited in CESPI 2000: 856, my translation).

created a national fund for migrant reception centres, to be set up and managed by local authorities. Regional authorities were made responsible for distributing national funds to different local authorities, in effect deciding where the migrants would be accommodated in each region, according to prepared plans. However, administrative and political obstacles often kept government funding from reaching the local level. Out of 30 million lire budgeted in 1990, only three million reached the Lazio region, of which only two million lire eventually reached Rome (Misiani 1999: 4). In 1998, Act 40 further decentralized Italian migrant policy, placing most of the responsibility for integration on the local level, funded via the regions. Again, Lazio Region was slow in its allocation, delaying national funding from reaching the city of Rome.[15]

Institutional problems characterize not only the Lazio region but the City of Rome as well. Palidda (1998: 124–5) has suggested a 'tentative typology' of integration in Italian cities, based on the local economic and institutional context. He contrasts between 'cities that are clearly benefiting from economic growth and with effective initiatives [for migrant integration] implemented by local authorities', such as Bologna, and 'cities with an underground economy that are still suffering the repercussions of administrative mismanagement in the past', such as Rome. That administrative mismanagement eventually led to the 1991 collapse of the ruling Christian Democrat coalition headed by Mayor Carraro.[16] However, Roman politics also reflected a general breakdown in the Italian political system in the early 1990s, when widespread corruption scandals led to the collapse of the Christian Democrat and Socialist parties (see Ginsborg 2001). In Rome, a second Carraro administration (1992) lasted less than a year. In response, the government appointed a transitional administration with an appointed Commissioner (not uncommon in Italy) for one year.

In November 1993, mayors were directly elected for the first time in Italy. In Rome, Francesco Rutelli was elected at the head of a Left-Centre coalition. Rutelli ruled for two terms, resigning in 2001 to run (unsuccessfully) for prime minister. His successor, Walter Veltroni, continues to rule with the same coalition. Thus, from 1993 onward Rome has been governed by a Left-wing majority in city council, with a Right-wing opposition headed by the Alleanza Nazionale. The watershed year of 1993 also marked a turning point in Rome's migrant policy, as we shall see below.

---

[15] Act 40 created a 'National fund for migration policy' to be divided between government ministries (about 20 per cent) and local authorities (about 80 per cent). To receive this national funding, regional authorities must submit budgeted proposals based on existing or planned local integration policies, by local authorities or civic organizations. However, the law's vagueness created uncertainty and overlapping competencies (CESPI 2000: 862–3, 875).

[16] In the mid-1980s Rome's Communist-led administration was replaced by a coalition of the Christian Democrats and Socialist Party.

4   Local Migrant Policies in Rome

4.1   Non-Policy, Mid-1970s to 1990

From the first appearance of labour migrants in the mid-1970s and throughout the 1980s the city of Rome had no real migrant policy. It is plausible that during the 1970s the municipality was simply unaware of the labour migrant presence as distinct from the many other transient residents in the city. But as their numbers increased in the 1980s, City Hall's attitude appears to have been one of wilful ignorance. Municipal actions toward migrants were limited to ad-hoc responses to minor crises, such as clearing migrant squats to avoid clashes with neighbours. A Caritas report (2000: 1481) describes this period of 'emergency policies' as 'spontaneity bordering on fatalism'. In 1986, as mandated by Law 943 (the first national regularization programme), a two-person unit was set up to assist applicants in obtaining residency and work permits.[17]

However, the growing migrant population did not go completely unnoticed, as shown by two studies undertaken by the city's research department. The 1983 Santori report, based on the latest census, outlined Rome's development into a multi-ethnic city and indicated the need for a long-range migrant policy. This was followed by a second study that noted the problems facing immigrants in Rome as well as the first expressions of xenophobia in the city, and put them down to the absence of an integration policy. Based on a comparison of policies in other European cities (including Amsterdam and Paris), the Ferrarotti report proposed a local policy that would extend various rights to immigrants, within the limits of Italian national policy. Both studies were effectively ignored (Misiani 1999).

In the same period a variety of non-governmental organizations increasingly turned their attention and resources to addressing the basic needs of the growing migrant presence. The most important of these was (and remains) the powerful Catholic organization Caritas, which set up reception and assistance structures for immigrants.[18] Other religious organizations (Evangelicals, Jesuits) as well as hundreds of religious charities in Rome (parish associations, convents) provided basic services such as food, shelters and medical treatment. They were supplemented by secular voluntary organizations and the powerful trade unions (CGIL, CISL and UIL). In the second half of the 1980s the three unions each established special sectors to deal with foreign workers. These evolved into offices in Rome advocating for migrant rights and offering various services of a mediatory nature, as well as supporting migrant associations with office facilities,

---

[17] According to Misiani (1999: 4), this unit was later dismantled; according to Accorinti (1998: 41, 44), a municipal 'Foreigners Office' (Ufficio Stranieri) continued to exist but with little or no effect.

[18] Caritas is the largest Catholic organization specializing in social issues, with branches throughout Italy and abroad. The Roman diocese of Caritas includes hundreds of lay employees and volunteers involved in social activism.

etc. Third sector activity in Rome was characterized by cooperation, if not actual coordination, between the many religious and secular organizations (Accorinti 1998: 38–56).

The municipality was aware of these activities and the needs they were addressing, but as with other problems, such as homelessness, it was easier to leave them to the better organized and more experienced NGOs, rather than attempt to tackle them directly. Political corruption may have also played a role in local authority negligence of this and other areas, in which there was no kickback money to be made (see Ginsborg 2001: 181–6). One example of Rome's Non-policy regards migrant children. An ever-growing number were placed in local charitable institutions that normally cared for Italian children rejected by the formal educational system due to behavioural and family problems. By the early 1990s some of these day-care centres, run by nuns and priests of religious charities, contained more migrant than indigenous children. The municipality limited itself to subsidizing this arrangement, ignoring new directives by the Ministry of Education that urged local authorities to integrate migrant children in public schools.[19] When older migrant children nevertheless enrolled in local schools, which then demanded help and extra resources, the municipality was 'caught unprepared' (interview P. Gabrielli). An interview with the Alderman for Social Affairs (Giovanni Azzaro, 1989–92) reveals the situation in the municipality at the end of the 1980s:

> ... there was no budget item regarding the specific question [of migrants]. There was no organizational structure, excepting an office of two junior employees who dealt above all with the question of refugees. There was no culture of assistance for migrants. When I became alderman, this problem was not presented to me as a priority nor did I receive indications of its emergence. In sum, the municipal administration was not in a condition to confront the problem that exploded in 1990, when I was told that the Pantanella building had been occupied by *extracomunitari*. (Misiani 1999: 4, my translation)

4.2   The Pantanella Crisis and Transition, 1990–92

The half-year-long occupation of the empty Pantanella factory near Rome's central station (July 1990–January 1991, see above) caught City Hall by surprise and eventually forced Mayor Carraro to request assistance from the Ministry of Interior to evacuate the migrants. For the first time, the city made a sustained effort to find lodging solutions for homeless migrants. In a crisis atmosphere, various ad-hoc solutions such as disused school buildings were considered. Finally, the municipality rented two hostels on the city outskirts for the Pantanella

---

[19] This policy was promoted through various circulars by the Ministry of Education from the early 1990s, but it was only in 1998 that Act 40 made local authorities responsible for obligatory education of all children aged 6 to 15, including migrant children (interview E. Todisco).

evacuees – an arrangement that turned out to be wholly inadequate. Charges were later raised of shady dealings between the hostel owners and the Carraro administration, and the hostels were later closed down by the Commissioner. In 1992 the municipality tried to set up an agency together with Caritas and the labour unions, to rent private dwellings and sublet them to migrants at subsidized cost. This attempt failed as well. Meanwhile, most migrants continued to live in rented flats, abandoned buildings, shelters run by civic organizations and in growing numbers on the streets. Rome's Termini train station became, and has remained, a focal point of migrant homelessness.

In the aftermath of Pantanella, public sentiment demanded that 'something be done'. Attitudes within the Municipality were also changing: City Hall began facing up to the possibility of a permanent migrant presence in the city. Under Mayor Carraro, however, the migrants were perceived primarily as a public order problem. It was only under the appointed transitional administration that migrants in Rome were redefined as a 'social problem that must be addressed with a long-term policy' (interview C. Rossi). At the end of 1992 the Alderman for General Affairs proposed that an office be established to deal specifically with Rome's foreign population. Just before Mayor Carraro was replaced by the Commissioner, City Council approved the establishment of the Special Office for Immigrants, laying the basis for the second phase in Rome's migrant policy.

4.3   Accepting Migrant Permanence, Moving toward 'Integration', 1993–2001

In 1993 the newly elected Rutelli administration announced the beginning of a long-term migrant integration policy, to be coordinated by the Special Office for Immigration (*Ufficio Speciale Immigrazione*, henceforth: USI). Since then, policies affecting migrants are largely decided within two departments: Social and Human Services Policy (Dept. V), and Education and Training Policy (Dept. XI). The alderman heading these departments and the acting director of USI (Carlo Rossi) remain the principle actors shaping Rome's integration policy.[20] The two terms of the Rutelli administration enabled a period of continuity so that we may speak of a single policy phase lasting from 1993 until at least 2001. Mayor Walter Veltroni (elected June 2001) appears to continue the policies of his predecessor.[21]

USI began operating in February 1993 as a quasi-autonomous unit within the Department of Social and Human Services, with its own budget, staff and separate premises. Although set up to deal with the migrant presence (overwhelmingly

---

[20] Aldermen (*assessore*) are appointed by the mayor from among the city councillors to head a municipal department. They are assisted by an appointed advisor (*consulente*) who is also involved in policymaking.

[21] In 2001 Mayor Veltroni appointed councillor Franca Coen to a new position, entitled 'Delegate for Multiethnic Policy' (*delegato* is a kind of alderman without portfolio), with Carlo Rossi as her *consulente* (advisor).

composed of labour migrants at that time), USI included sections dealing with gypsies,[22] refugees and asylum seekers, as well as returning Italian emigrés. The new office had a staff of just over 20, of which 10 dealt with *immigrati*; in practice, there was an overlap of services for labour immigrants and refugees/asylum seekers. Since 1993 the size of USI's staff has decreased slightly but its budget grew significantly, from 1.78 billion lire in 1993 to 12.76 billion lire in 2000 (USI Direzione, 2001).

Rome's migrant policy since 1993 adopts a two-pronged approach:

1. Making general welfare services (*l'assistenza sociale*), provided by national and regional law to all residents of Rome, accessible to eligible migrant residents. This is coordinated through USI.
2. Providing migrants with specific integration services (*sostegno all'integrazione*). This is done primarily through 'reception centres' which provide lodging and various integration services, 'education centres' for migrant children, and a vocational orientation agency. These services are provided by NGOs, in contractual agreements with USI. In addition, the city's Education Department provides pedagogical tools for schools with foreign pupils.

Rome's new migrant policy is based on a strategy of delegation, that is, institutionalizing the provision of integration services by local non-governmental entities. The role of USI is in large part to manage the outsourcing of migrant services to local NGOs (by channeling government and municipal funding to them), coordination and supervision. The daily management of the services is left up to the civic organizations. This delegation strategy is not particular to Rome's migrant policy, and characterizes social services policy in Italy since the 1980s.[23]

Within the new policy, two stages can be identified. During the first Rutelli administration (1993–97), the main goal was to establish a network of orientation structures and reception centres (below) that would prevent 'new Pantanellas'. By the mid-1990s an array of integration services had been outsourced to civic organizations, including a few migrant associations. Most of the integration services were provided through the reception centres, as mandated by Act 39/1990). In the second Rutelli administration (1997–2001), City Hall aimed to expand its migrant policy 'beyond reception'[24] to longer-term integration. Integration services were expanded and the municipality streamlined the channelling of government money provided through Act 40/1998 to civic organizations to which these services were outsourced. The Veltroni administration also aims at involving migrants in decision-making (see below).

---

[22] The gypsies (*nomadi*) were largely immigrants as well, arriving from the various parts of Yugoslavia, Albania and later from Romania.

[23] See e.g. Da Roit and Sabatinelli 2005.

[24] 'Beyond reception' (*Oltre l'accoglienza*) is the title of the USI brochure explaining municipal migrant policy, July 2000.

Although the new 'integration policy' declared by Mayor Rutelli in 1993 appears to depart radically from previous decades of Non-policy, the change may not be that clear-cut. To understand what has transpired since 1993, the following sub-sections describe the various components of Rome's new policy in more detail, using the ordering scheme of policy domains and issue areas proposed in the typology (see Chapter 3). Section 5 then analyzes this evolution in Rome's response to migration, again in terms of the typology.

4.3.1 Policies on civic status and representation

Civic status Italy's national immigration policy, as noted above, has resulted in a large proportion of immigrants living for years in an irregular status. Periodic amnesties opened the door for increasing numbers of undocumented migrants to become regularized, granting them temporary resident status and formal access to basic social services. Until now, civic organizations assisted migrants in the complicated bureaucracy that this involves. One of the aims of the new municipal policy is to facilitate this process. Since 1994, USI provides assistance directly to all new immigrants in Rome (who must register at its office), in obtaining residency status and information on rights. This is one of the few services that the municipality provides directly to migrants. However, it appears that the bulk of the work in this area is still delegated to civic organizations, through the NGO-run reception centres or in their offices. The difference is that now it is coordinated and subsidized through USI, which, in effect, channels government money to local civic organizations.

In the late 1990s USI set up a cultural mediators service to assist migrants in their contacts with public services and government agencies (see below). Trained cultural mediators may now be called upon by USI to accompany migrants encountering problems in various stages of the serpentine bureaucratic process, such as residency registration. However, this service only relates to regular (or regularizing) immigrants. Tens of thousands of undocumented migrants in the city continue to depend on civic organizations. The largest of these is Caritas, which provides all newcomers in Rome who register and pass an interview at its 'Foreigners Centre' (*Centro Stranieri*) with a Caritas 'identity card'. This not only gives them access to various Caritas services (health, soup kitchens, hostels, Italian courses, etc.) but also serves as a kind of alternative ID card. In 1999, 13,560 immigrants (regular and irregular) from 101 countries were thus registered, providing them with an informal semi-regular status that is recognized by various authorities, at least within Rome (interview M. Accorinti).

Migrant representation and organizations After the Pantanella occupation, the city of Rome could no longer ignore the fact that it had a very large, disenfranchized population. Today, few channels exist for minority residents to air their grievances and express their needs at the local level. Despite the size of the migrant population, only a few communities are well organized and there are only several dozen *active* migrant associations.²⁵ In part this has to do with the fact that Rome's migrants are fragmented into many communities, many are transient and many are irregular (Collicelli et al. 2000).

However, the weakness of migrant mobilization is also a result of the local political opportunity structure. When funding began to flow from the national and regional levels to local civic organizations in the 1990s, most migrant associations could not meet the formal requirements and bureaucratic procedures. In effect, they were unable to compete with Italian voluntary organizations which continued to monopolize the field of services to migrants. Migrant associations in Rome now limit their role to provision of cultural and social services. Some serve as intermediaries between their communities and Italian civic organizations. It is the latter who advocate in the name of the migrants vis-à-vis Italian institutions and the host society (Accorinti 1998, interview N. Tang).

Given the weakness of bottom-up migrant mobilization in Rome, the possibilities for establishing frameworks for representation include migrant representative(s) in city council, or some kind of consultative migrants' forum (the latter exist at the provincial and regional levels but are largely ineffective).²⁶ Regarding the former, a proposal was first raised in 1994 to assign one non-voting councillor who would represent all the foreign residents in the city. This was strongly opposed by the local Right-wing opposition, and the Alcanza Nazionale launched a court appeal (which was rejected) against the proposal. After prolonged debate the proposal was approved but never implemented. According to USI's director, despite the good intentions 'the idea became uninteresting' because one councillor could not possibly represent the needs of all the city's foreign communities, from labour migrants to EU nationals, foreign students, etc. (interview C. Rossi).

In 2001 the new mayor, Walter Veltroni, proposed to have four non-voting councillors (*consiglieri aggiunti*) who would represent only the non-EU residents in the city (EU residents already had local voting rights), plus one 'adjunct councillor' in each of the city's nineteen district councils.²⁷ This accorded with Veltroni's espoused policy of involving migrants in developing Rome's integration policy.

---

²⁵ Migrant mobilization in Rome began around the mid-1980s, with small organizations providing various services to their communities (cultural/recreational, advocacy and mediation with institutions). According to a survey by USI, as few as ten per cent of some 200 listed migrant organizations were active (Collicelli et al. 1998). A 1998 survey refers to only 48 associations, with an average participation of less than 100 persons per organization (cited in Pittau 2001).

²⁶ Consultative councils to represent migrants were set up in Italy in the second half of the 1990s. In the Province of Rome, a 'Forum of the Foreign Community' has existed on paper since 1996. Consultative councils at the regional level (created according to Act 40/1998, and including municipal officials, NGO representatives and migrant associations) also have little to no relevance.

²⁷ The city of Rome is divided into districts (*circoscrizione*) with elected district councils. City districts serve as the Municipality's 'front office' in direct contact with

In March 2004 Rome's *extracomunitari* residents elected for the first time four 'adjunct councillors' (from Romania, Peru, Morocco and the Filippines) to the city's municipal council. The impact of this remains to be seen, but it may mark a new chapter for migrant representation in Rome (*Altri/Others* 2004).

In the meantime, the municipality's relation to migrant associations is limited to 'occasional meetings' between Rossi and migrant associations, and an 'observatory' in USI that monitors the number and activity of migrant organizations in Rome. The absence of a formal structure mediating between the resident migrant communities and the municipality may be due in part to the relatively low level of migrant mobilization in Rome. No less important, however, is City Hall's tendency to relate to migrant associations not in terms of their representational potential but as potential service providers, in keeping with its delegation strategy (see below).

4.3.2 Socio-economic policies
Reception centres as lodging facilities The two most basic, immediate needs of migrants arriving in Rome are to find shelter and work. The first need is obvious, the second derives from the absence of any minimal income or welfare provision (welfare benefits are low to non-existent for Italians as well). The core of Rome's new migrant policy are 'reception centres' (*centri di accoglienza*) that provide new migrants with several months' lodging and meals, plus several services. In 1990, Act 39 made local authorities responsible for providing primary lodging to immigrants (including refugees/asylum seekers) for a period of up to nine months. The background to this was the disastrous housing situation of immigrants, soon after highlighted by the Pantanella crisis.

In this context Rome conceived a new lodging policy, based on a network of reception centres to be run by 'custodian organizations' (*organizzazioni affidatarie*) and supervised by USI, with funding provided by the city from the budget allocated by Act 39. In 1994 the first contracts were signed with several Catholic and lay organizations for a dozen centres providing about 300 beds. Most of the organizations run more than one reception centre, and there has been almost no turnover in the organizations involved (Caritas, Jesuit Refugee Service, Case dei Diritti Sociali, etc.). Every year or two USI announces a public tender to organizations to provide reception centres, with the services they should include (board, basic medical and orientation services, etc.). The organizations then submit proposals, including size and location of the centre, type of clientele (e.g. single men, families) and budget. If approved by the alderman, an annual contract is signed between USI and the organization.

Although the municipality claims to have developed the network of reception centres, in many cases it was the civic organizations that initiated and proposed a service to USI, or already ran an existing service which was adjusted to

---

residents. Decentralization has shifted more functions to the city districts, which have increasing autonomy primarily in providing social assistance.

meet municipal requirements. Often the services provided to migrants by the organization were greater than those required by the municipality. In such cases, the contract stipulates the number of beds, meals, etc. to be provided to migrants referred to the service by USI; concurrently, the organization continues to serve other clients (e.g. indigenous homeless) in the same structure.

In 2000, 15 reception centres offered lodging for some 1,200–1,500 people per year (Municipality of Rome, 2000). To qualify, migrants having a resident permit place a request at the USI office and are put on a waiting list. When a place is vacated, USI refers the next person on the list to a specific centre. But the huge gap between the demand and supply of places results in a waiting time of up to one and half years – precisely the period when newcomers most desperately need this service.

Reception centres as service centres The idea behind the reception centres as devised in 1993–94 was to provide primary lodging and reception services primarily to *labour migrants*. In addition to bed and board, the centres provide reception and orientation services: accompanying the migrant in his/her dealings with the Italian bureaucracy, basic medical and psychological aid, language courses, orientation toward job and house searching for adults, scholastic orientation for minors. Most of these services were developed over the years by the NGOs in response to the needs of migrants and then proposed for municipal funding within the contracts.[28] Others were initiated by USI. The target population of the *centri di accoliegnza* were labour migrants who had failed to find lodging and work on their own, and would 'end up in the street' if not helped. A 'personal project' was devised for each lodger (e.g. psychological and vocational counselling, orientation toward finding permanent accommodation), with the aim of eventual 'insertion' into Italian society. The lodging period was designated as three months followed by another eight if necessary.

This scheme, designed for the labour migrant population, became obsolete from the mid-1990s due to the influx of asylum seekers and refugees into Rome. As there were no specific lodging facilities for the latter (often arriving in desperate circumstances), USI directed them to the centres. As a result, by 2001 labour migrants occupied less than ten per cent of the places in the centres. Refugees and asylum seekers, however, have very different needs than the original target population. While the labour migrants were mostly young single adults, the new clients often include families, unaccompanied minors and elderly. Their needs are more immediate, and unlike most of the labour migrants, they do not have a minimal knowledge of Italian. The 3/8-month 'personal project' scheme did not fit this new population, and by 1997 the centres were 'in crisis' (interviews E. Serpieri, C. Rossi).

---

[28] For example, Italian language courses were originally initiated by NGOs using volunteer teachers. They are now partly funded by USI.

USI has tried to adjust to this new population by prolonguing the staying period to nine months. But for asylum seekers who now make up the majority of lodgers, this is insufficient. Altogether, the needs of this population are far greater than anticipated under the original reception centres scheme. This raises the costs per client beyond those calculated in the contracts by which USI funds the services, so that the NGOs are forced to cover the difference. Meanwhile, municipal funding for the centres, already considered insufficient by the organizations, is decreasing (interviews G. Russo, F. Campolongo, M. Accorinti).

As a solution, City Hall proposed opening a new refugee centre that would house asylum seekers and refugees for a short period. The municipality would then refer them to reception centres in other cities where the pressure is not as great, freeing Rome's reception centres to serve more labour migrants. In 2002 an abandoned station hotel at Termini Station was consigned for this purpose by Italy's National Railways to the Municipality of Rome and the Jesuit Refugee Service. The Municipality and JRS must find the funds to transform the building into a centre to be run by the latter, accommodating some 100 refugees.[29] While fitting into Rome's delegation strategy, this solution will still be insufficient.

A recurrent criticism regarding the reception centres policy is that all the services it offers are inaccessible to newcomers outside the centres, including those on the waitlist, i.e. during the first months when they are most needed. More seriously, the policy ignores the irregular migrant population, which makes up most of the homeless in the city. This means that the vast majority of migrants in Rome are left to their own devices to find work as well as shelter. While municipal homeless centres also take in migrants (regardless of legal status), it is largely the civic organizations that must address these needs as best they can.

Cultural mediators service One of the main initiatives of Rome's new migrant policy is a cultural mediators service, based on similar projects in other European cities. 'Veteran' migrants go through a months-long training programme run by CIES, an NGO, after which they work part-time at the USI office and the reception centres. The project began in the mid-1990s and included some 60 accredited 'linguistic-cultural mediators' by 2001. As the pool of mediators grows (by about twenty each year), the service should expand to include mediation services at the city district level. For 2002, the municipality budgeted some €1 million from national funding to provide cultural mediators in all the neighbourhood health clinics (interview E. Serpieri).

Labour integration service Unlike the guestworkers directly recruited into large industrial plants in northern European cities in the 1960s, labour migrants in Rome have had to find employment in a market dominated by small and medium-sized firms operating largely on personal connections, and a large shadow economy.

---

[29] Press release by Italian State Railways, 'E nato il Centro Padre Arrupe per i rifugiati politici', Rome, 8 May 2002.

While migrants can find work in various 'dirty/ dangerous/demeaning' jobs, they face difficulties finding work that suits their background and training. To improve the fit between migrants and the local labour market, the trade unions and USI established *Agenzia Chances* in 1995. This service is meant to provide migrants with information and orientation on finding work, as well as aiding potential entrepreneurs. Six branches in the city (most in trade union offices) receive some 10,000 migrants per year, creating a data bank on migrant work demands and skills. With a staff of 10, *Agenzia Chances* is jointly financed by the unions and the municipality (the latter budgeting nearly €250,000 for 1999–2001). The service also offers vocational orientation courses, but these serve a tiny proportion of unemployed migrants (some 350 a year) and entrepreneurs (80 individual and 12 cooperative enterprises set up with the agency's help, according to its director).

The effectiveness of this service is questioned by many. *Agenzia Chances* can only provide general orientation to (legal) migrants and its vocational training courses are considered inappropriate for most migrants who need to find immediate work of any kind. These shortcomings are not blamed on the service, which is prohibited by Italian law from mediating between employers and migrants, but on the national context, specifically the *de jure* or *de facto* inaccessibility to the legal labour market for most migrants. Regardless of its utility, *Agenzia Chances* signals an assumption on the part of the municipality that the migrants are 'here to stay' and must be incorporated into the local economy.

Education Catholic activists began raising public awareness of the problems faced by migrant children in Rome in the early 1990s. As noted above, the previous administration was unable and unwilling to cope with this problem, beyond subsidizing some of the charities. In 1993 the Rutelli administration proclaimed the integration of migrant children as one of the priorities in its new migrant policy. The new education policy toward migrants is based on two tracks. The first involves setting up separate educational facilities for migrant children, to address their specific educational and cultural needs, run by civic organizations. This began in 1994 with seven summer schools involving 150 children. By 2000 there were 24 annual educational facilities with over 800 children participating: six day-care centres for pre-schoolers and 18 'educational centres' for school-age children.[30]

All the centres are run by NGOs, including a few migrant organizations, with USI providing funds and supervising through yearly contracts. Since 1999, five educational centres run by migrant organizations are organized according to 'culturally homogenous regions' (sub-saharan Africa, South America, etc.). The migrant-run educational centres focus specifically on providing support to children with potential integration problems. The justification for this approach, according to a municipal publication (Municipality of Rome 2000: 4), reveals a clearly pluralist approach to integration:

---

[30] Municipality of Rome website 2001: www.comune.roma.it/dispsociale/prova/

If the awareness of one's own identity ... is not stable, then recognition [of others] becomes difficult, acceptance unclear, exchange impossible. In this case, the response may be of flight, of revenge, of assimilation, but not of integration. Based on this theme, five of the centres pay particular attention to reinforcement of the [children's] language and culture of origin ...

The second track of Rome's education policy relates to the integration of foreign-origin children within the public school system. In 2000–01 there were 12,368 migrant children (2.1 per cent of the student body) registered in schools in the Province of Rome, an increase of one third over the previous school year. Foreign pupils were found in some three-quarters of the schools in the city, with an average of only 5 per cent foreign pupils per school. However, some schools had 30 and even 40 per cent foreign students (possibly including students from wealthy countries). More importantly, an estimated 2500 foreign children remained outside the school system (Caritas 2001, Pittau 2001).

The aim of the new policy is to help schools adapt to a multi-ethnic student body by encouraging 'inter-cultural' activities. In the first Rutelli administration, the Alderman for Education, Fiorella Farinelli, initiated several projects including training teachers in intercultural pedagogy. During the first five years these initiatives were fragmentary and funded mostly from other programmes. In the second Rutelli administration a more systematic approach was adopted. In 1998 a small 'Intercultural Unit' was set up within the Education Department's Psychopedagogic Service. The Intercultural Unit produces teaching materials, multilingual pamphlets for migrant parents, coordinates courses for teaching Italian to foreigners, and is involved in various multicultural projects within the school system. The introduction of *hallal* menus in schools with a significant number of Muslim pupils was slated to begin in school year 2002–03. According to department officials, the aim was to 'go beyond the reception of migrant children, to raising consciousness of multiculturalism ... getting people used to pluralism in the schools' (interviews R. Attento, P. Gabrielli).

However, most of the initiatives for dealing with the presence of migrant pupils (e.g. setting up language labs) are bottom-up, originating in the schools themselves. The municipal Education Department appears to serve more as a support service for schools and a channel for government funding, rather than providing an overall strategy on how to integrate migrant children. The gap between Rome's espoused aims in this policy area and its actions may be due more to the municipality's limited capabilities and resources rather than a lack of willpower.

4.3.3 *'Cultural integration' policies*
Rome's migrant policy since 1993 is unabashedly Pluralist in its rhetoric. The long-term integration of migrants is described as a two-way process in which the municipality must 'come to terms with negative stereotypes and prejudices' by promoting the 'awareness of the conditions and culture of the others and making them aware of ours ...' (Municipality of Rome 2000: 6, my translation). Municipal

initiatives under the heading of 'cultural integration' include subsidizing courses for migrants on Italian language and culture at Rome's Popular University; a 'documentation centre on immigration and interculture' to document migrant culture in Rome, publish writings by migrants, etc.; and the cultural mediators service described above. Most of these initiatives are well-meaning but affect a very small segment of the migrant (and indigenous) population.

The municipality also claims credit for an 'Information and Consultation Centre on Migrant Women's Rights'. This project opened in 1999 on the premises of Caritas' 'Centro Stranieri', and is managed jointly by migrant and Italian women's organizations. This again raises the question, to what extent is this service a result of *municipal* policy, beyond the financial support the city provides? A 'multicultural centre' has also been proposed, but until now most organized meeting places for migrants are provided by civic organizations.

As noted above, the Education Department's Intercultural Unit also supports projects that raise awareness of multiculturalism among youth. The most ambitious project is a four-day multicultural *Festa de Intermundia* for schoolchildren in Piazza Vittorio, begun in 1999 (see Box 4.1, above). Another initiative, a planned 'cycle of monthly manifestations' (sports, debates and the like) was meant to 'promote the visibility' of the migrant communities in Rome in 2001 but had little visible impact (interviews P. Bacchetti, M. Migliano). Large cultural events – for which the City of Rome is famous – have rarely included the participation of artists and performers from the migrant communities. Rome's publicly organized expressions of multiculturalism tend to stress folkloristic features and are used more as touristic events. This appears to demonstrate an exploitative rather than a truly genuine embrace of difference. Meanwhile, the real campaigns in Rome to raise public awareness of the migrant presence and tolerance of their Otherness remain in the hands of the religious and secular civic organizations (Collicelli et al. 2000, Caritas 2000).

4.3.4 Housing policies

Finding shelter is probably the greatest difficulty facing newcomers in Rome. As noted above, the 'reception centres' provide short-term solutions to only a fraction of the migrant population. The city is characterized by a continual, severe housing shortage, with demand for low cost housing far exceeding supply. Non-Italian tenants (especially irregular migrants) are commonly exploited, and illegal practices such as overcrowding and overpricing are rampant.[31] Most of the migrants in Rome find lodging in overcrowded flats (often using informal kinship networks), some live in abandoned buildings, others in irregular settlements on the outskirts of the city, and an estimated 6,000–7,000 sleep on the streets. Of the latter, almost all are irregular migrants. Concentrations of migrants in

---

[31] For example, Bangladeshi migrants (both regular and irregular) rent flats in Esquilino for 150–250,000 lire per room, living as many as 20 in a flat (interview M. Brazzoduro).

public spaces in Rome have created 'stigmatized spaces' (Caritas 2000: 1526). An example is the Colle Oppio park overlooking the Coliseum, where hundreds of migrants congregate during the day and sleep at night under plastic awnings. The presence of homeless migrants in parks and other open areas, converted into small camps at night, is not unusual. For the most part, the municipality condones such 'irregular settlements', lacking any alternative solutions. In other areas the congregation of migrants is discouraged, especially if complaints by residents reach a critical mass.

Municipal policies toward migrants in regard to squatting and irregular settlements range from benign neglect (avoiding problems until they can no longer be avoided) to some rather symbolic changes. Traditionally, the municipality turned a blind eye to migrant squatting of abandoned houses, intervening only when conflict with local residents became too strong to ignore. Since the 1990 Pantanella crisis, and especially in recent years, City Hall has taken a stronger stance against squatting in the city centre. In outlying areas of the city, where illegal slums (*borgate abusive*) have existed for decades, municipal policy alternates between benign neglect, periodical regularizations and evictions. One example is the settlement of Casilino 700, an old airfield occupied by several thousand gypsies plus several hundred Moroccan migrants. In 2000 the city cleared out this settlement, transferring a thousand of the gypsy inhabitants to a newly constructed caravan camp nearby. The remaining squatters, among them the immigrants, had no alternative but to relocate to another *burgata* nearby (interview M. Brazzoduro).

Until recently, rent-controlled public housing in Rome was closed to non-EU residents. In 2000 the municipality opened a new waitlist for public housing planned or under construction. The waitlist eligibility criteria (determined at local level) include income levels and valid residency. This time the municipality specifically noted the eligibility of *extracomunitari* (non-EU) residents. But while symbolically important, this had no practical effect. The reason is that demand for public housing far exceeds supply, so that the chances of obtaining a rent-controlled flat are miniscule for newcomers (including Italians from outside Rome). Currently, public housing accounts for only 6–7 per cent of the housing stock in Rome. This stock is fully occupied and there is almost no turnover, at least such that reaches the social housing waitlists.[32]

In sum, social housing remains largely irrelevant for the migrant population. Nevertheless, the official opening of public housing to resident *extracomunitari* caused resentment among indigenous working-class Romans who felt that public housing should be reserved for Italians. The same resentment is felt when the municipality regularizes migrant squats in public housing in Rome's peripheral

---

[32] Due to the severe housing shortage in Rome and a native distrust of the allocation system, many flats were squatted immediately on (or even prior to) their completion. Eventually, the squatting was regularized. A system then developed by which social housing flats were handed over for a 'fee' by their occupants to the next occupant (ibid.)

neighbourhoods, in effect repeating the policies toward Italian squatters in the 1970s (interviews C. Conti, M. Brazzoduro).

5   Summary: From Ignoring to NGO-ing?

Rome's policy reactions to migrant settlement can be divided into two phases, separated by a two-year transition. The first phase can be summarized as 'Non-policy' in terms of the typology proposed in Chapter 3. The second phase, from 1993 onwards, is more difficult to identify. As noted in this chapter, significant settlement of labour migrants in Rome only began in the 1980s. For well over a decade (from the mid-1970s to 1990), the municipality was unaware of, or wilfully ignored, the growing migrant presence in the city. Despite two internal reports in the early 1980s it made no attempt to formulate, let alone implement, any long-term policy, preferring ad-hoc solutions only in specific cases. The city had no policy regarding the growing presence of migrants in the informal labour market, the housing market (overcrowding, squatting) or in schools.

What can explain such a long Non-policy response? One possibility is that the migrant needs were not of sufficient volume or urgency to arouse the attention of the municipality. This appears unlikely at least from the mid-1980s, when dozens of local non-governmental organizations set up (or expanded) services in response to just these needs. Indeed, the municipality subsidized some of these NGO services. A more plausible explanation is that Rome's municipality was simply *incapable* of dealing with the problems arising from the migrant presence, and preferred to leave them to civic society. This fits Palidda's (1998) third 'scenario of integration' (in this scenario, lack of integration) in cities characterized by a large underground economy and administrative mismanagement.

However, following the host-stranger relations model we can envisage another possibility, namely that municipal decision-makers were not unaware of the labour migrant presence in the city, but that they continued to regard it as *transient*. This is plausible, considering the city's role as a temporary station for labour migrants heading north, and the traditional dominance of transient foreigners (clergy, students, diplomats) in Rome. In other words, the dominant perception in City Hall was that labour migrants were one more type of Stranger passing through.

Indeed, much of Rome's migrant population until the mid-1980s can be characterized as transient, and even now temporary or pendular migrants make up a significant proportion of the city's foreign population. In this regard, Rome's Non-policy may be understandable, at least up to a point. However, from the late 1980s a noticeable gap appears between the growing numbers and needs of the migrant population, and the city's continued Non-policy response. This gap was partly compensated for by the extensive activity of non-governmental organizations. Indeed, the substitutive role of civic society is one characteristic of the Non-policy phase, as we will see in the following chapters.

Rome's transition from Non-policy to an avowedly Pluralist view of its migrant population was precipitated by the Pantanella crisis. In the following two years (1991–92) the permanence of the migrant presence was acknowledged and the basis laid for a new local policy. Since then, mayor Francesco Rutelli (1993–2001) and his successor Walter Veltroni have proclaimed Rome to be a multi-ethnic city whose migrants should be integrated without losing their cultural identity. In terms of *espoused* policy, this second phase in Rome's response is clearly of the Pluralist type.

However, Rome's *enacted* migrant policy (i.e. how it actually pursues the above aims) is based on a strategy of delegating most of the integration services for migrants to the Third Sector. The city's direct involvement in 'migrant integration' is very limited. How much of a difference, then, has the new policy made?

Several changes are noticeable since 1993. Through USI, the municipality now registers legal migrants as residents – the first step toward formal political participation. The election in 2004 of four non-voting 'adjunct councillors' to represent the city's *extracomunitari* residents is a clear indication of a Pluralist-type policy. However, the municipality's relations with migrant associations as representatives of Rome's foreign communities remain informal and ad-hoc. Instead, migrants remain largely dependent on Italian civic organizations to voice their needs vis-à-vis the authorities. A large gap still exists, then, between a clearly Pluralist aim to integrate the migrant population into the local civic-political system, and enacted policies in this domain.

Regarding socio-economic integration, USI provides migrants with some assistance in gaining access to the social services that are available to all legal residents. However, nearly all migrant-targeted services – from food-and-board to counselling and language courses – are delegated to civic organizations, usually within the framework of NGO-run reception centres. This delegation strategy is not problematic *a priori*, but the question arises: to what extent is City Hall taking credit for the work of others, and simply channelling the funding now provided by national government? Is the new policy simply a variation of Rome's traditional avoidance of responsibility, of letting civic society do the work?

As far as the municipality is concerned, the delegation of services is the most efficient way to meet migrant needs, considering the experience of local civic organizations and the weakness of local public services. Until 1993, the problem lay in the dispersed character of the NGO-run services, as various organizations had different agendas, clientele and resources. Under the new policy, the local authority sees its role primarily as initiating, coordinating and financing the migrant-targeted services, rather than providing them directly.

The civic organizations take a somewhat different view. There appears to be a consensus that the Third Sector is more capable than the public sector in providing migrant services. In Rome, both sides have a vested organizational interest in this arrangement. There is also agreement that the coordination and extra funding provided through USI has improved the provision of services for *legal* migrants. However, NGO representatives criticize municipal migrant policy on several grounds. First, they note that some, if not most, of the services that City Hall claims as part of its new migrant policy were developed by them and operating before 1993. Second, there is debate on the overall utility of USI's coordination efforts and the amount of financing provided by City Hall. According to some NGO representatives, the subsidies provided through USI, while theoretically covering all of the costs, only cover 40–50 per cent of the real costs of services provided to migrants, while creating more bureaucracy (interviews G. Russo, M. Accorinti). Some of the municipally-initiated services (e.g. *Agenzia Chances*) are seen as ineffectual or cosmetic.

The most damning criticism of Rome's migrant policy is that the overall basket of services set by the municipality (whether subcontracted to NGOs or provided directly by USI) is altogether insufficient in light of actual migrant needs. A primary example are the reception centres where many of the migrant services are provided. The 15 centres can only serve a fraction of the city's legal migrant residents and none of the irregular migrant population. The same can be said of Rome's policies regarding the 'cultural integration' of migrants. Municipal initiatives such as the migrant 'documentation centre' may be well-meaning but affect very few people. The activities of the Education Department's Intercultural Unit are similarly limited. Finally, there is a large gap between municipal rhetoric and enacted policy regarding the promotion of public awareness and tolerance of Otherness. Here the few municipal actions appear to be more public relations exercises than substantive efforts to sell the new vision of Rome as a multi-ethnic city.

Rome's inaction regarding migrant housing needs (manifested in the continued presence of squats and informal migrant settlements) appears to be a continuation of its previous Non-policy, alternating between benign neglect and evictions. However, this is largely due to the city's inability to affect the housing market (for non-migrants as well). Beyond the symbolic step of opening social housing waitlists to migrants, there is not much the city can do.

Clearly, Rome's migrant strategy since 1993 differs from the previous Non-policy phase: migrant settlement was acknowledged; a long-term policy has been adopted; a municipal office with a significant budget is coordinating the policy; various measures have been implemented. But a large gap remains between City Hall's declared intentions and its actions. Rome's espoused policy is clearly Pluralist, but the city's delegation strategy means that most of the implementation (in the broadest sense) remains in the hands of civic organizations. It would be overstretching the typology to identify Rome's response over the past decade as a Pluralist-type policy (as I do regarding Amsterdam's policy in the 1980s, below). Instead, I would characterize this phase as an *espoused Pluralist policy which has only been partially enacted*. Rome's policy change since Pantanella is not merely cosmetic: the municipality has come a long way in its perception of the migrant presence in the city. That this has not been sufficiently expressed in its actions may be understood in the local context: a relatively weak government, a strong and experienced Third Sector.

Chapter 5

Tel Aviv: The Limits of Liberalism in a Guestworker Regime

> Approximately 200,000 foreign workers reside today in Israel, many of them without permits. This disturbing statistic requires a response at the national level, however, until such policy is formulated, the responsibility for some 60,000 foreign workers in Tel Aviv-Yafo falls on our shoulders. We can no longer stand aside.
>
> Mayor Ron Huldai, MESILA brochure, July 1999

1 Introduction[1]

Since its establishment nearly a century ago, Tel Aviv has grown rapidly through the absorption of successive waves of Jewish immigrants coming from a widely varied diaspora. Most of today's Tel Avivians are first-, second- or third-generation immigrants from Europe, Russia, North Africa and the Middle East. But in the past decade this city of immigrants has had to cope with a different type of Newcomer, as Tel Aviv became a destination for non-Jewish labour immigration. From the early 1990s the labour migrant population ballooned from a few thousand to tens of thousands, estimated in 2001 at anywhere between 8–17 per cent of the city population. In this respect Tel Aviv is not so different from other 'new immigration' cities such as Athens, Lisbon and Rome. However, those cities have developed their policy responses within national immigration regimes that allow, even if reluctantly, some degree of labour migrant settlement. Southern European countries experiencing labour immigration since the 1980s have not repeated the kind of strict Guestworker-type policies that characterized their northern neighbours in the 1960s and early 1970s. It is therefore difficult to find a local authority among Europe's 'new immigration cities' that assumes its labour migrant population will simply be 'repatriated' one day.

In contrast, Tel Aviv presents a contemporary example of a city responding to labour immigration within an old-style national Guestworker regime. In 1993 the Israeli government began allowing the massive recruitment of overseas workers as a 'temporary substitute' for Palestinian workers. A decade later labour

---

[1] Parts of this chapter were published in earlier versions in Alexander 2001 and Schnell and Alexander 2002. The findings presented here refer primarily to the period up to 2002, just prior to a new government policy to limit the labour migrant presence, which included an aggressive deportation policy whose consequences are still unclear.

migrants had largely replaced the Palestinians, but unlike the latter, who commuted daily between Israel and the nearby Occupied Territories, the overseas labour migrants remained in the country. To prevent the possibility of their settlement, the government instituted a strict, exclusionary Guestworker-type policy. This policy resulted in a very high proportion of illegal labour migrants, many of whom live in Tel Aviv.

It is in this context that Tel Aviv has developed a local policy toward its labour migrant population, evolving in one decade from a Non-policy phase to what I call a 'liberal Guestworker policy'. This process can be seen as a pragmatic response by the municipality to the problems posed by a large irregular migrant presence, within an exclusionary national migration regime. But Tel Aviv's response also reveals a gradual change in attitudes and expectations within the local authority, regarding these non-Jewish newcomers. The question arises, to what extent have host-stranger relations in Tel Aviv deviated from those at the national level?

This chapter will address that question and in doing so, test the meaning behind Guestworker-type migrant policies. Section 2 describes Israel's exclusionary attitude toward non-Jewish labour migration on one hand, and its need for overseas migration to substitute for Palestinian labour, on the other. The result is a classic Guestworker regime. The local context is described in Section 3 (the city's immigration history, including the labour migrant population, local attitudes and the political/institutional context of policymaking). Section 4 describes the development of local migrant policies in Tel Aviv. Section 5 summarizes the evolution of Tel Aviv's policy response within the host-stranger relations framework.

2 The National Context

Two points are crucial to understanding official policy as well as general attitudes in Israel toward labour migrants. One is the nature of Israel as an 'ethnocracy' (Yiftachel 1993) that refuses to admit any permanent non-Jewish immigration. The other is the legacy of Israel's decades-long dependence on Palestinian workers. When Israel disengaged from this cheap, non-citizen labour force in the early 1990s, overseas labour migrants were recruited as a 'temporary substitute' for the Palestinians. These two opposing interests (one closed to non-Jewish immigration, the other pressing for it) are elaborated below. Together, they form the backdrop to Israeli attitudes and policies toward overseas labour migrants at both the national and local levels.

2.1 Host-Stranger Relations in the Jewish State

Israel's Zionist ideology and *raison d'etre* remain rooted in the idea of a Jewish State based on the 'ingathering of the Diaspora'. The state actively encourages Jewish immigration, and until a decade ago immigrants to Israel were overwhelmingly

Jewish.[2] The Law of Return (1950) grants Jews anywhere the right to immigrate to Israel and receive immediate citizenship, while an elaborate 'absorption' system provides Jewish immigrants with a variety of support services. For non-Jews, Israeli law and bureaucratic practice make it extremely difficult to obtain permanent resident status, let alone citizenship.[3]

Polar attitudes toward Jewish and non-Jewish immigration are reflected in Israeli terminology: Jewish immigrants are called *olim* (literally 'ascenders', from the Biblical Hebrew: to ascend to the Land of Israel). *Olim hadashim* (new ascenders/immigrants) is a social construct (the Jewish Newcomer) as well as an official status which confers various rights. Labour immigrants are called *ovdim zarim* (foreign/alien workers), a label that also has biblical connotations: in Hebrew 'alien work' also means paganism. '*Oved zar*' (singular) is also a social construct, connoting Otherness and transience (equal to the European *gastarbeiter*), as well as an official category ('foreign worker'). The neutral term *mehager* (migrant) is rarely used in Israel outside of academia.

At the risk of oversimplification, we may describe host-stranger relations in Israel's first 40 years (1948–88) largely in terms of Jewish-Israeli attitudes toward two basic types of Others.[4] The first is the Other-within-the-State, i.e. the indigenous Palestinian-Israeli minorities who make up 18 per cent of the population.[5] The second type of Other is the Jewish newcomer, i.e. *olim hadashim* who are expected to shed their Jewish-diaspora Otherness and in assimilating, become 'Israeli'. Until the 1990s there was virtually no non-Jewish immigration to Israel (although the last wave of *olim* from the former Soviet Union contained a significant proportion of non-Jews – see below). The massive entry of overseas labour migrants (over 240,000 at its peak in 1999) thus created the first significant non-Jewish, non-Arab presence in the country's history.

How has Israeli society contended with this new type of Stranger, the non-Jewish Newcomer? Until now, Israeli attitudes toward labour migrants appear to be based largely on their substitutive role, as temporary replacements for

---

[2] In 1995, 39 per cent of the Jewish population were first-generation immigrants and an additional 40 per cent were second-generation immigrants (Shuval and Leshem 1998).

[3] The most common way for non-Jews to obtain citizenship is through marriage to Israelis. Proposed changes in the Entry and Citizenship Law may soon narrow this 'breach' as well.

[4] Other ways in which Jewish-Israelis define themselves vis-à-vis Others reflect the sharp internal cleavages within Jewish Israeli society: by ethnic origin (Ashkenazi versus Sephardi Jews), by religious versus secular conviction, and by political beliefs (Right versus Left). However, these are less relevant in terms of host-stranger relations for this chapter.

[5] 'Arab Israelis' connotes Muslim and Christian Palestinians, as well as Druze, with Israeli citizenship. The 'Arab-Israeli' Other is regarded by some Jewish-Israelis as a potential Fifth Column, by others as a constant litmus test of Israeli democracy (see Smooha 1990 on Israel as an 'ethnic democracy').

Palestinian workers. The expectation of temporariness as well as their non-threatening status (in contrast to the Palestinian labourers) resulted in a generally positive view of foreign workers. Surveys in the mid-1990s showed that almost two thirds of the Israeli respondents approved of the labour migrant presence (approval ranged from agreement to legalize irregular migrants, to living next to them). Interestingly, it was the respondents' degree of religiousness (a common criterion in Israeli surveys) that most closely corresponded to negative attitudes toward labour migrants. The main factor appeared to be the desire to preserve the Jewish character of the state, rather than negative (racist) perceptions about the migrants, i.e. the migrants' non-Jewishness was sufficient. Approval ratings deteriorated between 1996–99 but still remained relatively high (Schnell 2001: 18–19).

Israeli attitudes toward foreign migrants are bound to change if the host society perceives their presence as a permanent one. Until recently, most Jewish-Israelis still regarded overseas labour migrants as a non-threatening substitute for Palestinian workers, rather than as competition for Israeli jobs. As the migrant presence lengthens and signs of settlement increase, host society attitudes may change as labour migrants are increasingly regarded as a threat to the country's Jewish character. Meanwhile, an aggressive deportation policy begun in 2002 appears to have allayed fears (or hopes) about the possibility of a new non-Jewish minority (see below). Indeed, government policy appears to be consistently more anti-immigrant than public opinion – even as successive governments since 1993 have allowed the recruitment of foreign workers into Israel. To understand why, we must look at the economic factors determining Israeli labour immigration policy.

2.2 Israel's Dual Labour Market: From 'Arab Work' to 'Foreign Workers'

From the mid-1950s to 1987 certain sectors in the Israeli economy, especially construction, agriculture and some services, became increasingly dependent on low-paid Arab labour, leading to the entrenchment of an ethnically-based dual labour market (**Figure 5.1**). Prior to 1967 'Israeli Arabs' filled many of the 'dirty, dangerous and demeaning' jobs. After the 1967 war, Palestinians from the newly occupied West Bank and Gaza Strip began to commute to work within Israel (and later also in Israeli settlements in the Occupied Territories). By the late 1980s some 120,000 Palestinian border workers commuted daily into Israel, over half of them without work permits. Altogether, they accounted for nearly one tenth of the labour force in Israel, but in the construction and agricultural sectors, these non-citizen labourers constituted 45 and 25 per cent of the workforce, respectively (Bartram 1998, Fischer 1999, Schnell 2001).

In 1987 the first Palestinian uprising (*intifada*) broke out, leading to frequent closures of the Occupied Territories. In the early 1990s the government effectively banned the employment of Palestinians inside Israel, leading to severe labour shortages in the secondary sectors. In 1993, under increasing pressure from employers, especially the powerful construction and agricultural lobbies, the large-

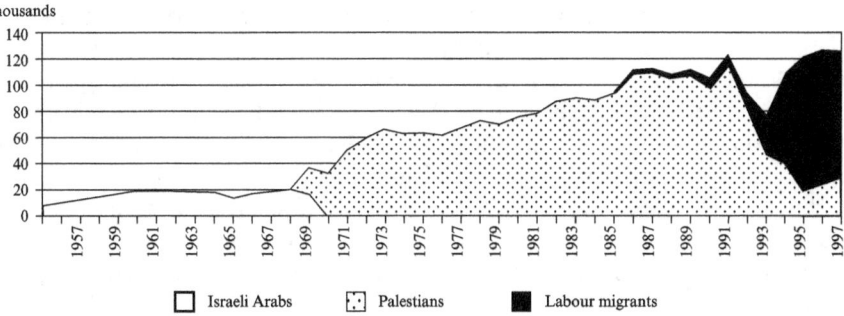

Figure 5.1 Development of the secondary labour market in Israel, 1956–99

scale recruitment of foreign workers from overseas was first allowed.[6] The number of overseas labour migrants entering Israel with legal permits escalated rapidly, from under 10,000 in 1993 to almost 70,000 in 1995, peaking at over 100,000 in 1996. Thereafter the number of legal foreign workers stabilized at around 80,000. Parallel to this, there was an increase in irregular labour immigration to Israel (see below). In the early 1990s irregular migrants in Israel were estimated at several thousands; a decade later they were estimated at 150,000.[7]

The unplanned detachment of the Israeli economy from its captive Palestinian workforce meant that in the mid-1990s Israel finally entered the global labour market – and did so rapidly. By 2002 the total number of overseas labour migrants (regular and irregular) was estimated at 247,000, or 13 per cent of Israel's workforce (Palestinians accounted for another 2 per cent). This is one of the highest proportions of labour migrants in the workforce among industrialized democracies. An estimated 60 per cent of the labour migrants are irregular[8] (Government of Israel 2004).

The recruitment of overseas labour migrants that began in 1993 was meant to be a temporary solution to the shortage of Palestinian workers 'until the situation stabilizes'. Instead, it marked the beginning of a *de facto* guestworker policy that came to resemble those of Germany, Austria and Switzerland of the 1960s. Today, Israel's restrictive guestworker regime is unique among western democracies and more closely resembles labour immigration regimes in the Persian Gulf states and Asia. The Israeli system is based on work/residence permits (valid for 1–2 years and

---

[6] At first, the government attempted to recruit Israelis and newly arrived Russian immigrants with various public recruitment campaigns and subsidization programmes, but these failed to fill the labour shortage in the secondary sectors.

[7] Irregular labour migrants include those who arrived on tourist/student visas and overstayed, and those who arrived on foreign worker visas and then left their employer, were dismissed, or were 'transferred' from one employer to another (see below) (Government of Israel 2004).

[8] Since the aggressive deportation policy begun in 2003, the government estimates the number of labour migrants has fallen to below 200,000 (ibid.).

renewable depending on the employment sector) that are issued not to the worker but to the employer. According to this 'binding arrangement' the migrant's legal status is tied to employment *at a specific employer* whose name is stamped on his passport upon arrival at the airport. The employer is henceforth responsible for the worker's housing, work conditions and health insurance, as well as ensuring he leaves the country. Employers can dismiss their workers at any moment – thus terminating their legal residency. The threat of early repatriation spells disaster for most foreign workers, who arrive in the country in debt to middlemen (payment for the right to work in Israel generally ranges from $3,000 to $10,000). Together with weak-to-nonexistent enforcement of foreign workers' rights, the binding system encourages massive exploitation of labour migrants in Israel.[9]

This has led to the paradoxical result that conditions for irregular labour migrants are often better than those of legal guestworkers. Irregular migrants risk deportation, but are free to choose their workplace, bargain over work conditions, find their own housing, etc. It is not surprising, therefore, that the majority of labour migrants in Israel are irregular. Of these, over half originally arrived as legal foreign workers, according to government estimates in 1999 (Kemp and Raijman 2003: 14).

Israel's national policy for the first few years effectively ignored the swelling irregular migrant population. In 1997 the government commenced a deportation policy but did not succeed in repatriating more than a few thousand migrants per year before 2002. Meanwhile, pressure from human rights organizations resulted in several minor (but important) changes regarding labour migrant rights.[10] Nevertheless, national immigration policy changed little in the decade between 1993 and 2002. Regardless of the changes in government (Rabin, Netanyahu, Barak, Sharon), Israel's exclusionary Guestworker regime continues to reflect the country's ethnocratic nature on one hand (excluding any possibility of non-Jewish permanent immigration), and its dependence on non-citizen labour (Palestinian and foreign workers) on the other.

---

[9] Israeli law extends many workers rights to foreign workers as well, however enforcement is weak to non-existent. In addition, the legislation refers to the employer's responsibilities, but many employers hire manpower agencies to recruit their foreign workers abroad and to handle their their work, payment, housing and insurance in Israel. Common abuses by employers and manpower agencies include confiscation of workers' passports upon arrival, salary deductions for fictitious costs, withholding salaries to prevent workers from 'escaping' deplorable lodgings, etc. Workers who complain are dismissed by their employers, which makes them automatically liable for deportation (Hotline for Foreign Workers 2002).

[10] In 2000 the law was amended to tighten employers' responsibilities for foreign workers' health insurance and housing conditions. In 2001 the Health Ministry introduced a formal arrangement to incorporate children of foreign workers (regardless of their legal status) into the national health insurance scheme. Civic rights organizations also succeeded in amending the Law of Entry to introduce a quasi-judicial review process into the detention and deportation of illegal immigrants.

The basic assumption behind government policy is that (non-Jewish) overseas labour migrants are temporary. Just as their Palestinian predecessors were expected to return to their homes in the Occupied Territories every night, overseas migrants are expected to return home after a few years. Meanwhile, they are bound to their employers and excluded from nearly all social and welfare systems. This has inadvertently encouraged a high proportion of 'illegal' migrants, living invisible lives. And with no periodic amnesties to reduce the number of illegals (as in Italy, France, Spain), undocumented migrants remain irregular. In Israel, the primary magnet for this population is Tel Aviv.

3   The Local Context

3.1   A City of Immigrants

Tel Aviv was founded in 1909 as the 'first Hebrew city' by 60 Jewish families from the nearby port city of Jaffa (Yafo in Hebrew). Its spectacular growth thereafter was based on waves of Jewish immigration which swelled the new town's population to 200,000 by 1948, on the eve of Israel's War of Independence. During the war – called by Palestinians 'the Disaster' – nearly all of Jaffa's 100,000 Arab inhabitants fled, and in 1950 Jaffa was annexed to what became officially known as Tel Aviv-Yafo. Today some 16,000 Palestinian-Israelis reside in Yafo, constituting about 4 per cent of Tel-Aviv-Yafo's population. After the war, waves of Jewish immigration from Europe and the Arab countries doubled the city's population to nearly 400,000 at its peak in the mid-1960s (**Figure 5.2**).

With the collapse of the Soviet Union, some 26,000 Russian immigrants settled in Tel Aviv (Menahem 1993). At about the same time (late 1980s to early 1990s), labour migrants from Africa and Latin America appeared in Tel Aviv in increasing numbers. Although the Russian *olim* included a high proportion of non-Jews,[11] it was the *ovdim zarim* (foreign workers) who were later seen as commencing the first non-Jewish immigration wave to Tel Aviv – a new type of newcomer in the city of immigrants.

Until 1993 labour migrants in Tel Aviv numbered several thousands, most having arrived on tourist visas and stayed on to work illegally. The first irregular migrants came from Africa and Latin America, and were later followed by others from Eastern Europe and the Far East. In addition, labour migrants from neighbouring Arab countries (Jordan, Egypt) managed to enter Israel via the Palestinian territories; in Tel Aviv they merged into the local Palestinian population of Jaffa (Schnell 2001). After 1993 the number of irregular migrants increased dramatically, as tens of thousands of legally admitted guestworkers

---

[11] Under the Law of Return, non-Jewish spouses, parents and children also receive *oleh* status. It later transpired that many Russian immigrants entered under false papers.

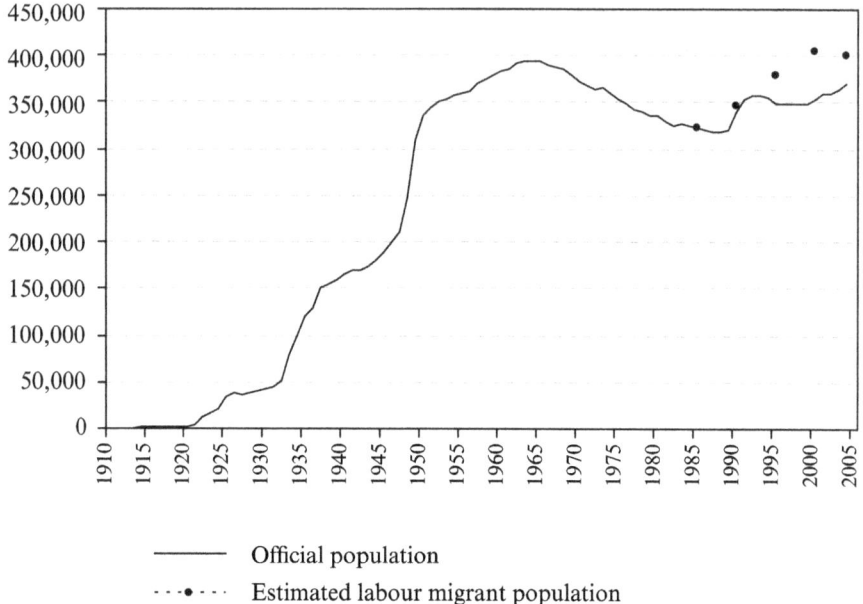

Figure 5.2 Population of Tel Aviv-Yafo, with estimated labour migrant population

Source: Official population compiled from Municipality of Tel Aviv Statistical Yearbook 2004 and National Statistics Bureau website 2005; labour migrant population based on author's estimate.

(mostly Romanians, Thais, Filipinos, Turks and later Chinese) became 'illegal' after overstaying their work visas, being dismissed by, or leaving, their legal employers (see above).

Tel Aviv soon became the focal point for irregular immigrants in Israel. The city's informal labour market offered work in cleaning, geriatric care, restaurants and small workshops. By 2000 Tel Aviv hosted a sizeable number of labour migrants, of which an estimated 70–80 per cent were irregular. The overall size of Tel Aviv's labour migrant population is unknown; official estimates by the municipality were (and remain) around 60,000, but the basis for these numbers is unclear.[12] Guess-estimates by researchers and local NGOs prior to 2002 varied from 30,000 to well over 60,000 labour migrants (Schnell and Alexander 2002). Since 2002, when the government began its aggressive deportation policy by

---

[12] In 1999 the Welfare Division estimated there were 30–60,000 labour migrants in Tel Aviv – a figure repeated in later municipal publications. Although most agree that since the deportation policy commenced in 2002 these numbers have gone down, the city's website in Hebrew still cited in December 2005 an estimate of 50–70,000 labour migrants (the English version cited 60–80,000!).

focusing on labour migrants in Tel Aviv, their numbers have declined significantly, although it is unclear by how much.[13]

The following pages describe the decade up to 2002, when labour migrants in Tel Aviv grew from a few 'invisible' thousands to an unavoidable presence of tens of thousands, or anywhere between 8–17 per cent of the city population (based on the estimate of 30–60,000). As in other 'new immigration' cities (Rome, Athens, Barcelona), this population was extremely diverse, with over 80 countries represented and no dominant ethnic group or continent of origin. Labour migrants from Eastern Europe and Russia probably accounted for one third of all migrants living in Tel Aviv, followed by those from Southeast Asia (perhaps another quarter). However, these can only be rough estimates of this largely undocumented population (**Figure 5.3**).

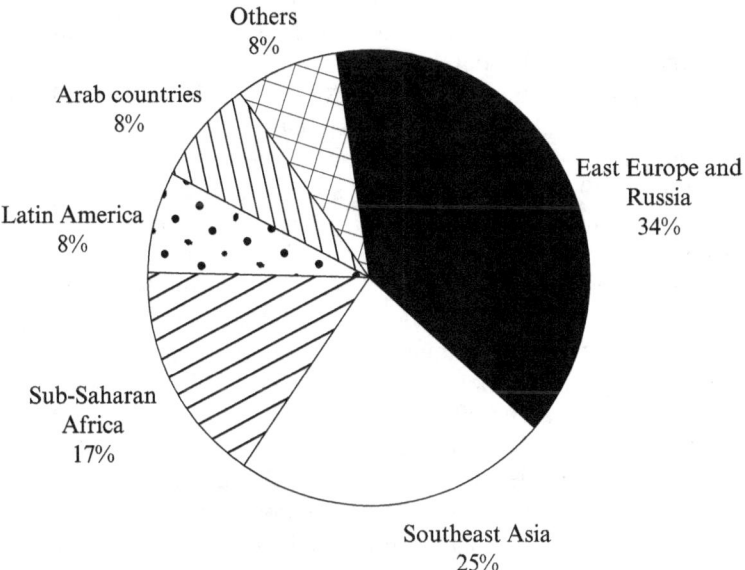

Figure 5.3   Estimated labour migrant population in Tel Aviv, by continent of origin, 2001

By the late 1990s the veteran African and Latino communities displayed signs of settlement and vigour, characterized by a high percentage of families with children and developed communal patterns of organization. These included various

---

[13] In mid-2005 one municipal official estimated 'off the record' that Tel Aviv's labour migrant population dropped by as much as 20 to 40 per cent since 2002. This is partly due to relocation by irregular migrants to nearby cities less targeted by migration police.

self-help networks and cultural associations, as well as dozens of 'underground' churches, some 30 creches (baby-sitting services) and one African 'school', operating informally in rented apartments or stores in southern Tel Aviv. Existing churches in Jaffa became important nodes of migrant association; pastors of migrant origin assumed leadership roles especially in the African and Filipino communities. A weekly football tournament at a seaside park with Latino music and food stalls became the locus of the South American community (Von Breitenstein 1999, Kemp et al. 2000). Since 2002, the deportation policy has drastically reduced Tel Aviv's African and South American communities, possibly by as much as half.

In contrast to the irregular migrant communities, legal foreign workers did not develop formal social organizations. One explanation is lack of motivation: legal guestworkers in Israel regard their stay as temporary (2–3 years at most). Mostly single men, they prefer to work long hours and live frugally for maximum savings. Moreover, the 'binding arrangement', as noted above, keeps them in constant fear of their employers, discouraging any form of mobilization. Thus, the Israeli guestworker regime led to a situation whereby irregular labour migrants enjoyed greater freedom than their legal counterparts.

The most remarkable reflection of this paradox was a short-lived but lively mobilization of the irregular African migrant population. With assistance from Israeli activists and parliamentarians, the African Workers Union was officially registered in November 1997 as a non-profit organization in Israel, although its 1,200 card-carrying members were nearly all illegal residents! For several years, in close cooperation with Israeli human rights organizations, the AWU lobbied the Knesset and appeared in the Israeli media as the public voice of the labour migrant community in Israel. Its strategy vis-à-vis the host society was to portray African workers as a respectable community with no intentions of settling in the Jewish state, seeking only temporary regularization. While successful in its public relations, the AWU had no effect on government policy and effectively disappeared with the onset of the deportation policy in 2002.[14]

The emergence of new, non-Jewish minorities in Israel was felt above all in Tel Aviv. Here the labour migrants' geographical concentration magnified their impact. The core area was in Neve Sha'anan, a neighbourhood that came to symbolize the migrant presence in Israel (**Box 5.1**). In 1999 possibly a third of Tel Aviv's labour migrant population resided in Neve Sha'anan and nearby neighbourhoods; another third (including the Arab labour migrants) resided in Jaffa's Ajami neighbourhood; and the last third (mostly Filipinos engaged in domestic and geriatric care) resided in the wealthier areas of central and northern Tel Aviv in proximity to their employers (**Figure 5.4**). In recent years, as police raids on illegal migrants began to focus on Tel Aviv and the 'bus stations area' in particular, there has been a marked degree of dispersion to outlying neighbourhoods and nearby cities.

---

[14] A similar attempt to set up a Latino Workers Union in 1998 (encouraged by Israeli activists) was abandoned after two of its leaders were deported (Rosenheck 1999, Kemp et al. 2000).

Box 5.1   Neve Sha'anan: the 'foreign workers neighbourhood' of Israel

The heart of Tel Aviv's labour migrant population is located in two southern Tel Aviv neighbourhoods, Neve Sha'anan and Shapira. Labour migrants began settling in these working-class areas in the late 1980s, attracted by low rental prices and easy access to public transportation. The construction of a massive Central Bus Station had aggravated the physical and economic deterioration of this district, which had among the highest negative migration rates in Tel Aviv. For the many irregular migrants who clean houses throughout the metropolitan area, however, living in the 'bus stations area' was an important asset.

After 1993 the settlement of foreign workers in Neve Sha'anan intensified, leading the municipality to define this as the 'core area' of the foreign worker population in Tel Aviv. In 1999 it contained up to 10,000 labour migrants, comprising 50 to 60 per cent of the area's population and up to one third of Tel Aviv's labour migrant population. With its foreign workers' cafes and meeting places, Neve Sha'anan also serves labour migrants living and working outside of Tel Aviv. Many of Israel's legal guestworkers, lodged in isolated construction sites and agricultural settlements during the week, converge on this area on weekends and holidays. Some even hire apartments together to serve as weekend homes.

Neve Sha'anan's location, adjacent to the central node of Israel's intercity bus system, had another effect: it magnified the labour migrant presence in the eyes of thousands passing daily through this urban gateway. The 'bus stations area', a gritty-but-sympathetic symbol of Tel Aviv for most Israelis, was transformed within a few years into a symbol of foreignness: 'You walk down the street and don't hear a single word of Hebrew!'. This expression is often followed by complaints about the area's sex shops, bars, etc.

The municipality of Tel Aviv is well aware of Neve Sha'anan's centrality. The failure of a previous renovation plan was partly blamed on the arrival of the labour migrants, symbolized in their 'takeover' of its pedestrianized main street. Later urban development plans proposed using the migrant presence as a springboard for the area's development, based on its 'ethnicity' (see below). However, since the deportation policy was renewed in 2002 hopes for the renaissance of Neve Sha'anan appear to have faded.

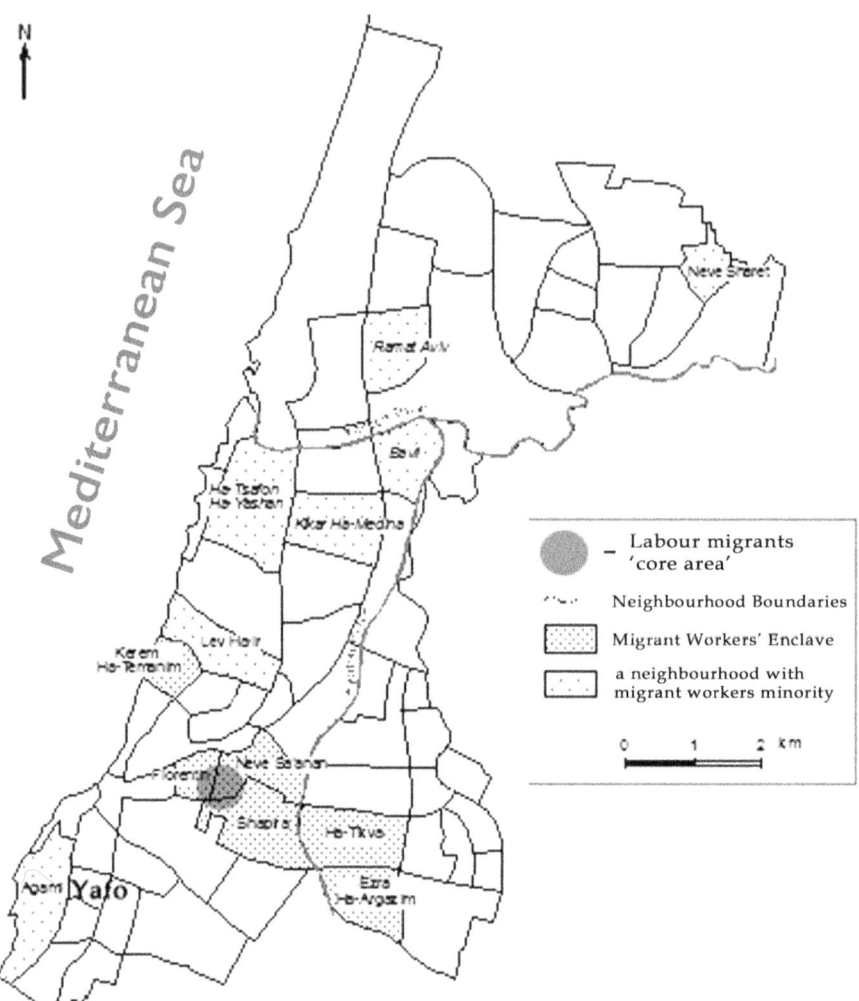

Figure 5.4   Labour migrant concentrations in Tel Aviv-Yafo, 1999

Source: Schnell 1999; Municipality of Tel Aviv 2002b.

3.2 Host-Stranger Relations in Tel Aviv

> It is amazing there is so little anti-migrant feeling in Tel Aviv, considering the Israeli context ... of ethnic-based fear (of Arabs) and insecurity about the future character of the Jewish state.
>
> Einat Fishbein, journalist, interview (my translation)

Tel Aviv likes to see itself as 'Israel's New York': a modern, cosmopolitan city that is open to the world, far ahead of the rest of the country in terms of secular values and tolerance of Otherness. Does this extend to tolerance regarding foreign workers? Without a city-wide survey it is unclear, but I would risk saying that attitudes toward labour migrants in Tel Aviv are relatively benign, for several reasons. The local press was one factor in creating public empathy among Tel Avivians toward 'their' migrant population. From the mid-1990s the main local paper *Ha'ir* published a weekly column presenting the human face of the foreign workers, their precarious living conditions and exploitation by Israeli landlords and employers.[15] The city is also home to the four human rights organizations that have been most active in raising public awareness of labour migrant rights in Israel: Workers Hotline, the Hotline for Migrant Workers, Physicians for Human Rights (PHR) and the Association for Civil Rights in Israel (ACRI). The (few) pro-migrant demonstrations organized by these NGOs all took place in Tel Aviv.

But above all, the benign attitude of most Tel Avivians toward labour migrants is due to the perception (shared by most Israelis, as noted above) that they are a non-threatening substitute for Palestinian workers, and that their presence is *temporary*. This perception of temporariness is constantly reinforced by government statements and policies that deny any possibility of settlement for the non-Jewish foreign workers. Nevertheless, as the large migrant presence in Tel Aviv stretched into the late 1990s, local attitudes appeared to be polarizing. A survey of attitudes in Neve Sha'anan and Shapira revealed a clear divide between lower- and higher-income residents in these neighbourhoods. The original, lower-class residents felt trapped and threatened by the labour migrant presence (Schnell 2000: 13–14). The newer residents who were gentrifying these neighbourhoods provided the most positive responses in the survey. Their 'embrace of strangers' was later demonstrated in interviews conducted by municipal planners during the public participation stage of a new redevelopment scheme for the area (see below). A typical answer to the question 'How do you feel living with foreign workers as neighbours?' was given by one such respondent who purchased his Neve Sha'anan flat in 1994:

> It's nice to have heterogeneity. They don't harm me, everyone does his own thing. Visitors tell me 'Listen, it's like living abroad here!' (Municipality of Tel Aviv 2002a: 117, my translation).

---

[15] 'The new Tel Avivians' (in Hebrew) by Einat Fishbein, *Ha'ir*, August 1996–June 1999.

In sharp contrast, in the traditional working-class neighbourhood of Hatikva, which experienced a substantial inflow of labour migrants from Neve Sha'anan in the late 1990s, the potential for xenophobia soon became apparent to municipal officials. As we will see, preventing an outburst of anti-immigrant feeling was one of the motivating factors behind Tel Aviv's local migrant policy.

4 Local Migrant Policies in Tel Aviv

The generally tolerant attitudes described above allowed the local authority to respond to the growing migrant presence with little public pressure. The local policy response first evolved within the municipal bureaucracy; later, the mayor and his advisors took a more active role. The period covered here includes two mayoral terms. From 1993 to 1998 mayor Ronnie Milo, a liberal maverik from the nationalistic Likud party, governed with a broad local coalition of parties. In the November 1998 municipal elections he was defeated by Ron Huldai, an independent candidate. In 1999 Mayor Huldai set up a wall-to-wall coalition, and was re-elected by a large margin in 2003. Huldai replaced the previous system of administration, in which different municipal divisions were headed by aldermen representing different coalition factions, with a more centralized system in which the divisions are headed by top civil servants who report directly to him. But even under the previous administration it was the mayor and his team, together with the top civil servants, who effectively made local policy, with little interference from city council.

The main, overriding parameter for Tel Aviv's policymakers has been the national policy toward labour migration. Israel is a highly centralized country in which national ministries routinely meddle in local matters. This is certainly true regarding labour migrants, most of whom are illegal residents. Nevertheless, Tel Aviv's size and economic base make its municipality relatively independent of central government.[16] This meant that the Huldai administration was able to openly espouse and implement an autonomous local policy toward labour migrants that often contradicted national policy. In fact, Tel Aviv's migrant policy under Huldai was the culmination of a process that began under the previous administration and took place largely within the municipal bureaucracy. This process is described in the following three sub-sections, corresponding to three policy phases.

4.1 Non-policy, Late 1980s to Mid-1990s

In the late 1980s–early 1990s the municipality was largely unaware of the foreign worker population, numbering a few thousand in Tel Aviv and nearly all

---

[16] Government payments accounted for only some 12 per cent of of the 1997 municipal budget.

undocumented. As their numbers grew, labour migrants increasingly came into contact with local service providers. From the mid-1990s a bottom-up practice evolved of informal provision of basic health, welfare and educational services to irregular migrants, especially children. By 1995 two 'Family Health clinics' in south Tel Aviv were informally providing preventive medical treatment to migrant children who were excluded from the national health insurance system and could not afford private treatment.[17] In 1996 these clinics treated 543 migrant families; in the Neve Sha'anan clinic half of all the clients were migrants. This practice was condoned by the director of the city's Public Health Administration, who later reported it to the deputy mayor as well. A similar norm developed at the main municipal hospital, Ichilov, where doctors liberally defined 'emergency treatment' and extended hospitalization days to uninsured migrants (interviews H. Nehama, R. Adout).

Social workers in the city's welfare department also began treating dozens of migrant children in what they defined as 'critical cases'. Similar treatment was extended to some homeless migrants by the municipal Homeless Unit (Municipality of Tel Aviv Welfare Services report, 11 April 1999). The municipal primary school in Neve Sha'anan, Bialik School, was another actor. Bialik's director not only opened the school to migrant children but also provided extra resources such as bilingual teachers. She, too, received the *post facto* approval of the director of the city's Education Division. Most other schools at this time refused to admit children who could not produce proof of residency – although this violated Israeli law requiring all children to be enrolled regardless of their legal status (interview Y. Yahalom).

These practices developed as a response by Tel Aviv's municipal workers to the needs of migrants whom they encountered on a daily basis. In lieu of any formal municipal policy, these actions were based on their professional ethics and then approved by their superiors, as described by the director of the city's Public Health Administration:

[W]e knew then that they were being treated [at the Family Health clinics], but we didn't yet know the breadth of the phenomenon....At that time there was no written policy regarding them. My attitude is that medical treatment should be given universally, without regard to status ... . I was aware of the practice and did not give a directive for or against [treating migrant children] ... The non-intervention [of the political level] and the fact that they did not try to stop this practice, is also a policy (interview Dr. H. Nehama).

---

[17] The Family Health clinics are managed by the city's Public Health Administration and staffed by municipal workers. The Ministry of Health covers 70 per cent of the local authority's costs. Israeli law requires the clinics to treat residents covered by the national health insurance scheme but does not prohibit treatment of other populations.

At this stage, then, street-level bureaucrats in Tel Aviv (Health Clinic nurses, social workers) fulfilled the same function as that of civic society professionals in Rome (Caritas lay workers, union activists), i.e. filling the vacuum created by Non-policy at the national and local levels.

4.2   Toward a Minimalist Guestworker Policy, 1995–98

The first comprehensive attempt to understand the labour migrant phenomenon in Tel Aviv occurred in the Long-Term Planning Department, which was developing a new master plan for the city. A 1995 draft report for the master plan included a subsection entitled 'Foreign workers in Tel Aviv-Yafo'. Based on interviews with social workers, nurses at the Family Health clinics and managers of neighbourhood renewal projects in the two main 'foreign worker neighbourhoods', this document provides an interesting snapshot of how they perceived the labour migrants. Interestingly, the irregular African community was praised ('a quiet and gentle population trying not to stand out') while the legal guestworkers (mostly Romanians) were described as a 'nuisance' due to their consumption of alcohol and prostitution and the conditions in which they were housed. Relations with the local population were not deemed as problematic as were the environmental effects, e.g. overcrowding. The report concluded that the massive presence of a 'foreign worker population' would have wide-ranging detrimental effects on the development of the weak neighbourhoods, and that the municipality must prepare a long-term strategy to cope with this phenomenon.[18] In 1996 another departmental report focused on the urban consequences of migrant enclaves developing in the southern neighbourhoods, referring to the experience of European cities.[19]

Using these reports, the City Engineer (heading the Planning Division) made several attempts to alert the political leadership, urging them 'to cope with the issue at the city level, to think of solutions to the short-term and the long-term problems'. He warned of the negative impact of labour migrant settlement in weak neighbourhoods in the short-term, but also noted their positive long-term potential. The 'realization of this potential (positive or negative)', he concluded, 'depends on local authority policy'.[20]

At first, the mayor resisted any assumption of responsibility, despite repeated urgings by the director of Welfare Services and the City Engineer. Mayor Milo insisted that labour migrants in Tel Aviv were not a municipal matter. After all, according to Israel's guestworker policy the government should ensure that

---

[18]   Long-Term Planning Department, 1995, *Master Plan for Tel Aviv-Yafo*, Stage 1, Report #3 (draft, Hebrew) by Orly Hacohen, pp. 42–5.

[19]   Long-Term Planning Department, 15 October 1996, 'Foreign worker settlement in Tel Aviv-Yafo: urban consequences' (Hebrew, written by the author).

[20]   City Engineer, memorandum to Deputy Mayor, 27 November 1996, 'Foreign workers in Tel Aviv-Yafo – the phenomenon and its urban consequences' (in Hebrew).

employers provided suitable conditions (lodging, health insurance) for their legal foreign workers, and it was government's responsibility to deport the illegal migrants – the bulk of Tel Aviv's foreign population.

Nevertheless, in mid-1996 a 'Committee on Foreign Workers' was established, including the directors of the Welfare Services and Planning divisions, and chaired by the deputy mayor. After preliminary research, the committee reached three conclusions: first, the labour migrants were *defined as a long-term phenomenon*, their presence in Tel Aviv an outcome of global processes and government policy. Thus, 'the local authority has almost no possibility for action' in regard to their arrival, settlement and concentration in certain areas. Nevertheless, '[t]he citizens of Tel Aviv see the municipality as the address to the solution of these problems'. Second, the labour migrants were *defined as an urban problem*. Their massive presence in the southern neighbourhoods was seen as obstructing municipal plans to rejuvenate these deteriorated neighbourhoods. The deputy mayor spoke of 'foreign ghettos which may result in our "losing" half the city' (i.e. southern Tel Aviv). Third, the labour migrant presence was *defined as a humanitarian problem*, especially with regard to children. The city should thus continue 'provision of services as required by law and international treaties' even if the government refused to recognize this obligation.[21]

Ultimately, Tel Aviv's policy response at this stage was a compromise between the activist stance of the bureaucracy, and the minimalist stance of the mayor. This led to a two-pronged strategy in the last two years of the Milo administration (1997–98). First, the previously informal provision of basic local services for labour migrants was formalized. Second, City Hall began lobbying the ministries to obtain funding for those services provided by the municipality (estimated in 1997 at over 9 million shekels)[22] and to change government migrant policies. These efforts produced no significant change at the national level.

In this second phase, the municipality officially acknowledged the migrant presence and, at least within the professional level, realized its *potential* long-term impact. But the political leadership under mayor Milo retained characteristically Guestworker-type attitudes and policies: labour migrants were a temporary phenomenon requiring a minimalistic, short-term response at the local level; ultimate responsibility for 'the foreign worker problem' rested at the national level.

Despite this official stance, the basis for a longer-term migrant policy began to take shape at this time within the municipal bureaucracy, specifically in the Welfare Services division. According to its director, Zeev Friedman, Welfare Services could no longer limit itself to ad-hoc provision of services to the migrant

---

[21] 'Summary of meeting of Committee on Foreign Workers', 19 August 1996; 'Subcommittee on foreign workers in Tel Aviv-Yafo – Intermediate Report', 5 September 1996 (in Hebrew).

[22] Cited in Kemp and Raijman 2000: 92.

population and must take the lead in formulating a local policy.[23] A social worker of religious background, he explained his stand regarding the labour migrants in professional as well as ethical terms:

> We [the Jewish people], after such a long journey in the Diaspora during which our rights were denied us, for us to return to the Land of Israel and to do to them exactly what others did to us?? Is this how we are [to be] 'a light unto the nations'? ... These are not just pretty words ... The Bible mentions 36 times the responsibility of Israel toward the gentiles living among us (interview Z. Friedman).

Henceforth, Friedman took the lead in emphasizing the city's moral responsibility toward its new population, as well as the practical necessity of formulating a local policy to deal with this challenge.

At this point the Welfare Division lacked information on the labour migrant population and had not yet 'ideologically internalized' the policy implications (ibid.). In 1997 a social worker was assigned to research the labour migrant communities. Based on her work, the Welfare Services division developed a model defining three concentric 'spheres of vulnerability'. The first 'sphere of vulnerability' was the migrant population; the second was the 'foreign worker neighbourhoods'; the third included the rest of the city. This analysis, while mindful of the migrants, defined their presence *above all in terms of host-stranger relations*:

> In essence, we have here a population that is isolated, a Fourth World within a modern city ... they create their own networks, and we end up with a city within a city, a community within a community. We saw this situation as one in which they endanger themselves, but they also endanger others. They affect the residents in the area ... those residents who cannot escape, who are trapped. And then we end up with an area of chaos (interview Z. Friedman).

Friedman's apprehension about the possible reaction by 'those residents who cannot escape, who are trapped' recalls Bauman's terms (Chapter 2, above), that is, the migrant presence presents a threat to social Order in the city.

The 'spheres of vulnerability' model was propagated by the Welfare Division in the last year of the Milo administration and the beginning of mayor Huldai's term. Toward the municipal elections in November 1998 Friedman met with the mayoral candidates and told them that 'Tel Aviv cannot have an ostrich policy, we must deal with the issue' (ibid.). The policy he proposed would include incorporating the labour migrants into existing services that could meet their immediate problems, preventing conflicts between migrant and indigenous residents, and systematically collecting information on their needs as a basis for longer-term solutions. To implement this, a municipal center should be set up in

---

[23] 'Summary of meeting on foreign workers, chaired by the Director of Welfare Services', 8 January 1997 (in Hebrew).

one of the migrant neighbourhoods (Welfare Services Division, draft report, 14 April 1999). Friedman's efforts bore fruit when the new municipal administration adopted his model and began implementing all the above recommendations.

4.3 Toward a 'Liberal' Guestworker Policy, 1999–2002

4.3.1 MESILA – Aid and Information Center for the Foreign Community

Shortly after his election, mayor Ron Huldai officially adopted the policy proposals formulated in the Welfare Division in the last years of the Milo administration. Tel Aviv's new migrant policy was launched publicly in July 1999 with the opening of the 'Aid and Information Center for the Foreign Community in Tel Aviv-Yafo' (MESILA in its Hebrew acronym). The establishment of a municipal centre to serve Tel Aviv's largely illegal labour migrant population marked a deliberate gesture of autonomy on the part of the new administration. At the opening of MESILA, Mayor Huldai expressly challenged the government's labour migration policy, declaring that the city would extend services to all its foreign residents, regardless of their legal status:[24]

> The men and women here came to Israel alone with the aim of making a living, got married and set up families. Some are parents to small children and infants .... Their temporary status deprives them of personal security and other elementary rights. If we remain deaf to their cry for help, the problem will worsen and a deterioration of the situation may endanger us all. The creation of MESILA is a necessity, not a luxury ... Tel Aviv-Yafo is the only city in Israel that has chosen not to continue ignoring the problem.

In a potent gesture, a church choir from the irregular African community was invited to sing at the opening ceremony. Government representatives were also invited but pointedly failed to attend.

In the months leading up to the opening of MESILA, the mayor established an advisory 'Forum on Foreign Workers', chaired by the City Manager. The Forum was meant to supervise the new policy and specifically to coordinate between local and national policies toward labour migrants. Lack of cooperation by government representatives and other problems made this impossible and after a few years it was informally abandoned. Instead, MESILA became the *de facto* agency of local policy formulation and implementation toward migrants, within the Social Services division.

The municipal migrant centre is unique in Israel. Located in the heart of Neve Sha'anan, MESILA operates as an autonomous unit of the Social Services (previously Welfare) Division, with its own professional staff (equal to five full-time positions) and some 60 volunteers. In its first years, MESILA's annual

---

[24] See epigraph, above. Both citations are extracts from Huldai's speech which appear in the MESILA brochure, 1999.

budget was approximately 500,000 shekels (ca. €100,000); since 2003 the Huldai administration has sharply reduced spending on all social services, including MESILA. As a result, MESILA's director plays an increasingly entrepreneurial role, involving NGOs and other entities in specific projects initiated and coordinated by the centre.

MESILA's original objectives were to provide information, counselling and guidance services to the labour migrant population, act as liaison between them and their Israeli neighbours, and provide 'preliminary intervention in critical situations involving foreign individuals/communities' (MESILA 1999). An additional aim (not mentioned in the publicity brochure) was 'to collect information and understand the foreign community phenomenon in a systematic and organized manner'.[25] In practice, the centre's activity has evolved over the years. At first, the centre focused on outreach to the migrant communities and handling individual requests for assistance. In the following two years MESILA streamlined its treatment of individual requests (averaging some 100 a month, handled largely by volunteers), freeing the professional staff to focus on community-related work, including migrant 'community empowerment' and outreach to Israeli communities (see below). Since 2003, the government's deportation policy has shattered the communal life of Tel Aviv's migrant population, and MESILA finds itself dealing once again with individual migrant emergencies, as in its first year (interviews E. Altar-Dembo).

Most, but not all, of Tel Aviv's new migrant policy takes place within the framework of MESILA. In the following pages I summarize the various actions of the municipality since 1999, following the policy domains and issue areas defined in the typology (Chapter 3).

4.3.2 Legal-political domain

Migrant rights, representation and 'community empowerment' The municipality continues to see Israel's exclusionary guestworker regime as responsible for the high proportion of irregular migrants in Tel Aviv. Without challenging this regime head-on, the Huldai administration has intensified the city's lobbying efforts to affect some changes in national immigration policy. Municipal officials regularly lobby the Knesset and relevant ministries (Health, Education, etc.) for specific changes to incorporate labor migrants in Israeli social legislation. MESILA's director appears before the parliamentary Sub-committee on Foreign Workers, and hosts visits by Knesset members and government representatives. In 2000 the city hired academic experts to prepare a document proposing changes to government policy, addressed to the prime minister and relevant ministries. Among the changes it proposed: issuing work permits directly to the foreign workers rather than to their employers (i.e., eliminating the 'binding arrangement'), and a regularization of some illegal residents (Municipality of Tel Aviv 2000). This had no discernible effect.

---

[25] Social Services division draft report, 14 April 1999.

However, the Huldai administration does not present these proposals as a step toward extending citizenship to the labour migrants. Instead, it bases its reasoning for their (partial, temporary) incorporation on 'practical necessity' as well as humanitarian and 'Jewish ethical' grounds. Thus, MESILA focuses on improving the migrants' daily lives in practical matters, such as access to healthcare. This strategy, according to some Israeli civil rights organizations, avoids the real issue behind most of the foreign workers' problems: the exclusionary nature of Israel's ethno-national regime toward all non-Jewish immigrants. A lawyer at the Association for Civil Rights in Israel describes Tel Aviv's stance vis-à-vis the government as: 'We are not saying anything about the rights of the migrants to remain, only that they must be taken care of as long as they are here' (interview M. Pinchuk). Indeed, 'as long as they are here' is a phrase often used by local officials, underlying the essentially temporary status of the labour migrant population.

Practical reasoning, too, lay behind the city's attitude toward migrant representation. Any kind of formal framework on the lines of 'migrant advisory councils' found in some European cities is out of the question in Israel's immigration regime. Instead, MESILA cultivated ties with what it defined as 'migrant community leaders' (activists, pastors) and maintained regular, informal contacts with them. MESILA also presents the 'migrant situation' to City Hall in regular reports using its own database, compiled from questionnaires and structured interviews with every migrant applying for help at the centre.[26] Municipal officials were satisfied with this top-down arrangement, whereby MESILA served as a channel between migrant leaders and the municipality – indeed, it was seen as one of the centre's principal roles (interviews Z. Friedman, E. Altar-Dembo).

This top-down manner of informal consultation also suited the main migrants' association, the African Workers Union, who feared that any formal representative arrangement would be viewed as a provocation by the government, to be avoided at all costs (interview N. Holdbrook). But while the municipality wants to keep abreast of migrant interests regarding *local issues*, the migrants themselves take a broader view. According to the AWU president,

> The most important thing is to change the government policy, to get the municipality to influence them. For example, the new order to deport a thousand migrants a month. We say, 'talk with the government, try to leave the Africans out of the deportations'. We know the municipality also has a limit, most of the things they do have to go through the government. Basically what we want is to get legalized... But anytime any small thing comes along, like the health insurance for children, we welcome it. We don't want to be seen as initiators. It's a game. (ibid.)

---

[26] The reliability of this data, however, is questionable. According to one researcher on South American migrants in Tel Aviv, they regard MESILA questionnaires with some suspicion, resulting in not-necessarily-truthful answers (Barak Kalir, personal communication; interview Maria).

This form of consultation was one reason behind MESILA's policy of 'community empowerment'. Apart from cultivating 'migrant community leaders' who could serve as a voice for the migrant population, the centre offered courses in which hundreds of migrant activists participated, in Hebrew, healthcare, etc. 'Community empowerment' was not meant to lay the basis for real migrant representation at some future stage. Rather, it should allow more effective local policy toward a largely undocumented population, in part by encouraging migrant communities to provide these services themselves, e.g. childcare arrangements (see below) (interview E. Altar-Dembo). The same reasoning lay behind MESILA's publication of a 'Guide to the Foreign Worker' on labour migrant rights in Israel.[27]

4.3.3 Socio-economic domain: health, welfare and education policies
Tel Aviv's policy since 1999 focuses on providing basic education, health and welfare services to the migrant population, 'as long as they are here'. This continues the policy begun in the mid-1990s, with two differences. First the use of MESILA as a front office for incorporating labour migrants, especially children, into existing services. Second, the development of specific services for the labour migrant population.

MESILA has come to specialize in migrant children's health, welfare and education, filling a niche that was relatively unattended by local non-governmental organizations. In the late-1990s the number of migrant children was estimated at 1500, of which about 1,000 were under age 6. Following an amendment allowing incorporation of migrant children into the National Health Insurance scheme, MESILA campaigned among migrant parents to register their children.[28] By February 2002, 500 of the 600 migrant children registered in Israel were registered at the centre (MESILA 2002b). It also held workshops to acquaint nurses at the Family Health clinics with the migrants' special needs.[29] MESILA also used its position as a municipal agency to mediate between its mostly 'illegal' clients and various governmental agencies, in individual cases involving health and welfare (e.g. children with disabilities).

Another focus of MESILA's activity were the underground, migrant-run creches located in dozens of rented apartments in southern Tel Aviv. Already in the mid-1990s the local press had exposed the unhealthy conditions in which

---

[27] MESILA, 'Guide to the Foreign Worker in Israel', May 2001 (Hebrew, English, Spanish and Romanian).

[28] In 2000 the law was amended to include migrant children regardless of their legal status (see above). While Israeli children are automatically registered upon birth, labour migrant children must be registered by their parents, who must also pay a supplementary fee. The child is then entitled to all the health services.

[29] The number of migrants treated at these clinics had risen steadily, reaching 856 families (1039 children) in July 2000 (Public Health Division, Report on migrants, July 2000).

hundreds of migrant children were kept during the long working hours of their parents. This had been one of the catalyzers for municipal involvement with the labour migrant population. Incorporating the illegal migrant creches into the formal education system was impossible, not least because of the migrants' fear of arrest for illegal residence. MESILA therefore concentrated on improving their conditions by holding a series of workshops for the migrant babysitters on proper childcare and pedagogy, as well as sending volunteer assistants. When the government accused 'the municipality's independent policy' as undermining its efforts against the irregular migrants, the director of MESILA responded that Tel Aviv was not challenging government policy, only doing the minimum necessary to allow migrant children basic education and a healthy development (interview, E. Altar-Dembo).

MESILA's strategy, often based on incremental improvements, is a result of its unique position as a municipal agency. The centre's director acknowledges that their treatment of individual cases without the ability to create large-scale change, is frustrating: 'In most requests by migrants we cannot help them beyond directing them to other agencies or NGOs ... at most we act as intermediaries' (ibid.). In contrast, non-governmental organizations dealing with labour migrants can be more openly critical of national policies, pressing for fundamental change through the courts and public pressure (see Kemp and Raijman 2000).

A relatively successful aspect of municipal policy has been the gradual incorporation of migrant children into the local public education system. Here local policy is backed by Israeli law, which requires school enrolment for all children from age six, regardless of their legal status. MESILA's outreach activities encouraged migrants to enrol their children in local schools, opening a registration service at the centre in 2001 and convincing the Education Ministry to allow two new kindergartens in that year specifically for migrant children. The kindergartens were opened on the grounds of the Bialik School, which provided multicultural learning materials and bilingual staff. From a handful of migrant children enrolled in the mid-1990s, by 2002 the number of migrant pupils in Tel Aviv's public kindergartens and schools surpassed 500 (MESILA bi-annual report, July 2001). Since the deportation policy was renewed in 2002, the number of migrant children has dwindled (to an estimated 1200 by 2005), but some 900 are still enrolled in local kindergartens and schools. The Centre also initiated extracurricular activities for older migrant children, involving other bodies to finance these activities[30] (interview, E. Altar-Dembo).

The flagship in Tel Aviv's school policy toward migrant children was Bialik primary school. By 2002, migrants accounted for half of Bialik's pupils. The school's charismatic director had early on decided to allow migrant pupils 'to

---

[30] In 2001 summer camps for 90 migrant children were organized and financed by youth movements and a kibbutz. MESILA even initiated an 'adolescents group' for migrant teenagers who met at the centre with youth counsellors – and obtained funding for the project through an anti-crime budget in the Ministry for Internal Security!

preserve their identity and language on one hand, and on the other hand to give them everything this country which they have chosen can offer, within our limited resources' (interview A. Yahalom). The 'limited resources' referred to a municipal request to the Ministry of Education, which provides extra funding to local authorities per *Jewish migrant* pupils, to do the same for the labour migrant pupils. When this was rejected, the municipal Education Division decided to cover the extra costs from its own budget.

In 2003 the Bialik School was moved out of its decrepit building for safety reasons, and relocated in two floors of a secondary school (Rogozin, which also has a significant presence of non-Jewish pupils) in a nearby neighbourhood. The multicultural curriculum and multi-ethnic student body of Bialik and Rogozin are unique: apart from the labour migrant children, most of the other pupils are Russian *olim* (not all are Jewish), as well as children of Palestinian collaborators relocated into Israel by the government. The schools have thus become symbols of Otherness in the local education system, a receptory for Outsiders. Municipal policy appears to willingly accept the self-selected concentration of non-Jewish pupils in these schools. This contrasts sharply with European cities such as Amsterdam that have tried over years to desegregate schools with a concentration of migrant-origin children.

In terms of host-stranger relations, the integration of migrant pupils at Bialik and Rogozin may signal their acceptance or their rejection by the host society, depending on how one looks at it. Certainly this is not a simple case of integrating migrant children into the general education system, as pointed out by Bialik's director:

> This school serves as the fig leaf covering the dilemmas of our state ... We never acknowledged ourselves as a country of immigration, a multi-cultural country. We remain a nation-state based on assimilation ... Now the foreign workers are holding a mirror up to us, reflecting our incapacity to absorb immigration, to contain Otherness (interview A. Yahalom).

4.3.4 *Cultural-religious domain*

Outside the hallways and courtyard of Bialik and Rogozin (covered with posters promoting multicultural values), Tel Aviv has little to show in terms of municipal support for the cultural and religious Otherness of its migrant population. Again, this must be understood within the general context of 'the Jewish State'. Indeed, Tel Aviv, the self-defined 'first Hebrew city', is more religiously homogenous than other mixed (Jewish-Arab) cities in Israel, such as Haifa. Notwithstanding Tel Aviv-Yafo's official hyphen, the Arab neighbourhoods of Jaffa remain largely segregated from the rest of the city. The visibly growing presence, therefore, of a Christian minority in south Tel Aviv had a greater impact than the actual numbers of migrants. The sight of African families dressed in their Sunday best on the way to church, soon became a part of the local scene in southern Tel Aviv. Publicized by the media, the presence of these Christian migrants was shocking to some

Tel Avivians and attractively exotic to others. In contrast, the increased presence of Muslim labour migrants (from Egypt, Jordan, Sudan, etc.), has gone largely unnoticed as they blend in the local Palestinian community in Jaffa.

The municipality was aware since at least 1995 of the large number of 'underground' churches operating in apartments and warehouses throughout the migrant neighbourhoods (in addition to swelling attendance levels in the established churches in Jaffa). Since the opening of MESILA, City Hall knows more about the religious needs of the labour migrant population. Nevertheless, until now the municipality has adopted a Non-policy of benign neglect, neither condemning nor condoning the underground churches. This may be due in part to Israeli sensitivity on maintaining religious freedom for Christian minorities. This is clearly an issue that policymakers in Tel Aviv prefer to leave to national authorities.

One incident throws light on the situation in which the municipality can find itself in any attempt to forge an independent policy in the cultural-religious domain. In 2001, it gave permission for a internationally known Nigerian singer to appear in the municipal amphitheatre, located in the city's largest park. The organizer of the event requested an entry visa for the singer, attaching a supportive letter from a municipal official stating that his appearance would hearten the Nigerian migrant community in Israel. The Ministry of Interior not only refused to issue the visa, but sent an angry letter noting that the Municipality of Tel Aviv was contravening government policy: the African labour migrants were illegals, not a community that should be entertained. 'Do we belong to two different governments?' asked the Interior Ministry official, as reported in the media (*Ha'aretz*, 30 July 2001: E7). The city's director of Social Services responded:

> We are talking about a clash of attitudes. The State's attitude is one of deportation, non-recognition of elementary rights. We, on the other hand, claim that there is a certain reality, and as long as these people are among us, a universal morality applies to them that crosses borders and nations ... There is no basis to the claim that by allowing them to enjoy their own culture we are encouraging them to settle (ibid.).

The Huldai administration was not pleased with this public dispute between ministry and municipality, especially after its supportive letter was cited by the Association for Civil Rights in Israel in an appeal to the Supreme Court against the Interior Ministry's decision. Following this incident City Hall lowered its profile and has distanced itself from the appearance of cooperation with the struggle of Israeli NGOs to extend civil rights to the labour migrants (interview M. Pinchuk).

A more low-key municipal venture in regard to migrant cultural needs is MESILA's support for La Escuelita. This is an after-school programme run by migrants from South America who want to preserve the Latino identity of their children, some of whom speak fluent Hebrew and faltering Spanish. Initiated by migrant parents, it first operated in the MESILA office before moving into premises at the Bialik School. In 2002 La Escuelita operated on Friday afternoons and included some sixty children divided into three age groups, taught by migrant teachers. Material and technical assistance was provided by Bialik. MESILA's support for La Escuelita can be seen as either a Guestworker-type or Pluralist-type response to cultural Otherness. The former seems more probable, i.e. the municipality sees the programme as preparing migrant children for an eventual return to their countries of origin, not as preparing them to become Israeli citizens with a strong cultural identity of their own (*Jerusalem Report*, 14 January 2002, pp. 12–17; interview E. Altar-Dembo).

The municipality's ambiguous attitude regarding a potentially new non-Jewish minority in Tel Aviv is reflected in the responses of key players in the new migrant policy, such as the director of MESILA:

> Very few perceive of Tel Aviv as a multicultural city...mostly people in the educational sector. The Municipality makes attempts to take into account the needs of the migrants, but compared to the liberal attitudes existing in European cities – we're still not there. There's still a lot of work to be done in changing public attitudes. *The religious issue is all the time in the background.* In this, Tel Aviv differs from the European cities (interview E. Altar-Dembo).

This ambivalence appears to be the reason why the municipality has taken almost no actions to affect public attitudes regarding the labour migrant population. The idea of accepting non-Jewish labour migrants as another minority culture has been left to local NGOs and, to some degree, the local media. Instead, municipal policy in this area is based on the need to avert potential crises in areas of migrant concentration – a basic fear expressed early on by policymakers (see above). Indeed, preventing conflict between the newcomers and Israeli residents in the migrant neighbourhoods was one of the original aims behind the establishment of MESILA. Since then, two attempts at 'community bridging' have met with little success. In Neve Sha'anan, local residents committees showed little interest. A second attempt in 2001 was planned more carefully, after xenophobic feelings were expressed in an eastern neighbourhood where migrants began settling as they dispersed beyond Neve Sha'anan. MESILA designed this project ('The new faces of east Tel Aviv'), together with local community workers, with the aim of legitimizing the migrant presence (interview A. Ezov-Amon). It was later abandoned following budget cuts in the welfare department.

4.3.5 Spatial policies toward migrant enclaves
As early as 1995, municipal planners perceived the presence of labour migrants as a threat to their renovation plans for the southern neighbourhoods. However, no action was taken in the Milo administration. In 1999 the Huldai administration initiated a 'Strategic Planning' process for the city, in effect re-starting the master plan begun under the previous administration. The Strategic Planning process began with a year-long public participation phase that included a series of

meetings between municipal planners, residents and others. This in itself was quite revolutionary in the normally top-down planning process characterizing Israel. Moreover, labour migrant 'representatives' were invited to participate in the meetings held in southern Tel Aviv – a precedent in Israeli planning. The labour migrant presence was among the issues raised in these meetings, which dealt with the problems, potentials and 'vision' for each neighbourhood. Residents expressed negative as well as positive feelings (see above), which were duly noted in later stages of the Strategic Plan (Municipality of Tel Aviv 2002a).

Concurrent with the long-term Strategic Planning Process, two non-statutory plans were advanced for two neighbourhoods in which labour migrants are concentrated. Both plans mention the migrant presence as a factor to consider in the areas' redevelopment. The *Strategic Plan for the Stations Area* (covering the migrant 'core area' of Neve Sha'anan) is the first Israeli plan to consider labour migrants as a significant springboard for urban renovation. The preliminary recommendations include 'transforming the foreign workers from "threatening" to "interesting" [in a] process of transforming [the neighbourhood] into a multicultural area' (Tayar/Asif presentation slides 2001). The final document, written after the deportation policy of 2002 had significantly reduced the local migrant population, insists that they will remain a significant presence in the area (Municipality of Tel Aviv 2004b). The plan proposes adopting an 'intercultural municipal policy' that takes into account 'the multicultural existence' of the migrants and other local populations – without specifying what that means. One section proposes to 'encourage local entrepreneurship by labour migrants' and a 'publicity/marketing campaign of the area as "ethnotown"'; another section notes that the entire plan will depend on coordination with government ministries, including the ministries implementing the deportation policy when the document was prepared! It is safe to assume that most of the proposals in this non-binding document will remain on paper.

5   Summary: 'As Long As They Are Here ...'

Tel Aviv's migrant policy has developed in the context of a national immigration regime that excludes the possibility of non-Jewish migrant settlement. For most of the past decade, the government effectively ignored the large irregular migrant presence that resulted from Israel's particular Guestworker regime. Since 2002, deportation of illegal migrants has become a central component of the national Guestworker policy. Tel Aviv is the only Israeli city to have developed its own migrant policy. In doing so, it has shown considerable autonomy, progressing from a Non-policy phase to what I call a 'liberal Guestworker policy'.

Tel Aviv's policy responses reflect changing attitudes and expectations within the municipality regarding the labour migrants. Prior to 1995 there was little or no awareness of their presence. From the mid-1990s a *de facto* bottom-up practice evolved, of informally providing some basic services to irregular migrants, mostly children. These procedures received the approval of higher levels in the municipal bureaucracy, who then began pressing the political level to formulate a long-term policy. At that time, the mayor refused to accept responsibility for the migrants, claiming it was a national-level problem. City Hall preferred to regard the labour migrant presence as a temporary phenomenon, resulting from the government's policy of substituting overseas workers for Palestinian workers 'until things calm down'.

Tel Aviv's Non-policy response, lasting from the late 1980s until the mid-1990s, differs little from other cities in the first phase of labour migration. Amsterdam, for example, went through a similar phase in the late 1950s and early 1960s. Rome deliberately ignored its labour migrant population from the 1980s to 1993. Other cities in self-declared 'non-immigration' countries (e.g. Athens) have responded similarly during the first decade of labour immigration.

Tel Aviv's second policy phase lasted from 1996 to 1998. In response to pressures from the professional level, City Hall formally acknowledged the labour migrant presence and approved the formal provision of minimal services 'as long as they are here'. This was based on the assumption of temporariness: legal guestworkers would return to their countries of origin within a few years, irregular migrants would eventually be repatriated. The mayor's stand remained that ultimate responsibility for Tel Aviv's 'foreign worker problem' rested in the hands of national government. In attitudes and actions, this phase marks a change from the previous (undeclared) Non-policy to a (declared) minimalist Guestworker policy. At the same time, however, the basis for a longer-term policy was being prepared at the professional level.

A third period began in 1999 with the election of a new mayor who adopted the policy concept conceived in the previous two years within the city's Welfare Division. The new policy recognized the labour migrant presence as a long-term (but not necessarily permanent) phenomenon. This required a more comprehensive local response, regardless of national policy. The new strategy was based on the establishment of a municipal 'Aid and Information Center for the Foreign Worker Community in Tel Aviv' (MESILA). The following years can be seen as a period of increasing incorporation of the labour migrant population into the city's services structure, without officially recognizing the permanence of the migrant communities (still largely composed of illegal residents). Instead, it tries to do 'what is possible' for them under the circumstances. This I termed a 'liberal Guestworker policy'.

Since 1999, Tel Aviv's local policy has openly challenged the government's immigrant policy. This is demonstrated most clearly by the fact that MESILA serves mostly illegal migrants. However, this challenge should not be exaggerated. While the Huldai administration criticizes the national Guestworker policy, it does not fundamentally challenge the basic assumptions of the Israeli immigration regime, which is based on the assumed temporariness of non-Jewish immigrants in Israel. Municipal representatives repeatedly stress that their goal is not to turn Tel Aviv's non-Jewish labour migrants into future citizens or even permanent residents, only to meet practical needs arising from their presence, needs that cannot be ignored 'as long as they are here'.

It appears that City Hall *recognizes* that there is a permanent new non-Jewish minority in the city, but has not *accepted* the full consequences of this. In this respect, Tel Aviv's response differs substantially from the policies adopted by local authorities in Europe in the 1980s–90s. Following the abandonment of national guestworker programs after 1973, many European cities developed policies that aimed, in one way or another, at integrating their newly-acknowledged ethnic minorities (Rogers and Tillie 2001, Alexander 2004).

Such a policy response would appear premature in the case of Tel Aviv, considering Israel's national immigration regime. Even the permanence of the labour migrant population remains an open question. Since the deportation policy was renewed in 2002, the number of labour migrants in Tel Aviv has dropped by perhaps a third, although this is but one rough estimate. The veteran African and Latin American migrant communities have nearly vanished. Nevertheless, they have been partly replaced by more labour migrants from eastern Europe. Many, if not most, labour migrants no longer expect to settle permanently in Israel. At the same time, it does not appear that Palestinian border workers will soon replace overseas labour migrants. In short, some long-term labour migrant presence in Tel Aviv appears *probable* although it is too early to regard it as *irreversible*. In these circumstances, the city's current policy appears to be a sensible one. Indeed, since 2002 MESILA has shifted its focus from community-based activities back to solving individual problems arising from the deportations (separated families, etc.). This may signal a new phase in local policy, although it is too early to tell.

But is Tel Aviv's 'liberal guestworker policy' only due to external limitations, i.e. the national guestworker regime? I would argue that it is also a consequence of ambivalent attitudes *within* the municipality, at both professional and political levels, in regard to the (non-Jewish) labour migrant population. This ambivalence is expressed in the city's actions (and inaction) across the various policy domains. Regarding the migrants' civic status, Kemp and Raijman (2000) argued that Tel Aviv's policy of incrementally incorporating (mostly irregular) migrants into the Israeli welfare system presented a real challenge to Israel's migrant regime. Without openly questioning the government's authority on the migrants' civic status, the city was blurring the line between citizen and non-citizen, legal and illegal resident. According to them, Tel Aviv had adopted a 'concept of "urban citizenship" that does not follow the national definition nor is it subservient to it' (ibid.: 93). But according to the director of MESILA, their 'community empowerment' strategy was simply a way to improve the flow of information from the migrants to the municipality. The aim was a more efficient provision of services, not to prepare the migrants as potential political actors at the local level.

In the Socio-economic domain, too, the role of MESILA is primarily as a referral and mediation service between migrants and other (public or Third Sector) agencies. Very few migrant-specific services have been developed by the city. This can partly be attributed to the government's refusal to subsidize any local services to labour migrants. But it is also an expression of the ambivalent attitude of the Municipality and within MESILA, regarding the extent to which labour migrants should be incorporated into the Israeli welfare system.

In the Cultural-religious domain, municipal actions have been few, especially when compared to the policies of many European cities that are eager to demonstrate (even if superficially) their multiculturalism. Tel Aviv's inaction regarding the migrants' non-material needs cannot be attributed to ignorance: the municipality has been aware for years of the 'underground churches' in southern Tel Aviv. However, any real action in this area would signal an acceptance of the fundamentally *religious* nature of the labour migrants' Otherness (as Christian or Muslims). While local officials acknowledge, and may even empathize with, the migrants' religious/ethnic Otherness ('we know what it's like to be a minority'), this is not translated into intentions to support this Otherness – as a Pluralist-type policy would imply. Neither is assimilation a possible option, since the newcomers are not Jewish. These attitudes characterize the Guestworker policy phase, in which Otherness is tolerated, not supported.

Some of the sharpest changes in municipal rhetoric are found in its urban planning documents. Until the mid-late 1990s, labour migrant enclaves were perceived by planners as a threat and an obstacle to urban renovation. In 2002, the first report of Tel Aviv's 'Strategic Plan' was published, as the basis for articulating a new vision of the city (Municipality of Tel Aviv 2002). The report presents the labour migrant presence in the southern neighbourhoods as both 'a problem' and 'an opportunity'. However, its proposal to 'utilize this heterogeneity [to] strengthen the area as a touristic-ethnic magnet' (p. 118) appears to express the kind of Pluralist attitudes that Bauman and Levinas warned of, i.e. embracing Strangers for their aesthetic/market value, rather than being truly sensitive to their Otherness.[31] The chance that these general planning proposals will actually be implemented appears at this time highly doubtful.

In sum, the latest phase in Tel Aviv's response displays some Pluralist characteristics in espoused as well as enacted policies, but it cannot be characterized as a truly Pluralist policy according to our criteria. Above all, it remains ambiguous regarding the permanence of the labour migrants and support for their Otherness. The fact that Tel Aviv remains in a Guestworker policy phase, albeit a liberal version, cannot be attributed solely to the (very real) restraints imposed by the national migrant regime. It is also a consequence of ambivalent attitudes within the municipality in regard to the permanence of the labour migrant population. A Pluralist attitude implies the acceptance of the migrants' presence, as well as acceptance of their Otherness, as a permanent feature in the city. This view can be found among some activists in Israeli NGOs fighting for a fundamental change in the Israeli migration regime. It implies that Israel should

---

[31] See Chapter 2, section 3, above.

open itself to non-Jewish immigration, regularize illegal immigrants and allow eventual citizenship for those that remain.

Such a view is unacceptable to most Israelis, including key actors in the municipality. Among the principle policymakers of the new migrant policy there remains a reluctance to accept the full consequences of Pluralism. This would mean that local authority policies would aim at the long-term integration of the non-Jewish labour migrant population, while supporting its religious and ethnic Otherness. The 'first Hebrew city' is not yet ready to expand its self-definition as a tolerant, pluralistic city to the point of incorporating a permanent new non-Jewish minority.

Chapter 6

Paris: A Century of Assimilation

[The] general impression of disorder and destructurization ... [of east Paris] contrasts strongly with the grand elements of urban composition, organization and coherence of the built areas and public spaces that mark, altogether, the central and western quarters of Paris.

APUR, *L'aménagement de l'Est de Paris*, 1987 (my translation)

[W]henever building-order-by-design is on the agenda, certain inhabitants of the territory to be made orderly in the new way turn into strangers that need to be eliminated.

Zygmunt Bauman, 'Making and Unmaking of Strangers', 1995

1   Introduction

The city of Paris appears a strange choice for a case study of municipal migrant policies. First, its unique status within the French political system (until 1977 the capital was administered directly by government-appointed prefects) raises the question of whether Paris had any *local* policy prior to 1977. Second, policymaking in Paris has traditionally been framed in universalist terms ('unsanitary housing', 'social exclusion') that avoid any mention of migration or ethnicity *per se*. However, this is characteristic of the type of response to immigration that this chapter explores. Indeed, Paris was chosen to illustrate Assimilationist-type policies precisely because its response to ethnic diversity has remained so consistently loyal to the French republican model of integration – even as other cities in France moved toward more 'ethnicization' of their policies toward migrants.

Indeed, Paris's policy response to immigration has remained fairly consistent throughout the twentieth century: the underlying aim was to distance the working-class population from the city centre to the periphery. Over time, the indigenous proletarian Other was replaced by the labour migrant from abroad. Although the ethnic element was rarely mentioned, the displacement of certain minority populations was implicit in the overall vision of creating urban, social, political and economic order in the capital. The results are clear: although greater Paris has long served as a magnet for immigrants, the bulk of the migrant population in the metropolitan area is today found in the *banlieues*, the cities surrounding the capital. Consequently, it is Paris's *banlieues* that have attracted most of the research on migrants and migrant policies,[1] and it is there where the recent upsurge of violence by second-generation migrant youth took place. It is not by chance that this occurred just 'outside the walls' of Paris, symbolized by the *périphérique*, the ring highway that separates the capital from its suburbs.

Nevertheless, Paris itself always retained a significant migrant/minority population *intra muros*, due to its sheer size and its role as a gateway city.[2] This chapter will explore those urban policies that distanced Paris's working-class migrant population ever farther from the centre and eventually 'beyond the city walls', as well as local policies affecting those migrants who remained within Paris. To use Bauman's term, we will discern how local policymakers have waged a 150-year 'war of attrition' against Strangers. We begin with the national context (Section 2), followed by a summary of immigration to Paris and migrant settlement patterns (Section 3). The bulk of the chapter follows the evolution of urban development policies (the Spatial domain – Section 4), while Section 5 describes local policies toward migrants in the other policy domains. Section 6 discusses Paris's new 'integration policy' since 2001, which appears to break from previous migrant policy. Section 7 summarizes continuity and change in Parisian policies toward migrants.

2   The National Context

2.1   Challenges to the Republican Model

The question of 'what it is to be French' is intertwined with how the French perceive and define their Strangers. According to Brubaker (1992: 163), the prevailing 'statist, assimilationist idiom of nationhood' in France 'remains political rather than ethnocultural', however, immigrants are expected to conform to host society norms and values. 'Political inclusion has entailed cultural assimilation' (ibid.: 1). French secular Republicanism, in particular, demands that religious differences be confined to the private sphere. From the 1980s onwards the debate over the integration (or exclusion) of immigrants in France (now roughly 10 per cent of the population, including some five million Muslims) has dominated the political discourse. Countering the dominant ideology, the Far Right has revived a popular 'counteridiom' of French nationhood that stresses cultural homogeneity and the Catholic roots of French culture, asserting the 'unassimilability of immigrants' (ibid.: 163).

---

[1]   See Ireland (1994) on policies affecting migrant mobilization in La Courneuve; Gaxie et al. (1998) on migrant policies in Saint-Denis, Montreuil, Gennevilliers and Antony; Kastoryano and Crowley (2001) on Saint-Denis, Saint-Ouen, Epinay-sur-Seine and Clichy.

[2]   Nowadays, a third of the migrants in the Paris region first settle inside Paris before moving to cities around the capital, notably in the Seine-St Denis department.

Although the republican model of integration is no longer as powerful as a structural framework for policymaking, it still 'retains powerful ideological significance' (Kastoryano and Crowley 2001: 179). This means that the *official* discourse in France is different from that in, say, the UK or the Netherlands. While the latter openly debate the ethnic and racial dimension in host-stranger relations (e.g. on social exclusion), in France this is either absent or concealed in socio-economic and territorial code-words such as 'marginalized youth' and *banlieues*. French institutions do not recognize 'ethnic minorities', differentiating only between French citizens by birth or naturalization (*Français/Français par acquisition*), and non-French citizens (*étrangers*, i.e. foreigners).[3] Ethnic minorities (including second-generation migrants) are often concealed in French statistics, research and espoused policies. Ethnicity and race relations are also largely absent from the French academic discourse.[4]

In everyday use, however, ethnic categorization is as rampant in France as elsewhere. *Etranger* and *immigré* are used interchangeably to refer to people of foreign origin, including those with French citizenship. *Deuxième génération* is used in the media and elsewhere to connote people born in France of migrant parents. In street language, *beur* and *black* are commonly used slang terms designating people of Arab and African origin, respectively. In the past two decades politicians on the Extreme Right have used the ethnic dimension openly and to great advantage, as have some migrant/minority groups themselves (Thranhardt 1995, Mamadouh 2002).

Immigration and the integration of minorities became important political issues after 1974 and especially since the early 1980s, when ethnic divisions replaced class-based divisions as the main factor in host-stranger relations. Previously, class had served as the dominant cleavage in French society, but as the proportion of foreigners increased among blue-collar workers in France (while the indigenous working class steadily diminished), a large and growing gap developed between French- and foreign-origin workers. Thus, the ideological construct of the 'unified working class' has been replaced by the ethnically-based construct of the *immigré* (Rhein 1998b: 53). But *immigré* does not usually refer to all foreign workers, rather, it is linked in the eyes of the host society to certain populations, e.g. Africans and Arabs, but not Americans or Japanese.

In the early 1980s France was rocked by a series of public disorders originating in the public housing estates in the suburbs or outskirts of cities. In the following decade the *banlieues* became linked in the public eye with a breakdown of social

---

[3] In the national census, *étranger* refers to 'persons declaring a nationality other than French' (INSEE 1999). In 1990 the national statistics institute (INSEE) added *immigré* as an operational term, defined as 'persons born abroad with non-French nationality at birth'. *Immigré* appears in national-level analyses but not in the census, which is based on self-declaration according to one of the three official terms noted above (Simon 2002).

[4] Damian Moore notes (2001: 55, based on Geisser 1997) that 'the notion of ethnicity is almost absent in French sociology' (my translation).

order: high crime rates, attacks on social workers, occasional looting and clashes with police. Official public discourse described this as a reaction of 'marginalized youth' in these areas to economic, social and physical exclusion. However, the *crise des banlieues* was closely linked from the start to religion and ethnicity, and to the apparent failure to integrate second-generation migrants of Arab and African origin.[5]

During the 1980s, growing political consciousness among second-generation migrants led to ethnically-based mobilization, most prominently in the *beur* marches of 1983. Some welcomed these manifestations as a chance for France to move away from the increasingly unrealistic Republicanist discourse, as they saw it, in a multicultural society. Others saw these '*nouvelles ethnicités*' (Geisser 1997) as a threat to the French social model of universal rights and its rejection of communitarianism. Thus, 'multicultural concerns have moved from the margins to the mainstream' in the French discourse on host-stranger relations (Kastoryano and Crowley 2001: 194).

While these issues are debated largely at the national level, they are played out at the local level. Thus the 1989 headscarves affair (the right of Muslim schoolgirls to cover their heads in a public school) escalated from a local incident into a national issue of first magnitude. This long-running debate (culminating in the controversial 'headscarves law') demonstrates the continued salience of the republican model as well as increasing criticism of it in France. As the local and the national have become inextricably intertwined in French host-stranger relations, urban policies have become central in the national-level response to ethnic diversity.

2.2 National Immigration/Integration Policies

France became the premier country of immigration in Europe in the nineteenth century. Immigrants from neighbouring countries was followed by newcomers from overseas colonies. In the postwar period, national policies facilitated movement into the country to fill the demographic deficit and meet manpower demand, resulting in large-scale labour immigration, especially from Portugal and Algeria. France's *laissez-faire* Guestworker policy ended in 1974 with the economic recession. However, new restrictions on labour immigration only led to increased family reunification, especially from non-European countries. This came to be seen by some of the public as a threat to social cohesion. In response, the government adopted a 'double strategy' of increasingly strict controls on entry, together with measures to integrate the newcomers already legally resident in the country (Brochmann 1998).

Since the 1980s, French immigration policy has largely developed in response to the success of the Extreme Right to translate (and broaden) anti-immigrant

---

[5] For analyses of this substitutive labelling, see Hargreaves 1996, Geisser 1997, Body-Gendrot 2001, Simon 2002.

sentiment into electoral results. To counter the rise of Le Pen's *Front Nationale*, governments on both Left and Right formulated successively stricter immigration policies.[6] These were accompanied by various attempts to integrate migrants already in the country, many of whom had acquired French nationality. Here the (sub)urban and local dimension in national policy has been pivotal.

In 1981, the new Socialist government responded to the *crise des banlieues* by creating a number of national frameworks and forums to formulate, in effect, a national strategy. One result was the devolution of responsibility for migrant integration to the local level. Together with other measures,[7] this evolved over time into a national urban policy that came to be known as the *Politique de la ville* (henceforth: *Pdlv*). The paradigm through which urban problems came to be defined and addressed was that of territorially-based social and economic 'exclusion' rather than racial or ethnic relations (Kastoryano and Crowley 2001). Accordingly, *Pdlv* strategy is based on promoting economic, political and social 'participation' of residents in designated 'areas (neighbourhoods) of exclusion'. This served as the national framework for local migrant policies from the 1980s on.

The decentralization of policy resulted in a large variety of pragmatic policies initiated by local authorities and supported by national-level funding, aimed at incorporating excluded populations. While France's republican ideology still demanded that the *problematique* be addressed within an ethnically neutral discourse, a growing number of cities displayed increasing sensitivity to the *ethnic dimension* of exclusion (ibid., Geisser 1997). The ethnicization of local policies was not consistent across France. In large part it depended on the local context, which in turn expressed local host-stranger relations.[8] As we will see, the Municipality of Paris steadfastly opposed this trend in its local policies, at least up to 2001.

2.3 The Algerian Factor[9]

The Algerian immigration to Paris and its impact on local policies deserves special attention for two reasons. Not only are Algerians probably the largest ethnic minority in Paris (see below), but the trauma of the Algerian conflict, including

---

[6] The most important are the 1989 law of entry and residence, reform of the nationality code in 1993, and the 1993 Pasqua law. However, various internal and external restraints including the French constitution, European laws and bilateral treaties have limited the extent to which France can restrict immigration.

[7] In 1983 the *Zones d'Education Prioritaires* (ZEPs) policy was created. In 1992, again in response to violent local incidents, a Minister for the Cities was appointed.

[8] For example, Gaxie et al. 1999 note the varieties of explicit and implicit forms of ethnically-sensitive local policies toward migrants/minorities in cities such as St Denis, Montreuil and Gennevilliers. Mazzella 1996 and Moore 2001 show how local policies in Marseille's migrant neighbourhoods reveal a clear 'ethnicization of policy' beneath their universalist rhetoric (see also Geisser 1997, Ireland 1994).

[9] This sub-section is based largely on Peggy Derder's book (2001) *L'immigration algérienne et les pouvoirs publics dans le département de la Seine, 1954–1962*.

bloodletting on the streets of Paris, remains an important undercurrent in French society. France annexed Algeria in 1946; a year later the '*Français musulmans algériens*' were accorded full citizenship rights and could move freely between this 'overseas department' and metropolitan France. By the mid-1950s there were 50,000 Algerians living in Paris, mostly young men with no determinate plans for settlement, including many seasonal migrants. Notwithstanding their civic status, relations between the indigenous French and the Algerian migrants demonstrated a profound mutual misunderstanding. According to Derder (2001: 42), the Algerian community in Paris lived in 'veritable social and spatial segregation', a situation reinforced by the spill-over of the Algerian War (1954–62) onto the streets of Paris. Consequently, the authorities initiated various policies to combat Algerian separatism at the local level **(Box 6.1)**.

Box 6.1   Policies toward Algerians in Paris: the 'second front'

Between 1958 and 1962 the French authorities vied with the Algerian Front de Libération Nationale (FLN) for the allegiance of the Algerian guestworker community in France. In Paris, this 'second front in the war' was fought in the city's streets with propaganda as well as violent confrontations between Algerians loyal to the opposing sides, claiming hundreds of casualties. In October 1961 an FLN demonstration was repressed by Parisian police with numerous casualties; four months later, another pro-independence demonstration resulted in eight deaths at the Charonne metro station.

In response to the separate social structures imposed by the FLN on the Algerian community, the French government developed a strategy of incorporating Algerian residents into the national welfare system. In the Department of the Seine (Paris and surrounding suburbs), a network of social services was set up for the Algerian population. Staffed by specially trained personnel, often themselves of Maghreb background, the services were provided through hostels, a 'reception and information centre' as well as a network of 'social counsellors' in the migrant neighborhoods.

According to Derder, this social action policy in the Paris area was one component in the French policy to repress Algerian separatism. For example, local offices set up by the Prefecture of the Department of the Seine provided some of the social services noted above, while also conducting a local propaganda war with the FLN, administering detention centres and conducting surveillance on the Algerian community. After Algeria's independence, this network of social support structures was slowly dismantled, however, several vestiges remained. These evolved into agencies that presently coordinate national integration policy (FASild) and housing policy (SONACOTRA) toward all migrants.

Sources: Derder 2001; L'Histoire 1999.

The 'fear and hostility' (ibid.: 46) underlying relations between the French authorities and Algerian migrants in the late 1950s remains relevant to an understanding of later migrant policies. In the past two decades xenophobia toward non-European immigrants, and Muslims in particular, have been on the rise in France as elsewhere. These have been aggravated by a variety of incidents, from the 'hot summer' of 1981 to the most recent riots in the *banlieues*, from terrorist bombings by Arab militants in 1986 and 1995 in Paris, to rising Islamic fundamentalism and the ongoing headscarves controversy. But what official documents continue to refer to as 'social exclusion' is for many indigenous French (one in five regularly support Le Pen) the problem of allegiance of Muslim migrants to France (Rhein 1998b, Hargreaves 1996, Brubaker 1992). According to Wihtol de Wenden (1998: 107), 'Maghrebians and their sons (mainly Algerians) are fulfilling a need in security terms for a new enemy in Western Europe'. In Paris, memories of the Algerian 'second front' lend weight to the image of non-European and especially North African migrants as the new Strangers within the city walls. In the following section I suggest that this fear and hostility toward the Other was a fundamental element in Parisian policymaking long before the arrival of non-European, Muslim immigrants.

3   The Local Context

3.1   Immigration to Paris

Paris has long been the primary magnet for immigrants from within and beyond France (**Figure 6.1**). Newcomers fitted into the city's existing class-based and

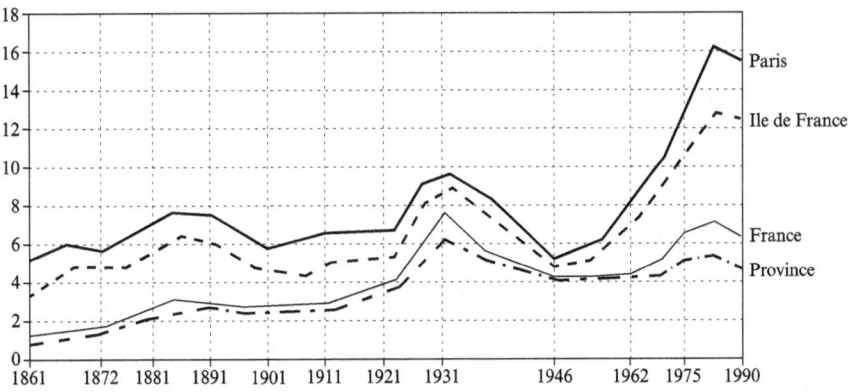

Figure 6.1   Immigration to Paris and France, 1861-1990 (% foreign resident population)

Source: Poinsot 2000, p. 4, based on Guillon 1992.

geographic cleavages and reinforced them with an ethnic character. In the first half of the nineteenth century the municipal population doubled (to one million inhabitants by 1844), largely due to immigration from the French countryside. By 1901 provincial migrants made up over half of the city's population, creating conditions similar to those of Third World cities today: slums, disease and social unrest. For the Parisian bourgeoisie, the provincials were clearly Outsiders threatening the established order. This fear of the provincial-turned-urban proletariat, as one historian noted, was itself not new: 'On the eve of the French Revolution there existed a veritable social fear by Parisians of [the] floating and unemployed population'.[10]

European immigrants began settling in Paris in large numbers from the late nineteenth century onwards, swelling the city's population to 2.9 million by 1911. From the 1950s to the early 1970s the demand for foreign labour together with decolonization resulted in the first large-scale arrival of non-Europeans. Postwar migration was dominated by guestworker and post-colonial migrants, who arrived in unprecedented numbers. By 1954 there were nearly 100,000 Algerians in the Department of the Seine, half of them in Paris. During the 1960s Portuguese guestworkers recruited by the French automobile industry replaced Algerians as the capital's largest foreign community. Paris's migrant population at this time displayed typical guestworker characteristics (predominantly single, male adults intent on saving their earnings and returning home), although the more veteran migrants showed signs of settlement already in the 1960s.

After 1974, following the government decision to restrict immigration, family reunification increased and Paris's migrant population gradually lost its guestworker characteristics. In the following decade economic migrants and refugees came increasingly from sub-Saharan Africa and southeast Asia. Immigration from Eastern Europe, the Balkans and the Far East characterized the 1990s. At the turn of the twenty-first century, China was the single largest source of migration to the Paris region (Musterd et al.1998, Kastoryano and Crowley 1999).

Altogether, the proportion of registered foreign residents in Paris tripled between 1954 and 1999 (from 4.8 to 14.5 per cent) (**Figure 6.2**). But these figures ignore the growing number of naturalized ethnic minority residents (below), and do not take into account irregular immigrants, estimated at several tens of thousands in Paris. In addition, the presence of tourists, business people and other transient strangers in the city approaches 100,000 on peak days. Ambroise-Rendu (1987: 95) estimates that altogether 'over a quarter of the people found in the capital are foreigners'.

Considering the definitional problems noted in Section 2.1, we can only roughly estimate the total size of Paris's resident migrant/minority population. According to the 1999 census, over 22 per cent of the population (nearly 465,000

---

[10] Fierro, A. *Histoire et dictionnaire de Paris*, 1996, Lafont (cited in Pinçon 2001: 42).

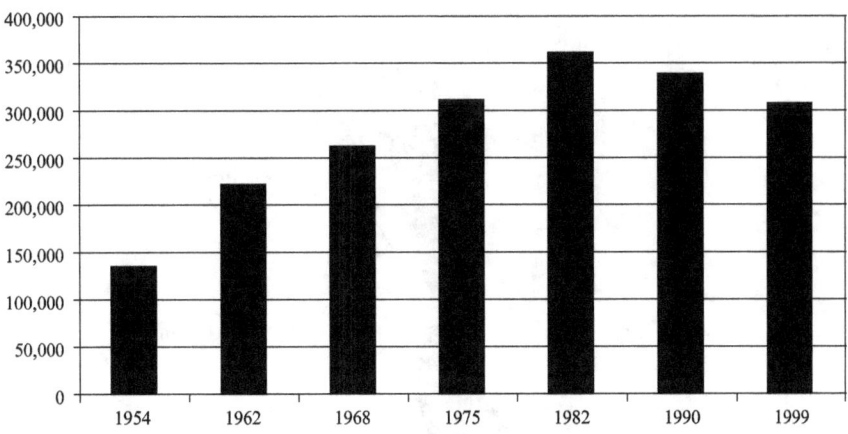

Figure 6.2 Foreign resident population in Paris, 1954–99

Source: Data compiled from INSEE 1999.

residents) was of foreign origin. Of these, over 308,000 were registered foreign residents and another 156,000 were self-declared naturalized French citizens (INSEE 1999). Adding to this figure an estimate of second-generation migrants in Paris who declared themselves 'French by birth', we arrive at some 872,000 residents of ethnic origin (first and second generation), or 41 per cent of the city population.[11] Based on this estimate, Paris's proportion of ethnic minorities is high, even in comparison to other veteran immigration cities in Europe (see Table 1.1, above).

The ethnic breakdown presented below (**Figures 6.3a–b**) should be treated with caution, as it relates only to the 308,000 registered foreign residents, representing less than half of the estimated ethnic minority population in Paris. Nearly 217,000 foreigners are non-EU nationals, representing 70 per cent of Paris's registered foreign population and 10 per cent of the city population (APUR 2002, INSEE

---

[11] I estimated the size of Paris's 'hidden second generation' (which does not appear in municipal census figures) based on calculations made at the national level by Tribalat, who estimated around 85 per cent of the children of migrants born in France appear in the statistics as 'French'. Deriving from her calculations, we can estimate a statistical relationship between the first and second generation of immigrants in France. Applying this to the census figures for Paris, we arrive at a figure of 484,634 second-generation residents (as opposed to less than 77,000 self-declared 'second generation' residents appearing in the census, i.e. those born in France who declared themselves as non-French) (INSEE 1999, Table 2 bis). The number of first-generation immigrants in Paris ('born abroad' but excluding those born abroad with French nationality, e.g. the '*pieds noirs*' from Algeria) is 387,707. Together, the first- and second-generation migrants equal 872,341 persons. I thank Patrick Simon for assisting me in these estimates.

124 *Cities and Labour Immigration*

a)   **Percentages**

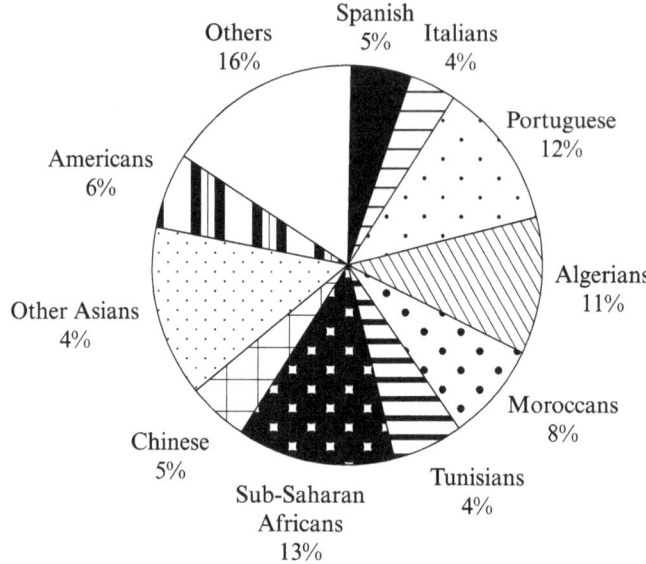

b)   **Absolute numbers**

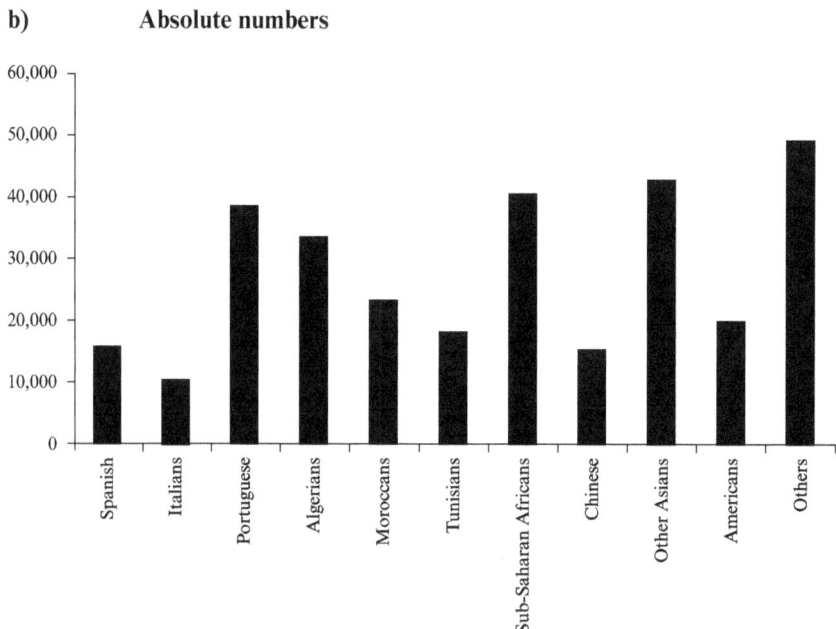

Figure 6.3   Foreign resident population in Paris, by country of origin, 1999

1999).[12] Adding the naturalized second-generation migrants, Paris's migrant/minority population is overwhelmingly non-European, with Algerians probably constituting the largest single ethnic minority.

3.2 Postwar Migrant Settlement Patterns in Paris

Postwar migrants settled into, and became a part of, the socio-economic geography of Paris that was established during the nineteenth and early twentieth century. In 1945 the bourgeois/working class division of Paris was already in place (Rhein 1998a: 440).

The middle- and upper-class neighbourhoods (*beaux quartiers*) were located on the Right Bank, especially in the northwestern districts, while on the Left Bank a large working class population, formed largely by previous migrations, was densely housed in the proletarian neighbourhoods that formed a giant crescent across the east of Paris. This '*croissant populaire*' (Toubon and Messamah 1990: 43) included the eastern half of the seventeenth district and much of the 18, 19 and twentieth districts, with some neighbourhoods already established as migrant strongholds, such as the Goutte d'Or (**Figure 6.4**). But it was during the postwar period that Paris's *quartiers populaires* became increasingly identified as *quartiers d'immigration*. This process is described below.

Figure 6.4 The croissant populaire: working class quarters in east Paris, 1990

Source: Yankel Fijalkow, based on data from INSEE 1990.

---

[12] The largest contingents of registered foreign residents are the Portuguese (38,455), followed by Algerians, Moroccans, Tunisians, Spanish and Chinese. Of the non-EU foreign residents, over half originate from the African continent (75,000 from the Maghreb, 41,000 from sub-Saharan Africa), 58,000 from Asia and 20,000 from the Americas (ibid.).

During the 1950s–60s Paris suffered an acute housing shortage, as the private housing stock could not accommodate the massive influx of newcomers. Some postwar migrants found accommodation in cheap, dilapidated hotels and flats in the working class quarters of central and eastern Paris. Others were housed in half a dozen *foyers* (worker hostels) provided by the government, but most improvised their own lodgings. This resulted in the growth of informal shantytowns (*bidonvilles*) 'under the tolerant eye or indifference of the municipality' (Derder 2001: 39). The growth of Paris's *bidonvilles* in the 1960s was accelerated by family reunification among the veteran Algerian migrants.

Gradually, a succession process occurred in the proletarian neighbourhoods, as migrants moved into housing vacated by working-class and lower-middle class residents, who moved to newly constructed social housing, much of it outside Paris. From the 1960s onward, Paris underwent increasing gentrification and polarization. According to Catherine Rhein (1998a: 445–6), a double process of economic and ethnic polarization has taken place in the Paris metropolitan area, with an increasing concentration of foreigners in the working-class suburbs accompanied by their decreasing presence in the middle- and upper-class neighbourhoods inside Paris (and its wealthy suburbs) (**Figure 6.5**).

Variation in the percentage of blue collar workers within active population

0 to + 2%
0 to –2%
–2 to –4%
–4 to –6%
over –6 %

Figure 6.5   The *embourgeoisement* of Paris and its suburbs, 1982–90

The migrant/minority population inside Paris can now be classified into several broad types, based on their socio-economic status (Rhein 1998b). The first includes foreign residents in the highly skilled category, mostly from OECD countries, who reside in the *beaux quartiers* (especially the 16th district). Next are the upwardly mobile European labour migrants from the 1950s–60s (Italians,

Spanish, Portuguese) who have joined the ranks of the *petit bourgeoisie*, pursuing a home-ownership strategy. The third and largest category comprises migrants/minorities of guestworker and postcolonial origin who reside in the working class neighbourhoods, mostly in eastern Paris.

During the 1980s–90s, the foreign population increasingly shifted from the city to the *banlieues*, and within Paris from the central to the peripheral eastern districts (Pinçon 2001: 44) (**Figure 6.6**). This was due not only to free market forces creating the polarization that characterizes all global cities, but also, as we shall see below, a result of deliberate gentrification policies (Rhein 1998b, Body-Gendrot 1996, Carpenter et al. 1994). From the 1980s onward, Paris experienced the first *absolute* decline (excluding the war years) in its foreign resident population. In particular, the number of non-EU foreigners has declined since 1990 in all but one of the Paris districts (APUR 2002).

As socio-economic segregation strengthened in the capital, working-class migrants were increasingly restricted in their housing choice. Within Paris, certain ethnic groups are increasingly concentrated in particular areas and types of housing stock. Thus, Maghrebians and Africans are concentrated in lower rungs of the social housing stock and in specific neighbourhoods, mostly in the east of the city (Simon 2002). By 1999 the foreign presence in some *quartiers* reached up to 30 per cent, almost twice the city-wide average of foreign residents per district (15.8 per cent). In the eastern and central districts one in four residents was foreign (Poinsot 2000).[13] However, Paris's dense urban structure means that there is almost no quarter with a majority of minorities or with just one ethnic minority (Body-Gendrot 2000: 185). Nevertheless, some neighbourhoods have a distinctly 'ethnic character', including the Goutte d'Or (twentieth district), Belleville (11th) and Paris's 'Chinatown' around the Place d'Italie (13th).[14]

3.3   Local Host-Stranger Relations

In large part, Paris has avoided sharp ethnic conflict by exporting its migrant population to the suburbs. Historically, the capital has not experienced conflict between different ethnic groups or between migrants and veteran Parisians (Body-Gendrot 1996). This may also have to do with the city's dense urban structure: on the level of daily interaction, even the most 'ethnic' neighbourhoods in Paris do not approach the conditions of exclusion and isolation that engendered the cycle of violent expression and repression that characterized, for example, the northern quarters of Marseille, the suburbs of Lyon, or the public housing estates of La Courneuve, northeast of Paris. But while Paris itself did not experience the disturbances of the *banlieues,* it was not isolated from what occurred just beyond

---

[13]   Districts include four *quartiers*. The highest proportion of *non-EU residents* (over 20% of the population) is now found in the 10th, 18th and nineteenth districts, followed by the 3rd, 11th and twentieth districts, i.e. the north-east of Paris (INSEE 1999).

[14]   On Paris's Chinatown, see Box 7.1 in Chapter 7.

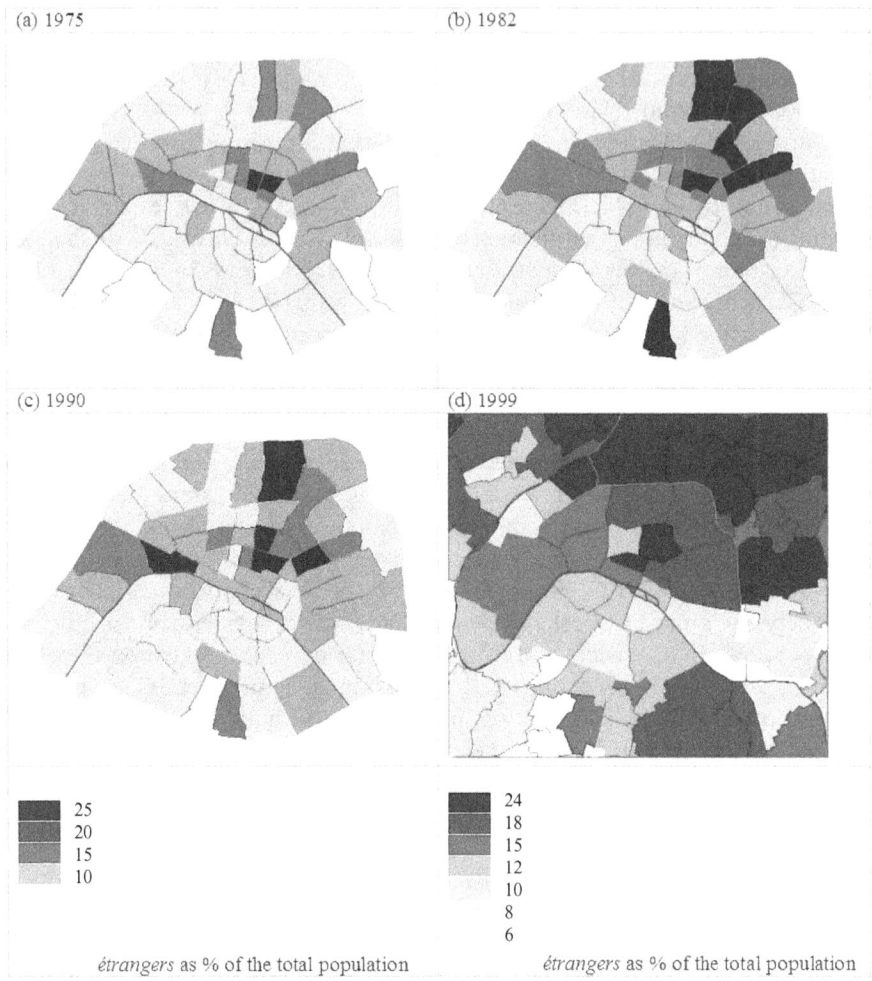

Figure 6.6   Distribution of foreign population in Paris, 1975–99

Note: (a), (b), (c): Paris by quartiers; (d): Paris by arrondissements and banlieues.

Source: INSEE 1999.

the municipal boundary. In the 1980s the national *beur* marches, originating in the provincial cities and amassing in Paris's *banlieues*, culminated in the streets of the capital. Meanwhile, the *Front Nationale* was garnering 17–18 per cent of the vote in the adjacent Seine-St-Denis department. Clearly, Parisian policymakers made the connection between ethnic segregation, the threat of ghetto formation and the potential for disorder.

In the 1990s some traditional migrant neighbourhoods such as Belleville underwent gentrification. As more and more new residents of middleclass French origin moved in next to the veteran residents of working-class migrant origin, another *problematique* emerged. This was phrased in terms of *'mixité sociale'* ('social diversity') and the challenges of *'cohabitation'* in residential blocks and local public spaces. Again, the ethnic element was not explicitly mentioned in the official discourse, but was clearly there. But who was now the Outsider? The problems of *mixité sociale* within Paris raised again the issue of diversity on the local policy agenda (Fijalkow and Oberti 2001: 18–19). However, these pale in comparison to the *problematique* of host-stranger relations in the *banlieues*. The riots of November 2005 were the worst since the Algerian conflict. Although the violence began in the suburbs (hundreds of cars burned, massive police turnout), it eventually spilled into the streets of the capital, albeit on a smaller scale. This dashed any sense of complacency in Paris that the threatening Other had been exiled beyond the city walls. Comparing the violence-and-repression of 1958–62 (first-generation migrants) with that of 2005 (second-generation Arab and African migrants), it appears that Paris's decades-long policy of exporting its most problematic Strangers to the suburbs was partially, but not wholly, 'successful'.

3.4 Institutional and Political Context: L'état, la ville, la foule

Isolating local policymaking in Paris requires an understanding of the special relationship between France's central government and its capital city. French central authority, embodied in the *ancien regime* by the king and his administration, and after the Revolution by Napoleon I and later Napoleon III, mistrusted and feared the Parisian populace. They had good reason: the uprisings of 1789, 1848 and 1870 were all specifically Parisian events, led by local leaders and backed by the Parisian mob, *la foule*. The demonstrations of 1968 (once again, Parisian paving stones used as barricades and weapons) showed again that disorder on the streets of Paris can directly threaten the stability of central government.

The French state has responded by keeping a tight hold on its capital city: after 1884 Paris was ruled directly by the government's representative, the Prefect of the Seine Department, and after 1964, through the Prefect of Paris.[15] In most cases, the prefect managed to balance between his two roles, as governmental representative and as appointed mayor of Paris, by taking into consideration the opinions of city council, over which he presided (see Nivet 1992). Considering the dual role of Paris's prefect, local policy in Paris prior to 1977 can be defined as those policies initiated by the city council, as well as those policies set by the

---

[15] Prefects are the Minister of Interior's representative at departmental level, but the Prefect of Paris is appointed directly by the President. A separate Prefect of Police is responsible for security in the capital. France is divided into some 100 *departements*. In 1964 the huge Seine-St Denis department was divided into four new departments: Department 75: the City of Paris, and Departments 92, 93, 94: the inner suburbs.

prefect in which the council had significant influence. This influence changed over different periods, as the state's involvement in local matters waxed and waned (see below).

The above *tutelage* arrangement lasted until 1977, when the prefect was effectively replaced by a mayor elected through the city council. Since the voting system ensures that the mayor always presides over a majority in city council and in the city districts, local policy from 1977 has effectively been mayoral policy.[16] Especially during the 18-year mayoral reign of Jacques Chirac, Paris's city council was reduced to a debating forum (see below). In 2001 the Left came to power in Paris for the first time, capturing 13 of the 20 city districts. Bertrand Delanoë (Socialists) was elected mayor at the head of a Left-Green coalition whose platform promised change, including in local policies toward migrants (section 6, below).

4   Urban Policy in Paris: 150 Years of Distancing the Other

Despite regime changes and shifting city-state relations, urban policy in Paris has shown remarkable continuity in one objective: the physical distancing of disorder and Otherness. As we will see, the role of threatening Other was first designated to the indigenous poor ('*les classes dangereuses*'), but in the postwar period it was increasingly associated with non-European immigrants. The results of this policy were a progressive distancing of the working classes, migrants and ethnic minorities. These undesirable populations were pushed ever farther from the city centre, first to the outlying neighbourhoods and eventually beyond the city walls. In the postwar period this meant relocating populations beyond the *périphérique*, Paris's ring road and municipal boundary.

In keeping with the assimilationist model of integration (and the French republican model in particular), policies avoid dealing *explicitly* with ethnic diversity. Instead, the French authorities have traditionally responded to migrant settlement and its consequences through territorially-defined policies. This section will therefore be devoted to migrant policies in the Spatial domain (other policy domains are covered in section 5). The following pages trace the history of urban renovation in the capital from the mid-nineteenth century onwards, to demonstrate the emergence of a specifically *Parisian* policy. The sub-sections below summarize the evolution of this policy.

---

[16]   Councillors are elected by city districts (*arrondissements*) from party lists drawn up by the mayoral candidates. A mayoral candidate whose lists win the majority of districts is then elected as mayor. Paris's 20 districts are primarily responsible for some local services but have little influence in overall municipal policymaking.

4.1 Foundations of Parisian Urban Policy: Haussmannian Renovation, 1853–70

The widescale urban development carried out by Baron Haussmann, Prefect of the Seine from 1853 to 1869 under Napoleon III, laid the foundations for later urban policy in Paris. The aim of this policy was the deliberate *embourgeoisement* of the city through urban renovation. Haussmannian 'renovation' entailed the massive destruction of poor, overcrowded neighbourhoods, vestiges of medieval Paris, and their reconstruction as modern residential quarters. This involved the massive transfer of poor residents – many of them provincial migrants – from the central neighbourhoods to the outer *faubourgs* (the outlying towns and villages incorporated into Paris in 1860). In their place were built the famous Haussmannian avenues and apartment blocks, embodying in their order and respectability 'the triumph of the rental bourgeoisie' (Lacaze 1994: 77, my translation).

Haussmann's unprecedented renovation policy contained a double agenda. The explicit objective was to transform Paris, then a city of extreme overcrowding and unsanitary conditions (even by mid-nineteenth century standards), into a modern capital. To this end, water and sewage systems were reconstructed, streets paved, building height regulations set, etc. The implicit agenda was to reconquer the city for the middle classes that had deserted the city centre and who constituted the political support of the regime. With the 1848 uprising just over, Napoleon III meant to displace, once and for all, the unwanted populations from areas too geographically close to the seats of power. Haussmannian renovation specifically targeted the poor populations in certain quarters that had long troubled the authorities, such as the Cité, Les Halles and Faubourg St Antoine (the Bastille).[17] 'The price', according to Lacaze (1994: 77–8), 'was paid by the people of Paris, whose exodus toward the periphery was knowingly organized' (my translation).

4.2 Emergence of Local Urban Policy: Hygiénisme and Renovation, 1870s–1950s

The implementation of Haussmann's urban policy was patchy and incomplete, but it set the basis for municipal policymaking that increasingly replaced state policy in Parisian affairs from 1871 to 1958 (the Third and Fourth republics). In this 'local parenthesis', the newly independent city council extended and adopted Haussmann's modernization scheme into the twentieth century (Fijalkow and Oberti 2001, Cole 1999). The explanation for this unusual continuity in policy despite regime changes, bridging between the centralistic Haussmann and the local Parisian councillors, can be found in their ideological common ground: the belief in modernity, Order and 'hygiene'.

---

[17] L. Chevalier's *Classes laborieuses, classes dangereuses* (1958) is the classic work describing the political and class-related basis of this policy. See also Lacaze 1994.

The ideology of *hygiénisme* (and its physical expression in urban renovation) emerged in full force at the beginning of the twentieth century. As a basis for urban policy, this was rooted in the distinctly modernist urge of the late nineteenth and early twentieth centuries, to quantify, measure and territorialize social patterns in general, and social deviancy in particular. In France, social deviancy was defined by 'social hygienists' such as Lefebre; in America, by the Chicago School sociologists (Simon 1994: 125). *Hygiénisme* was a belief whose time had come: between 1872 and 1913 Paris's population surged from 1.8 million to 2.8 million and tuberculosis became widespread. The spread of contagious diseases was believed to be due to overcrowding, lack of light and air, and bad social hygiene habits among the working classes. According to the hygienists, disease, poverty and social disfunctions (such as promiscuity of the working classes) were not only interrelated, they could also be mapped and treated.

In 1894 the city council established the *Casier sanitaire des maisons des Paris* to locate specific *îlots insalubres*, 'unhealthy street-blocks requiring demolition' (Carpenter et al 1994: 219, citing Bastié 1984). By 1905 the municipal *Casier* had identified six *îlots* with 1600 buildings destined for demolition, by 1918 it had defined seventeen *îlots* (**Figure 6.7a**). These blocks were destined for '*rénovation*', i.e. demolition and relocation of the local population to new social housing. The scale was even greater than under Hausmmann, envisaging the displacement of nearly 187,000 residents (Lucan 1992)!

Ostensibly, the policy of demolition-and-relocation was based on public health reasons, e.g. the number of tuberculosis cases per block. However, Yankel Fijalkow (1994, 1998) has shown that the main criteria for designating an area for 'renovation' were *not* the condition of the buildings or frequency of tuberculosis, but the *character of the resident population*, described variously as 'dangerous', 'contagious' and 'hostile to hygiene'. Thus, *Ilot 1* (Les Halles) had a 'floating population', *Ilot 2* (in the Marais quarter) was a Jewish 'ghetto', *Ilot 3* (on the Left Bank) was the rag-pickers area, another was 'a proletariat fortress', etc. (ibid., Fijalkow and Oberti 2001: 11). According to Patrick Simon (1994: 126), *hygiénisme* was used to demarcate the geography of Otherness in Paris and prepare it for disappearance, either by physical displacement or by re-educating the inhabitants through a renovated environment.

Toward this second aim, the city established (1911) a municipal office for the construction of low-cost public housing. This policy was also politically motivated: left-wing councillors began to suspect that the massive displacement of working-class residents beyond the municipal borders would deprive them of their electoral constituency (Nivet 1992: 297). Social housing within Paris was thus meant to supplement the renovation/displacement policy. However, most of the social housing intended for displaced residents from the inner quarters was built on the eastern outskirts of the city, further distancing the proletariat from the centre. Furthermore, from the 1920s onward the city's social housing policy became oriented toward lower-middle class rather than working-class residents.

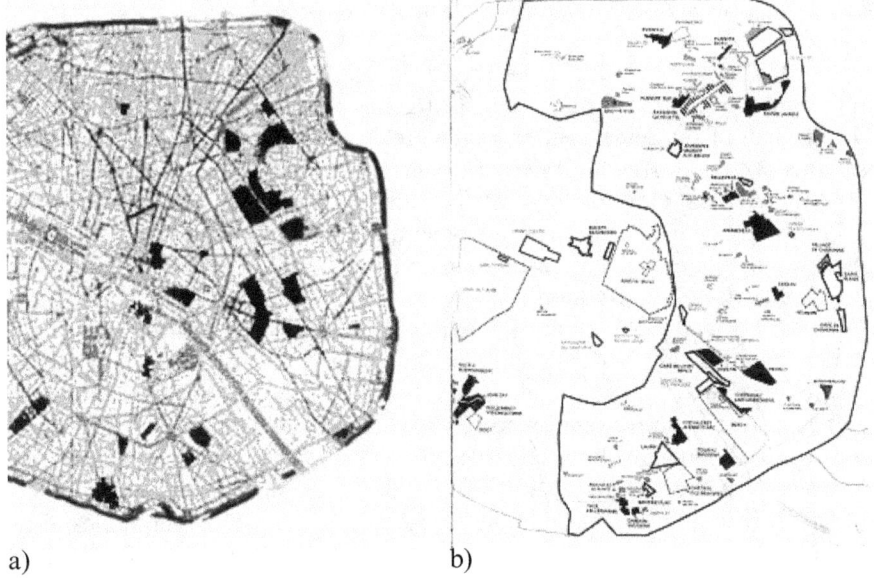

Figure 6.7 Planned renovation areas in Paris, 1938 and 1987

Construction of costlier social housing meant that truly affordable public housing for the lower classes became rare within the city (Fijalkow and Oberti 1994).

Lacaze (1994: 78) notes how Haussmann's original aim of renovation and modernization, with its resultant dispersal of unwanted populations, 'would be pursued, patiently and methodically' by the city. What was stated explicitly in the mid-nineteenth century (the *embourgoisement* of Paris, i.e. replacing unwanted populations with desirable middle-class residents) was concealed in the twentieth century within discourses of public hygiene and urban incompatibility (Simon 1994: 128). Thus, the planned renovation areas were given increasingly vague labels, evolving from *îlots tuberculeux* into *îlots insalubres* (unhealthy blocks) in the early twentieth century. By 1954 only three *îlots* had been partially destroyed or renovated, due to the weak economy and the intervening wars. Later, the remaining *îlots* and other renovation areas reappeared as 'priority zones for urbanization' in the urban development plans of the 1950s–70s, 'renovation sectors' in 1967 and 'zones for concentrated management' (ZACs) in the 1980s (**Figure 6.7b**). Despite the changing labels, the areas designated for renovation remained remarkably constant until their transformation from pockets of disorder to complementary parts of the Parisian cityscape was completed to the planners' satisfaction. Les Halles, for example, was finally renovated in the late 1970s, while the Faubourg St Antoine (east of the Bastille) was finally conquered through gentrification in the 1990s.[18]

---

[18] See Fijalkow and Oberti 2001, Simon 1994: 124–5, Dumont 1994: 27, Lucan 1992: 76.

4.3 Hierarchical Renovation Policy, Mid-1950s–Mid-1970s

From 1958 to 1969 the state under President De Gaulle became heavily involved in local matters. Parisian policies were largely formulated by bureaucrats in the Department of the Seine, headed by the prefect. However, these policies largely accorded with the hierarchical view of urban renovation that evolved within Paris's city council in the 1950s (below). At this time the Gaullists formed the majority in Paris's city council as in the government, assuring 'a fusion of national and local urban policy, with a powerful desire on all sides to proceed with renovation policy' (interview J.-C. Toubon).

In the postwar years questions were raised in city council regarding the extent of renovation policy in Paris. While the modernists favoured 'hard' *rénovation* (destroying the existing urban fabric and rebuilding), the traditionalists favoured 'soft' *restauration* (improvements to existing buildings defined as having aesthetic and historical value). By the early 1950s a consensus was reached in city council: the peripheral districts in eastern Paris should undergo *rénovation* while some quarters in the centre and Left Bank should undergo *restauration*. This hierarchical view of the city was based on (subjective) criteria of architectural and historic value. But it also implicitly reflected a hierarchical view of the resident populations in the various neighbourhoods. Thus, bourgeois residential quarters were designated for *restauration*, while build-and-destroy *rénovation* policies were applied to the predominantly working-class *faubourgs*, mostly in east Paris.[19]

Like Napoleon III, De Gaulle came to power after a period of prolonged instability, with the Algerian conflict spilling onto the streets of the capital (above). Like Napoleon III, De Gaulle's policies for Paris combined an urban agenda and the need to establish order.[20] By this time the Paris agglomeration had some of the worst slums in Europe. During the 1960s-70s the main priority of urban policy was to clear the slums and *bidonvilles* populated largely by Algerian migrants, and replace them with better housing. The two master plans of this period (the 1957 PUD and 1967 SDAU)[21] envisaged 'a quasi-total demolition of the existent urban structure' in the peripheral neighbourhoods (interview M. Cougougliene). This meant a further relocation of much of Paris's working class population to suburbs and new towns beyond the municipal borders, thus fulfilling the aims of the previous renovation policies, but on a larger scale (Simon 1994: 127). The

---

[19] See Lucan 1992, Nivet 1994: 278–93.

[20] To carry out his policies De Gaulle created in 1965 a new District of Paris, headed by Director General P. Delouvrier, described as 'De Gaulle's Haussmann' (Lacaze 1994: 98).

[21] The 1957 *Plan d'Urbanisme Directeur de Paris* (PUD) was created by the prefectural planning department. This evolved into the 1967 *Schema directeur d'amenagement et urbanisme de la region de Paris* (SDAU), the Master Plan for the Paris region.

aim, in the words of the chief planner for the region, was (again) the 'reconquest of Paris'.[22]

To lodge the poorest populations (which now included a significant proportion of labour migrants) that would be displaced by urban renovation, the City of Paris purchased lands in neighbouring municipalities just beyond the *périphérique*. These were destined for construction of low-cost social housing (*habitations à loyer moderé* – HLMs). Built *à la* Corbusier, with high-rise buildings surrounded by open areas, these *Grands Ensembles* were often isolated from existing neighbourhoods, and were considered a great improvement over the slums. In this way, *bidonville*-style disorder was replaced by Modernist-style order. Social housing policy thus fulfilled two agendas: distancing the Other and 'improving' his environment.

Significant amounts of social housing were also built inside Paris, with the specific aim of retaining *some* of Paris's working-class and lower-middle class population. However, as Parisian policy became increasingly oriented toward bourgeois needs, the public housing built in the renovated areas accommodated higher economic strata, while the poorest residents displaced by the renovation were relocated to HLMs outside the city.[23] As a result, the proportion of working-class residents in HLMs inside Paris is only 16 per cent, half of that for HLMs in the Ile-de-France region (Fijalkow 2002: 55).

Different explanations have been advanced regarding the motivation behind urban renovation policies in this period, which led to a progressive gentrification of Paris from the 1960s onward. Castells and Godard (1974) showed statistically that the most common factor uniting the renovation areas was the *proportion of immigrants*. They concluded that renovation policy expressed a deliberate strategy of depopulating the migrant neighbourhoods (cited in Simon 1994: 131). This intentionality argument is not widely accepted among French scholars today. Most claim that the main motivation behind urban policy in the 1950s and 1960s was economic and that planners did not distinguish between indigenous and migrant populations.[24] Whatever the motivation, there is consensus regarding the results of these policies. First, Paris's working class population was distanced even further from the older, central neighbourhoods to new, outlying areas. Second, the proportion of foreign residents in the renovated areas was reduced.

It is difficult to ascertain the role that host-stranger relations played in this period. In particular, did renovation and social housing policies from the 1950s through the 1970s express Assimilationist attitudes toward migrants/minorities in the areas designated for renovation? Paul Nivet's detailed analyses (1992, 1994) of city council protocols of this period reveal a republicanist and class-based discourse, with no explicit references to the ethnic dimension. This raises two

---

[22] P. Sudreau, named in 1955 as chief planner for the Parisian region, in Godard et al. 1973: 13 (cited in Simon 1994: 128).

[23] Interview, J.-C. Toubon. See Simon 1994 for a detailed analysis of this process in the Belleville neighbourhood.

[24] See for example Coing 1962.

possibilities: either the ethnic factor was genuinely not taken into account, or as Castells and Godard claimed, Paris's renovation policies *deliberately* dispersed unwanted minorities and concealed this agenda behind the logic of urban planning and economy. In either case, this conforms to what I defined in Chapter 3 as an Assimilationist-type spatial policy.

4.4 Gentrification Policy under Chirac and Tiberi, 1977–2001

From the 1970s onward decentralization in France steadily shifted planning powers to the local authorities. In Paris, the new municipal planning agency APUR (*Atelier Plan d'Urbanisme de Paris*, created in 1967) began to promote its own line of thinking in urban policy, gradually replacing the departmental and regional planners. Following compromises reached in city council in the early 1970s, APUR promoted a 'softer' renovation policy, expressed in the new master plan for Paris, the 1977 SDAU. But while the plan's objectives 'aimed ... to offer decent housing to the least well-off groups in society such as the elderly and migrants', its results were social housing at higher rents and further displacement of the poorest residents from renovated areas (Carpenter et al. 1994: 223). Whatever the intentions of APUR, it provided the tools with which Mayor Chirac was to pursue an aggressive policy of gentrification in the 1980s-90s.[25]

In 1977 Jacques Chirac was elected mayor and ruled with an overwhelming majority until 1995, when he successfully ran for the presidency of the Republic. After a campaign that emphasized the need to control immigration, Chirac carefully played on popular fears of the Other, using illegal immigrants as a cue. His image of 'fair but tough' (on illegal migrants) steered just wide enough of Le Pen-ist xenophobia:

> France is a good mother, but she no longer has the means to support a throng of foreigners [*une foule d'etrangers*] who abuse her hospitality. Using the means at its disposal, the City of Paris has decided to fight against the proliferation of irregular aliens. This policy will lie between two extremes: neither racism nor laxity (*Le Monde*, 15 July 1983, cited in Thranhardt 1995: 341, my translation).

According to Thranhardt (pp. 328–9), the mayor 'introduce[d] a pattern of bureaucratic harassment of non-European immigrants who, at every interface with the city services – police, kindergarten, schools, social care – had to prove that they were in the country legally'. According to Ambroise-Rendu, Chirac understood the public mood regarding immigrants, and acted accordingly – a

---

[25] According to a veteran APUR planner 'one cannot reduce the intentions of the [SDAU] to gentrification', but he admits that 'in hindsight' the plan's methods of implementation, including construction of social housing by private developers in the renovated areas, were 'inadequate and benefited mostly the strongest' (interview M. Cougougliegne). Currently, only a third of the residential function in the renovated areas (ZACs) is slated for low-rent social housing. (Fijalkow 2002: 102–6)

strategy that brought him electoral success in successive municipal and national elections (interview M. Ambroise-Rendu).[26]

Chirac's 18-year reign effectively neutralized the influence of city council. Paris's policy was henceforth mayoral policy, although under Chirac's protégé Jean Tiberi (mayor from 1995 to 2001), there was some limited opposition in city council.[27] Under the Chirac and Tiberi administrations, Paris's urban policy was characterized by expanding gentrification to new areas of the city, particularly the poorer quarters in the 'eastern crescent' where most of the migrant/minority concentrations remained.

In 1983 Chirac presented his vision for the 'valorization' of eastern Paris, the *Plan Programme de l'Est de Paris*, which expressly targeted migrant concentrations. The 'Plan for the East of Paris' gave a strategic push to the upgrading of designated areas to attract middle- and upper-income residents, placing increasing pressure on the original inhabitants. This deliberate gentrification was aimed at the remaining low-income areas in the old *faubourgs* such as La Villette and Faubourg St Antoine (renamed Bastille-Opera) (White and Winchester 1991: 40). As in the previous plans, some of the designated renovation areas were chosen 'more because of their high concentrations of immigrants than because of poor absolute standards of housing' (Carpenter et al. 1994: 225) (**Box 6.2**).

In some of these areas, resistance to the city's renovation plans ultimately led to softer renovation and less displacement of the original inhabitants. Ironically, this resistance was led by recently arrived residents (the bourgeois-bohemians, or 'bobos') who did not want to see the social heterogeneity of their 'ethnic' neighbourhood completely destroyed. Such opposition to municipal renovation plans can be seen as a bottom-up expression of what I termed the 'embrace of Otherness', in response to what is perceived as a top-down, homogenizing policy.[28]

According to some, Chirac's urban policy was not *deliberately* aimed against ethnic minorities. Rather, the mayor's objective of upgrading Paris's social composition in keeping with its status as a global capital, required policies whose internal logic resulted in an ethnic population change (interview M. Ambroise-Rendu). Others claim that this gentrification policy contained a clear ethnic dimension. In order to 'valorize' the capital, Chirac's municipal policy pursued

---

[26] Chirac ruled Paris for three consecutive terms using the centre-right RPR party, which he created and dominated. In the municipal elections of 1983 and 1989 Chirac's candidates took all twenty city districts, assuring him an absolute majority in city council. In 1986 the RPR won in the legislative elections and Chirac became Prime Minister while continuing to serve as Paris's mayor, as allowed in the French system.

[27] In the 1995 elections the Left recaptured six districts (all of them in the 'eastern crescent' of Paris) which contained large migrant/minority populations and were targeted by Chirac's gentrification policies (below).

[28] See Chapter 2, footnote 7. Such resistance occurred in the 1980s in Belleville (cf. Simon 1994, 2000) and the Goutte d'Or (cf. Toubon and Messamah 1990) and in the 1990s in Faubourg St Antoine (interview Y. Fijalkow; Pinçon and Pinçon 2005).

> **Box 6.2 Bringing order to the 'eastern crescent'**
>
> The 1983 Plan Programme de l'Est de Paris describes the eastern quarters of Paris as the city's 'new frontier'. In a truly Baumanesque comparison of the two halves of the city, it contrasts the 'general impression of disorder and destructurization' of east Paris with 'the grand elements of urban composition, organization and coherence of the built areas and public spaces that mark, altogether, the central and western quarters of Paris.' The disorder in Paris's eastern crescent is presented as an opportunity for 'development' and 'valorization'.
>
> Although couched in planning terminology, the Plan Programme is as much about creating social order as it is about urban design. The East is described as having various 'handicaps' including most of the remaining 'îlots sensibles'. Many of these remaining vestiges of pre-renovation Paris have 'a marked overpopulation, being the reception areas of an especially poor population and particularly of many immigrants'. With uncharacteristic frankness, the Plan notes the high proportion of foreigners in certain quarters and schools.
>
> According to the document presented to city council, the planners intend to maintain the 'uniqueness of this part of the city in…its social and economic diversity'. But the Plan's economic logic is a blueprint for gentrification. According to the renovation strategy, new housing in the renovated areas will be developed privately and aimed primarily at the middle class, rather than the original residents of whom a significant proportion, as noted above, are foreigners.
>
> *Source*: APUR 1987.

the de-ethnicization of certain migrant enclaves that were not in keeping with the desired image of Paris (interview P.-F. Salviani). Thus, 'one of the objectives of renewal [was] the dispersal of foreigner concentrations' (White and Winchester 1991: 40). Patrick Simon (2000: 109) notes how the municipality's renovation plans systematically tried to modify the social composition of Belleville, a neighbourhood 'which the authorities perceive as too "immigrant"'. What is undeniable is that between 1982 and 1990 Paris experienced its first decline in a century in the proportion of foreign residents, with a further drop between 1990-1999 (see section 3.2, above). Not surprisingly, the decline was greatest in regard to foreigners of non-EU origin (Pinçon 2001: 44).

4.5 Paris and the Politique de la Ville

While Paris continued on the path of renovation policy, a shift in thinking occurred in the 1980s at the national level. In response to the urban disturbances of the early 1980s, the government launched a nationwide programme of positive discrimination for selected 'problem neighbourhoods'. Conceived as a 'Marshall Plan for the *banlieues*' (Moore 2001: 105), the *Politique de la ville* thereafter developed into France's overall coordinating framework for urban policy.

The *Pdlv* aims at strengthening the autonomous social development of designated neighbourhoods with a bottom-up approach to be adopted by local authorities in partnership with local civic associations. Although it does not break with the territorially-based (and therefore, universalist) model of integration, the *Pdlv* does include explicit references to the ethnic dimension of exclusion. Thus, a 1999 *Pdlv* evaluation report on the Ile-de-France region notes the 'important function of interaction [and] reception of immigrant populations' in several neighbourhoods in Paris, and suggests that 'the public actors must henceforth recognize the de facto "ethnicization" of these in fact of these territories and adapt their policies in consequence' (Bravo 1999: 60, my translation). The *Politique de la ville* is thus expressing a change in attitudes toward some recognition of the ethnic minority presence – a shift, in effect, in French host-stranger relations.[29]

This new approach to tackling urban problems (implied in the new designation for urban renovation areas: '*dévelopement sociale des quartiers*') did not fit in with Chirac's policy. As noted above, the Chirac administration was interested in pursuing its urban 'valorization' agenda in a top-down approach that emphasized physical renovation. In contrast to the bottom-up, socially-sensitive criteria of *Pdlv*-funded projects, Paris's policies at best ignored the migrant population, and at worst targeted it for dispersal.

As mayor of a wealthy city, Chirac could afford to largely ignore *Pdlv* funding and maintain his own urban policy line. For this reason, Paris only became truly involved in the *Pdlv* framework from the mid-1990s, a decade later than most cities.[30] The one exception was the Goutte d'Or neighbourhood, designated as a *Pdlv* area already in 1983. However, the differences between the Parisian approach (an Assimilationist-type renovation policy), and the *Pdlv* approach (a more Pluralist-type policy) soon became apparent, and the project quickly became an area of political contention between municipal planners and local actors

---

[29] According to Moore (2001: 116) the evolution of the *Pdlv* combined three 'models of local development' which express conflicting ideologies. He describes these as 'a Republican integration model, a communitarian development model and a social cohesion model.' In terms of our typology, the first two can be identified respectively as the Assimilationist and the Pluralist types of policy response to ethnic diversity.

[30] The *Pdlv* is based on 'city contracts' that are signed between national, regional and local authorities, the *Fonds d'Action Sociale* (FAS) and local civic associations. Selection of eligible neighbourhoods is authorized at the national level, and the state provides some 80 per cent of the funding. Local authorities are expected to propose new areas and projects to be included in the programme. Chirac also opposed signing a *contrat de ville* to avoid staining the capital's image by association with the *Pdlv*, which was linked to problem neighbourhoods in the *banlieues* (interview M. Allal).

empowered through the *Pdlv*. Although it was not stated explicitly, the fact that the Goutte d'Or was the most visible African-Maghrebian enclave in Paris made it an example of different policy intentions regarding the migrant presence (**Box 6.3**).

Box 6.3 **The Goutte d'Or: the politics of renovation in a migrant neighbourhood**

The Goutte d'Or neighbourhood (18th district) has absorbed migrants since the nineteenth century, when it hosted newcomers from the provinces (as described in Zola's novels). In the 1950s it became the main refuge for Maghrebian migrants. For the past two decades it has become the main African enclave in Paris; its open market is perhaps the largest ethnic market in the city.

The neighbourhood has long been known for its dilapidated housing, crime, and a concentration of poor and transient populations. In 1983 the Goutte d'Or was the only neighbourhood listed as eligible for Pdlv funding in the capital. In the early 1980s the municipality prepared a ZAC plan (*Zone d'aménagement concerte*) for an area that included 5,300 residents, of which 58 per cent were registered foreigners. As with previous municipal plans in other migrant neighbourhoods, the ZAC was based on 'renovation' that would require most of the migrant population to be relocated, i.e. dispersed. This reflected previous municipal plans in other migrant neighbourhoods.

However, in the Goutte d'Or the municipality was thwarted by local opposition, led by several residents' associations that took advantage of the consultation procedures required by the Pdlv framework. These associations were composed mostly of recent residents of French origin who wanted to maintain the 'ethnic' character of the area (while improving conditions for gentrification). The outcome was a revised plan in which 'a consensus was reached against a radical social transformation of the area'. The new ZAC thus aimed at maintaining some of the original, ethnic-origin inhabitants.

Nevertheless, most of the destroy-and-build projects planned for the area were eventually implemented, forcing many of the veteran ethnic businesses to relocate. The city thus succeeded in carrying out most of its original renovation policy within the *Pdlv* framework.

Sources: Toubon and Messamah 1990; interviews J.-C. Toubon, M. Neyreneuf and S. Brial-Cottineau.

The complications of the Goutte d'Or project (not least, an upsurge in local civic mobilization) served as a warning signal to the Chirac administration. With a few minor exceptions, City Hall avoided signing other *Pdlv* contracts for the remainder of the 1980s. Instead, local urban policy followed the format established by the 1977 master plan (SDAU). As noted above, this meant destroy-and-build 'renovation' that resulted in the displacement of local residents (many of migrant origin) from the targeted areas. Only in 1995, at the end of Chirac's last term, did Paris fully enter the *Pdlv* framework, signing a *convention* (less binding than the 'city contracts') for six new areas. This did not signal a turnabout in urban policy as much as a political manoeuvre by Mayor Chirac (then campaigning for president), whose gentrification policies had come under fire (interview E. Bailly).

Under the Tiberi administration local urban policy did not change markedly. In the next national round of *Pdlv* contrats (2000-06) Paris signed one contract that designated six new areas, all situated in the northern/northeastern neighborhoods. It is commonly held that Mayor Tiberi succeeded in maintaining his predecessor's policy of gentrification and the dispersal of migrant concentrations, albeit less forcefully than in Chirac's time, within the framework of the *Politique de la ville* (interviews M. Neyreneuf, S. Brial-Cottineau).

5 Other Policy Domains

Beyond the urban policies described above, most other policy domains affecting migrants are dominated by national agencies. Nevertheless, decentralization and in particular the *Pdlv* framework have encouraged local authorities throughout France to develop 'ethnically sensitive' policies over the past two decades, for example in schools. Paris, meanwhile, has remained staunchly Assimilationist in its response to ethnic diversity. The following pages illustrate the city's universalist approach toward migrants in the Legal-political, Socio-economic and Cultural-religious domains, from 1977 to 2001. Changes initiated by the Delanoë administration from 2001 are described in section 6, below.

5.1 Legal-political Domain

Following the republican model of political participation, the local authorities in Paris have regarded acquisition of French citizenship as the one and only path for migrants to express their civic rights. Under the Chirac and Tiberi administrations, City Hall discounted the possibility of any other channels for political participation outside the formal system. This attitude was not exceptional: less than a dozen towns in France have experimented with participatory frameworks such as migrant advisory councils, of which only one (Strasbourg) is of significant size. In regard to migrant associations, however, national policy has diverged somewhat from the republican model and allowed more flexibility. In 1981 French law first allowed foreign residents to form their own associations, and thereafter public agencies began funding migrant/minority organizations, as part of President Mitterrand's policy to promote 'local democratization'. In Paris, *Pdlv* support for migrant/minority associations in the 1990s resulted in a surge of associational activity (Poinsot 2000:13).

The municipality, however, continued to oppose ethnic-based mobilization. Migrant-based associations had a long history in Paris, but they were always discouraged from engaging in any form of political activity, and focused instead on cultural activities (ibid.). After family reunification in the 1970s, some migrant organizations evolved into service providers in their communities. However, City Hall refused to fund or otherwise recognize ethnic-specific activities or organizations as such, classifying them according to general functions, e.g. women's or sports associations. Informally, officials in the municipal bureaucracy have recognized migrant associations as such for years, but it is 'not a declared policy' (interview R. Bercovici).

It is difficult to determine if the ethnic identity of a migrant association is officially ignored or actually *discouraged*, for example, in allocating municipal subsidies to organizations. One indicator is the number of local organizations that identify themselves (or are identified by others) as ethnic-based associations. In the Goutte d'Or neighbourhood, which has a large, mobilized ethnic minority population, only two among some thirty local associations were identified by staff of the Local Development Team (EDL)[31] as 'ethnic associations' (interview S. Brial-Cottineau). Other local associations which clearly have a migrant/ethnic specific function and nature do not promote themselves as such (see below). Is this an internalization by migrant/minority activists of the universalist model, or a tactical consideration in the face of municipal policy that discourages ethnic-based mobilization?

5.2 Socio-economic Domain

Welfare policy in France is determined largely at the national level and implemented locally through national agencies.[32] In Paris, the municipal Welfare Division 'follows the policy determined by elected officials, which continues to be provision of services according to socio-economic criteria, certainly not ethnic criteria' (interview M. de Brunhoff). The one exception, in terms of a municipal migrant-targeted service, is the provision of French language courses, provided through neighbourhood 'Social Centres'. But this service, by its very nature, is assimilationist.

Nevertheless, there is growing awareness within the municipal bureaucracy of the need for ethnically-sensitive solutions to specific needs of the migrant/minority population. Although it is not officially acknowledged, an informal practice has developed since the 1980s of delegating specific services to migrant and 'solidarity associations' (French NGOs aiding migrants). In addition, the role of mediating between migrants and public agencies is increasingly delegated

---

[31] The EDL ('local development team') was established within the *Pdlv* framework.
[32] The government also has a national immigrant reception policy, including primary lodging centres (*foyers*), language education for new immigrants and vocational training. These services are all managed by national agencies (FAS, SONACOTRA, etc.).

to migrant NGOs. Thus, a Turkish migrants association receives some municipal funding for a service supporting Turkish women abandoned by their husbands (interview M.-J. Minassian). This subsidization, however, appears in municipal records as 'support for women'. While the amount of funding provided by the municipality to migrant-related activities or migrant associations is thus concealed within universal budget items, officials agree that substantial sums are involved (interviews R. Bercovici, J. Adriant-Mebtoul, K. Bourcart).

Some migrant activists support the city's universalist policy, fearing that ethnic-specific assistance would stigmatize them in the eyes of the host society. At the same time, they denounce the 'schizophrenia' and 'hypocrisy' of the system, which disguises migrant-specific services within the needs of non-ethnically defined (and therefore legitimate) populations such as 'youth' and 'women' (interview G. Patek-Salom). Paris's Assimilationist-type services policy appears especially outdated when compared to some of the neighbouring municipalities with large migrant populations. For example, Montreuil has enacted an 'integration policy' since 1978, coordinated by its Municipal Immigration Service. While Montreuil deliberately avoids setting up migrant-specific services, it openly formulates policies toward specific ethnic groups, e.g. its large Malian community (Gaxie 1998: 257–77).

Education is another state-dominated policy area, with local government primarily responsible for school facilities. The French system follows strict universalist principles, making no distinction between French and foreign pupils, except in the area of language education. Since the 1980s, however, a national programme of 'Education priority areas' (*Zones d'Education Prioritaires* – ZEPs) has provided opportunities for more local authority involvement as well as for migrant-specific educational actions in some schools. As part of the *Politique de la ville*, the ZEP policy takes a global approach to scholastic failure in schools within a designated area. One of the criteria for designating a ZEP is a high proportion of foreign-origin pupils. In cities such as Marseille, ZEPs provide a framework for ethnically-sensitive local education policies that go far beyond helping migrant-origin children to improve their French (Mazzella 1996). In Paris, however, language education remains the primary, if not the only, policy tool that the municipality regards as necessary to integrate migrant pupils in the school system. This again expresses an underlying assimilationist attitude toward integration.

5.3 Cultural-religious Domain

The 'distrust of anything that is ethnically-specific', as one official put it (interview P.-F. Salviani) translates into a minimalist policy regarding the cultural and religious needs of migrant communities. For a city that prides itself as a cultural capital, Paris has largely avoided supporting ethnically-specific cultural activities. When it comes to religious needs, the municipality takes a minimalist stand. According to French law, local authorities are responsible for the physical upkeep and construction of places of worship. In a city like Marseille, the local authority has been negotiating for years with local Muslim communities over the construction of a symbolically prominent mosque. In contrast, Paris's official city mosque is a modest building dating back to the 1920s, tucked away behind the municipal botanical gardens. The main Islamic monument in the capital is the *Institut du Monde Arabe*, a building that is neither local nor religious, but a gesture of the state (specifically, of President Mitterrand) toward Islam as a culture. Meanwhile, 'the grass-roots faith is practiced in impoverished prayer-halls and converted warehouses in gloomy suburbs' (Le Quesne 2000: 62).

In the Goutte d'Or neighbourhood, local authorities prefer to disregard the cultural and religious needs of the large Muslim population. According to an EDL official, the inadequacy of exiting mosques is 'an enormous problem' which remains 'taboo' (interview S. Brial-Cottineau). The 18th District Municipality (which is directly responsible) has expanded the area's only mosque building and recently bought a building to house another, but the deputy district mayor takes a minimalist stand:

> We have a duty to provide all residents with the conditions for practicing their religious freedom as guaranteed by the constitution. It doesn't go beyond that (interview M. Neyreneuf).

The prevalent Assimilationist attitude also means that inter-ethnic tensions are ignored by the local authorities, despite what the EDL official describes as a 'very, very serious problem of racism between the different communities' (interview S. Brial-Cottineau). Again, this contrasts with initiatives taken by other cities, such as Lyon and Marseille, which have set up inter-communal 'conciliation councils' (*La Gazette* 2002).

6 The New Integration Policy, 2001 – ...

> We are approaching a new phase ... how should we imagine the new municipal policy? Should Paris see itself as a cosmopolitan city, or should it continue to close its eyes to [the migrant] phenomena? We are raising all the questions ... we have no taboos.
> Interview M. Allal, *Diagnostic* coordinator.

Paris has historically been ruled by parties of the Centre-Right, with the Left as opposition. In 2001 a Left-wing coalition came to power for the first time, on a platform of change for Paris. Bertrand Delanoë's promise to promote 'local democracy', including an integration policy for the city's foreign residents, played a significant role in the municipal campaign of the Socialists and their coalition partners, the Greens. After he was elected mayor in March, Delanoë appointed an activist of Algerian origin, Khedidja Bourcart, as 'Deputy Mayor for Integration and Non-EU Foreigners' (*Adjointe au Maire de Paris, chargée de l'intégration et des étrangers non-communautaires*). In June 2001 Delanoë and Bourcart announced the main lines of their integration policy at a press conference; in November a *Mission Intégration* was established to implement the new policy on a daily level; in January 2002 a 'Citizenship Council for Non-EU Parisians' was proposed by the mayor and approved by the new city council.

Thus, for the first time in Paris's history, the integration of migrants was defined as a policy area within the municipal structure. Bourcart heads the new *Délégation à l'intégration*, responsible for formulating overall policy. On the administrative side, the *Mission Integration* coordinates policy implementation on a daily basis.[33] The *Mission* has a small staff and a budget of €500,000 (2002), of which €350,000 for subsidizing associations that provide migrant services. The new integration strategy is based on three 'policy axes', summarized in the following subsections (Municipal press release, 19 June 2001).

6.1 'Comprendre et informer'

The first policy axis ('understanding and informing' the foreign resident community) is based on the realization (repeatedly expressed by municipal officials that I interviewed) that the municipality knows almost nothing about its migrant population and their needs. To address this problem a year-long '*diagnostic*' was initiated in December 2001. The diagnostic included a statistical analysis of the city's foreign population, a mapping of existing 'integration services and actors', and an 'evaluation of the dynamics of integration' emphasizing strong and weak points in the existing situation. It was to culminate in a 'programme of concrete actions' to be presented to the city's political leadership by the end of 2002 (APUR 2002: 6–11).[34] Coordinated by APUR, the *diagnostic* is meant to prepare the basis for developing Paris's new migrant policy.

The budget[35] and comprehensiveness of the *diagnostic* imply that City Hall takes the issue seriously. According to its director, the evaluation programme should be the basis for a fundamental rethinking of local policy toward migrants and minorities:

> We must rethink the traditional French model of integration, and find a solution that is compatible with the French characteristics of universalism and so on, and the realities of today, including the persistence of [migrant] unemployment and housing problems (interview M. Allal).

---

[33] Deputy mayors are city council members appointed by the mayor to oversee a policy area. A *delegation* consists of the deputy mayor and her staff, and is meant to cut across the administrative divisions of the municipal bureaucracy. *Missions* are administrative units set up to implement a multi-sectoral policy issue.

[34] In mid-2003 most of the *diagnostic* was still incomplete and unavailable to the public.

[35] The estimated budget of €290,000 is jointly funded by the municipality and national authorities.

However, the independence of this evaluation is unclear, not least because it is coordinated within APUR, the municipal planning agency responsible for much of the local policies that are supposed to be critically evaluated. Although APUR engaged an independent sociologist (Mourad Allal) to direct the evaluation, the 'diagnostic teams' include representatives of various local and national agencies that may be unwilling to propose radical changes to the current system. Allal raises one example: should the new integration policy target only *étrangers* (alien residents), or include second-generation migrants, thus breaking with the republican model (APUR 2002: 31)?

In any case, the *diagnostic* shows that Mayor Delanoë has tried to involve all the relevant actors in this stage of policy formulation (including representatives of the Prefecture, state agencies, district mayors and civic associations), with the aim of coordinating expectations among all the actors regarding the new policy (interview M. Allal). This partnerial style is characteristic of French policymaking since the 1980s, but it also appears that Delanoë has no intention of formulating his new integration policy singlehandedly.

6.2   'Soutenir' – Services Policy

The second policy axis is meant to improve local social services for foreign residents. In France, social services have been decentralized since the 1980s, often by delegating implementation to civic organizations. But as noted above, Paris's subsidization policy concealed any municipal support for migrant-related activities within general budget items, e.g. 'scholarization'. The new policy is meant to make the integration/ethnic element explicit, with the aim of improving coordination between the many local and national-level agencies involved in the delegation and subsidization of migrant-related services. According to deputy mayor Bourcart, currently 'the mechanisms are in place' but migrants are uninformed of their rights and have difficulty accessing local services. Among the new measures she plans are training sessions for municipal employees in services that come into frequent contact with migrants (for 'a minimal sensitization to cultural differences'), and a guide on migrants' rights and local services to be published in several languages (interview K. Bourcart).

This marks a certain departure from Paris's traditional policy of avoiding explicitly migrant-targeted services. Nevertheless, the current administration does not intend to *increase* municipal funding for such services nor to establish new services specifically targeting migrants (the latter would signal a shift to a truly Pluralist-type policy in this domain). *Au contraire*, the Deputy Mayor for Integration is *opposed* to migrant-specific services, except French-language teaching. According to her, 'the key to integration' is fluency in French and this will be a central element in the integration policy (ibid.). By late 2002 (a year into the new policy) no real changes were noted by local migrant associations providing social support services, which still received a minute part of their budget (often less than 10 per cent) from the municipality (interview M.-J. Minassian). In short, the Delanoë administration continues the social services policy that evolved in the previous decades, but intends to make the migrant integration element explicit, and thus more efficient.

6.3 'Associer' – the Citizenship Council

The clearest break from Paris's traditionally Assimilationist policy toward migrants is to be found in the third axis of the new policy: the 'Citizenship Council of non-EU Parisians' (*Conseil de la Citoyenneté des Parisiens non-Communautaires*). Paris is one of the very few cities in France (after Grenoble and Strasbourg) to establish a consultative council for non-EU residents. The Council is expected 'to formulate advice and propositions on municipal questions regarding [the foreigners'] life in Paris [as well as] applying itself to any problems of local interest, beyond questions of integration'.[36] Presided by the mayor, the new body comprises ninety appointed members from 36 countries, all of them non-EU citizens legally residing in Paris for at least one year.

Delanoë's objective in establishing the Citizenship Council is clearly symbolic and 'militant'. According to Bourcart, 'More than an instrument of integration, the council is a means of recognizing those people that the electoral law continues to ignore' (*Libération*, 14 January 2002). On the occasion of its establishment the mayor repeated his demand to the government, to extend local voting rights (given to EU residents) to non-EU residents as well. Until then, the Citizenship Council is presented as an interim channel of participation for the city's non-EU residents. In a direct challenge to the republican notion of citizenship (and no less importantly, to the policy of President Chirac), Mayor Delanoë proposed a notion of urban citizenship (*citoyenneté dans la cité*). At the same time, the new administration goes out of its way to deflect claims that it is fostering ethnic-based communitarianism: 'we are not speaking of a council of communities' stipulates Bourcart (ibid.).

The Citizenship Council was set up in a process supervised by a special committee comprising representatives of civic associations, local politicians and other 'qualified persons' (most of foreign origin). 'Citizenship meetings' were held in the city districts, at which foreign residents were called to propose themselves as candidates. A 'candidature commission' then selected a list of 90 members that was approved by the mayor. Their criteria included gender parity, proportional representation of the different districts and countries of origin, and diversity in 'socio-professional milieues and motivations' of the members.[37]

In November 2001 the proposal for establishing the Citizenship Council came before city council. The ensuing debate focused less on its utility and more on its

---

[36] 'Objet: Creation du Conseil de la Citoyenneté des Parisiens non communautaires. Projet de deliberation', November 2001, Secretariat General, Municipality of Paris.
[37] Ibid. footnote above.

symbolic significance, revealing conflicting notions of citizenship. Mayor Delanoë made no attempt to hide the political significance of the proposal:

> By giving the voice to those who have been deprived of it, our ambition is to favour a true citizenship based on residence which is indispensable to the revitalization of our local democracy (Municipal Council protocol, Meeting of 19–20 November 2001: 1358).

The Greens' representative added that 'it is no longer possible to speak of a true politics limited only to the national territory'. On the contrary, 'this notion of foreigners (*étrangers*) appears to us more and more strange' (ibid.: 1364–5). The opposition RPR representative accepted the 'necessary and legitimate' objective of encouraging 'the participation of foreigners in the life of the city where they live,' but objected strongly to the term 'citizenship' in the proposed title:

> [Delanoë] may contest or disagree, but since 1789 citizenship and nationality are linked in an unchangeable manner in our specific national tradition ... this council is everything except a council of citizenship (ibid.: 1358–60).

Indeed, opposition councillors were willing to support the proposal, if the title was amended to '*Participation* Council of non-EU Parisians'. This semantic change was rejected by coalition councillors, for whom the proposed Council represents a new kind of local *citizenship* 'dissociate[d] from nationality' (ibid.: 1368). Rarely, if ever, have host-stranger relations been discussed so explicitly in Paris's *Hôtel de Ville*.

On 12 January 2002, the Citizenship Council was ceremonially opened in City Hall. The event drew local and national media attention and was used by all as an opportunity to repeat their support or opposition in terms that went far beyond the local context. Mayor Delanoë spoke of separating between notions of 'nationality' and 'citizenship in the city' (*Agence France Presse*, 14 January 2002), while an RPR councillor warned: 'The way to integration is not through this false citizenship!' (*Le Parisien*, 14 January 2002). Interestingly, the Citizenship Council's new members raised very different expectations regarding their role. A Chilean councillor saw it as an opportunity to advance democratic ideals; a Chinese councillor hoped to raise the problems of her community; a Bulgarian councillor warned that the Council would 'not be a playing card for the Left' (*Libération*, 14 January 2002).

In its first year, the Citizenship Council (with an annual functioning budget of €106,000 and a permanent secretary) had elected a steering committee and various sub-committees (housing, social affairs, etc.) which met regularly to draw up specific proposals. If approved by its plenary, these would be raised before Paris's city and district councils. Outside the political elite, however, the Citizenship Council remained largely unknown. In City Hall, a 'wait and see' attitude prevails.

For Bourcart, the Council's importance lies in its awareness-raising function more than its ability to address the practical needs of migrants in Paris:

> The aim is not to set up a 'secondary council', but to utilize this legal instance as an instrument through which the foreigners can feel that they are part of the city (Interview K. Bourcart).

6.4 Other Policy Domains

According to one migrant activist, the main change felt 'in the street' since Delanoë took office has been in the cultural domain, e.g. a multicultural festival organized in the twentieth district (interview Patek-Salom). Mostly, however, the new integration policy is expressed in symbolic gestures that reflect the new administration's main concern: to promote a 'cultural recognition' of the foreigners in Paris. These included the first official reception in City Hall for the Muslim community, and a declaration (October 2001) of a 'Cultural Year on the contribution of migrants and immigration to the historical development of Paris'. Behind the longwinded title, however, were only a few actions of a very academic nature.

In the Spatial domain, there has been no significant change in urban policy under the new administration (interviews M. Allal, E. Bailly). Indeed, gentrification has intensified in Paris since 2001, with rental prices increasing over 5 per cent annually, and a rise in housing prices that is unprecedented in the past 30 years. If continued, this could lead to a further decline in the proportion of rental households in Paris, from 75 per cent today to 60 per cent within two decades, of whom only 15 per cent will belong to the working class (where migrants are predominantly found).[38] Gentrification is not a result of urban policy alone. But according to Fijalkow, Delanoë's current policy of 'valorizing Paris's hyper-centrality for the urban classes' through festivals, cultural events, etc. clearly contributes to the capital's continuing gentrification. So, too, does the continuation of local renovation policies that are meant to eliminate dilapidated housing (interview, Y. Fijalkow). According to Allal, urban policies in Paris within the *Politique de la ville* still do not recognize the ethnic dimension, demonstrating a 'continued hypocrisy' (interview M. Allal).

7 Summary: '*Plus ça change, plus c'est la même chose*'?

Traditionally, immigrants in Paris were perceived by the host society in terms of class more than ethnicity. In the postwar period, however, as immigration became increasingly non-European, ethnic rather than class differences became the basis for host-stranger relations in France. Since the 1980s, the persistence of social and

---

[38] Personal communication, Y. Fijalkow. See Fijalkow 2004.

economic exclusion among second-generation migrant youth have undermined the validity of the French model of integration. Urban disturbances in areas of migrant concentration and the rise of ethnic mobilization are seen as a threat to the French model. I identified this model with the Assimilationist type proposed in Chapter 3, according to which immigrants are expected to lose their Otherness through individual assimilation into the host society.

Some cities in France have reacted to these changes by developing ethnically-sensitive integration policies toward their migrant/minority populations. This 'ethnicization' of local migrant policies, i.e. a partial abandonment of the French republican model of integration, occurred largely within the framework of the *Politique de la ville*, as demonstrated by Moore, Gaxie and others. In Paris this has not been the case. Applying the criteria of the typology, this chapter shows that local policies in the capital have remained consistently Assimilationist across all the policy domains, at least until 2001. The Assimilationist approach applies to policymaking toward migrants both before and after 1977 (the end of direct state rule in Paris), indicating a particularly Parisian response to ethnic diversity.

One characteristic of Assimilationist-type migrant policies is that they are hidden within general policies; in the French case this usually means territorially-based policies. As we have seen, Paris's urban development policies have served a political-social agenda going back 150 years. This (usually implicit) agenda can be summed up as distancing the poor and other 'dangerous' populations to areas progressively farther from the centres of power and privilege, and attracting more desirable residents in their place. The intentional *embourgeoisement* of Paris began under Haussmann in the 1850s and was continued vigorously under council-led 'renovation' policies into the twentieth century. It was then expanded to the outlying areas of the city through the master plans for Paris of the 1950s–60s, and accelerated in the mayoral-led urban policies of the 1980s–90s. The Chirac and Tiberi administrations, in particular, succeeded in gentrifying the remaining areas of lower-class migrant concentrations in Paris, resulting in a steady decline in the city's foreign resident population over the past two decades. In keeping with the universalist policy discourse, the ethnic dimension of this 'valorization' of Paris was rarely made explicit.

Using the host-stranger relations model, we can discern the underlying similarity (as well as the differences) between urban policies implemented in Paris over the past 150 years. The common thread running through this period is the attempt to bring Order to disorderly environments. The difference lies in the policymakers' definition of what (and who) constitutes the threatening Other. In the nineteenth century, the historical fear and repugnance felt by the French elite toward the Parisian masses was replaced by the fears of the local bourgeoisie toward the new proletarian (largely provincial migrant) population. Later in the twentieth century their place (and space in the city) was increasingly occupied by non-French immigrants. The Algerian War rekindled the threat of the ethnic Other *intra muros*. Consequently, Paris's renovation and public housing policies effectively relocated much of this population 'beyond the city walls', to the *banlieues*. In the 1980s, the threatening Other became associated with second-generation ethnic minority youth who had grown up in the suburban housing estates. The recent (sub)urban riots have demonstrated not only the failings of the French model of integration, but also the consequences of Paris's policy of 'exporting' unwanted migrant populations beyond its boundaries.

What characterized Paris's policymakers, from Haussmann through the urban planners of the 1960s to Chirac, were their systematic attempts to rid the city of undesirable Others and replace them with more desirable residents. These renovation/gentrification policies consistently targeted neighbourhoods (from the Cité and Les Halles to Belleville and the Goutte d'Or) whose resident population was perceived by policymakers as incompatible with the status and prestige of the capital. Beyond their explicit universalist aims (from fighting disease to upgrading Paris's global competitiveness) we can discern an implicit *modernist strategy*. To use Bauman's terms, this was meant to eradicate Otherness by physically distancing Strangers. Those who remained were expected to lose their Otherness, i.e. assimilate. Housing policies adopted by city council in the twentieth century can be seen as an attempt at replacing disorderly environments (from the *îlots* to the *bidonvilles*) with planned environments that correctly socialize their inhabitants. The replacement of disorder with (physical/urban/social) order is a recurring theme in Parisian urban planning, from Haussmann to the 1983 Plan Programme for the East of Paris.

The ethnic dimension in this distancing of Otherness was rarely made explicit. Indeed, the extent to which Paris's policymakers did or did not *intentionally* target migrant/minority populations remains an issue of debate among French scholars. Did urban development plans from the 1950s onward *deliberately* result in the distancing of migrants from Paris? Or, was this only a by-product of ethnically-neutral renovation and gentrification policies? In either case, the sidelining of ethnicity in Parisian urban policies, intentional or not, expresses an Assimilationist-type response according to our model.

Paris has pursued Assimilationist-type policies in the other policy domains as well. Thus, ethnic-based migrant mobilization was long ignored or discouraged by City Hall. Since the 1980s, municipal support for migrant-targeted services and associations is minimal and implicit, with the exception of French language teaching. Similarly, the city's response to the religious needs of its growing Muslim population is minimalistic and couched in universalist terminology. In sum local policy in Paris was dominated by modernist attitudes in both rhetoric *and* daily practice, until recently.

Since 2001, the new municipal administration has espoused a change from the traditional Parisian attitude toward migrants. Its new 'integration policy for foreign residents of non-EU origin' openly challenges the republican model of integration by proposing to 'dissociate citizenship from nationality', as symbolized in the Citizenship Council. However, it appears that this new policy emphasizes changes of a symbolic more than a structural nature. Thus, French language acquisition will remain the primary integration instrument, since other ethnically-specific measures are 'stigmatizing'. Delanoë's policy for managing ethnic diversity appears to be based on adapting existing universal services and working within existing frameworks (e.g. the *Politique de la ville*) rather than creating new ones. The exception is the new Citizenship Council, criticized by some as a largely symbolic entity, whose impact is still unclear.

In any case, City Hall avoids any suggestions that it is pursuing an ethnically-based, communitarian policy. Instead, new measures toward Paris's minority residents are justified in universalist terms such as 'ensuring access to rights' and 'the fight against discrimination'. The new integration policy may thus not present such a break from the past. The main change appears to be symbolic: legitimizing the presence, needs and contribution of the capital's migrant/ minority population. This does not mean that Paris has adopted what we would identify a Pluralist approach toward integration. Rather, it appears that the new administration proposes to *change the basis for the city's Assimilationist policy*, from the republican model (tied to French citizenship) to some kind of 'citizenship in the city'. It remains to be seen whether this new policy signals a real departure from the past.

Chapter 7

Amsterdam: Pluralism and its Discontents

Almost half of all Amsterdammers do not originate from the Netherlands. In Amsterdam live young and old, homos and lesbians, people with handicaps, Muslims, Buddhists and atheists. And that's fine, that people are so different. Amsterdam is truly a diverse city.

Amsterdam leeftsamen, municipal brochure (my translation)

1   Introduction

Amsterdam's migrant policies over the past half-century provide a textbook example of changing host society attitudes toward Otherness, and how these changes are expressed in the policies of one city over time. Looking back over the past fifty years we can identify four phases of labour migration and policy response. The first wave of labour migrants (late 1950s) was largely ignored by the municipality. From the mid-1960s to mid-1970s, City Hall recognized their presence as a temporary phenomenon, as expressed in a decade of Guestworker policies. The 1980s saw an official acceptance of their permanence and a redefinition of migrants as 'ethnic minorities'. This was expressed in a Pluralist-type 'Minorities Policy' (pursued well into the mid-1990s) that recognized and supported ethnic-based difference. Amsterdam's current 'Diversity Policy' signals a reaction against the perceived failure of the multicultural model. This latest policy phase is neither Pluralist nor does it correspond to the Assimiliationist type of policy response (see Chapter 3, above).

Amsterdam's local policies toward migrants are embedded in particular attitudes toward newcomers and Otherness that evolved over centuries. Within the city's trajectory of shifting attitudes we can also discern a certain continuity. Specifically, we can distinguish certain *attitudes toward Strangers* that stem from two longstanding traditions. One is a particular kind of 'Dutch-style tolerance' toward Otherness, rooted in the Netherlands' history of co-existence between separate, indigenous religious communities. The practice of tolerating difference by 'looking the other way' (at which Amsterdammers were particularly adept), was later applied to non-Dutch newcomers, as was the Dutch 'pillarization' system (below). In contradiction to these practices, however, we can also discern a pattern of institutionalized paternalism (a kind of 'Dutch bear-hug approach') toward

154   *Cities and Labour Immigration*

those defined by the host society as *problematic Others*. This practice, originally applied to Dutch 'anti-social families' and then to post-colonial immigrants, later resurfaced in migrant policies directed at (officially defined) 'ethnic minorities'. Finally, the Netherlands' long colonial history also affected host society attitudes toward ethnic Otherness, and policies toward migrants.

These various aspects of Dutch host-stranger relations are elaborated below, together with the broader context of postwar immigration to the Netherlands and national policy responses, in Section 2. Section 3 describes the local context of immigrant settlement in the city. Section 4 follows the evolution of Amsterdam's response to postwar immigration, from Non-policy in the late 1950s to the current Diversity Policy. The lion's share of section 4 is devoted to Amsterdam's 'Minorities Policy' of the 1980s, which illustrates the Pluralist-type of local policy response that is the focus of this chapter. Section 5 summarizes and analyzes this 60-year policy trajectory, in light of the typology.

2   The National Context

2.1   *Gedogen and the Pillar Approach*

> One Dutchman – one theologian; two Dutchmen – a Church; three Dutchmen – a schism.
>
> Proverb

Co-existing with the Other is a Dutch tradition, rooted in historical necessity going back at least as far as the sixteenth century. At that time the Republic of the United Provinces was formed as a confederation of cities and regions, ruled by a mercantile bourgeoisie of different religious and political persuasions, and lacking a central authority that could impose the will of one group over another. The survival and eventual flourishing of the Republic (and its successor the Kingdom of the Netherlands) can be seen as one long, delicate balancing act involving a series of careful compromises between several indigenous minorities.[1] These compromises were often expressed in practice rather than in law. For example, the Treaty of Utrecht (1579), which signalled the unification of the Protestant rebels against the Catholic rule of Spain, officially forbade Catholicism. In most cities, however, the Catholic minority was allowed to continue worshipping 'in secret', while their Calvinist neighbours pretended not to notice. This passive tolerance had previously been applied by the Catholic elites toward the Lutherans and other reformers, despite pressure from the Spanish crown to persecute Protestants.[2] This

---

[1]   See Schama 1987 (especially Chapter 2) on the formative period of the Dutch.
[2]   This is not to say however that discrimination and segregation based on religious differences did not exist (cf. Knippenberg 1992).

Dutch manner of living with difference by 'looking the other way when necessary' became known as *gedogen*, roughly meaning 'illegal but officially tolerated'.

This exceptional tolerance came to characterize the Dutch Republic in the seventeenth century, attracting minorities fleeing persecution elsewhere in Europe. Many settled in the port city of Amsterdam, where the practice of *gedogen* was already well entrenched, and was applied to the newcomers as well. The idea that each person should be 'sovereign in his own domain', i.e. allowed to believe and practice as he pleases (as long as he respects the rules binding the host society and does not disturb the neighbours), remains to this day central in Dutch attitudes toward Others (Van der Horst 2001), particularly in Amsterdam.

In the late nineteenth century, the idea of separate-but-equal co-existence at the communal level was institutionalized in what Lijphart (1968) termed the 'pillarization' (*verzuiling*) of Dutch society. Each of the four official pillars (Protestant, Catholic, Socialist and Liberal) had its separate political parties, schools, newspapers, etc. – autonomous worlds in which the members of each community lived, with interaction and political compromise occurring between each community's elites. Pillarization can be seen as the modern equivalent of the system applied since the Dutch Republic: co-existence with the Other despite ideological differences, for the benefit of all.

Social pillarization all but disappeared in the 1960s, but its institutional vestiges remain the basis of modern Dutch consociational democracy.[3] Pillarization also played an important role in how newcomers were later perceived and incorporated into Dutch host society. In particular, it facilitated the institutionalized Pluralism that characterizes the Dutch response to ethnic diversity, e.g. publicly supported denominational schools. Pillarization can thus be seen as the Dutch variant of communitarian strategies for living with Strangers (see Chapter 2, above).

2.2   The Institutionalized Problematization of Strangers

> The way in which, nowadays, immigrant ethnic minorities (the exterior 'others') are ideologically represented displays remarkable similarities with the way in which anti-social families (the interior Others) were represented in an earlier historical phase.
>
> Jan Rath, '[...] a Dutch treat for anti-social families and immigrant ethnic minorities', 1999, p. 165

Another factor to consider in understanding policy reactions to immigration in the Netherlands is the paternalistic aspect of Dutch host-stranger relations, expressed

---

[3]   The mainstream political parties originated in this system, although their constituents may no longer identify themselves with the original pillars. The religious pillars were represented by Protestant and Catholic parties which united in 1980, becoming the Christian Democrats (CDA). The Socialist and Liberal pillars are represented by the Labour (PvdA) and Liberal (VVD) parties, respectively. The rise of new parties such as the Green-Left (Groen Links) and the Pim Fortuyn List (LPF) symbolizes the continued weakening of pillarization in Dutch society.

in an often unspoken attitude of superiority.[4] Jan Rath (1999, citing Dercksen and Verplanke 1987, and De Regt 1984) describes the attitudes and policies of the Dutch middle classes toward indigenous 'anti-social families' that were later applied to immigrants. The institutionalized problematization of the new urban proletariat in the late nineteenth century originated in the 'moral repugnance' of the Dutch liberal bourgeoisie, 'but also from fear of revolt by the impoverished mob' (p. 153). The approach to Otherness as a kind of behavioural deviancy that can be corrected through intensive re-education was common not only in the Netherlands at this time (see Chapter 6, above). What characterizes the Dutch case was the extent and the way in which this was *institutionalized*. During the first half of the twentieth century, some families from the lower proletariat were defined as socially deviant, and became the target of reformist re-education policies. Public policies soon followed in poverty relief, education, social housing and health care. This was particularly popular in cities ruled by social democrats, who were interested in the 'moral improvement ... of the working class' (ibid.: 153–4).

Over time, 'the emancipating groups had less and less sympathy for those that refused to fit into the norms of respectable working-class families, in terms of neatness, thrift, neighbourly relations, etc. Gradually, their moral improvement acquired a less voluntary character' (ibid.: 154). After the Second World War, local authorities set up 'a series of institutions for special family and neighbourhood work for anti-social families' (ibid.: 157). In Amsterdam, municipal housing officials identified 'anti-social families' and defined them as 'inadmissible for council housing'; special residential areas were then established, supervised by wardens and psychiatrists who were responsible for educating the 'deviant' families. As in France, the ideology of 'hygienism' played an important role. 'The diagnosis was now often couched in epidemiological terms: anti-socials were socially diseased and threatened to affect the stability of the whole society' (ibid.: 155–7).

In the 1950s this paternalistic approach toward indigenous Others was redirected toward newcomers, namely Dutch-Indonesian immigrants. During the 1960s–70s, as the host society opened up to various different lifestyles, such re-education policies faded away. By the early 1980s, behaviour that deviated from Dutch norms, e.g. the wearing of headscarves by Muslim women, was regarded as a legitimate expression of cultural Otherness (below). But the multicultural policies of the 1980s also expressed a certain paternalistic attitude toward the new minorities and their expected eventual integration, as will be shown below. A decade later, when migrant integration was not fulfilling expectations, a reaction set in. This reaction finds expression in current policies toward migrants, which

---

[4] See Schama 1997, Chapter 2, on the moralistic streak in Dutch culture and its Calvinist roots. For a comparison of Dutch (paternalistic) and Italian (laissez-faire) attitudes in the treatment of Serbian refugees, see Korac 2003.

display many of the characteristics of Dutch re-education policies applied a century earlier.⁵

2.3 The Colonial Legacy

> The collective memory [...] of the colonies is still with us at all levels. It helps to determine the way in which the Dutch respond to foreigners, ethnic minorities, immigrants, non-Dutch nationals or whatever other name is given to them. No one consciously makes the connection, but for unprejudiced outsiders, it is clearly visible.
>
> Han van der Horst, *The Low Sky*, 2001: 274–5

Until 1949 the Netherlands was the world's third colonial power, after Britain and France, in terms of colonized area and population. Dutch overseas trade had evolved into three centuries of colonization in the East Indies (1619–1949) and in the Caribbean (1613–1975).⁶ In the late nineteenth century the rest of the Indonesian archipelago was conquered in violent military operations by the Dutch colonial army. Decolonization in the mid-twentieth century involved a bloody war against Indonesian nationalists, followed by Japanese occupation of Indonesia and internment of the Dutch settlers in concentration camps. This traumatic conclusion to the colonial enterprise in the Far East was brought home, literally, with the repatriation of some 300,000 Dutch-Indonesian immigrants after the Second World War (below).

The Netherlands' colonial legacy is a mixed one in terms of its effect on host society attitudes toward racial and cultural Otherness. On one hand, the mercantile tradition exposed the Dutch to different cultures at a time when most European peoples were still living in relative isolation. In the seventeenth century Amsterdam was the busiest port in the world and arguably the most cosmopolitan city in Europe. Overseas trade brought Otherness literally into Dutch homes, for example in the East Indian spices that became a staple in the Dutch kitchen. On the other hand, extended contact with foreign customs did not necessarily make the Dutch more open to Otherness, as the colonial experience fed into pre-existing assumptions of moral superiority. Well into the twentieth century most Dutch perceived *their* colonialism as bringing civilization and progress to the colonized (Van der Horst 2001).⁷

---

⁵ See Section 4.5, below, on Amsterdam's obligatory 'Civic Integration' programme for newcomers.

⁶ In the seventeenth century the main islands of the Indonesian archipelago came under commercial and military control of the Amsterdam-based East Indies Company (VOC). In the eighteenth century the Dutch crown took over direct control from the VOC. In the Caribbean, the Dutch colonized Surinam on the coast north of Brazil, and six islands including the Netherlands Antilles.

⁷ 'After 300 years of rule over the largest Muslim country in the world, we learned at school about our colonization of Indonesia but nothing at all about Islam' (Jeroen Doomernik, personal communication).

Nevertheless, in the Netherlands' history of contact with Far Eastern cultures (as opposed to the Caribbean) there appears to have been a respect for the colonized Other that was rare among other Europeans in regard to 'their' colonial Strangers. In 1860 a former colonial official exposed the exploitative side of Dutch colonialism as well as his empathy with the Javanese, in a novel that 'sent a shiver through the country'.[8] In 1899 the notion of Holland's 'debt of honour' to its colonies was popularized by the liberal politician Conrad Deventer, while in the early twentieth century an influential group of scholars at the University of Leiden propagated a 'culturally sensitive' policy of colonial administration based on understanding and even admiration for the indigenous cultures (Van der Horst 2001: 281–3).[9] The 'debt of honour' that many Dutch still feel toward non-Europeans partly explains the political correctness that characterized host-stranger relations in the Netherlands up to the late 1990s. It also throws light on the overtly (some say overly) multicultural policies toward migrants and ethnic minorities in the postwar period.

The colonial legacy has also left its mark on Dutch definitions of 'insiders' and 'outsiders' (Lucassen and Penninx 1997). Until the nineteenth century it was not uncommon for Dutch settlers to marry native women and return with their children to Holland, so that *some* dark-skinned people became a part of Dutch society relatively early. Today, it appears that cultural capital (especially fluency in Dutch) is more important than skin colour *per se* in how the Dutch define different types of Strangers. Thus, Indonesian-origin Dutch are not included in the official 'ethnic minorities' category 'because they are considered wholly assimilated to the Dutch culture and society' (Phalet, 2001: 3). While second-generation Indonesians and Surinamese are considered insiders in the host sociey, European residents who are ethnically closer to the Dutch (e.g. Germans and British, the two largest EU communities in Amsterdam) can still feel like outsiders after years in the country.[10]

Nevertheless, informal discrimination against ethnic minorities (particularly Moroccans and Turks, but also Africans) is still common, although the racist as opposed to the xenophobic element in this is difficult to ascertain (see below). One indicator is that racist parties have never attained a significant portion of the national vote (the highest level was 4 per cent, by the Dutch National Socialist

---

[8] *Max Havelaar, or The Coffee Auctions of the Dutch Trading Company*, by Multatuli (E.D. Dekker) was an immediate bestseller and remains a 'must read' book for the Dutch. The quote (citing a speaker in the Dutch parliament at that time) appears in the Introduction by R.P. Meijer to the Penguin edition, 1987: 12.

[9] C.S. Hourgonje, the leading scholar of the Leiden group, may have secretly converted to Islam. His followers codified the indigenous Indonesian legal systems, the *adat*. However, this knowledge of indigenous cultures was also used as an instrument for furthering Dutch colonial expansion (ibid.).

[10] Based on personal communications with various foreign residents in Amsterdam as well as with Dutch of Surinamese and Indonesian origin. Another indicator is the relatively high rate of interracial marriages (11 per cent) in The Netherlands. In Amsterdam the figure is considerably higher.

party in the 1930s). This may now be changing, as religion (specifically: Islam) becomes the main delineator in host-stranger relations (see below).

2.4 Postwar Immigration Flows and National Immigration Policies

The various elements described above have all affected host society attitudes toward the different types of immigrants that settled in the Netherlands. Postwar immigration to the Netherlands can be divided into five types: postcolonial migration (1945–79); guestworkers (late 1950s–73); family reunification (1970s–80s); asylum seekers (primarily 1980s–90s); and economic migrants from other industrialized countries (primarily since the 1980s) (Musterd et al. 1998: 15–16). Postcolonial immigrants first arrived from the Dutch East Indies: between 1945 and 1962 some 300,000 Dutch nationals were 'repatriated' to the Netherlands. Most were descendants of Dutch settlers, among them 180,000 '*indos*' (of mixed Eurasian origin). In addition, over 10,000 Moluccans (an Indonesian people that had served in the Dutch colonial army, and their families) arrived in Holland in 1951. Over the next 20 years, the Dutch-Indonesian repatriates were integrated into the host society in an intensive assimilation process (below).[11]

Immigration from the West Indies (Surinam and the Antilles) increased in the 1960s and peaked during the 1970s.[12] Surinamese holding Dutch passports and speaking Dutch had migrated to the Netherlands in a small but steady stream for decades. The first flows, predominantly of Creole origin and middle-class background, were 'almost automatically incorporat[ed] into Dutch society' (Van Amersfoort and De Klerk 1984: 201). But the rush of migrants in the mid-1970s included many lower-class Surinamese of Hindustani and Javanese-origin as well as poor rural Creoles who were much less easily integrated into Dutch society. These waves (1973–75 and 1979–80) coincided with economic restructuring in the Netherlands which hampered their integration into the labour market. Subsequently the Surinamese and Antillean migrants were included in the official category of disadvantaged 'ethnic minorities' (see below).

Postwar *gastarbeiders* (guestworkers) were recruited by sectors such as mining and industry in the late 1950s and early 1960s, primarily from Spain and Italy.[13] Between 1964 and 1973 national Guestworker policy included government-

---

[11] Lucassen and Penninx (1997: 146) note that in the 1980s questions were raised about the 'myth of success' of the Eurasian integration. For the Moluccans, integration has been a much longer and more difficult process.

[12] Surinam became independent in 1975. Aruba and the Dutch Antilles remained a part of the Kingdom of the Netherlands, and their residents can travel freely between the islands and the Netherlands. This pendular migration follows economic shifts, with a high rate of return migration.

[13] At the same time, a labour surplus led to the emigration of nearly half a million Dutch citizens to Canada, the USA, Australia and New Zealand (between 1946–62). This points to the development of a segmented labour market in the Netherlands from the 1960s onward.

regulated recruitment from other Mediterranean-basin countries. These migrants were predominantly male, unskilled and semi-skilled workers of rural background, living frugally and sending their savings home. Between 1965 and 1973 their numbers rose from some 40,000 to nearly 130,000 (Penninx 1979: 94).

Following the 1973 energy crisis the government halted foreign labour recruitment, however bilateral arrangements allowed guestworkers already in the country to bring over wives and children. Many labour migrants (especially Turks and Moroccans) did this, leading to a change in the ethnic composition of the guestworker population, from predominantly south European and Catholic to predominantly non-European and Muslim. Family reunification reached a peak in 1980 and effectively ended in the early 1990s. Today Turks and Moroccans constitute the largest ethnic minorities in the Netherlands after the Surinamese (Lucassen and Penninx 1997, Van der Leun 2003).

Refugees and asylum seekers account for much smaller, but still substantial, migrant flows. Their numbers increased steadily in the 1980s and peaked in 1994 (53,000 admitted), thereafter asylum policy became increasingly restrictive. At the same time, immigration to the Netherlands from other developed countries increased as a result of globalization and the robust Dutch economy. The 'new migration' (see Chapter 3) of the past two decades thus includes a variety of migrants, among which are a growing number of irregular migrants. Altogether, immigrants and their direct descendents make up roughly 9 per cent of the population in the Netherlands (Van Amersfoort 1998, Van der Leun 2003).

In sum: the Netherlands experienced a brief period from the late 1950s to the mid-1960s of informal labour migration from southern Europe. Much of this may be characterized as transient, in that most of the labourers returned home after a brief period. From 1964 to 1973 a guestworker period occurred, followed by family reunification from the mid-1970s to the mid-1990s. Postcolonial migration occurred in several waves between 1945 and the late 1980s, with the largest single influx arriving from Surinam in the mid-1970s. In terms of host-stranger relations, the first waves of postwar immigrants (labour migrants from southern Europe as well as the Dutch-Indonesians) are now considered as fully integrated into Dutch host society.

In contrast, the guestworker migrants and their families, as well as the Surinamese migrants from the 1970s and immigrants arriving in the past two decades from various non-European countries, have not sufficiently integrated in the eyes of many Dutch. Roughly speaking, migrants from the Caribbean now occupy a midway position between the 'successful' migrants from the Dutch East Indies at one end, and labour migrants from the Mediterranean-basin countries at the other end, with Moroccans often singled out as the most problematic (see below).

2.4.1 Postcolonial immigration policies, 1950s–70s

In the postwar period the Netherlands 'emphatically did not consider itself to be an immigration country' (Lucassen and Penninx 1997: 142). National policies reflected the official view that the country was hosting 'short-stay migrants'. Newcomers were referred to as repatriates, overseas citizens, foreign workers or refugees – not as 'immigrants'. At first, even the repatriates were assumed to be temporary, and 'diligent efforts were made to find a final destination for them "elsewhere", at least for some of them' (ibid.).

This attempt was soon abandoned and the government adopted a reception policy for the Dutch-Indonesian population that developed into an intensive indoctrination programme, with social workers instructing the newcomers in various aspects of Dutch middle-class norms, from housekeeping to childrearing. This policy of forced integration recalled the previous actions toward Dutch 'anti-social families', including '[s]ocial counselling and spiritual guidance', which were delegated to mostly church-affiliated civic organizations (ibid.: 142). Rath notes (1999: 160) that the migrants housed in hostels rented at government expense 'had particular difficulty in escaping from' well-meaning social workers.

National policies in the 1950s–70s toward postcolonial and guestworker migrants were also based on assumptions of temporariness:

[F]or as long as these migrants were to stay in the Netherlands some degree of adaptation and operation in society was thought necessary. Fitting in 'while retaining their own identity', as it was called for a long time, was not, however, seen in terms of a prolonged or even permanent stay, but was based on the assumption that they would return home (Lucassen and Penninx 1997: 143).

The myth of return guided national policy toward the Moluccan migrants in particular. Until 1954 the Moluccans were housed in isolated camps, with a special office responsible for all their basic needs, from food to pocket money. Later they were dispersed through the country in specially built communities which were meant to preserve their indigenous culture. This only prolonged their segregation and eventually led to an outburst of violence among the second generation.

2.4.2 Guestworker policy, 1964–73

In 1964 the Netherlands enacted a national guestworker policy, signing agreements with six sending countries between 1964 and 1970.[14] The bilateral treaties stipulated the work hours, health insurance and housing to be provided by employers in the first year. Guestworkers received temporary residence permits that were automatically renewable each year, and were allowed to bring first-order family members. After five years they could apply for a permanent residence permit. Nevertheless, both the government and the foreign workers assumed their stay was temporary (Van Amersfoort and De Klerk 1984: 201). Government policy addressed only their minimal needs, leaving the rest to the employers and civic organizations, often Church-based associations. They were thus spared the kind

---

[14] Portugal and Turkey (1964), Greece (1966), Morocco (1969), Tunisia and Yugoslavia (1970). Earlier agreements were signed with Italy (1960) and Spain (1961).

of intensive, paternalistic measures applied earlier to the Dutch-Indonesian and Moluccan immigrants. The assumed temporariness of the labour migrants meant that 'there was as yet no excessive pressure for their adjustment, and they had scope to develop their own communities' (Rath 1999: 161).

2.4.3 Accepting permanence: Minorities Policy, 1980–94

The turnaround in Dutch perceptions toward immigrants, from an assumption of temporariness to an acknowledgement of permanence, occurred at the end of the 1970s. Between 1966–77 a number of occupations and train hijackings by disenchanted Moluccan youths served as a wake-up call to Dutch society that it had a 'minority problem'. After 1973 it also became apparent that many 'guestworkers' were settling permanently, as family reunification increased (Lucassen and Penninx 1997: 149–50). In 1978 the government officially recognized the permanence of the Moluccan minority. In 1979 a government-commissioned 'Ethnic Minorities Report' redefined 'guestworkers' as permanent 'ethnic minorities' and proposed group-targeted policies for them as well as for the other 'ethnic minorities' (Penninx 1979: xi). A Minorities Policy was formulated in 1981 and formally adopted in 1983, confirming the Netherlands as 'an immigration country'.

The national 'Minorities Policy' (*Minderhedenbeleid*) targeted specific population groups whose disadvantaged position should be corrected through public policy. This created an official classification system of Strangers that was both ethnic-based and policy-oriented. The 'minority target groups' included Moluccans, Surinamese, Antilleans, refugees, gypsies, caravan dwellers and labour migrants from eight recruitment countries. Immigrant groups that were not considered socially disadvantaged (Indonesians, EU nationals, etc.) were classified within the broader category of 'allochtones', a technical term used to distinguish them from ethnic Dutch 'autochtones'. In 1993 this classification was adjusted, resulting in eight categories: Surinamese, Antilleans, Turks, Moroccans, South Europeans, Other non-industrialized, Other industrialized, and Dutch. The first six groups (i.e. migrants from poor countries) fall into the official rubric of 'ethnic minorities'.[15] At this point, the distinction between Strangers of postcolonial origin and those of guestworker origin largely disappeared within the label of 'ethnic minorities', and migrants of Dutch-Indonesian origin officially disappeared as a category of Strangers in Dutch society.

The Minorities Policy proclaimed the Netherlands to be a multiethnic society that recognizes the social and economic problems facing its 'ethnic minorities'. The basis of the new policy was to enable minorities to integrate while retaining their own cultural and ethnic distinctiveness, i.e. accepting their Otherness. In terms of

---

[15] The new definition is based on the native country of the individual as well as of each parent. Countries are classified according to three categories: Netherlands (A), Other Rich Countries (A2) and Other Countries (B). Individuals from B countries are considered as a potential target population for policy, of which the so-called B1 are the actual target groups. (Musterd et al. 1998)

host-stranger relations, this reflected a Pluralist attitude to migrant integration. In practice, it extended existing arrangements within the Dutch pillar system to include the new ethnic minorities. The latter were encouraged to establish ethnic-based associations, seen as crucial to the 'maintenance and development of their own culture and identity' (Lucassen and Penninx 1997: 151).

Combining pillarization and a welfare state approach to ethnic minority needs, the Dutch state applied communitarian solutions supported through public funding. This included support for ethnic-based organizations, Muslim and Hindu schools, ethnic-based radio stations, etc. Until 1984 mosques were also subsidized, following the precedent of churches and synagogues. The new policy also eased naturalization procedures, extended local voting rights to all foreign residents with over three years' residency, and encouraged local authorities to establish migrant advisory councils.

The second aim of the Minorities Policy was to eliminate existing gaps between indigenous Dutch and the designated ethnic minorities, particularly in housing, education and the labour market. Government policies were accordingly adjusted to take into account the social and economic disadvantages of designated minority populations. In education, for example, the government introduced a system of extra funding to schools based on the number of 'ethnic minority' pupils, in addition to a national education programme (OETC) to support mother-tongue classes.

2.4.4 *Reaction to Minorities Policy, 1994–present*

The Netherlands' transformation into a multiethnic society was less accepted in the host society than government policy might imply. The realization that Holland had become home to permanent ethnic minorities also led to a rise in anti-immigrant feelings, but this 'undercurrent of racism was long ignored by officialdom' (Van der Horst 2001: 301). It was only in the 1990s that a public debate emerged on majority-minority relations in the Netherlands, and in particular on the perceived separatism of the country's 650,000 Muslims.[16] As the media increasingly linked social problems and crime with immigration and ethnic minorities, second-generation Moroccan youth were singled out as the embodiment of the threatening Other. Anti-Muslim feelings were also fed by external events throughout the 1990s, as in the rest of Europe. After 1992, illegal immigration to the Netherlands became a particular cause of public concern (see below).

The political outcome first became visible at the local level: in 1990, only 11 Far Right candidates gained seats in local councils throughout the Netherlands; by 1994 there were 87 councillors (Mamadouh 2002: 11). At the national level, the mainstream parties managed to effectively marginalize anti-immigrant sentiments for two decades (Van der Horst 2001: 308–9). This politically correct consensus was finally broken by an outsider to the political system in 2002. Pim Fortuyn

---

[16] For one climax of this debate in the media, see P. Scheffer, 'Het multiculturele drama', *NRC Handelsblad*, 29 January 2000.

reframed the discourse on host-stranger relations in the Netherlands, depicting Islam as the religious, intolerant Other threatening the secular-liberal, tolerant Dutch host society. Fortuyn did not run on an anti-migrant platform *per se*, rather he articulated popular views regarding 'the "failure of the multicultural society"', focusing on the perceived separatism of the Muslim minorities (Mamadouh 2002: 12).

In March 2002 the newly formed Pim Fortuyn List (LPF), gained a spectacular victory in the Rotterdam local elections. In May 2002, Fortuyn was assassinated by an animal rights activist. In the national elections that followed, the LPF shook the political system, leading to the formation of the Netherlands' first Centre-Right government in the postwar period.[17] The 'Fortuyn phenomenon' opened the door to an unprecedented, no-holds-barred, often populistic debate on immigration. After decades of technocratic policymaking, the integration of migrants/minorities became politicized as never before. A sense of crisis appeared in Dutch host-stranger relations, especially after the religiously motivated murder of filmmaker Theo Van Gogh by a second-generation Moroccan migrant in Amsterdam (November 2004). This was seen by many as further proof of some fundamental failure in the Pluralist model of integration.

Indeed, public criticism of the Pluralist approach as espoused in the Minorities Policy had already surfaced in the late 1980s. Indirectly, this was connected to another debate, over reform of the Dutch welfare state. While unemployment among Dutch workers declined during most of the 1980s and 1990s, it remained stubbornly high among Turks and Moroccans who were left behind in the restructuring of the economy. This highlighted the apparent inefficiency of the Minorities Policy: after a decade of massive spending, minority shortfalls in labour and education had not been significantly diminished. Critics tied this failure to the government's over-sensitivity to the specific needs of ethnic minorities. Rather than promoting the integration of ethnic minorities, they claimed, the minority-specific measures stigmatized the target groups as passive beneficiaries of the welfare state, and encouraged separatism.

Consequently, from the mid-1990s the Netherlands shifted away from ethnically targeted policies and toward a more universalist approach. In 1994 the government issued new guidelines incorporating most of the specific measures aimed at combating ethnic minority arrears into general social policies. The new approach restricted welfare measures, devolved policymaking from national to local authorities and shifted funding to more Assimilationist-type programmes. In 1998 a national Newcomers Policy was adopted, including a Newcomers Civic Integration Law that made Dutch-language and civic courses compulsory for all immigrants of non-EU origin. This policy change was first initiated by local

---

[17] The new coalition (VVD and Pim Fortuyn List) collapsed in October 2002. The January 2003 elections restored the strength of the mainstream parties, while the LPF without Fortuyn won only seven seats.

authorities unhappy with the perceived failure of the Minorities Policy (Section 4.5, below).

3 The Local Context

> In this city there is nobody who does not trade in something ... Everyone is so preoccupied by his own profit that I could live here for all my life without ever being noticed by anyone.
> R. Descartes, newcomer to Amsterdam ca. 1635, cited in Mak 1999: 100.

Amsterdam's reputation as a cosmopolitan city goes back at least 400 years. During the city's Golden Age (1600–50) French Huegenots, Portuguese Jews, Antwerpan merchants, German peasants and others tripled the population from 50,000 to 150,000. By the mid-seventeenth century Amsterdam was a veritable 'city of outsiders', with over half its residents born elsewhere (ibid.). Newcomers were tolerated as long as they were seen as contributing to the city's economic growth, and Amsterdam's ruling classes were careful to accommodate religious and ideological differences as long as they did not endanger the city's carefully built prosperity. Geert Mak describes (pp. 77–8) 'the manner in which Amsterdam's administration reacted to dissident [religious] groups over the centuries', noting that already in the fifteenth century local authorities applied a policy of *gedogen* in avoiding the application of its own strict penal codes in matters of morality (brothels, for instance). 'In political matters, too, the city administrators gave priority to the avoidance of potential unrest. Battling it out for the sake of principles was left to others' (ibid.).

In recent decades Amsterdam has regained its reputation as a gateway city. Postwar labour immigration to Amsterdam was slow at first, due to the city's small industrial base. In the late 1960s Amsterdam hosted possibly 2000 Italian and Spanish guestworkers; by 1973 Turkish and Moroccan labour migrants accounted for another 9000 legally resident migrants, or just over 1 per cent of the city's population. After the 1973 ban on further recruitment, the Turkish and Moroccan population rose sharply through family reunification, approaching 25,000 *documented* residents by 1978 (nearly 3.5 per cent of the city population) (Penninx 1979). Surinam's independence in 1975 resulted in the city's largest single influx, when 10,000 Surinamese settled in Amsterdam (see below).

In the 1980s–90s, asylum seekers and refugees became a significant element in the migrant population, along with economically-motivated migrants from around the world. Altogether, Amsterdam's migrant/minority population more than doubled between 1961 and 1981, with an annual increase of 1 per cent in the share of non-native residents through the 1980s (**Figure 7.1**). This levelled off during the 1990s, but in that decade some 30,000 native Dutch left the city. As a result, Amsterdam now has one of the highest proportions of migrant-origin populations among European cities: of its 738,763 residents (in 2004), 359,632

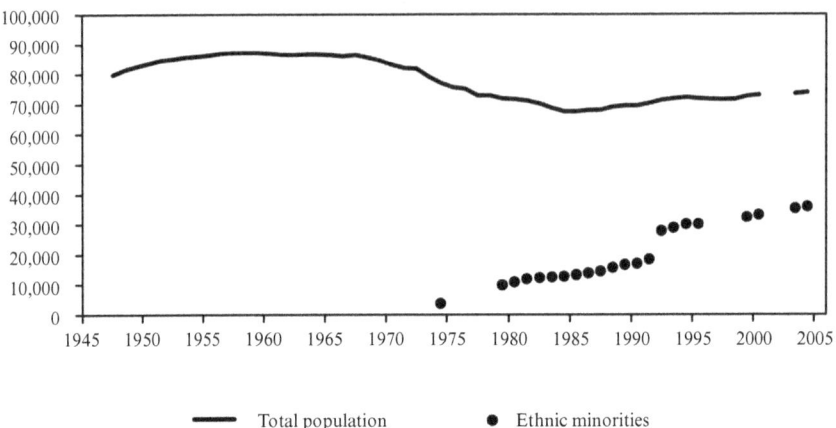

Figure 7.1 Population of Amsterdam and 'ethnic minorities', 1947-2004

Note: Data vary according to the definition of 'ethnic minorities'. Between 1947-1979 no precise data are available; in 1975 there were an estimated 38,000 'ethnic minorities'. Since 1979 'ethnic minorities' is defined by specified countries according to family head; from 1992 it includes all residents born in or with at least one parent from Category B countries. Surinam, Antilles, Turkey, Morocco, South Europe, and Other Non-industrialized Countries.

Source: Data compiled from Amsterdam Research and Statistics Bureau 2005; Wintershoven 2001.

were of non-Dutch origin, or 48.7 per cent of the population (Amsterdam Research and Statistics Bureau 2005). In addition, some 18,000 illegal immigrants were estimated to reside in Amsterdam (Van der Leun 2003: 15).

Amsterdam's migrant/minority population is extremely diverse, reflecting the city's role in the global economy (Nijman 2000). Eight out of 10 migrant/minority residents came from non-industrialized countries (288,000 residents, or 39 per cent of the city population); another 72,000 (a tenth of the city's population) came from industrialized countries.[18] The three largest ethnic minority populations are Surinamese-and-Antilleans, Moroccans and Turks (**Figure 7.2**). Among Amsterdammers below the age of 25, some 50 per cent are already of non-Dutch origin (of whom, two-thirds were born in the Netherlands). Within two decades at most, ethnic-Dutch residents will be a minority, albeit the largest, in Amsterdam (Municipality of Amsterdam 1999: 5) (**Figure 7.3**).

---

[18] In 2002, Amsterdam's largest contingents of foreign-origin residents were from Surinam (72,000), Morocco (59,000), Turkey (36,000), former Dutch East Indies (21,000), Germany (17,000), Antilles/Aruba (12,000), Ghana (10,000) and UK (8,000) (Amsterdam Bureau of Statistics 2003).

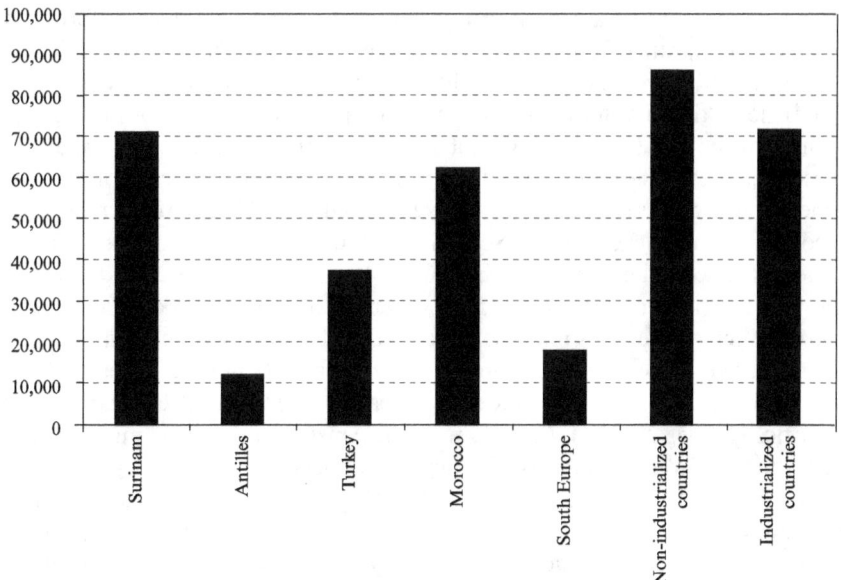

Figure 7.2   Resident population in Amsterdam, by country of origin (numbers)

Source: Data compiled from Amsterdam Research and Statistics Bureau, 2005.

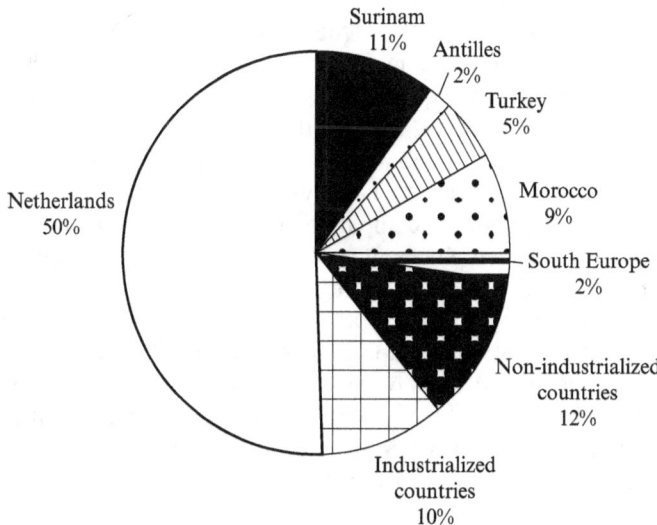

Figure 7.3   Resident population in Amsterdam, by country of origin (%)

Source: Amsterdam Research and Statistics Bureau, 2005.

Since Amsterdam's espoused and enacted migrant policies differentiate between immigrants from industrialized countries (Category A countries, see above) and those from non-industrialized countries (the officially targeted 'ethnic minorities'), this chapter focuses henceforth on the second type of Strangers as defined by the host society (see Chapter 2, above). In Amsterdam this population presents a clear picture of permanence. In 2001, over 44 per cent of the first-generation migrants had resided in the Netherlands over 15 years; over a third were second-generation (born in the Netherlands with at least one immigrant parent). Among the second generation, nine out of 10 are under 25 years old, meaning they are either in the school system or entering the labour market (Feijter et al. 2001). Much of the city's migrant policy is directed at this age cohort.

As noted above, socio-economic disadvantage is a built-in criterion in the official definition of 'ethnic minorities', creating a problem of circularity in the statistics (Phalet 2001: 4). Clearly, though, Amsterdam's ethnic minorities are below the city average in terms of educational levels and labour market position. In the Netherlands, pupils are separated into vocational and higher-education tracks already in secondary school, with minority children highly overrepresented in the vocational track. In addition, minority youth suffer a higher drop-out rate. In Amsterdam, second-generation children are narrowing the gap but shortfalls still exist (Phalet 2001, Musterd 2002a).

In the labour market, too, a significant gap exists between ethnic minorities and native Dutch. As Amsterdam has shifted from an industrial to a services-based economy, the economic polarization between native and migrant-origin residents has grown. In particular, unemployment among ethnic minority youth is now three times higher(!) than their Dutch age cohorts.[19] One positive indicator is the rise in ethnic entrepreneurship over the last two decades: in 1994 migrants were responsible for nearly a quarter of all new businesses in Amsterdam (see Kloosterman and Van der Leun 1999, Rath 2000).

In terms of residential distribution, public housing has played a dominant role in Amsterdam, mitigating the negative impacts of economic restructuring on the minority population. A comparison of nine European cities found that despite relatively high unemployment levels among Amsterdam's ethnic minority residents, the level of residential segregation is relatively low, with 'very few small pockets of poverty' in the city (Musterd et al. 1998, Musterd 2002b: 6). Nevertheless, different ethnic groups are unevenly distributed across the 16 city districts. While the four districts of central and southwestern Amsterdam have the lowest proportions of ethnic minority residents (17–25 per cent), in several districts in west and east Amsterdam the proportion more than doubles, to 48–56 per cent. In the southeastern district of Bijlmermeer, over 61 per cent of

---

[19] Between 1991 and 1998 the unemployment rate of Amsterdam's native Dutch residents fell from 12 to 5 per cent, while unemployment rates for Turkish, Moroccan and Surinamese residents fell, respectively, from 30 to 21 per cent, 30 to 17 per cent and 25 to 9 per cent (Burgers and Musterd 2002).

the residents are 'ethnic minorities' (Amsterdam Research and Statistics Bureau 2000) (**Figures 7.4, 7.5**).

The current pattern of distribution reflects different processes of migrant settlement and residential choices over the past decades (Van Amersfoort and De Klerk 1984). In the 1960s labour migrants concentrated in the city centre where hostels and cheap flats were available. In 1973 the majority of Turkish and Moroccan migrants still resided in the city centre and parts of the surrounding nineteenth century inner belt. A decade later, many had moved to social housing in the outer neighbourhoods. This was due to family reunification on one hand, and the increasing availability of the public housing stock on the other hand (due to suburbanization and local housing policy, see below). Over the past 20 years the rather uneven dispersal of the migrant population from central Amsterdam to the outer neighbourhoods has continued, resulting in 'clusters' of Moroccan and Turkish concentrations in the western and eastern neighbourhoods (Musterd and Deurloo 2002).

The Surinamese pattern of settlement was somewhat different, as their arrival in Amsterdam coincided with newly constructed housing projects in the Southeast district (Bijlmermeer). Many subsequently remained in 'the Bijlmer', creating Amsterdam's most visibly ethnic neighbourhoods (**Box 7.1**). But even in these concentrations the segregation levels are not very high and Amsterdam's three largest minority groups are 'certainly not establishing ethnic ghettos' (ibid.: 502).

The absence of highly ethnically-segregated neighbourhoods is a direct legacy of Amsterdam's long-term urban policy. In the nineteenth century, when Haussmannian-style policies were setting future patterns of segregation in Paris and other European capitals, Amsterdam 'failed' to carry out similar massive renovation of its historic areas, for a variety of reasons (see Wagenaar 1993, 2001). From the early twentieth century onwards and until recently, the city council pursued a consistent policy of public housing construction across all parts of the city. This resulted in relatively low levels of residential segregation despite the widening economic gap between Dutch-origin and ethnic minority residents. Amsterdam's public housing policy, combined with more general suburbanization trends, has meant that the city's main fault-lines of residential segregation run between families with children (Dutch and minority-origin) and non-family households, rather than strictly along ethnic lines.[20]

---

[20] The overall division of residential patterns in the city thus falls into three main housing types: minority family households, Dutch family households, and non-family households (largely Dutch), rather than strictly along ethnic lines (Van Amersfoort and De Klerk 1984: 220; Clark et al. 1992).

170   *Cities and Labour Immigration*

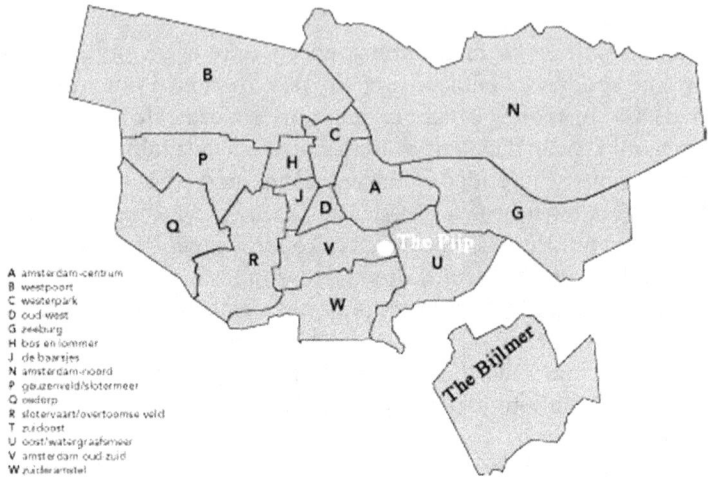

Figure 7.4   Amsterdam, city districts

Source: Amsterdam Research and Statistics Bureau 2003.

Figure 7.5   Geographical distribution of migrant/minority population in Amsterdam

Note: '% of foreigners' refers to the percentage of first- and second-generation residents of non-Dutch origin, per sub-district. The numbers in parentheses refer to the total number of sub-districts in each percentile.

Source: Amsterdam Research and Statistics Bureau 2003.

Box 7.1 The Bijlmer: Amsterdam's ethnic district

In the late 1960s the Bijlmermeer area was planned and constructed as a massive residential project to ease Amsterdam's housing shortage. Physically separated from the rest of the city, the new Southeast district contained high-rise tower blocks with spacious apartments surrounded by green areas. These modernist planning principles, however, did not attract the Dutch families for whom 'the Bijlmer' was intended, and thousands of flats remained vacant. When the first wave of Surinamese immigrants arrived in 1974–75 they quickly settled in the area, leading to further out-migration of the Dutch residents. The second Surinamese influx (1979) made the Bijlmer 'Surinam's second largest city'. Altogether, over 30,000 Surinamese and Antilleans reside in this district – by far the dominant ethnic group of any area in Amsterdam.

The Bijlmer suffers from a concentration of social problems, high unemployment and crime rates. But it also serves as a starting base for many migrant businesses and is the centre of Caribbean and African cultural life in Amsterdam. In the 1980s–90s low-rise and single-family houses were constructed in the district's newest neighbourhoods, attracting middle-class Surinamese and Dutch residents. Meanwhile, newer immigrants (mostly from Africa), continue to settle in the older, poorer parts of the Bijlmer.

In 1992 a cargo plane from nearby Schiphol airport crashed into one of the Bijlmer apartment blocks, killing 40 residents, mostly undocumented immigrants. Following an initial wave of sympathy, the authorities offered a one-time amnesty to illegal residents near the crash site. It soon turned out that hundreds of undocumented migrants from other areas were exploiting the amnesty offer. This fanned anti-immigrant sentiments and henceforth the Bijlmer came to symbolize illegal immigration as an increasingly politicized issue in the Netherlands.

The creation of the Bijlmer bears resemblance to the development of Paris's 'Chinatown' in that city's 13th district. There, a wave of immigrants from Asia turned an unattractive 1960s high-rise residential project that was intended for middle-class Parisians, into a thriving ethnic enclave. However, Paris's Chinatown is located well inside the city, while the Bijlmer is located 'outside the city walls', making it more similar to the public housing estates outside Paris.

Sources: Van der Horst 2001; Pinçon 2001.

4   Migrant Policies in Amsterdam

4.1   Political-institutional Context: Council-led, Consensual, Left-wing

Three features of policymaking in Amsterdam have a direct bearing on that city's local migrant policies. First, in contrast to the other cities in this book, policymaking is council-led, rather than mayoral. The second feature is a consensual style of governance, which partly accounts for minimal opposition to local policies. Third is Amsterdam's particularly left-wing political scene, which explains in part the city's response to ethnic diversity.

Amsterdam is governed by a City Council (*Gemeenteraad*) of 45 members, elected for four years. Overall municipal policy is decided by the Council, with permanent 'advisory committees' (chaired by an alderman) formulating policies in specific areas, e.g. education. Ongoing policy decisions and coordination occur in the Council's executive (the *College*), which consists of eight aldermen who are appointed by the coalition parties. The Council and College are chaired by the mayor, who is appointed by the Crown for a (renewable) period of six years. His responsibilities include public order and the municipal police, as well as External Relations. The mayor's role is both symbolic and functional, serving as a kind of mediator above the council's coalition politics.

In 1990 local policymaking was decentralized, transferring considerable authority and resources from City Hall to the city's 14 District Councils. The latter (elected during municipal elections, with each council then electing a district mayor) are now responsible for many issue areas, including education, culture, housing and public facilities. While the central municipality remains in charge of long-term strategic policy, police and health care, major infrastructure and housing (to some extent), decentralization has considerably diminished the effectiveness of City Hall's official minorities policy in the past decade, as the different districts vary in their policies toward migrants (see Wolff 1999).

The Dutch style of governance is based on consensus-building, with decisions usually reached after extensive consultation at all levels. A high degree of formal centralization is combined with a highly interdependent system of policymaking at the national, provincial and municipal levels. Thus, some 90 per cent of local authority budgets come from the national government (including funding calculated according to the city's 'ethnic minorities' population), but each local authority spends this money as it sees fit. In Amsterdam, consensus-building takes place in numerous advisory committees and other channels of participation. This process is long and often laborious but it facilitates the co-optation of outside elements into the system (a lesson learned from the city's confrontational politics in the 1960s–70s). Since then, Amsterdam's decision-making process has taken place 'in an open-government style': council debates are broadcast live on local cable radio, public hearings are often held before important decisions and preparatory committee meetings are open to the public (Kraal and Zorlu 1998: 26). Even the architecture of Amsterdam's new City Hall is meant to convey openness and transparency (see Box 1.1, Chapter 1 above).

Some feel that the various participatory mechanisms do not genuinely open the decisionmaking process, but act primarily as channels for letting off steam and gaining legitimacy for policies that are ultimately made by municipal politicians and technocrats. Since the 1980s, Amsterdam's various advisory councils, open hearings and so on served to diffuse potential opposition to migrant policies, either from Right-wing parties or ethnic minority groups. In the case of the latter, generous allocations of public money have also been used to co-opt potential troublemakers (see below) (interviews E. Adusei, A. Menebhi; Pirschner 2002: 102).

Amsterdam's city council has long been dominated by the PvdA (the Labour Party), which formed broad coalitions that left out the extreme Left and extreme Right. In fact, until the mid-1990s Amsterdam's council had no representatives of the extreme Right. In 2002, while Amsterdammers followed the siren call of Fortuyn in the national elections, they did not swing to the right in the municipal elections. Thus, the PvdA retained its 15 seats in the new city council, and there was little change in the other parties (although one extreme-Right list did gain a seat in 2002).[21]

In 1985 the Netherlands extended local voting rights to non-citizen residents. Since then the number of ethnic-origin councillors in Amsterdam has steadily increased, from three in 1986 to 11 in 1998. Today all the major lists in Amsterdam contain minority-origin representatives (Berger et al. 2001: 39–40). The role of ethnic-origin councillors is ambivalent. They are clearly recruited by local party lists as ethnic representatives (whether this expresses a sincere belief in the need for minority representation, or a cynical attempt to draw 'the ethnic vote', depends on one's point of view). Yet, once elected they are not supposed to behave as sectarian representatives, as this would smack of clientilism (Van Heelsum 2002). In the current city council (2002–06) ethnic-origin councillors (Surinamese, Moroccan, Turkish and Ghanaian) reflect the proportion of those ethnic groups in Amsterdam, but not the overall ethnic minority population which corresponds to another 2–3 councillors. There is only one ethnic-origin alderman.

4.2 *From Non-policy to Guestworker Policies, Late 1950s to Mid-1970s*

In the late 1950s and early 1960s small numbers of foreign workers began arriving in Amsterdam from Italy and Spain. Most of them returned home after a short time, although some gained permanent resident status. In terms of our typology, this can be identified as the first, 'Transient', phase in postwar migration to

---

[21] One reason for this was that Pim Fortuyn did not field any candidates in Amsterdam's local elections and distanced himself from the extreme anti-immigrant list, *Leefbaar Amsterdam*. The city council of 2002–06 is headed by the PvdA in coalition with the Conservative Liberals (VVD) and Christian Democrats (CDA).

Amsterdam. The municipality was aware of their presence (by the early 1960s up to a thousand workers were lodging in cheap accommodations, mostly in the city centre), but refrained from any specific policies. After all, housing was the responsibility of their employers (mostly large industries), and for other needs they could turn to local churches and other institutions of the 'Catholic pillar'.

In the mid-1960s a national guestworker policy was initiated and the number of foreign labourers in Amsterdam grew to several thousands. Soon workers from Turkey and North Africa outnumbered those from southern Europe. Despite early signs of family reunification, the local authorities as well as most of the labour migrants shared the myth of return: after a few years the *gastarbeiders* (guestworkers) would surely go home. This assumption framed the city's policies until the mid-1970s, as expressed in the area most crucial to newcomers: housing. National policy required employers to provide guestworkers with lodging during their first year. Workers were lodged mostly in boarding houses as well as a few specialized accommodations arranged by large-scale employers. The largest of these was 'Camp Ataturk', a barracks set up in 1966 by the shipbuilding company NDSM, which accommodated between 400 to 500 Turkish workers for almost a decade, near the port in North Amsterdam (Van Amersfoort and De Klerk 1984).

In principle, labour migrants with more than two years of legal residence in the city could also access Amsterdam's large stock of social housing.[22] But the nature of the allocation system shut out migrants from all but the most marginal housing. Although the formal criteria were universal, the social housing corporations, each representing a different 'pillar' in the host society, had a wide margin of discretion which allowed widespread discrimination against outsiders.[23] Belonging to none of the existing pillars, labour migrants were at the bottom of the ladder in social housing allocation. Most therefore found lodging either in the lower end of the private (rent-controlled) market or in the worst of the public housing. Although both sectors were theoretically under municipal supervision, the city took no action against the often illegal lodging of guestworkers. Illegal subletting of rooms in social housing was rampant: around 1970 an estimated 2000 or more Moroccans and Turks were living in illegal boarding houses, mostly in the city centre and surrounding nineteenth-century belt. The municipality also ignored the overcrowding resulting from migrants renting rooms intended for single occupancy, and then lodging family members as they arrived (Van Amersfoort and De Klerk

---

[22] From the beginning of the twentieth century, municipal housing policies created a large social housing stock, which today accounts for some 60 per cent of all housing in Amsterdam. The cheapest stock is council housing, while the better social housing stock is owned and managed by (non-profit) local housing corporations. In addition, much of the private rental housing is rent-controlled, so that the large majority of housing in Amsterdam is formally under municipal supervision.

[23] Amsterdam's housing corporations were established in the early twentieth century following the pillarization system, i.e. one housing corporation was linked to the Socialist 'pillar', another to the Catholic 'pillar', etc.

1984: 202). This *gedogen*-like policy had several causes. First, a severe housing shortage limited the city's ability to provide alternatives. Second, the presence of labour migrants and their dependents was considered temporary. Thus, City Hall's inaction regarding migrant housing was a matter of inability *and* lack of will.

Local officials also viewed the social and economic needs of the labour migrant population through the Guestworker framework, assuming minimal responsibility. The bilateral agreements signed between the Netherlands and the sending countries gave guestworkers access to basic health and welfare services. For other (social and cultural) needs, the municipality assumed that churches and other civic organizations would address these, based on experience with the earlier Spanish and Italian migrants. Indeed, as the number of labour migrants from Muslim countries grew, some outreach efforts were made by churches toward these newcomers.

4.3   Accepting Permanence: Migrant Policies from the Mid-1970s

During the 1970s, as it became less and less viable to ignore the signs of permanent settlement and mounting needs of the guestworker population, the assumptions and expectations in City Hall regarding this population began to change. The shift in Amsterdam's response began with limited measures regarding housing needs and migrant associations, and culminated in 1982 with a local 'Minorities Policy' that officially sealed the Guestworker phase.

Housing

In the 1970s the dire housing situation of labour migrants gained increasing attention at both the national and municipal level (Musterd et al. 1998: 35). In the 'hot summer' of 1972 riots broke out in a Rotterdam working-class neighbourhood between local residents and Turkish and Moroccan migrants, on the backdrop of general social unrest. In Amsterdam, several fatal fires in overcrowded lodgings highlighted the dangerous conditions in which foreign workers were housed. Amsterdam's city council decided it had to avert a possible crisis. The city began with lodging controls and inspections in the municipally-owned social housing sector. Some illegal lodgings were upgraded, others were closed and their tenants moved to council housing units, often in blocks designated for eventual demolition. However, these ad hoc solutions could not solve the basic housing needs of a growing population.

In 1975 the municipality began to regulate the housing situation in earnest. In particular, the presence of migrant families lodging in tiny flats was recognized, and attempts were made to find suitable solutions.[24] At first, migrants who were

---

[24]   Until the mid-1970s, labour migrants wishing to bring over family members faced a Catch-22 situation: the Aliens Law allowed reunification only if adequate accommodation had been found for the family, but housing regulations stipulated that in order to apply for a larger flat one's family had to be legally resident. As a result, labour migrants housed their families illegally in flats that they rented as singles.

housing family members in 1–2 room social housing flats were allowed to apply for family-size units. This was not an official policy decision; instead, the municipality applied pressure on the housing corporations to open up their stock of larger flats to labour migrants and their families. The corporations resisted, but after a report commissioned by the municipality (1978) revealed their discriminatory allocation practices, they began to cooperate with City Hall to regularize the migrants' housing situation.

Amsterdam's policy in social housing allocation complemented two other factors to ease the housing situation for migrants. The first was suburbanization, which opened up more of the social housing stock to newcomers, enabling guestworkers and their families to move out of their small dwellings in the city centre to larger ones in surrounding neighbourhoods. This succession process was especially dramatic in the new public housing neighbourhoods in west Amsterdam where the original Dutch inhabitants were migrating to the new suburban towns.

The second factor was urban renovation. From the mid-1970s and throughout the 1980s the government funded cities to upgrade their deteriorated public housing stock. The 'building for the neighbourhood' programme then gave local residents priority in renting the renovated (or new) housing. Though not ethnically-targeted, this policy clearly benefited minority residents due to their prominence in the designated areas. Amsterdam's dispersed pattern of social housing and relatively compact size meant that its renovation policy was uniformly applied across the whole city. This in turn meant that the movement of some of the migrant populations, as a result of the higher rents in post-renovation areas, did not cause the kind of spatial polarization that occurred in other cities following renovation, as we saw in Paris.

Migrant mobilization
In another sign of labour migrant settlement, Moroccan and Turkish associational activity increased in the 1970s. In this policy area, however, the municipal response was hesitant, at least in comparison with Amsterdam's policies toward its postcolonial migrants. As early as 1968 a newly founded Surinamese organization 'received a leading role [by City Hall] in the provision of social policy to Surinamese in Amsterdam' (Vermeulen 2002). In 1972 subsidies were provided to a rival association. Thereafter, an 'impulsive local policy' threw money to quell increasingly militant demands by competing Surinamese organizations, amounting to over 5 million guilders a year between 1975 and 1984 (ibid.: 15–16). In contrast, Moroccan and Turkish mobilization did not arouse City Hall's interest, although some municipal funding did trickle down to a few labour migrant organizations that applied for subsidies. Still, in 1978 public funding for Turkish organizations was less than 2 per cent of the subsidies allocated to Surinamese organizations (ibid.). Such a discrepancy can only be explained by contrasting expectations regarding the presence of postcolonial and guestworker migrants in the 1970s. While Amsterdam officially acknowledged the permanence of its Surinamese

population in 1974 (preceding the national government by four years), it still regarded its Turkish and Moroccan migrants on the whole as 'guests'.

Summing up the first two decades of municipal responses to labour immigration, we can identify a period of Non-policy from the late 1950s to the mid-1960s, followed by a Guestworker-type response from the mid-1960s to the mid-1970s. At that point, the municipality began regularizing the housing situation of migrant families, reflecting a growing realization among local officials of the *possibility* of long-term settlement. Nevertheless, a new housing policy was not formally put into place until the 1980s. Meanwhile, the municipality largely ignored the growing activism of Turkish and Moroccan organizations during the 1970s. In contrast to the attention lavished on the Surinamese associations, official recognition of guestworker associations would only come in 1981. Unofficially, however, municipal expectations were clearly changing in the late 1970s, toward a full recognition that Amsterdam's guestworker population would not return to their countries of origin.

4.4 'Minorities Policy', 1980 to Mid-1990s

Amsterdam's first official acknowledgement of labour migrant permanence appeared in a 1978 'Policy memorandum concerning foreign workers in Amsterdam' which stated that local policy must begin with 'the fact that the presence of a considerable number of foreign employees in Dutch society is of a permanent nature' (cited in Musterd et al. 1998: 35). Two draft reports followed on policies toward migrants in housing and education, leading to a 1981 decision to institute a comprehensive local policy toward the city's ethnic minorities. In 1982 the city published its 'Memorandum concerning an integrated minorities policy'. This process roughly paralleled the shift at the national level (above), where the government formally accepted the permanence of the ethnic minorities in 1980.

Echoing the government's policy, Amsterdam's new Minorities Policy acknowledged not only the permanence of the city's new population but also its Otherness, 'based on the idea that minorities should integrate while also maintaining their cultural identity' (Kraal 2001: 20). From this point on, local migrant policies would not distinguish between migrants of postcolonial or guestworker origin. Instead, City Hall adopted the government's definition of five broad categories of Strangers, or 'ethnic minority target groups': Surinamese and Antilleans, Turks, Moroccans, South Europeans, and migrants from other non-industrialized countries. The policy's declared aims were to integrate these minorities through an equal-rights membership in society, by reducing minority disadvantages in the labour market, education and housing.

In practice, the first years following the 1982 memorandum were marked by few specific actions. In 1984 the newly elected alderman responsible for the minorities policy (Peter Jong) established a 'Minorities policy coordination bureau' to formulate specific actions for each of the 'ethnic minority target groups' and oversee their progress. The new bureau, numbering a handful of civil servants headed by a woman of Turkish origin, remained relatively isolated. According to Jong's successor, it 'did not try to change the mindset of the civil servants in the different departments' (interview J. Van der Aa). Instead, it formulated a policy document proposing some 150 actions that was approved by the College and city council, sent to the departments, and then ignored by the municipal bureaucracy. Jong's successor notes that the proposed actions (e.g. an affirmative hiring policy) were often vaguely worded and their implementation 'would have required a complete reorganization of the municipality' (ibid.).

Nevertheless, during the 1980s and 1990s the municipality did initiate a variety of actions, expressing a clearly Pluralist view of ethnic minority integration. These are described below, following the order of policy domains proposed in the typology (Chapter 3).

4.4.1 Legal-political domain

Ethnic minority advisory councils In 1985 Amsterdam established three ethnic-based 'minority advisory councils' to advise the city council on existing and proposed policies affecting minority communities. This occurred a year after the government extended the right to vote in local elections to non-citizen residents. Clearly, city council did not consider individual voting rights an adequate guarantee of migrant/minority incorporation in the local polity. The advisory councils thus reflected a communitarian attitude to integration based on communal representation (the city also established advisory councils for women and the gay community).

The minority advisory councils were composed of representatives of pre-selected migrant organizations from each community, ratified by the College and then appointed by city council. They were housed in City Hall, accorded their own budgets and secretarial staff. Their proposals were to be taken into account by councillors, aldermen and the mayor. In practice, the three advisory councils never attained substantial influence, as noted in several municipal reports (Vermuelen 2002: 24, Pirschner 2002: 84). Mounting dissatisfaction with their representativeness and effectiveness led to a restructuring in 1991, resulting in five new councils: TDM (Turks); SRM (Moroccans); SAAMGha (Surinamese, Antilleans/Arubians, Moluccans and Ghanaians); ZEG (South Europeans); and VluChiPa (Refugees, Chinese and Pakistanis).

Nevertheless, contentious relations between the ethnic advisory councils and the municipality re-surfaced and remained strong, until their dissolution in 2002. Municipal councillors and officials complained that the advisory councils were not functioning properly and insufficiently involved in presenting concrete advice. Advisory council members felt that they were not given sufficient resources to maintain ongoing contact with their communities (most of this was done by volunteers) and that their advice was never taken seriously in City Hall (Berger et al. 2001: 46, Pirschner 2002: 83).

According to one alderman, just as the municipal Minorities Bureau was out of touch with elected officials and bureaucrats, the advisory councils made up of the older first-generation activists were out of touch with their constituencies in the street. Following decentralization, the situation improved: 'When the districts got responsibility, they sought contacts directly with their residents, including minority residents, mosques, young activists...' (interview Van der Aa). For some, this made the advisory councils appear even more redundant (below).

Empowering migrant associations A central element in Amsterdam's Minorities Policy was encouraging migrant organizations to serve as vehicles of minority empowerment. Migrant associations were expected 'to promote and preserve cultural identities, to emancipate their constituencies and to serve as advocacy groups' (1984 *Gemeenteblad,* cited in Vermeulen 2002: 23). By the 1970s pillarization was considered rather irrelevant in regard to relations among the Dutch. But with the acknowledgement of new minorities in the country, the consociational approach, with its empowerment of civic minority organizations, was seen as the obvious way of integrating the newcomers. In the eyes of the host society, public support for ethnic-based organizations was considered the most natural way of accomplishing integration (just as in France it was seen as the most unnatural way of accomplishing integration).

To support migrant associations as leading players in the integration process, the municipality institutionalized their function as intermediaries between the host society and the migrant communities. In the early 1980s the 'Amsterdam Centre for Foreigners' (ACB) was established to provide organizational support and services to migrant organizations. Moroccan and Turkish organizations were largely overlooked at first. It took until the mid-1980s for the municipality to officially recognize the *labour migrant* associations 'as providers of certain services to their communities' (ibid.). A significant increase in municipal and state subsidies followed, totalling some 500,000 guilders annually for Turkish organizations alone in the second half of the 1980s.[25] Unlike in Rome, in Amsterdam the delegation of social and welfare services to migrant organizations supplemented, rather than replaced, the provision of targeted services provided directly by the municipality.

4.4.2 Socio-economic domain
Welfare services Service provision to migrants/minorities by the city's welfare department developed in two phases. In the first half of the 1980s the city acknowledged that its ethnic minority residents faced specific problems but there was still little experience or resources for migrant-targeted measures. In 1986 the Alderman for Welfare, P. Jong, instituted a new policy of 'general services where possible, targeted services where necessary'. By 1990 the municipality had established various migrant-targeted projects as well as ethnically-specific services (interview R. Van Oordt). The overriding motivation for this policy was practical rather than ideological, based on the alderman's assumption that fighting the

---

[25] Communication with Floris Vermeulen.

180   *Cities and Labour Immigration*

array of problems faced by the city's ethnic minorities could not be accomplished without 'target-group activities'. After 1990, most of the competencies in welfare policy devolved to the city districts, making it more difficult to speak of a 'municipal policy' in this area (see below).

Labour market policies The restructuring of the Netherlands into a post-industrial economy led to massive layoffs in traditional industries such as shipping and automobiles where many labour migrants were employed. In the Amsterdam area, restructuring resulted in a loss of some 60,000 jobs in industry between 1970 and 1995, a decrease of 40 per cent (Kraal 2001: 20). With their low educational levels and less-than-fluent Dutch, the labour migrants were left behind in the ensuing prosperity of the 1980s–90s. Structural unemployment hit first-generation immigrants especially hard. Regarded as productive labourers in the 1960s, the former guestworkers came to be seen by many native Dutch as an economic liability.

Getting minorities back into the labour market is thus presented nationally and locally as a key to successful integration (Burgers and Musterd 2002). Amsterdam specifically targeted its migrant population in two areas of labour policy. The first was an affirmative hiring policy within City Hall, one of the largest employers in the city. This had, at best, mixed results: at the end of the 1990s 'targeted ethnic minorities' accounted for 16.2 per cent of municipal personnel, mostly in lower positions, although they made up 26 per cent of the local labour force (Berger et al 2001: 41–3). Another project involved training migrants in the construction industry.

The second area was in the promotion of ethnic entrepreneurship. For example, one project (1987 to 1990) gave unemployed residents of ethnic minority origin short training courses in street vending and offered them hotdog stalls (for which there are normally long waiting lists). Another project was an 'Oriental market' developed by the municipality on a new waterfront site, with stalls rented out exclusively to ethnic minority residents. This was meant to replace a lively market in a migrant neighbourhood that the authorities had closed for sanitation reasons. The 'Oriental market' opened in 1992, after years of bureaucratic problems and heavy opposition from the local market vendors union. It proved an economic and political flop, closing within a year (Musterd et al. 1998: 40). These projects created a backlash against affirmative action, and the next city council (1994–98) abandoned any idea of ethnically-targeted labour market policies.

Education policies Amsterdam's schools policies have by and large followed national education policy. In the Netherlands' pillarized education system, local authorities are responsible for allocating buildings for 'public municipal' schools, 'public denominational' (i.e. Catholic, Protestant) schools, and 'special schools' (Islamic, Montessori, etc.). All are supervised and funded by the Ministry of Education, which covers over 80 per cent of their budget. The remaining 20 per cent is covered by the municipality and since 1990, by the city districts. In terms of local policy, the Alderman for Education must rely primarily on his 'powers of persuasion' before the school boards and directors (the latter are appointed by the alderman only in the public municipal schools) (interview J. van der Aa). Since 1990, this policy area has in large part devolved to the city districts.

Local schools policies in Amsterdam have been directed at three issue areas, namely segregation, multicultural education, and Islamic schools, discussed below. Segregation became a major issue in the 1980s, when the proportion of ethnic-origin pupils reached a critical mass in some schools, which became known as 'black schools' (*zwarteschool*). As the proportion of minority pupils grew, more Dutch parents enrolled their children in nearby 'white schools' (*witteschool*). As a result, Amsterdam's level of school segregation is higher than its residential segregation.

Minority-origin pupils now make up over half of the city's school population. Ironically, the term 'black school' normally means that most of the pupils are Moroccan and/or Turkish, although neither Moroccans nor Turks consider themselves 'black', and resent this labeling. At the same time, many black Surinamese parents avoid the *zwarteschool*, which they connect to lower educational achievements and unruly behaviour, preferring to enroll their children in mixed or 'white' schools. Apparently, Dutch parents (white as well as black) do not regard *zwarteschool/witteschool* as racial terms, although they clearly designate the pupils' ethnic background.[26]

The municipality of Amsterdam first addressed the 'black schools problem' in the mid-1980s. City council 'found it unacceptable that a small number of schools should have all the practical problems derived from the presence of large numbers of non-Dutch students, and they feared that "white flight" would further reinforce racist attitudes in Amsterdam' (Clark et al. 1992: 97). A proposal by the Alderman for Education, to require parents to enroll children in their neighbourhood school, was vigorously opposed by parents (native as well as minority-origin) and the municipal bureaucracy. Instead, the city council decided to direct extra resources to designated schools that were suffering from white flight. This so-called 'magnet school' policy was meant to bring back Dutch pupils through various incentives such as small classes and enriched extracurricular activities. Although two studies later commissioned by the municipality concluded that parents' choice of school in Amsterdam was based more on class than on ethnic differences (ibid.: 99–101), the issue of black/white schools has remained on the public agenda.

Intercultural education is another area where the municipality has had some leverage. In 1985 a national 'educational priority policy' was implemented, allocating additional funding to schools in designated disadvantaged areas, or with

---

[26] Interview, J. Roosblad. These terms also appear in public discourse and official documents and are not considered racist. For example, the national newspaper *NRC Handelsblad* headlined an article comparing schools in Amsterdam: 'No-one puts her white Anita in a black class' (*Niemand zet zijn blanke Anita in een zwarte klas*), 5 November 2002, p. 3.

a high proportion of minority pupils (Amsterdam had 11 'education priority areas' in 1986) (Musterd et al. 1998: 39). The government also offered funding to schools for providing mother-tongue classes, classes on minority religions, etc. (Phalet 2001). Amsterdam supplemented these policies with its own initiatives, diverting municipal funding from its social/cultural budgets to targeted schools. This policy came under increasing scrutiny in the 1990s and was abolished in 1994 (see below).

Another issue for local policymakers emerged in the mid-1990s, when several Islamic schools in the city expanded and demanded extra facilities, in effect competing with neighbouring public schools. As noted above, the pillarized educational system facilitates the establishment of 'specialized schools' by minority communities. Amsterdam alone has some 15 Islamic schools, out of some 260 schools in the city. Since 1990 the city districts are responsible for providing the appropriate facilities including the building, as required by Dutch law. Different city districts have responded differently, but like mosques, Islamic schools in Amsterdam were not considered a particularly controversial issue until recently.

4.4.3 Religion

Amsterdam hosts the largest Muslim population of any city in the Netherlands (some 180,000 residents, mostly Moroccans, Turks and some Surinamese). During the 1970s Muslims led a largely hidden existence in Dutch society. After the 1983 revision of the constitution guaranteed equality between all religions, Muslims could demand the same government resources previously doled out to the Catholic and Protestant pillars. However, that constitutional revision was intended to create a separation of Church and State, putting an end (in theory) to government financing of religious institutions. The result was that public support for minority places of worship was left largely for local authorities to decide.

At first, the debate on how to relate to Muslim institutions and practices (mosques, primary schools, ritual slaughter, cemeteries) was confined to local policymakers and bureaucrats, with little public involvement (Rath et al. 2001, 2004). Gradually, the presence of Islam in the Netherlands became an issue of broader concern, following events such as the 1989 Rushdie affair. During the 1990s, however, political correctness constrained the public debate on 'minority religions', a code-word for Islam. It was only after the 9/11 attacks (2001) that Pim Fortuyn placed the issue of Muslims' integration in Dutch society on centre stage (see above).

Against this background, Amsterdam's relatively tolerant policy toward Muslim institutions is another sign of that city's Pluralist attitudes. As Rath et al. showed, different local authorities in the Netherlands have shown different attitudes toward the institutionalization of Islam and its public practice at the local level.[27] After the November 2004 murder of Theo Van Gogh by an Islamic

---

[27] Rath et al. (2001, 2004) describe how Rotterdam defined its Muslim residents as *ethnic* minorities and thus eligible for public support, while Utrecht defined them as a *religious* minority and withheld municipal support for mosques, etc.

extremist in Amsterdam, Mayor Job Cohen expressed satisfaction that the city had not witnessed the kind of Christian-Muslim violence that occurred in other towns following the killing. He saw this as evidence that Amsterdam had been right in supporting Muslim institutions over the past decade to serve as intermediaries between their communities and the host society.[28]

Going back several decades, we can see how this policy evolved. During the 1960s the municipality ignored its Muslim guestworkers. At first, the faithful prayed in hostels, factories, etc. but as their numbers grew, it became clear that other solutions were required, especially during Ramadan. In the mid-1970s some municipal workers became privately involved in a voluntary 'Mosques Workgroup', established to locate temporary places of worship. From the late 1970s and into the 1980s the municipality tolerated improvised mosques set up by Turkish and Moroccan associations in various places, such as abandoned school buildings, although formally such mosques were illegal (Doomernik 1999). This arrangement recalls Amsterdam's *gedogen* policy toward unofficial Catholic churches some four centuries earlier.

By the mid-1980s the permanence of the Muslim minorities had been recognized; furthermore, Amsterdam's Muslim population had grown and splintered, creating a growing demand for mosques. City Hall responded by locating disused public buildings to serve as mosques and approving sites for the construction of purpose-built mosques. In the late 1980s, despite opposition by local residents, it approved a request by the Moroccan community to build its first mosque with a minaret, in east Amsterdam. The number of Turkish mosques alone grew from one in 1976, to six in 1981, to 10 in 1988 (ibid.).

Following the 1983 constitutional reform separating Church from State, the municipality decided to stop further subsidies for new religious facilities. At that time Amsterdam's Minorities Policy provided generous subsidies to migrant associations, but withheld municipal funding from religious organizations (Vermeulen 2002). However a considerable number of migrant associations were in fact of a religious nature (known as 'mosque associations'). A debate ensued in city council on municipal aid to the mosque associations and their role in the city. Some council members feared that funding religious organizations would strengthen separatism; others felt that isolating the Muslim communities was more dangerous.

To address the issue, a 'work group on religious facilities' was established and produced a typical compromise: the municipality would not subsidize religious facilities or organizations as such, however, the latter could apply for municipal funding for any non-religious activities.[29] To fit the new criteria, religious associations redefined themselves as social-cultural organizations, and applied for municipal subsidies for activities (ranging from computer classes to a course

---

[28] 'The new Dutch model?', *The Economist*, 2 April 2005: 22–4.
[29] 'Municipal policy regarding religious facilities of ethnic minorities', 1985 (cited in Landman 1992).

for teaching Moroccan women to ride bicycles) held inside the mosques. Since there was little to no monitoring of these activities, in effect the municipality continued to indirectly subsidize the mosques (Landman 1992: 289–90). This *gedogen* solution seemed to suit everyone involved.

In the 1990s the mosque issue was delegated to the city district councils. Generally, these have tried to balance between the demands of Muslim organizations and those of local residents (including some Muslims) who oppose additional mosques. One example is the conflict in the Baarsjes district in west Amsterdam (**Box 7.2**).

Box 7.2   The Aya Sofya Mosque conflict

In 1990 the Turkish mosque association Milli Gürüs proposed to construct a large (4000 m^2) mosque on a disused plot in the Baarsjes district, in west Amsterdam. The Baarsjes hosts a large Turkish and Moroccan population and already has a Moroccan mosque. The district had just prepared a zoning plan proposing the establishment of a smaller (1000 m^2) Turkish mosque on a different site. The Milli Gürüs proposal provoked a NIMBY reaction (Not In My Back Yard) among local residents, worried about the traffic and parking problems that such a large mosque would generate. The Aya Sofya mosque was also opposed by Left-wing Turkish residents who viewed Milli Gürüs as a fundamentalist organization.

The Baarsjes district council rejected the Milli Gürüs proposal, since the proposed site was designated for residential use. Milli Gürüs then bought the plot despite the zoning restriction. The district council saw this as flaunting its authority (a sensitive issue in the Baarsjes, whose council had been waging a long campaign against lawlessness in the area). After several years and court litigation, a compromise was reached: Milli Gurus would sell most of the plot to a housing association, and construct a smaller mosque on the remaining area.

Lindo concludes that the Baarsjes district council was not opposed to a visible Islamic presence *per se* in the neighbourhood. Rather, the long-running argument over the Aya Sofya mosque presents a planning conflict over competing land uses.

Sources: Lindo 1999; interview F. Lindo.

4.4.4 Housing and urban renewal policies
During the 1980s public concern with urban poverty and crime increased in the Netherlands as elsewhere. A succession of national policies channeled vast sums of money to the cities for carrying out urban renewal and tackling their social problems. The aim was to coordinate new and existing measures and territorialize them for maximum effect. A package of measures was to be

drawn up by local authorities for specific areas, including physical renovation, strengthened neighbourhood social services, extra resources for schools, etc.[30] These programmes emphasized the need for a social component in the urban renewal of the designated areas, recalling the *Politique de la ville* in France at the same time (see Chapter 6).

Unlike the other domains noted above, housing and urban renewal are officially 'ethnically blind' policy areas in the Netherlands, i.e. the ethnic element was not explicitly taken into account. For example, the proportion of ethnic minority residents was not included as a criterion in designating urban renewal areas. But the language of these policies referred to an 'accumulation of problems' in those areas, implying also the concentration of 'ethnic minorities' (which were defined according to low socio-economic status, as noted above). According to one scholar, 'The ethnic minorities were always seen as part of the problem [of urban decay], but not as the cause'. Following this reasoning, urban policies were designed to attract middle-class Dutch-origin residents to designated areas rather than dispersing the existing residents (interview L. de Klerk). This can be termed a gentrification policy that aims to limit dispersal of the existing resident population.

Unlike in Paris, in Amsterdam dispersion policies are officially forbidden, nor is such a policy pursued informally. Since 1979 such an option has not even been debated in Amsterdam, while proposals to apply dispersion policy to schools (desegregation) never got past the debating stage (Musterd et al. 1998: 37–8). Musterd et al. concluded (p. 40) that most housing policies in the city 'do not have a specifically ethnic component; ethnic groups profit just like autochton inhabitants.' Nevertheless, the ethnic element was *implicitly* there, due to the over-representation of ethnic minorities in the neighbourhoods designated for urban renewal. Thus, although the kind of ethnic targeting that characterized Amsterdam's Minorities Policy was not applied in local housing and urban development policies in the 1980s, they were nevertheless *perceived* as channeling public money toward ethnic minorities in this domain as well.

4.5   Reacting to Multiculturalism: 'Diversity Policy' from Mid-1990s

The 1994 elections signalled the beginning of a new phase in Amsterdam's response to migration (although a new policy was officially proclaimed only in 1999). But it was not the *objective* position of minorities which lay behind this change so much as a shift in *host society attitudes toward newcomers*. After a decade of Pluralist-type policies and officially promoted multiculturalism, there was a growing perception in the Netherlands that its ethnic minorities were not integrating according to plan. The 1994 elections expressed a feeling among the public as well as some policymakers that the Minorities Policy had failed. The

---

[30] Minister for Urban Policy and the Integration of Ethnic Minorities, *Grotesteden en integratiebeleid*, 2001.

belief in a Pluralist-type response to ethnic diversity was giving way to a more individualist, universalist approach to integration (Pirschner 2002; Musterd et al. 1998: 41). In Amsterdam this change in the political climate was tersely summed up in a Minorities Policy Memorandum:

> after a decade of efforts of both government and private initiatives the position of ethnic minorities groups seems not improved ... the effects of the minorities policy ... appear not to be encouraging (cited in Wolff 1999: 28).

Attitudes toward the city's Minorities Policy differed at this time. While the Pluralist approach was credited with raising the issue of ethnic diversity on the local agenda, its ethnically specific policies were criticized for highlighting problems in the targeted communities and stigmatizing them. Others felt that migrant policies had failed because City Hall did not take them seriously enough. Representatives of the veteran migrant communities felt the city should focus on social issues rather than ethnic background in coping with problems such as youth unemployment. Finally, representatives of the newer groups complained that they were overlooked by policies designed for the needs of the postcolonial and guestworker migrant communities (Municipality of Amsterdam 1999; Pirschner 2002: 85–6).

Following the 1994 elections the new alderman, Jaap Van der Aa (PvdA), determined to change the city's approach to its ethnic minorities. During his two terms as Alderman for Minorities Policy (1994–2002), Amsterdam moved from an ethnic group-targeted approach to more general policies. Van der Aa's universalist approach was based on his previous experience in 'managing ethnic diversity', as director of a school with a large minority presence. However, the decision to abandon the Minorities Policy 'was not just philosophical but also political'. During the election campaign Van der Aa had been told by too many voters that 'the PvdA has only been helping the minorities.' The unprecedented four council seats subsequently won by the conservative Centrum Partij served as a clear signal of public dissatisfaction. After the elections, Van der Aa found general support for a policy change in city council. This was facilitated by the replacement of mayor Ed Van Thijn (1983–94), who had been a strong advocate of the Minorities Policy (interview J. Van der Aa).

The change did not occur overnight. It was only in 1997 that City Hall initiated a year-long process of consultation and consensus-building, to officially re-evaluate its Minorities Policy. A special committee was set up to consult with key actors (including the various advisory councils) and draw up recommendations.[31]

---

[31] The consultation process included two reports, one by the five ethnic advisory councils and one by the women's advisory council, who were asked to propose concrete changes in existing policy. The entire process and its conclusions appeared in a report entitled '*Amsterdam heeft de wereld in huis*' (loosely translated: 'The world at home in Amsterdam').

This culminated in eight public evenings, a closing conference and a televised debate.

The resulting Diversity Policy (*Diversiteitbeleid*), as it came to be known, was formulated in 1999 in several policy reports. These present Amsterdam's 'diversity' (defined not only ethnically but also in terms of sexual orientation, etc.) not as a liability, but as a strength to be promoted (Municipality of Amsterdam 1999). The reports recommend that local policies should henceforth focus on 'citizens' and particular problems (e.g. delinquency), not on predefined ethnic target groups, with 'participation' replacing 'integration' as the keyword. Three main policy aims were identified. First, guaranteeing equal opportunities for all. This means addressing existing shortfalls in education and labour through general, problem-oriented policies (although group-specific policies may still be necessary in some cases). Second, combating discrimination and encouraging 'mutual respect among the city's diverse residents'. Third, promoting participation at the *individual* level in all aspects of city life (ibid.; Wolff 1999: 28–31).

In 1999 a small 'Diversity Unit' was created by combining the old Minorities Policy Coordination Bureau with similar units for women's, handicapped and gays policies. This is now located in the Department for Social, Economic and Cultural Affairs (MEC), within the Division of General Affairs. However, like its predecessor, the Diversity Unit appears to have minimal influence in actual policymaking. In part this is due to the devolution of most policymaking affecting migrants/minorities to the district level. But it also has to do with bureaucratic resistance to change. Much of City Hall's remaining 'local migrant policy' is formulated and implemented in other municipal divisions, primarily the Welfare Division (DWA). According to a former DWA department director (and current 'strategic advisor'), there is 'a complete separation between our content [DWA's policies] and what they talk about in the MEC, Diversity Policy' (interview T. Bolten).

To what extent, then, does the Diversity Policy differ from the Minorities Policy? The following pages describe the changes in the two policy domains that have been most affected.

4.5.1 Legal-political domain: promoting 'participatory citizenship'
Since the early 1980s Amsterdam had encouraged newcomers to participate actively in local politics, with campaigns for voter registration and civic education. Nevertheless, minority turnout rates in municipal elections fell between 1994 and 1998.[32] Prior to the 1998 election, City Hall provided funding to migrant organizations and ethnically-based media to get out the vote among minority residents (Berger et al. 2001: 46; Van Heelsum 2002). This appears to continue the Pluralist approach to the political incorporation of minority residents. The

---

[32] The rate for Turks, who had the highest voter turnout among ethnic minorities, fell from 67 to 39 per cent between 1994 and 1998 (voting rates also decreased in the general public) (Berger et al. 2001: 15).

difference is only in emphasis: if the Minorities Policy stressed the communitarian basis of participation, above all through the ethnic advisory councils, the new policy promotes 'participatory citizenship' on an individual basis, through the ballot box. While the Diversity Policy does not oppose ethnic-based mobilization, it encourages (and expects) migrant/minority associations to create opportunities for their members to interact *beyond* their own ethnic communities. This is expressed in the kinds of associational activities that the municipality is now willing to subsidize. Delegating civic education of potential voters to migrant/minority organizations thus remains a legitimate instrument.

At the same time, the new policy states that the ethnic advisory councils should be maintained only as long as other general frameworks of political participation do not reflect the city's ethnic diversity. As a first step, the city's five ethnic minority advisory councils should be replaced by one advisory council representing all the ethnic minorities. This has taken place, however some of the old councils appear to continue in another capacity.[33] The confusion (and apparent disinterest) regarding the advisory council's current status indicates that this channel of participation is no longer considered especially relevant by municipal officials or migrant/minority activists. With decentralization, the focus of migrant/minority political participation may also be shifting to the district councils, where 52 ethnic-origin councilors were elected in the 1994 elections.

4.5.2 Socio-economic policies

During the 1980s, the municipal Welfare Division (DWA) was directly involved in implementing social policies affecting minorities, allocating the substantial government and municipal funding earmarked for minority-targeted programmes and projects. Since the 1990s many if not most of the social policies have been initiated and implemented by the city districts. In youth policy, for example, the welfare and education departments of each city district decide what actions to take and initiate their own projects. Nevertheless, Amsterdam's Welfare Division remains a huge bureaucracy: between 250 and 300 staff (none of whom are actively involved in street-level social work) are engaged in formulating and coordinating social policy at a city-wide level and providing assistance to the city districts.

In accordance with the new approach, many welfare projects no longer target specific ethnic minorities, although DWA staff 'take into consideration the integration aspects' when necessary (interview T. Bolten). However, Amsterdam's Welfare Division has not completely relinquished its appetite for ethnically-specific projects. For example, the DWA's Youth Education department proposed a specific programme to identify and counsel Antillean 'problem youth'. The DWA also develops ethnic-targeted projects that are initiated by city districts, such as a proposed old-age home for residents of Indonesian origin. Ethnic-targeted

---

[33] The Moroccan Advisory Council (SMR), for example, is still functioning in its capacity as an NGO, but its position vis-à-vis City Hall is unclear.

projects are seen as 'temporary measures' that are required for addressing specific problems that will eventually disappear.

> We are not going back to Minorities Policy, but we are not afraid to have some [ethnic] target-group policies ... Target-group policies are generally avoided, but sometimes it's inevitable (ibid.).

A more universalist approach has also been adopted in the city's labour market policy. Unemployment among migrants is no longer addressed as an ethnic minority issue but as a symptom of low educational qualifications. After the heyday of minorities-targeted projects in the 1980s, the only remaining such project in Amsterdam is a small support centre for small and medium businesses. Aimed toward (but not exclusive to) ethnic entrepreneurs, it is run by a local NGO funded jointly by the municipality and the EU – a far cry from the ambitious municipal projects of the previous decade.

A similar shift has occurred in school policies. In the 1990s the focus in national education policy shifted from ethnic minority children to targeting socially disadvantaged children based on non-ethnic criteria (Phalet 2001: 7–8). In 1994, Amsterdam's new Alderman for Minorities Policy also held the education portfolio. Van der Aa quickly abandoned the previous 'magnet schools' policy, claiming that ethnic-based actions were not the solution to failing students or problem schools. Instead he advocated a universalist approach:

> My experience as a school director showed me there were as many differences as similarities between Moroccan students, and programmes targeted at Moroccans missed the mark. We had to concentrate on those pupils who needed special attention, whether they were Moroccan or Dutch.

Instead of targeting 'black schools', Van der Aa proposed that all below-average schools in Amsterdam should concentrate on individual pupils rather than on ethnically-targeted measures. But as noted above, the alderman had few means to promote this policy on a city-wide basis. In effect, school policy now falls within the competency of each city district (**Box 7.3**).

4.5.3 Civic integration policy

Another component in Amsterdam's response to continued immigration in the 1990s, and to the perceived failure of the Pluralist approach of the 1980s, is its 'Civic Integration' (*inburgering*) policy. This developed separately from, but was incorporated into, the city's Diversity Policy. Civic integration programmes were initiated by several municipalities in 1993 and later adopted by Amsterdam and a dozen other cities. Targeting the same 'ethnic minorities' defined by the government, this represented a response by local authorities to the perceived failure of the Minorities Policy. The *inburgering* approach stresses elements of individual assimilation into the host society as a key to successful integration.

Box 7.3 From a 'black school' to a 'Community School' in the Pijp

The Pijp is an ethnically diverse neighbourhood located south of the historic centre. The phenomenon of 'black/white schools' appeared in the early 1980s as labour migrant families settled in the Pijp and Dutch families moved out, or enrolled their children in schools outside the neighbourhood. In De Edelsteen primary school, enrolment dropped from 170 to 75 children, with 80 per cent of the remaining pupils being Moroccan. De Edelsteen's transformation into a '*zwarteschool*' resulted in its abandonment, first by Dutch and then by Surinamese and Turkish pupils, according to the school's current director.

In 1998 the local district council decided to fight this trend. The school was closed and re-opened in 2000 in a renovated location. The newly-named 'Community School' (based on the American concept of the same name) includes the primary school plus a kindergarten and community centre. The latter two components are run by a local semi-public NGO (Combiwel), which maintains links between parents, the school and the local community.

The Community School was developed with the expressed aim of attracting Dutch as well as other minority children back to the neighbourhood. To this end it offers an enriched programme of extra-curricular activities, smaller classes and no less importantly, a new image. As a result, enrollment has risen to over 100 pupils. The proportion of Moroccans is now 40 per cent, with the remaining pupils originating from Surinam, Turkey, Tunisia, etc., as well as a dozen 'white' pupils.

Despite this ethnic diversity, the school does not emphasize its multicultural character. During Islamic holidays, for example, Muslim pupils are allowed to leave early and celebrate with their families at home, but Dutch holidays are celebrated in the school. The policy is to be sensitive to the children's family (rather than ethnic) background, thus teachers emphasize Dutch vocabulary since most pupils have parents who speak limited Dutch. The school's director explains this in practical terms: Dutch fluency is what the pupils need most, and emphasizing multicultural aspects (e.g. celebrating Islamic holidays) would only scare away the non-Muslim parents.

Sources: Interview, T. Rek; Combiwel 2002–03; 'Een basisschool en een buurthuis in een gebouw', www.democratenmuiden.nl/pol-communityschool.

In 1998 a national 'Newcomers Civic Integration Law' established the formal framework of the policy, requiring all adult newcomers belonging to the targeted 'ethnic minorities' to complete an '*inburgering* trajectory' within 12 months of arrival in the Netherlands. Implementation was delegated to the local authorities, which became responsible for immigrant registration in each city, overseeing the required educational courses, outsourcing the other services involved, coordination and monitoring.

Amsterdam's Civic Integration Policy has gone beyond this framework. It includes a 'Newcomers' programme, an 'Oldcomers' programme (for pre-1998 immigrants) and an 'Adult Education' programme, described below. This confusing mix is expressed in an equally confusing organizational structure that has undergone several revisions.[34] Currently, all three programmes are coordinated by an 'Education and *Inburgering*' (E+I) unit in the department of Instruction, Youth and Education, within the Welfare Division.

Newcomers Civic Integration policy Amsterdam made its 'Newcomers Civic Integration' programme obligatory in 1995. The policy's declared aim was to 'advance the self-sustainability of immigrants' in education, the labour market and daily life in the city, by combining the existing potpourri of integration measures (some optional) into a *comprehensive and compulsory process*. In wording reminiscent of the approach to immigrants in the 1950s, the municipal website claims that 'Newcomers *must* be given the possibilities for a *systematic* civic integration' (www.e-i.amsterdam.nl, my italics). The *inburgering* process includes several stages which newcomers must pass over a period of approximately 18 months. Significantly, it applies only to immigrants belonging to the category of Strangers entitled 'targeted ethnic minorities' (**Box 7.4**).

In his review of this policy, Edward Adusei (2000: 57) found that less than one in 10 of the migrants who participated actually completed the entire *inburgering* programme. The reasons included the course hours and locations which were unsuitable for many migrants (who work long hours and are too tired to learn Dutch in the evenings). Childcare presented an obstacle for women. Not surprisingly, only a small percentage pass the proficiency exams on schedule, and absenteeism levels are high.

Oldcomers and Adult Education policies The stated aim of these two programmes is 'to overcome arrears in education and the labour market for Amsterdam residents, integrating them into the modern city' (www.e-i.amsterdam.nl/pages/nieuws). Both programmes are optional, offering courses in Dutch, 'orientation in society' and computer literacy. These are meant to supplement the Civic Integration programme. Thus, the 'Oldcomers' policy targets pre-1998 migrants who are not eligible for the Newcomers programme (over 1,500 participants by 2003). Some of the courses are ethnic-specific, e.g. a Dutch language and computer course for Turkish women. The 'adult education' policy offers similar courses to all residents regardless of origin, but over 80 per cent of the participants are ethnic minorities.

---

[34] At first the 'integration process' for newcomers was coordinated by a special unit within the Welfare Division ('Amsterdam Newcomers Bureau', later 'Newcomers Instreaming Amsterdam', or INKA). In 2002 INKA was combined with other units into an enlarged 'Education and Inburgering' (E+I) unit, comprising some 15 staff within the department of Instruction, Youth and Education.

> **Box 7.4 'Links in the chain' of the inburgering process**
>
> The Newcomers Civic Integration process begins with an *inburgeringscontract* signed between the new immigrant and the municipality. This specifies his/her 'trajectory of activities which must be concluded satisfactorily (e.g. testing level, diploma) within a predetermined period.' The municipal website describes four 'links in the chain'(*schakels in de keten*) of the integration process (the irony of these terms appears to have been lost on the integration professionals).
>
> In the first stage ('Selection and Identification'), the newcomer is registered at the municipal registry, gets a 'welcome talk' and is assigned a 'trajectory guide' who will escort him/her throughout the process. The second stage ('Assessment and placement') includes 'intake talks' by the guide and a 5-6 week (!) *inburgeringdiagnoseprogramma* of language and other tests conducted by a 'research unit', providing the city with comprehensive statistics on its migrants. Based on this, the guide proposes an individual 'integration trajectory' for the migrant.
>
> The third stage is the individual 'educational programme' that each migrant must undertake, including instruction in Dutch (averaging 600 hours) and a 'social-occupational orientation' course (70 hours). At the end the migrant must past proficiency tests in order to receive his *inburgeringcertificaat* from the municipality. The fourth stage is 'Referral', in which advice is provided to the migrant for further steps to integration, including a recommended work or study trajectory, as well as 'social participation or social activity'. Following the advice is not mandatory.
>
> *Sources*: www.e-i.amsterdam.nl/pages/uitvoering/inburgering.htm; Adusei 2000.

In effect, the Adult Education and Oldcomers programmes serve as frameworks for continuing ethnically-specific and targeted measures.

The various courses in these three programmes are subcontracted through the city districts to non-governmental organizations. This includes some migrant associations, who may also propose specific courses based on demands from their clientele. In practice, most courses are outsourced to Dutch organizations. According to an official responsible for outsourcing courses in the Southeast district (himself a veteran migrant), most migrant associations 'are not yet qualified to implement' the courses and 'don't believe themselves in these policies' (interview E. Adusei). But according to the representative of one migrant association involved, 'we teach our migrants better than [the Dutch teachers] and we do it for less money, but they [the Municipality] won't admit it' (interview R. Yuksul).

Amsterdam's Civic Integration policy acquaints newcomers, if not with the local host society, then with the vast machinery of social workers, instructors and bureaucrats involved in such programmes. These include (a partial listing): the Foreigners Police, the City Registrar, the district Newcomers Bureaus, the regional employment bureau and various quasi-governmental NGOs subcontracted for other components of the *inburgering* process. Over time the policy has expanded to include childcare facilities for parents taking the required courses, a municipal 'Fund for newcomers expenses' and an ombudsman to handle complaints. Combining paternalistic good intentions, compulsory arrangements and institutional self-sufficiency, the civic integration programme continues a century-old tradition in Dutch social policy of 'assisting' those Strangers whom the host society does not expected to integrate of their own accord.

5   Summary

Amsterdam's policy trajectory over the past half century demonstrates how that city's migrant policies corresponded to changing attitudes and expectations in the host society toward Strangers. Until a decade ago, these subjective, attitudinal changes followed the actual trajectory of migration phases (from transience to temporariness to permanence) quite closely. National and local policies evolved correspondingly, from Non-policy to Guestworker to Pluralist policies. Thus, Amsterdam's response to the largely transient presence of labour migrants from southern Europe in the late 1950s was to ignore them, leaving civic (particularly Catholic) institutions to take care of those who chose to remain.

From the mid-1960s the city experienced a decade of Guestworker migration during which the labour migrant presence was transformed in quantity (to many thousands) and in terms of ethnic origin (to predominantly Turkish and Moroccan migrants). Their stay was expected to last longer, but the myth of return remained the basis of local attitudes toward these newcomers. The Guestworker phase was accompanied by short-term local policies that overlooked illegal rental practices in the housing market, and relegated responsibility for most migrant needs to the employers. Guestworkers had formal access to basic social services and even to social housing, although the latter remained on the whole inaccessible to them. The municipality also overlooked manifestations of the migrants' cultural and religious Otherness (be they ethnic associations or makeshift mosques). All these point to the prevailing assumption that this was a temporary presence.

This expectation began to change in the mid-1970s, although City Hall formally acknowledged the permanence of the labour migrant permanence only in 1979. This shift was first manifested in housing policy, where the municipality adopted informal long-term solutions geared toward migrant families. In other domains the policy change was slower. Thus the municipality largely ignored Turkish and Moroccan associations, although it recognized and generously subsidized Surinamese associations. This expressed different attitudes toward different types of newcomers: postcolonial immigrants were expected to remain; guestworkers were expected to leave.

This distinction was erased at the beginning of the 1980s with the official definition of 'ethnic minorities'. The Pluralist policy phase of the 1980s paralleled the settlement phase of labour migration. Following national policy, Amsterdam's new Minorities Policy espoused a vision of the city as a multiethnic society in which Otherness was not only accepted, but embraced. The legacy of pillarization legitimized and facilitated a communitarian approach to the integration of the newcomers: local policies were henceforth based on the assumption that empowering ethnic communities was the best way to integrate migrants while preserving their cultural distinctiveness. This expresses a particular Dutch brand of host-stranger relations, of co-existence between distinctive-yet-equal communities.

While many local policies were implemented within the framework of the national Minorities Policy, Amsterdam was especially zealous in its application of Pluralist-type migrant policies. In the Legal-political domain, the city encouraged ethnic-based organizations and set up ethnic advisory councils, to serve as intermediaries between individual migrants and the local polity. In the Socio-economic domain, it initiated various ethnically-targeted policies to reduce migrant arrears in education and in the labour market. In the Cultural-religious domain, City Hall supported minority religious and cultural activity and delegated migrant services to ethnic-based organizations.

The 1990s witnessed a reaction against the Pluralist approach, nationally as well as locally. This may be seen as a reaction in the host society to an overly pervasive presence of Strangers. This perception feeds on popular sentiments that newcomers in the Netherlands have not sufficiently integrated, i.e. accepted host society norms. Muslim separatism, in particular, is blamed on policies that were too protective of cultural and religious Otherness. One response to the perceived failure of the Minorities Policy is to press for integration policies that encourage migrants/minorities to conform more closely to host society norms, e.g. regarding the status of women. The new approach is not Assimilationist in the modernist sense, in that it does not aspire to *eliminate* Otherness (see Chapter 2). Rather, it claims to strike a balance between the right to be different, and majority norms.

In Amsterdam this new approach underlies the city's Diversity Policy, officially adopted in 1999. The new policy advocates a more universalist approach, focusing on problems rather than 'problem groups', individual rather than ethnic criteria. This was expressed in a certain move away from specific (migrant-targeted) to general policies in the Socio-economic and Cultural-religious domains. In the Legal-political domain, the focus moved to individual civic integration. The Civic Integration programme, in particular, displays a more assimilationist approach.

Unlike the previous phases, Amsterdam's latest change in migrant policy does not appear to correspond to a significant change in the *objective* situation of the migrant/minority population. Rather it reflects *a subjective shift in host society attitudes toward Strangers*. If the 1980s were characterized by tolerance toward Otherness, at least among policymakers, the following decade saw growing public impatience with such Pluralist attitudes. Newcomers are not expected to assimilate completely, but they are increasingly expected to conform to host society norms.

However, a closer look at Amsterdam's *enacted* policies since 1999 reveals that the move away from the Pluralist phase has not been so radical. One reason can be found in the decentralization process that began in 1990. The new Diversity Policy was formulated at the municipal level, but local policies affecting migrants are increasingly determined at the city district level, where a variety of approaches exist. In addition, it appears that bureaucrats in the Welfare Division, who still have a say in migrant policymaking, are slow to abandon their Pluralist approach to integration. The continuation of ethnic-targeted policies, however, may have more to do with paternalistic tendencies toward Strangers in Dutch welfare institutions.

The Diversity Policy, then, presents a reaction against the Pluralist approach, yet it cannot be identified with the Assimilationist type in our model. This new approach can be identified in other cities as well, raising the possibility of a *fifth* type of local policy response to ethnic diversity, not covered in the original typology proposed in Chapter 3. This possibility is discussed in the following chapter.

Chapter 8

Summary and Conclusions

1 Introduction

The reader expecting to discover in this chapter which city has most successfully responded to labour immigration (and how) is in for a disappointment. Alas, there are no set formulas for 'managing labour migrant settlement'. Instead, the previous chapters have shown that each city dealt with this phenomenon in its own way, and that the local policy response to this phenomenon is thoroughly embedded in the particular as well as the national context of each city. The findings from the four case studies and the preceding survey present a very complex picture. Local policies toward migrants involve different policy domains, they change over time, and may or may not be accompanied by organizational changes in the municipality. City Hall's strategy in dealing with ethnic minorities may be openly espoused or hidden behind more general policies (e.g. 'urban renewal'). Local authorities may choose to ignore migrant needs, provide them with specific services, or leave the responsibility to civic organizations; they may ignore, support or restrict ethnic-based mobilization, encourage or discourage manifestations of cultural and religious Otherness; relate to 'ethnic neighborhoods' as a threat or an opportunity, etc.

One aim of this book has been to make sense of such variety by focusing on one dimension, namely, host-stranger relations. This concept refers to the way in which 'each kind of society produces its own kind of strangers' (Bauman 1995: 1), i.e. how different societies define, and relate to, their 'newcomers', 'interior Others', 'guestworkers', etc. (Chapter 2). Specifically, I hypothesized that *local migrant policies can be understood as an expression of local authority attitudes and expectations regarding the temporal and spatial presence of the migrant population and regarding their Otherness* (Figure 2.1, above).

This aspect of policymaking has never been systematically explored in the literature on local migrant policy, although it appears in some theories on *national* immigration regimes. However, the latter (e.g. Castles' 'citizenship regimes', on which my model is partially based) have been rightly criticized as too deductive. To bridge the gap between the overly abstract national-level theorizing and the overly inductive local-level research, I proposed an analytical framework which elaborates the link between host-stranger relations and specific policy responses at the local level. The resultant typology should make it possible not only to compare *how* different cities have reacted to the arrival and settlement of migrants, but also provide an understanding of *why* they responded as they did, when they did.

The typology space presented in Chapter 3 proposes four archetypes of local policy responses, corresponding to four types of host-stranger relations (Transient, or Non-policy, Guestworker, Assimilationist and Pluralist), as well as grouping all potential policies into four local *policy domains*, subdivided into *issue areas*. The aim is to provide an overall picture of a city's migrant policies at any given time (Table 3.1, above). Based on a survey of actual policies in some 25 cities, as well as deductive reasoning, specific policies were suggested as manifestations of each response type (or phase) in each issue area, creating the full typology at this stage of the study (Table 3.2, above).

To what extent is such an analytical framework viable, as a method for comparing between different cities? Can such a comparison lead to a more general understanding of local policymaking toward migrants, that goes beyond any particular city? To test this, I followed the development of local policymaking in four cities, using the host-stranger relations model and the typology (Chapters 4–7). The following pages summarize the findings from Amsterdam, Paris, Rome and Tel Aviv (Section 2, below). Section 3 presents the overall conclusions from this comparison. In light of the findings, Section 4 proposes an additional policy response phase to the typology. I conclude with the theoretical and practical implications of applying the analytical framework proposed in this book.

2 Summarizing the Case Studies

The four case study cities were chosen to represent each one of the four types of local policy responses to labour migrant settlement. Rome and Tel Aviv, two 'new immigration cities' that experienced significant labour immigration relatively recently, were chosen to explore the Non-policy and Guestworker responses, respectively. Paris and Amsterdam, two 'veteran immigration cities', represent the Assimilationist and Pluralist response types, respectively. Beyond this, each case study followed the evolution of that city's migrant policy over time, from just over a decade in Tel Aviv to over a century in Paris. This revealed a trajectory of policy phases in each city, as suggested by the typology, but also highlighted where the typology must be fine-tuned to fit the observed policy responses.

Rome

Although labour immigration to Rome became 'visible' in the 1980s, City Hall displayed a Transient-type attitude throughout the decade (see Chapter 4). Non-policy toward migrants continued until 1991, despite two internal reports in the early 1980s that warned of the consequences of ignoring the migrant population. What can explain the municipality's inaction for so long? A political-institutional analysis would point to the weakness of the local authority on one hand, compared with the city's well-organized Third Sector. Municipal inaction can then be seen as one more instance in which City Hall abdicated responsibility for marginalized populations to non-governmental organizations. This is plausible, but the host-stranger relations model adds a further nuance: Rome was *particularly* unwilling to address the growing needs of labour migrants due to the municipality's persistent Transient-type attitude toward this population. The assumption that the migrants were 'just passing through' can be understood in light of Rome's historic role as a gateway city and its large presence of transient strangers of various types. It was the 1991 Pantanella crisis (including the collapse of the local administration) that finally brought an acknowledgement of the permanence of labour migrants at the local and national level, ending the Non-policy phase.

Since 1993 Rome has been ruled by a Centre-Left administration that espouses a clearly Pluralist attitude toward immigrants. However, our review of enacted policies over the past decade reveals that this was only partially translated into actions. Policy changes occurred primarily in the Legal-political and Socio-economic domains, with much of the implementation delegated to civic organizations. Municipal actions in the Cultural-religious and Spatial domains have been largely symbolic. This raises questions regarding the extent to which City Hall is willing to take on the responsibility ensuing from its declared aims of Pluralist-type integration. Nevertheless, the past decade cannot be described as a continuation of Rome's old Non-policy dressed in a new Pluralist rhetoric. Instead, the new integration policy may be best understood as an *intended Pluralist* policy.

Despite a clear shift in the city's *espoused* policy, from a Transient to a Pluralist attitude toward migrants, Rome cannot be regarded as having fully entered a Pluralist phase in its *enacted* policy. This gap can again be given an institutional-political explanation revolving around the relation between national government, local authorities and civic society in Italy. The weakness of Rome's municipality, in management ability and resources, have meant that much of its espoused migrant policy remains on paper or is delegated to civic organizations. The relative strength (and willingness) of non-governmental organizations in Rome allows the municipality to pursue its new integration policy using the proven method of delegating responsibility to, or simply depending on, the Third Sector.

Tel Aviv

In the case of Tel Aviv, the local authority response to labour migrant settlement evolved in less than a decade from a Transient-type attitude to what may be called a 'liberal Guestworker attitude'. Chapter 5 describes how the municipal bureaucracy became aware of the migrant presence in the first half of the 1990s and eventually persuaded the political level to acknowledge this at least as a 'temporary problem', in 1996. City Hall thus moved from a Non-policy response (which included some informal provision of services) to a characteristic Guestworker policy in the second half of the decade. This meant addressing the minimal, immediate needs of the largely irregular labour migrant population, especially regarding migrant children. Beyond this, the city did not concern itself with the foreign workers' self-organization and manifestations of cultural Otherness. The growth of ad hoc churches and crèches was regarded as a temporary phenomenon, until the government would 'solve the foreign worker problem'. The municipal response was thus limited to short-term measures and lobbying the government to provide long-term solutions.

Tel Aviv's minimalist policy can be understood in the context of Israel's exclusionary immigration regime toward non-Jewish newcomers. National policy allowed the recruitment of overseas workers as a temporary substitute for Palestinian labourers but resulted in a large illegal migrant population. Tel Aviv's professional bureaucracy soon realized that it faced a potentially long-term irregular migrant presence. In the second half of the 1990s the city's welfare department prepared a more comprehensive local migrant policy. This was adopted by the newly elected mayor in 1999, commencing another phase.

While outwardly critical of the national guestworker regime, the new policy presents an ambivalent position toward the city's labour migrant population. Since 1999 this can be summarized as acknowledging the probability of a permanent non-Jewish minority in the city, without fully accepting its consequences. Tel Aviv's espoused and enacted policies reflect the continued predominance of Guestworker-type attitudes within the municipality, premised on the need to make life as comfortable as possible for the migrant communities 'as long as they are here', without preparing for their long-term integration in the local society, economy or polity. In contrast to the city's previous policy (and to the ever harsher national policy), this may be labelled a 'liberal Guestworker response'.

Paris

Paris (Chapter 6) illustrates the continuity of an Assimilationist approach in local policy that stretches back to the mid-nineteenth century. Historically, migrants were accepted as permanent settlers (thus the absence of a Non-policy and Guestworker policy phase), but French republican ideology demanded that newcomers assimilate into the host society and unilaterally give up their Otherness. As Paris's migrant population swelled the ranks of the poor, 'dangerous classes', the authorities waged 'a war of attrition against the strangers and the strange' (to use Bauman's phrase), in their fear of social and spatial disorder in the capital.

Another characteristic of the French context is the prevalence of territorially-based spatial policies. Historically, Paris's response to immigration was concealed within urban renewal policy, making it particularly difficult to isolate 'local migrant policies'. Nevertheless, two conclusions emerge in this chapter. First, we can discern a continuous thread in the urban policy agenda of both national (prefectural) and local (council and mayoral) policymakers in Paris. This can be summarized as the progressive *embourgeoisement* of the capital, i.e. distancing the poor and other undesirable populations (often including migrants) progressively farther from the city centre, and replacing them with respectable residents and monumental spaces that symbolize the desired Order. A secondary agenda was to upgrade the environment of the poor who were displaced, as well as those who remained. Beyond the practical aspects (improved sanitation), this can also be seen as an attempt to replace disorder (disease, social marginality, 'inappropriate urban forms', etc.) with a new social and urban Order befitting the status of France's capital city.

Second, Paris's urban policies significantly affected the dispersal of its migrant/minority population, most of which is now found 'outside the city walls', in the *banlieues*. That Paris still hosts a large number of migrants testifies to its continuing role as a gateway city. There is still debate on whether the dipersal of unwanted minorities was an unintended result of *embourgeoisement*, or if the universalist rhetoric of urban renovation concealed an ethnic agenda. In any case, the ethnic element was *explicitly ignored*, despite the obvious impact of these policies on migrants – a characteristic of the Assimilationist response to ethnic diversity. Assimilationist-type policies were consistently pursued in other policy domains, e.g. in the provision of local services. When ethnically-sensitive policies gained acceptance in many French cities in the 1980s–90s, Mayor Chirac and his successor maintained a staunchly universalist approach in their espoused as well as enacted policies.

In 2001 the newly elected Centre-Left administration announced an 'integration policy', marking an apparent break from Paris's 150 years of Assimilationist tradition. The establishment of an advisory 'Citizenship Council of non-EU Parisians' signalled Mayor Delanoë's intention to promote a 'citizenship based on residency' – contradicting the republican model equating political participation with French citizenship. The impact of this measure is still unclear. In the other policy domains, the new strategy is based on making existing general services and policy frameworks 'ethnically sensitive', rather than creating migrant-specific services.

While the new administration has criticized the strictly Assimilationist approach of its predecessors, it is still early to evaluate Paris's new integration policy. However, it is already apparent that it does not conform in the full sense to my definition of a Pluralist-type response to ethnic diversity. City Hall avoids any hint of supporting communal or ethnic-based actions, and the 'integration' of newcomers continues to be seen as an individual, largely one-sided, process. While the new policy rhetoric contains some Pluralist elements, it remains largely within the universalist discourse characterizing Assimilationist attitudes toward migrants.

Amsterdam

The Amsterdam case study (Chapter 7) was chosen as an example of the Pluralist policy response, but it also illustrates how the typology can be used to understand change as well as continuity in one city's migrant policies over time. From the 1950s to the mid-1990s we identified three different phases, with a strong correlation between actual phases of migration (e.g. family reunification) and changes in local policy. Thus, as the Transient phase of migration was replaced by a 'classic' Gestworker phase in the mid-1960s, so the city's response changed from Non-policy to Guestworker policies, e.g. in housing. When the 'guestworkers' showed signs of permanent settlement in the mid-1970s, Amsterdam's migrant policies shifted to what can be identified as a Pluralist phase. During the 1980s Amsterdam's 'Minorities Policy' embraced multiculturalism, encouraged the preservation of ethnic Otherness and supported communal- rather than individual-based integration. This avowedly Pluralist approach was expressed in ethnically-targeted policies across all the policy domains.

Amsterdam's latest policy shift (beginning in 1994 and formalized in 1999) has, unlike the previous phases, *not* come about as a response to any substantial change in the objective situation of the city's migrant population. What, then, explains the replacement of the Minorities Policy with the new 'Diversity Policy'? A political-institutional approach would point to the devolution of policymaking from municipal to city district level in the 1990s. The Diversity Policy can then be seen as an attempt by City Hall to create a new framework for coordinating district-level policies toward migrants. This explanation reveals only part of the picture.

What is more significant is the transformation in Dutch attitudes toward the presence of migrants in the 1990s. This can be summarized as a reaction in the host society to the Pluralist approach of the 1980s, toward a more restricted understanding of ethnic diversity in which minorities are expected to conform more closely to host society norms. This can also be seen as a reaction against the perceived pervasiveness of Strangers: after nearly two decades of Pluralist-style integration, minorities are perceived as 'still too different'. While most Dutch recognize the permanence of ethnic minorities as well as their right to retain a certain degree of difference, they also expect a degree of assimilation.

The Amsterdam case study shows the change in the city's migrant policy to be a direct expression of this shift in host-stranger relations. However, the persistence of some minority-targeted and ethnically-based actions reveals that in *enacted* policies (primarily in the Socio-economic domain), the new policy retains some Pluralist characteristics. Again, host-stranger relations can help to explain this anomaly, by highlighting a paternalistic tendency that has characterized Dutch attitudes toward Strangers, especially among social policy professionals. This approach was earlier manifested in Assimilationist policies toward interior Others ('anti-social families') and Indonesian repatriates, and later, in the 'bear hug' approach toward labour migrants. The Minorities Policy can then be seen as a Pluralist version of the Dutch 'problematization of Otherness'. While Amsterdam's (over)abundance of ethnically-targeted policies may have expressed a genuine sensitivity toward the migrants' Otherness, it also expressed a paternalistic policy approach that is embedded in Amsterdam, with its tradition of social-democratic rule. The case study findings point to a continuation of this attitude toward ethnic minorities, despite the more universalist rhetoric of the new Diversity Policy.

Summary and Conclusions 203

Amsterdam retreat from Pluralist-type policies over the past decade is not unique. The survey of local policies (Chapter 1) found responses in cities such as Birmingham and Stuttgart that were similar to Amsterdam's Diversity Policy: not completely abandoning multiculturalism, nor completely embracing assimilationism. Signs of this approach also appear in the new 'integration policies' of Rome and Paris. This suggests the emergence of a new phase of local policy response to ethnic diversity, to be addressed below.

3 Comparison and Generalization

Two sets of research questions were raised at the beginning of this book. The first related to the *what* and *how* of local policy responses to labour migrant settlement; the second, to the *why*. In addition, I noted that local migrant policies may throw a light on changing city-state relations. Using the host-stranger relations model and typology, it is possible to make a comparative analysis of the case studies and begin to address these questions. The following generalizations should not be taken as definitive conclusions, but as preliminary observations and directions for further research.

3.1 How Cities Respond to Labour Migrant Settlement

3.1.1 Identifying general types of policy response
Despite the wide variety in many contextual variables (including different national migration regimes, scales of city, governance style and migration histories), the case studies show that it is possible to identify general types of local policy response to labour migrant settlement in particular cities and periods, following the criteria of the typology (see Summary sections in Chapters 4, 5, 6 and 7). The findings also show that most policies in a given city usually fall into the same general type of response in a given period. Thus, the Non-policy response was identified in Amsterdam in the early 1960s, in Rome during the 1980s and in Tel Aviv in the early 1990s. A Guestworker policy phase was identified in Amsterdam from the mid-1960s to the mid-1970s and in Tel Aviv from the mid-1990s. The Assimilationist response was identified in Paris at least until 2001.The Pluralist response was identified in Amsterdam from the mid-1970s to the mid-1990s, and a variation of it was identified in Rome after 1993. Finally, findings from Amsterdam from the mid-1990s raise the possibility of a fifth type of local policy response.

3.1.2 Identifying local policy trajectories
Preliminary findings from the literature survey indicated that there may be typical trajectories (paths of local policy responses to migrant settlement) that repeat in different cities. In three of the case studies, the municipality adopted a 'Non-policy' in response to the arrival of labour migrants. But the case of Paris suggests that in states where labour immigration is regarded as a permanent

phenomenon from the outset, Non-policy is not an option. In such countries, the typical trajectory would likely be from an Assimilationist policy to some form of more Pluralist response, as already noted in the national-level literature, and as suggested by Paris's recent integration policy. An historical comparison with cities in other traditional immigration countries such as the US or Canada may provide an answer.

Unlike France, most European states perceived labour migration as a *temporary* measure, to address short-term shortages. Here the case studies as well as the policies survey point to several possible *local* policy trajectories. In veteran immigration countries that adopted national guestworker policies in the 1960s, local authorities moved from Non-policy, to a local Guestworker policy, to their own brand of more-or-less Pluralistic policies (in the 1980s–90s). In Amsterdam this was clearly the case. In Tel Aviv the municipality moved from Non-policy to a Guestworker policy phase, but is not yet willing (and cannot) move beyond that, due to a strict national immigration regime that limits the local authority's policy options. In this sense, Tel Aviv may be closer to other cities in countries characterized by strict guestworker regimes such as Japan or the Gulf States.

In Rome, the city 'leaped' directly from Non-policy to some version of a Pluralist-type policy toward its migrant population. Rome's trajectory may typify other 'new immigration cities' that became destinations for labour immigration in the 1980s, when national Guestworker policies had lost favour in Europe. Since the Assimilationist model of integration is also considered unviable in most European countries, moving from Non-policy to a Pluralist-type policy (or a variation of it – see below) may become the rule in new immigration cities in Europe.

3.1.3 *Local policy phases and transitions*
Local policy responses to migration change, as attitudes in the local authority evolve. This may be a bottom-up or top-down process. In Rome and Tel Aviv the first signs of change (from a Transient attitude) occurred at the bottom, as the professional level tried to alert the political level to the fact that labour migrants where not a passing phenomenon. In both cities the warnings from below were dismissed at first (in Rome a crisis was required to bring about a policy change). However, a more common determinant of local policy change appears to be electoral change. In mayor-led municipalities this means the election of a new mayor with a new agenda, as happened in Rome in 1993, Tel Aviv in 1999 and Paris in 2001. In all three, new mayoral administrations initiated new phases of local migrant policy. Tel Aviv illustrates how the shift in attitudes that precedes significant migrant policy change may occur within the municipal bureaucracy prior to elections, but that electoral change may be necessary to realize this potential. In all three cases the electoral change was from a Centre-Right to a Centre-Left administration, but we cannot generalize from such a small sampling. Indeed, Amsterdam shows that significant policy change can occur after an election even when the same party continues to rule.

3.1.4 Relating between policy phases and policy domains

Are certain types or phases of local migrant policy characterized by more municipal activity in particular issue areas? According to the typology, the local policy response in the Non-policy and Guestworker phases is characterized by municipal inaction, or limited to meeting the minimal immediate needs of the labour migrant population. In the case studies, municipal actions during these phases occurred primarily in the areas of social services and housing. Inaction characterized the other issue areas in the Non-policy and Guestworker phases, especially in the Legal-political and Cultural-religious domains. This was confirmed by findings from the policies survey and from Amsterdam in the late 1950s–early 1960s, Rome in the 1980s and Tel Aviv in the 1990s.

In the Assimilationist phase, it appears that municipal actions in the Legal-political and Cultural-religious domains are primarily negative, e.g. discouraging ethnic-based mobilization. Similarly, the Socio-economic domain is less important, except in the area of language education. The Paris case suggests that the Spatial domain is the main arena for local policymaking affecting migrants, but it is unclear if this derives from the Assimilationist type or from the French context. If Paris moves into a Pluralist phase in the coming years, it will be interesting to see if this will be expressed in more municipal activity in the other (non-spatial) policy domains.

In the Pluralist phase, migrant-related policies in the Socio-economic domain remain important but are supplemented by municipal activism in the Legal-political and Cultural-religious domains. This may be because the latter provide a low-cost, high-visibility way to demonstrate City Hall's multicultural attitudes. Also, these are domains that were relatively neglected in the previous phases. This is borne out by our survey as well as the Amsterdam case and the more recent findings from Rome and Paris.

In sum, it appears that regardless of the policy phase, the primary arena for local policymaking toward migrants is the Socio-economic domain. Municipal activity in the Legal-political and Cultural-religious domains appears to be more phase-sensitive. Spatial policies (housing, urban development) are obviously crucial, but the extent of local policymaking in this domain may be more sensitive to other contextual variables, e.g. the public housing system or national urban policies.

3.2 Understanding Local Migrant Policies in Terms of Host-Stranger Relations

So far, I have shown that the typology proposed here can be a useful analytical framework for summarizing, comparing and ultimately theorizing about the *what* and *how* of local migrant policies. I now return to host-stranger relations as a useful concept for understanding the *why* of local responses to labour migration. In the introductory chapter I noted that much of the national-level theorizing on immigration policies is actually based on distinctions between different host-stranger relations at the nation-state level, even if other terms are used ('inclusionary versus exclusionary citizenship regimes', etc.) If this variable helps determine different types of migrant policies at the national level, the same appears likely at the local level.

Indeed, this study has shown that the concept of host-stranger relations can enrich our understanding of municipal policymaking toward migrants/ethnic minorities. This approach is meant to complement, not compete with, the institutional-political explanations that are common in local-level analyses. In particular, the focus on host-stranger relations reveals an aspect of policymaking that is often concealed within official discourses on service provision, urban renewal, etc. This hidden dimension is made explicit by recalling some of the points raised in Chapter 2, in light of the case study findings.

The first point is that immigration – in particular the settlement of newcomers with a very different background from the host society – challenges the host city beyond the practical impacts of such settlement. In coping with these challenges, local policies reflect prevailing attitudes and expectations toward the presence of Strangers. This was most apparent, perhaps, in Tel Aviv, where the foreign worker presence was perceived as temporary and problematic due to the migrants' non-Jewishness. This fundamental Otherness (as defined by Israeli host society) continues to shape national as well as local policy responses toward labour migrants, despite Tel Aviv's relative cosmopolitanism.

In contrast, in Rome it was not the labour migrants' religious or ethnic Otherness, but the underlying assumption that *all* foreigners were essentially transient, together with a local *laissez-faire* attitude toward Strangers, that explains in part Rome's decade-long Non-policy. Once the permanence of labour migrants was acknowledged, a Pluralist policy was fairly easily adopted – although its implementation has proven much more difficult. In Paris, local policies affecting labour migrants can be understood as part of an historic approach toward Otherness, of trying to distance undesirable populations from the city, or else assimilate them into the acceptable social norms by 'improving' their living environments. In Amsterdam, changes in local migrant policies (e.g. from Minorities Policy to Diversity Policy) express changing levels of tolerance for cultural difference in the local host society.

Second, the way in which immigrants are perceived – indeed, defined – by the host society shapes migrant policies at least as much as (if not more than) the newcomers' innate characteristics. Again, the case studies illustrate how each society creates its own categories of Strangers and how this has affected local policies toward labour migrants. In Rome, the civic status of migrants is crucial: local integration policy since 1993 is inclusionary in regard to legal foreign residents but basically ignores the city's irregular migrant population. In contrast, Tel Aviv's migrant policy is aimed at the 'foreign workers communities' – code words for all non-Jewish labour migrants, regardless of their legality. In Paris, socio-economic and spatial criteria were, until recently, the yardstick in defining target populations, while the ethnic element was denied explicitly, if not implicitly. In Amsterdam, the communitarian approach to dealing with Otherness (institutionalized through Dutch pillarization) shaped how policymakers categorized different groups of newcomers/minorities as targets of different policies.

Third, a host society's perceptions of one type of Stranger influence its response to the arrival of other types of Strangers. This means that local authority reactions to labour migrant settlement should be seen in the context of historic and current local host-stranger relations, i.e. how the host society has interacted (and continues to interact) with different types of interior as well as exterior Others. In Rome, the traditional prevalence of various kinds of (usually transient) foreigners can explain the city's Transient attitude toward labour migrants as well. In Tel Aviv, the Israeli attitude toward newcomers (Jewish = permanent, non-Jewish = temporary sojourner) allowed City Hall to adopt a particularly tolerant approach toward labour migrants. If the latter are ever perceived as a permanent and significant new minority in the city, their religious Otherness may then become threatening, and the whole edifice of Tel Aviv's liberal policy may disappear.

Paris's historic experience with assimilating previous waves of French provincial and later European immigrants, and the relation to Interior Others ('*les classes dangereuses*') served as a backdrop to the Assimilationist approach of the local authorities toward labour migrants in the postwar period. To this was added Paris's experience with its Algerian immigrants, when the 'second front' of the Algerian war was fought in the city's *bidonvilles*. Their largely migrant population was later displaced to housing estates in the *banlieues*. This served as an unspoken backdrop to the urban policies of the 1980s–90s, when the remaining ethnic enclaves (inhabited largely by African and Muslims immigrants) were targeted for *renovation* and *mixité sociale*, i.e. reducing the veteran ethnic-origin population through gentrification. In Amsterdam, the reformist zeal that drove local policies previously aimed at indigenous 'anti-social families' and repatriated Indonesians, was later redirected toward labour migrants.

Awareness of local host-stranger relations also directs our attention to the importance of residents' feelings of relative power or powerlessness vis-à-vis newcomers. The more that local residents feel 'trapped' in their neighbourhood, the more they are likely to react negatively to the settlement of labour migrants. These newcomers not only present competition for scarce resources (cheap housing, services, public spaces) but also pose a threat to the local way of life. In contrast, wealthy residents who may choose when and where to come into contact with immigrants are more likely to regard them as useful and exotic: their Otherness can be sampled at will. This results in a more tolerant (and possibly exploitative) attitude toward the newcomers.

Municipal policymakers and planners are aware of these situations, as reflected in various local policies. Tel Aviv, for example, explicitly justified the establishment of MESILA as a way to defuse potential tensions with indigenous residents. Similarly, Paris's new integration policy may be motivated by the desire to avoid the kind of inter-ethnic conflicts that periodically flare up in the *banlieues*. More optimistically, proposed plans for urban regeneration in Tel

Aviv's migrant 'core area' describe the potential of the foreign worker presence as a kind of local attraction, noting examples from abroad. Indeed, Amsterdam (and other cities) marketed its ethnic diversity for years, as part of its strategy to attract international investment.

3.3 Local Migrant Policies and City-State Relations

Although it is not the focus of this book, several generalizations can be made regarding the interaction between local and national governments in the field of migrant policy. The case studies illustrate the extent to which local authority responses to immigration are embedded in the national context. However, they also demonstrate that national-level dominance does not exclude local variations. This holds true for host-stranger relations: local attitudes toward newcomers broadly follow those at the national level, but they also reflect the particular history of the city. Similarly, each country's immigration regime (ideology, laws, institutions, policies), welfare regime, and other national-level structures and characteristics profoundly affect *how* local authorities respond to labour migrant settlement. This not only means that phase-shifts in host-stranger relations and migrant policy at the national level stimulate similar changes at the local level. It also means that the manner in which the different cities act out these phases often reflect national characteristics.

The contrast between the Pluralist phase in Amsterdam and Rome is one example. In Amsterdam, Pluralist-type policies (1980s to mid-1990s) were expressed in a large variety of municipal actions that targeted ethnic minorities, supported migrant associations, etc. This was rooted in the pro-active Dutch approach to dealing with social/economic problems in general, and the institutional-professional manner of dealing with Otherness in particular. In Rome, the Pluralist phase (since 1993) has involved relatively few municipal actions (although still significantly more than in the past). Instead, the municipality prefers to delegate actions to non-governmental organizations – reflecting the weakness of public agencies and relative strength of the civic sector in Italy.

However, the agenda of local authorities can sometimes diverge from national-level policies, as demonstrated by the migrant policies adopted by Tel Aviv (since 1999) and Paris (since 2001). Thus, Paris under Chirac pursued an Assimilationist approach in local urban policies throughout the 1980s–90s, even as the national *politique de la ville* was moving toward a legitimization of ethnically-sensitive policies. Since 2001, the Delanoë administration signals an even greater independence in Paris's migrant policy, but now it steers toward a more Pluralistic approach than that of the (Chirac-led) national government.

It is also clear that significant in-country variations exist in local migrant policy. Shifts from one response phase to another do not happen in all the cities at the same time – apparently, some municipalities are policy leaders, others are followers. In Israel, Tel Aviv is the only city to have adopted a local policy toward labour migrants. Other cities with substantial labour migrant populations such as Jerusalem and Eilat remain in a Non-policy phase. In France, Paris's migrant policy differs significantly from some of its neighbouring municipalities as well as from Marseille's, etc. These local variations may be general or limited to particular policy areas, e.g. regarding migrant political participation (Ireland 1994), social services (Gaxie et al. 1998), or the relation to Islamic institutions (Rath et al. 2001).

The case studies also shed light on the interaction between local- and national-level policymaking. In the case of Amsterdam there is overall consistency between national and local migrant policies. Some national policies were initiated by local authorities and later adopted by the national government, e.g. the 'Civic Integration' policy. In the Netherlands, then, a clear direction (top-down or bottom-up) in migrant policymaking is not obvious. At the other extreme is Israel, where national policymaking is clearly top-down. Tel Aviv's local migrant policy is exceptional, but it too has had to adapt itself to the parameters of the national guestworker regime. Nevertheless, Tel Aviv's relatively liberal policies toward 'its' labour migrants have also affected national policymaking, e.g. in regard to migrant children.

Finally, the case studies reveal the important role played by civic organizations in some cities in the development and implementation of local migrant policies. This suggests that rather than seeing the policy response to immigrant settlement and ethnic diversity as a top-down, binary system of government (national → local), it should be understood as a recursive, interactive process of governance, involving several levels of government and civic society (including migrant/minority mobilization) as well as supra-national actors. Such an approach demands attention to the dissonance that may occur between espoused and enacted policy. National-level explanations have tended to overemphasize espoused policy, while local-level explanations have focused on enacted policy. The theoretical implication is that a more integrative, holistic approach should be adopted in future research on migrant/minority policy, regarding it more as an open system of governance, rather than a policy area dominated by the state, or conversely, as an area of relative autonomy for local authorities.

4   Rethinking the Typology: A New Policy Phase?

We have seen that the typology can be used to describe complex and changing situations in terms of general types/phases of local policy response, as long as we are willing to amend these ideal types to fit local circumstances. Here the distinctions between espoused, intended and enacted policies are particularly important. This allows us, for example, to identify Amsterdam's Minorities Policy in the 1980s (espoused as well as enacted) and Rome's post-1993 integration policy (espoused, less enacted) as a Pluralist-type response to migrant settlement, despite their differences. I chose to label Rome's an 'intended Pluralist' response, to differentiate it from Amsterdam's full 'Pluralist' response. Similarly, I termed

Tel Aviv's policies since 1999 a 'liberal Guestworker' response, to distinguish it from the 'limited Guestworker' response of the previous administration and to indicate that the city has not entered a Pluralist phase. The typology has proved to be sufficiently robust and flexible to allow such variations without losing its fundamental quality of clarifying complex situations.

The most significant revision in the typology comes in light of the findings from the Amsterdam case study (specifically, the city's Diversity Policy from the mid-1990s), as well as other recent policies noted in the survey. In several veteran immigration cities such as Amsterdam and Birmingham, a reaction to Pluralist-type policies has led to what are often labelled 'intercultural' policies over the past decade.[1] Some new immigration cities, e.g. Barcelona and Turin, which only recently acknowledged a permanent labour migrant presence, have moved directly from Non-policy to similar rhetoric and actions that fit neither the Pluralist nor the Assimilationist types proposed in the typology. I therefore propose adding a *fifth* policy response: the 'Intercultural' type or phase (**Table 8.1**).[2]

The Intercultural vision of integration, although not reverting to Assimilationist-type goals, stresses the need for more common ground in a multiethnic city. This represents a reaction to Pluralist policies that are now seen as unwittingly perpetuating the stigmatization and segregation of ethnic minorities, by overemphasizing the cultural difference of the targeted populations. The perceived dangers of sectarianism (especially Islamic separatism) play an important role here. Hence this policy steers toward interaction between individuals *across* different communities. In contrast to the Pluralist approach, which tends to lump migrants together according to ethnic background, the Intercultural approach to ethnic diversity highlights individual differences (e.g. gender, lifestyle) *within* groups and is more sensitive to constraints that ethnic communities may place on their individual members (especially women). Nevertheless, the role of ethnic communities in the integration process is not dismissed, as in the Assimilationist approach. Rather, the aim is to empower individual migrant/minority residents to choose among multiple identities, including (but not limited to) their ethnic identity.

In the Legal-political domain, Intercultural policy is expressed by opposition to ethnically-based consultative structures; instead, 'mixed' advisory councils (with migrant as well as indigenous representatives) are acceptable. Birmingham, for example, replaced its powerful, ethnically-based Standing Consultative Forum (established 1990) with a mixed advisory forum in 1999. Stuttgart established a mixed advisory council already in 1994. Amsterdam, too, is in the process of unifying all the advisory councils. Municipal support for migrant organizations shifts away from supporting activities that strengthen ethnic identity, to activities that strengthen 'integration skills' such as language fluency.

---

[1] The designation 'intercultural' appeared in the 1990s in various policies, programmes and projects, see below.

[2] This table repeats Table 3.2 with the addition of the last column.

Table 8.1 Revised typology of local policies toward migrants/minorities

Host-Stranger Relations: Attitudes/assumptions of local authority	Migrants as TRANSIENT	Migrants as TEMPORARY 'guestworkers'	Migrants PERMANENT but their OTHERNESS is TEMPORARY	Migrants PERMANENT, their OTHERNESS will and should REMAIN	Migrants PERMANENT, ETHNIC OTHERNESS should not be emphasized
POLICY TYPES/ PHASES:	NON-POLICY	GUESTWORKER POLICY	ASSIMILATIONIST POLICY	PLURALIST POLICY	INTERCULTURAL POLICY
DOMAINS/issue areas					
LEGAL-POLITICAL					
Civic status	–	Lobby the government to regularize illegals (*Tel Aviv*)	Facilitate naturalization (*Berlin, Cologne*)	Support regularization (*Oeiras*), Extend local enfranchisement (*Turin, Bologna*). Lobby gov't to regularize illegals (*Paris '01*)	Naturalization contingent on minimal assimilation (*Amsterdam mid-'90s*)
Consultative structures	–	–	Reject, or mixed (non-ethnic) advisory councils (*Paris, Lille, Liege*)	Initiate/support ethnic-based advisory councils (*Frankfurt, Amsterdam '80s, Birmingham '80s*)	Prefer 'mixed' councils (*Stuttgart, Birmingham '99*)
Migrant associations	Ignore migrant associations (*Rome '80s, Athens*)	Informal cooperation with migrant associations on limited issues (*Barcelona, Tel Aviv*)	Co-opt or exclude migrant associations; delegation to migrant associations is implicit (*Paris, Lille*)	Support migrant associations as agents of empowerment (*Amsterdam '80s, Birmingham*). Delegate services to associations (*Amsterdam, Birmingham*)	Support migrant associations as agents of integration with host society (*Amsterdam mid-'90s, Birmingham '99, Cologne, Zurich*)
SOCIO-ECONOMIC					
Social services (health, welfare, etc.)	Ad-hoc access to some services (*Athens*)	Formalize access to selected local services (*Tel Aviv mid-'90s*)	Equal access to all services (ignore ethnic-based needs) (*Brussels, Barcelona*)	Reception/orientation service (*Rome '90s, Tel Aviv '00s*). Ethnically-targeted specific services (*Amsterdam, Birmingham, Stuttgart*)	Sensitivity to minority needs (e.g. cultural mediators) but minimize ethnic-based measures (*Amsterdam late '90s*)

Table 8.1 cont'd

POLICY TYPES/ PHASES:	NON-POLICY	GUESTWORKER POLICY	ASSIMILATIONIST POLICY	PLURALIST POLICY	INTERCULTURAL POLICY
Labour market	Ignore black market activity (*Rome '90s, Tel Aviv*)	Minimal regulation of legal work conditions. Limited vocational assistance	Anti-discrimination policy. General vocational training (non-ethnic criteria) (*Lille*)	Affirmative hiring policy (*Antwerp*). Ethnic-based vocational training and entrepreneurs policy (*Amsterdam '80s*)	Anti-discrimination policy. Minimize ethnic-based measures (*Amsterdam '00s*).
Schools	Ad hoc access for migrant children (*Rome '80s, Tel Aviv '90s*)	Possible home-language classes (*Berlin '70s*)	Spatial dispersal (school desegregation) (*Berlin*). Support national-language tutoring (*Zurich*)	Extra support to schools based on ethnic pupil ratio (*Turin, Amsterdam*). Home-language classes (*Berlin*), religion/culture classes (*Birmingham*)	National language classes, home-language tutoring
Policing/Conflict resolution	Ad hoc reaction to conflict situations	Municipal police as agents of migrant regulation	Area-based policing (possible implicit targeting of migrants)	Police as social agents with migrant-targeted projects (*Rotterdam*). Pro-active anti-racism enforcement (*Leicester*)	Police as agents of inter-ethnic conflict management (*Stuttgart*)
CULTURAL-RELIGIOUS					
Minority cultural/ religious practices and institutions	Ignore ad-hoc places of worship	Informal acknowledgement of ad-hoc places of worship (*Amsterdam '70s, Tel Aviv '90s*)	Discourage religious institutions (*Utrecht '80s, Marseille*)	Support religious institutions as agents of integration and empowerment (*Amsterdam '80s, Birmingham*)	Minimize support for religious institutions, emphasize intercultural activities (*Amsterdam late '90s, Stuttgart*)
Minority religion in school	—	—	Ignore/discourage religious practices in school (*Paris*)	Support religious practices in school (*Birmingham*)	Discourage religious practices in school
Public awareness/ Communication policies	—	—	Anti-racism/anti-discrimination campaigns	Multicultural projects 'celebrating diversity' (*Berlin, Frankfurt*)	Emphasize intercultural communication (*Stuttgart, Turin*)

Table 8.1 cont'd

POLICY TYPES/ PHASES:	NON-POLICY	GUESTWORKER POLICY	ASSIMILATIONIST POLICY	PLURALIST POLICY	INTERCULTURAL POLICY
SPATIAL					
Housing	Ignore housing problems, ad hoc reaction to crises (*Rome '80s*)	Possible short-term solutions (guestworker lodging (*Berlin '60s, Amsterdam early '70s*)	Equal access to social housing (universal criteria). Ignore ethnic-based discrimination in housing market (*Marseille*)	Anti-discrimination policy including ethnic monitoring (*Bradford, Birmingham*)	Equal access to social housing Anti-discrimination policy incl. ethnic monitoring
Urban development, relation to ethnic enclaves	Ignore ethnic enclaves, disperse if crisis arises (*Rome '80s*)	Ethnic enclaves considered temporary (*Amsterdam '70s, Tel Aviv '90s*)	Ethnic enclaves seen as urban problem; dispersal policy (*Berlin, Frankfurt '70s*); gentrification policy (*Cologne, Brussels, Paris*).	Recognize potential of ethnic enclaves (*Tel Aviv*). Renewal with residents policy (*Frankfurt*)	Ethnic enclaves seen as problematic
Symbolic uses of space, public spaces	Ignore in peripheral locations, discourage in central locations (*Rome*)	Ignore in peripheral locations, discourage in central locations (*Tel Aviv*)	Oppose physical manifestations of Otherness ('mosques w/out minarets') (*Utrecht, Paris*)	Support physical manifestations of Otherness (minarets, monuments, museums,) (*Amsterdam, Cologne*)	Emphasize intercultural symbolic uses of space

In the Socio-economic domain, Intercultural policies remain sensitive to minority needs but steer away from ethnic-specific actions. In Birmingham, ethnic-targeted policies (begun in the mid-1980s) are being replaced with general policies in areas such as health, employment and housing. In the Cultural-religious domain, the emphasis is on strengthening inter-ethnic activity. Thus Stuttgart organizes encounters between Turks, Kurds and other minorities, and established an inter-religious forum in 1994. Turin set up an 'Intercultural Immigrant Women's Centre' in 1996 which 'aims to promote dialogue between cultures through a series of initiatives' (Allesino et al. 1999: 29). Rome's Education Department established an 'Intercultural Unit' in 1998 with similar aims.

The distinction between Pluralist and Intercultural policies is not always clear-cut, be it in veteran cities (Amsterdam, Birmingham, Stuttgart) or new immigration cities (Turin, Rome, Barcelona). In some cases the Intercultural response clearly represents a reaction to the apparent failings of Pluralist policies. In others it is difficult to establish whether a significant policy change took place, or if the designation 'intercultural' has simply replaced 'multicultural'.[3] More research is needed to substantiate the hypothesis that the Intercultural response expresses a truly different approach to coping with ethnic diversity, and is not just a rhetorical variant of Pluralist policies.

5 Implications for Research and Policy

5.1 Directions for Further Research

National-level theorizing on immigration and integration policies has been criticized as overly deductive, based on *a priori* explanations that overlook local variations and are insufficiently grounded in actual findings. These criticisms are aimed especially at models emphasizing cultural traits and national identity, i.e. host-stranger relations. On the other hand, local-level analyses of migrant policy are usually rich in content but overly specific. Yet the need for a more general, comparative perspective of local migrant policies is growing, as cities become the primary arena in which the 'management of ethnic diversity' is played out, for better or worse.

I have attempted to address this gap by proposing an analytical framework for analyzing and comparing policies toward migrants *at the local level*. While the focus on local-level policies allows more grounded, empirically-based research, the host-stranger relations model relates the findings to a broader theoretical context which has previously been applied only at the national level. Based on this model, the typology proposed here can lay the basis for further research in the field of

---

[3] The "intercultural' label became especially popular in Italian cities (Turin, Milan, Rome) after it appeared in national policy documents, e.g. an Education Ministry directive stressing the need for 'intercultural education'.

local migrant policy, be it in unexplored cities or through comparative analyses of findings from research already carried out, such as individual case studies. The four case studies in this book present a first test of the robustness and flexibility of the typology, demonstrating how it may be applied to in-depth research. Additional research may result in further adaptations (e.g. restructuring the division of policy domains and issue areas, adding policy types/phases), without undermining the overall validity of the typology as a theoretical framework.

The findings of the case studies, and the comparative analysis and generalizations made in this chapter, point to several possibilities for further research. One, as noted above, is testing the hypothesis that some cities are moving into a new phase, beyond Pluralism, in their policies toward migrants/ethnic minorities. Another is the possibility of additional response types that were not identified in this study. Third, the probability that there are common trajectories of local policy responses suggests that new immigration cities may follow the path of veteran immigration cities. To further test this hypothesis requires a comparative analysis of a set of 'veteran cities' (to establish a number of typical trajectories) and 'new cities' (after a minimal period of migrant settlement).

Another intriguing question that could not be sufficiently addressed here relates to the role of host-stranger relations in shaping local policy responses to immigration, *in relation to other variables*. These include the local political-institutional context, the role of the state and its frameworks (national welfare regimes, urban policy frameworks, etc.) and cultural-historical 'traits' (e.g. the Italian laissez-faire approach to social problems). This means identifying not only shifts in host-stranger relations and phases of local migrant policy (as done in this study) but also charting the changes in the other variables noted above (in-depth research of a city usually uncovers all these elements at the same time). We may then begin investigating the *causal relations* between different contextual variables and local responses to immigration, addressing questions such as: are there common factors that explain certain policy trajectories?

5.2 Policy Implications

This study deliberately did not address the question of 'what works and what has failed' in local migrant polices. Evaluating the *effectiveness* of policies would not only require a massive effort, it would also raise theoretical and methodological problems that distract from my original focus on host-stranger relations.

Nevertheless, as immigration flows spread to a growing number of cities, local authorities are showing increasing interest in *comparative* research on local migrant policies.[4] Clearly, cities can and are learning from each other's experiences in dealing with ethnic diversity. For example, elements of the Intercultural approach have appeared in new immigration cities, suggesting that these cities

---

[4] This is demonstrated by the growth of city-to-city research networks in this area (see Chapter 1, footnote 14).

are deliberately avoiding Pluralist-type policies, in light of the latter's perceived failings.

The analytical framework proposed here may thus have practical relevance by enabling policymakers to systematically compare their situation with that of other cities. Using the typology, they can clarify where their city is situated in terms of their own migrant policies: what phases of policy response have they undergone, in what phase are they now, toward what phase do they appear to be heading? In this way policymakers can conduct reflexive learning based on their previous policy responses. They can then compare their own attitudes (host-stranger relations) and actions (migrant policies) with those of other cities before formulating future policies. The modular format of the typology allows such a comparative learning process to be carried out in one, several, or all the policy domains. Especially in the case of new immigration cities, local policymakers (as well as others involved in migrant policy, e.g. civic organizations) can use such comparison to gain insights from the (often hard-earned) experience of others. In particular, the typology makes it easier to distinguish if there is a fit (or misfit) between a particular policy response and a particular migration phase.

This book has shown that beyond the particular conditions of any city, municipal policy responses to labour migrant settlement are comparable, indeed, are often similar. This holds true for cities that experienced labour immigration decades ago, as well as those that have only recently 'joined the club' of labour migrant destination cities. This means that cross-city comparison is worth the effort, for those actively involved in shaping local migrant policies, particularly in new immigration cities. Understanding the process that veteran immigration cities underwent, as they coped with the challenges posed by the arrival of these Strangers, should highlight the possibilities and pitfalls open to policymakers in the earlier stages of migrant settlement. In the process they may also learn something about themselves.

Appendix: List of Interviews

ROME (May 2001, September–November 2001)

Academia and State

Marco Brazzoduro	Politica sociale, Università La Sapienza
Cinzia Conti	Demografia, Università La Sapienza
Enrico Todisco	Studi Geoeconomici, Università La Sapienza
Mario Petrini	Official, Ministry of Education

Municipality of Rome

Francesca d'Amore	Coordinator, Special Office for Immigrants (USI)
Rosetta Attento	Scholastic director, Bonghi Elementary School
Paola Bacchetti	Official, Intercultural Unit, Education Department
Paola Gabrielli	Senior Advisor (*consulente*) to Alderman for Education
Anamaria Marconi	Teacher, Bonghi Elementary School
Magda Migliano	Official, Intercultural Unit, Education Department
Claudio Rossi	Acting Director, Special Office for Immigrants (USI); Senior Advisor (*consulente*) to mayor's alderman (*delegato*) for Multiethnic Policy
Enrico Serpieri	Senior Advisor (*consulente*) to Alderman for Social Affairs

Third Sector

Marco Accorinti	Director, Centro Stranieri via Zoccoletta, Caritas di Roma
Francesca Campolongo	Information Officer, Centro Astalli, Jesuit Refugee Service
Grazia Curalli	CIES (Centro Informazione Educazione e Sviluppo)
Germana Monaldi	Former staff, Centro Astalli, Jesuit Refugee Service
Franco Pittau	Director of Research, Caritas di Roma
Giulio Russo	Director, Casa dei Diritti Sociali
Angela Scalso	Director, Agenzia Chances
Nellie Tang	Coordinator of daycare centre, CFMW (Filipino NGO)

TEL AVIV (January–April 2002; June 2005)

Municipality of Tel Aviv-Yafo

Edna Altar-Dembo	Director, MESILA (Aid and Information Center for the Foreign Community in Tel Aviv-Yafo)
Varda Dickstein	Community worker, Welfare Division
Adi Ezov-Amon	Staff, MESILA
Hedva Finish	Planner, Long Term Planning Department, Planning Division
Zeev Friedman	Director, Welfare Division (Social Services Division)
Tammy Gavriely	Director, Long Term Planning Department, Planning Division
Haim Nehama	Director, Public Health Division
Amira Yahalom	Director, Bialik Primary School
Ran Zafrir	Manager, Ichilov Hospital administration

Third Sector

Rami Adout	Director, Open Clinic, Physicians for Human Rights
Dana Alexander	Advocate, Association for Civil Rights in Israel
Naana Holdbrook	President, African Workers Union
Michal Pinchuk	Advocate, Association for Civil Rights in Israel
Hanna Zohar	Director, Workers Hotline

Other

Einat Fishbein	Journalist, *Ha'ir* and *Ha'aretz*
Maria (pseudonym)	Labour migrant from Ecuador

PARIS (June–September 2002)

Academia and Media

Marc Androise-Rendu	Former journalist, *Le Monde*
Sophie Body-Gendrot	Université de Paris, Sorbonne
Yankel Fijalkow	Université de Paris VII / formerly at APUR
Christine Lelevrier	IAURIF
Patrick Simon	INED (Institut Nationale des Etudes Demographiques)
Jean-Claude Toubon	Ecole des Hautes Etudes de Sciences Sociales

Municipality of Paris

Jocelyn Adriant-Mebtoul	Director, Integration Mission, *Délégation à la Politique de la ville et l'intégration*
Mourad Allal	Coordinator, *Diagnostic Intégration*, APUR
Emeline Bailly	Official, Local Development Team – Belleville
Rivka Bercovici	Director, Mission for urban requalification programmes - Château Rouge/Goutte d'Or sector, *Secrétaire Générale*
Khedidja Bourcart	Deputy Mayor for Integration and Non-EU Foreigners
Stephany Brial-Cottineau	Official, Local Development Team – Goutte d'Or
Marianne de Brunhoff	Director of Social Action, Social Integration Mission
Michel Cougougliegne	Assistant mission director, APUR
Michel Neyreneuf	Deputy district mayor (18th *arrondissement*), responsible for housing; former chairman, *Association Défense des Habitants*, Goutte d'Or
Pierre-Francois Salviani	Coordinator of project directors, *Délégation à la Politique de la ville et l'intégration*; former project director–Goutte d'Or

Third Sector

M. Diara	Director, *Unité de Réflexion et d'Action des Communautés Africaines* (URACA)
Marie-José Minassian	Coordinator, *Migrations et cultures de Turquie* (ELELE)
Fabrice Nicol	Director, *Association Dialogue et l'Orientation Sociale* (ADOS)
Gaye Patek-Salom	Director, *Migrations et cultures de Turquie* (ELELE)

AMSTERDAM (June–July 2001, October 2002–January 2003)

Academia

Hans van Amersfoort	AME and IMES
Gert Dijkink	AME
Jeroen Doomernik	IMES
Henk de Feijter	AME
Anja van Heelsum	IMES
Eva van Kempen	AME
Leo de Klerk	AME

Flip Lindo	IMES
Virginie Mamadouh	AME
Catelijn Pool	University of Nijmegen
Jan Rath	IMES
Judith Roosblad	University of Amsterdam
Pieter Terhorst	AME

AME: Amsterdam Study Centre for the Metropolitan Environment, University of Amsterdam (since 2005: AMIDST)
IMES: Institute of Migration and Ethnic Studies, University of Amsterdam

Municipality of Amsterdam

Jaap van der Aa	Former Alderman for Minorities Policy and Education
Jeanette Nijboer	Diversity Policy official, Department of Social, Economic and Cultural Development (MEC), General Affairs Division
Joris Rijbroek	Former staff, Welfare Department, Baarsjes City District
Edward Adusei	Official, Social Development Sector, Southeast City District
Theo Bolten	Senior Advisor, Welfare Division
Ton Rek	Director, the Community School

Third Sector

Abdou El Menebhi	Director, *Euro-Mediterranean Centrum Migratie en Ontwikkeling* (EMCEMO)
Roemer van Oordt	Staff, *Amsterdam Centrum Buitenlanders*
Boafi Owusu-Sekyere	Chairman, SIKAMAN (Ghanaian NGO)
Rejet Yuksal	Social worker, *Amsterdam Turkiyeli Kadinlar Birligi* (ATKB)

Bibliography

Accorinti, M. (1998) *Servizi per gli immigrati a Roma. Progetto: Lire, écrire, s'insérer.* Unpublished final report for EU Horizon Programme.
Adusei, E. (2000) *Conditions for a Successful Newcomers Policy: A Case Study of Policy Implementation in Amsterdam.* Unpublished thesis presented for Master of Arts in Public Policy and Administration, Institute of Social Studies, The Hague.
African Workers Union (1999) *AWU Newsletter.* Tel Aviv, August 1999.
Alexander, M. (1999a) *City Template Tel Aviv-Yafo,* MPMC. http://www.unesco.org/most/p97.htm.
—— (1999b) *Progress Report Tel Aviv-Yafo.* Report presented at MPMC workshop, Liege, 30 October–2 November 1999.
—— (2001) 'Tel Aviv: A Migrants' City Copes with a Different Type of Migrant', in Rogers, A. and Tillie, J. (eds), *Multicultural Policies and Modes of Citizenship in European Cities.* Aldershot: Ashgate, pp. 199–223.
—— (2003) 'Local Policies toward Migrants as an Expression of Host-stranger Relations: A Proposed Typology', *Journal of Ethnic and Migration Studies,* 29 (3): 411–30.
—— (2004) 'Comparing Local Policies toward Migrants: An Analytical Framework, a Typology and Preliminary Survey Results', in Penninx, R., Kraal, K., Martiniello, M. and Vertovec, S. (eds), *Citizenship in European Cities. Immigrants, Local Politics and Integration Policies.* Aldershot: Ashgate, pp. 57–84.
Altri/Others magazine, Rome (1) May–June 2004. http://altri.it/pdf/1Num/.
Ambroise-Rendu, M. (1987) *Paris-Chirac.* Paris: Plon.
APUR (Atelier Parisien d'Urbanisme) (1987) *L'aménagement de l'Est de Paris. Paris Projet* (27–28).
—— (2002) *Le diagnostic local d'intégration de la Ville de Paris: Rapport d'étape.* Unpublished draft report, October 2001–January 2002.
Barlow, M. (2000) 'Amsterdam and the Question of Metropolitan Government', in Deben L., Heinemeijer, W. and Van der Vaart, D. (eds), *Understanding Amsterdam.* Amsterdam: Het Spinhuis, pp. 249–99.
Bartram, D. (1998) 'Foreign Workers in Israel: History and Theory', *International Migration Review,* 32: 303–25.
Bar-Zuri, R. (1999) 'Foreign Workers Without Permit in Israel, 1998'. Jerusalem: Ministry of Labor and Welfare, Manpower Planning Authority (in Hebrew).
Bauman, Z. (1988) 'Strangers: The Social Construction of Universality and Particularity', *Telos,* 78: 7–42.

—— (1995a) 'Making and Unmaking of Strangers', *Thesis Eleven*, 43: 1–16.
—— (1995b) *Life in Fragments: Essays in Postmodern Morality*. Oxford: Blackwell Publishers.
Berger, M., Fennema, M., Heelsum, A, Tillie, J. and Wolff, R. (2001) *Politieke participatie van etnische minderheden in vier steden* (in Dutch: Political participation of ethnic minorities in four cities). Amsterdam: Institute for Migration and Ethnic Studies.
Blommaert, J. and Martiniello, M. (1996) 'Ethnic Mobilisation, Multiculturalism and the Political Process in Two Belgian Cities: Antwerp and Liege', *Innovation*, 9 (1): 51–73.
Boal, F. (1978) 'Ethnic Residential Segregation', in Herbert, D. and Johnston, R. (eds) *Social Areas in Cities: Processes, Patterns and Problems*, New York: Wiley, pp. 57–95.
Bochner, S. (1982) *Cultures in Contact: Studies in Cross-cultural Interaction*. Oxford: Pergamon Press.
Body-Gendrot, S. (1996) 'Paris a "Soft" Global City?', *New Community* 22 (4): 595–605.
—— (2000) *The Social Control of Cities?* Oxford: Blackwell.
—— (2001) 'The Politics of Urban Crime', *Urban Studies*, 38 (5–6): 915–28.
—— and Martiniello, M. (eds) (2000) *Minorities in European Cities*. London: Macmillan.
Bousetta, H. (1997) 'Citizenship and Political Participation in France and the Netherlands: Reflections on Two Local Cases', *New Community*, 23 (2): 215–31.
—— (2000) 'Political Dynamics in the City: Three Case Studies', in Body-Gendrot, S. and Martiniello, M. (eds) *Minorities in European Cities*. London: Macmillan, pp. 129–44.
—— (2001) *Immigration, Post-immigration Policies and the Political Mobilization of Ethnic Minorities: A Comparative Case-study of Moroccans in Four European Cities*. Unpublished PhD dissertation, Katholieke Universiteit Brussel.
Bravo, M. (1999) *Instance d'évaluation de la politique de la ville en Ile-de-France: Rapport Final*. Prefecture de l'Ile-de-France et Conseil Generale de l'Ile-de-France.
Breen, A. and Rigby, D. (1994) *Waterfronts*. New York: McGraw-Hill.
Brenner, N. (1999) 'Globalisation as Reterritorialisation: The Re-scaling of Urban Governance in the European Union', *Urban Studies*, 36 (3): 431–51.
Brochmann, G. (1998) 'Controlling Immigration in Europe: Nation-state Dilemmas in an International Context', in Van Amersfoort, H. and Doomernik, J. (eds) *International Migration*. Amsterdam: Institute of Migration and Ethnic Studies, pp. 22–41.
—— and Hammar, T. (eds) (1999) *Mechanisms of Immigration Control: A Comparative Analysis of European Regulation Policies*. Oxford: Berg.
Brooks, D. (2002) *Les Bobos*. Paris: Le Livre de Poche.

Brubaker, R. (1992) *Citizenship and Nationhood in France and Germany*. Cambridge, MA: Harvard University Press.
Calavita, K. (1994) 'Italy and the New Immigration', in Cornelius, W., Martin, P. and Hollifield, J. (eds) *Controlling Immigration: A Global Perspective*. Stanford: Stanford University Press, pp. 303–26.
Caritas di Roma (1998) *Nuova Legge sull'immigrazione: spunti di riflessione sulla legge 40/98*. Rome: Caritas di Roma.
—— (2000) 'L'immigrazione a Roma: l'esperienza della Caritas'. Extract of report in *Migrazioni: scenari per il XXI secolo, Dossier di ricerca, Vol. II*, International Convention, Rome 12–14 July 2000.
—— (2001) *Immigrazione: Dossier Statistico 2001*. Rome: Caritas.
—— (2005) *Immigrazione: Dossier Statistico 2005*. Rome: Caritas.
—— and Camera di Commercio di Roma (2005a) *Osservatorio Romano sulle Migrazioni, Primo Rapporto – 2004*. Rome: Caritas di Roma.
—— and Camera di Commercio di Roma (2005b) *Osservatorio Romano sulle Migrazioni, Secondo Rapporto – 2005* (final draft). Rome: Caritas di Roma.
Carpenter, J., Chauviré, Y. and White, P. (1994) 'Marginalization, Polarization and Planning in Paris', *Built Environment*, 20 (3): 218–30.
Castells, M. and Godard, F. (1974) *Monopolville: l'entreprise, l'Etat, l'urbain*. Paris: Mouton.
Castles, S. (1995) 'How Nation-states Respond to Immigration and Ethnic Diversity', *New Community*, 21 (3): 293–308.
—— and Miller, M. (1993) *The Age of Migration: International Population Movements in the Modern World*. New York: Guilford Press.
CESPI (Centro Studi di Politica Internazionale) (2000) 'Migrazioni e politiche locali: l'esperienza italiana nel quadro europeo', in *Migrazioni. Scenari per il XXI secolo, Dossier di ricerca, Vol. II*, International Convention, Rome 12–14 July 2000, pp. 848–948.
Chevalier, L. (1958) *Classes laborieuses, classes dangereuses*. Paris: Hachette.
Clark, W., Dieleman, F. and Klerk, L. (1992) 'School Segregation: Managed Integration or free choice?', *Environment and Planning C: Government and Policy*, 10: 91–103.
Cloke, P., Philo, C. and Sadler, D. (1991) *Approaching Human Geography: An Introduction to Contemporary Theoretical Debates*. London: Paul Chapman.
Coing, H. (1962) *Rénovation urbaine et changement sociale*. Paris: Editions Ouvrier.
Cole, R. (1999) *A Traveller's History of Paris*. Gloucestershire: Windrush Press.
Collicelli, C., Arosio, F., Sapienza, R. and Maietta, F. (1998) *City Template Rome*, MPMC. http://unesco.org/most/p97.htm.
—— (2000) *Progress Report Rome*. Report presented at the MPMC workshop, Liege, 30 October–2 November 1999.
Combiwel (Stichting Welzijn Amsterdam Oud Zuid). *Information brochure 2002–2003* (in Dutch).

Cooke, P. (1988) 'Modernity, Postmodernity and the City', *Theory, Culture and Society*, 5: 475–92.
Cornelius, W., Martin, P. and Hollifield, J. (eds) (1994) *Controlling Immigration: A Global Perspective*. Stanford, CA: Stanford University Press.
Da Roit, B. and Sabatinelli, S. (2005) 'Il modello di welfare mediterraneo tra famiglia e mercato. Come cambia la cura di anziani e bambini in Italia', *Stato e Mercato*, 2/2005.
Davis, C. (1996) *Levinas: An Introduction*. Cambridge: Polity Press.
Davis, M. (1985), 'Urban Renaissance and the Spirit of Postmodernism', *New Left Review*, 151: 106–13.
—— (1992) *City of Quartz: Excavating the Future in Los Angeles*. New York: Vintage Books.
Derder, P. (2001) *L'immigration Algérienne et les pouvoirs publics dans le département de la Seine, 1954–1962*. Paris: L'Harmattan.
DIECEC (Development of Intercultural Education through Cooperation between European Cities) (1996) *Learning from Diversity: Language Education and Intercultural Relations in the Inner City*. Report by Arturo Tosi. Brussels: Eurocities.
Dijkink, G. (1990) 'The Political Geography of Policing: The Experience of Amsterdam', *Journal of Police Science and Administration*, 17 (3): 155–62.
Doomernik, J. (1999) 'Turkse moskeeën en maatschappelijke participatie' (in Dutch: Turkish mosques and societal participation). *Nederlandse Geografische Studies*, 129: 1–194.
Dumont, M.-J. (1994) 'Du vieux Paris au Paris nouveau: abécédaire d'architecture urbaine', *Le Débat*, 80: 5–35.
ELAINE (European Local Authorities Interactive Network for Ethnic Minority Policy) (1996) *Local Authority Policies for Ethnic Minority Entrepreneurs*. Report of the ELAINE workshop, Utrecht, 27–29 June 1996. Maastricht: European Centre for Work and Society.
—— (1997a) *Celebrating Exchange: The First 12 ELAINE Workshops (1991–96)*. Maastricht: European Centre for Work and Society.
—— (1997b) 'Political Participation of Migrants and Ethnic Minorities in the Local Authority'. Preparatory draft by Hein de Haas. Maastricht: European Centre for Work and Society.
Elias, N. and Scotson, J. (1994) *The Established and the Outsiders: A Sociological Inquiry into Community Problems*, 2nd edn. London: Sage Publications.
Faist, T. (1996) 'Immigration, Integration, and the Welfare State: Germany and the USA in a Comparative Perspective', in Baubock, R., Heller, A. and Zolberg, A. (eds) *The Challenge of Diversity: Integration and Pluralism in Societies of Immigration*. European Centre Vienna/Avebury, pp. 228–57.
Favell, A. (2001) 'Integration Policy and Integration Research in Europe: A Review and Critique', in Aleinikoff, T. and Klusmeyer, D. (eds) *Citizenship Today: Global Perspectives and Practices*. Washington DC: Brookings Institution Press, pp. 249–99.

Feijter, H., Sterckx, L. and Gier, E. (2001) *Nieuw Amsterdams Peil: wonen, werken, leven in een multiculturele metropool*. SISWO Instituut voor Maatschappijwetenschappen.

Fennema, M. and Tillie, J. (2004) 'Do Immigrant Policies Matter? Ethnic Civic Communities and Immigrant Policies in Amsterdam, Liège and Zurich', in Penninx, R., Kraal, K., Martiniello, M. and Vertovec, S. (eds), *Citizenship in European Cities: Immigrants, Local Policies and Integration Policies*. Aldershot: Ashgate, pp. 85–106.

Fijalkow, Y. (1994) *Mesurer l'hygiène urbaine: logements et îlots insalubres, Paris, 1850–1945*. Unpublished PhD dissertation, Ecole des Hautes Etudes en Sciences Sociales, Paris.

—— (1998) *La construction des îlots insalubres – Paris 1850–1945*. Paris: L'Harmattan.

—— (2002) *Sociologie de la Ville*. Paris: Editions La Découverte.

—— (2004) 'Diagnostic partagé et groupes sociaux dans quatre quartiers parisiens en réhabilitation'. Presented at Congrès de l'association Française de Sociologie, February 2004.

Fijalkow, Y and Oberti, M. (2001). 'Urbanisme, embourgeoisement et mixité sociale à Paris', *Mouvements*, 13: 9–24.

Fischer, H. (1999) 'Foreign Workers: Current Situation, Formal Framework and Government Policy' (in Hebrew), in Nathanson, R. and Achdut, L. (eds) *The New Workers: Wage Earners from Foreign Countries in Israel*. Tel Aviv: Hakibbutz Hameuchad.

Foucault, M. (1965) *Madness and Civilization* (transl. Howard, R. 1988). New York: Vintage Books.

Friedmann, J. (1986) 'The World City Hypothesis', *Development and Change*, 17: 69–83.

—— and Lehrer, A. (1997) 'Urban Policy Responses to Foreign In-migration: The Case of Frankfurt-am-Main', *Journal of the American Planning Association*, 63 (1): 61–78.

Gale, R. and Naylor, S. (2002) 'Religion, Planning and the City: The Spatial Politics of Ethnic Minority Expression in British Cities and Towns', *Ethnicities*, 2 (3): 387–409.

Garbaye, R. (2000) 'Ethnic Minorities, Cities and Institutions: A Comparison of the Modes of Management of Ethnic Diversity of a French and a British City', in Koopmans, R. and Statham, P. (eds), *Challenging Immigration and Ethnic Relations Politics: Comparative European Perspectives*, Oxford: Oxford University Press, pp. 283–311.

Gaxie, D. (1999) 'Les politiques municipales d'intégration des populations d'origine étranger', *Migrations Etudes*, 86. Paris: ADRI.

——, Laborier, P., de Lassalle, M., Obradovic, I., Taiclet, A.-F. (1998) *Rapport Final de l'Enquête sur les Politiques Municipales d'Intégration des Populations d'Origine Etrangère*, Vol. 1. Université de Paris I, Département de Science Politique.

La Gazette, 'Tensions religieuses: les maires en première ligne', No. 16, 22 April 2004: 16–19.

Geisser, V. (1997) *Ethnicité Républicaine: les élites d'origine maghrébine dans le système politique française*. Paris: Presses de Sciences Po.

Ginsborg, P. (2001) *Italy and Its Discontents: Family, Civil Society, State 1980–2001*. London: Penguin.

Godard, F. (1973) *La rénovation urbaine à Paris: structure urbaine et logique de classe*. Paris: Mouton.

Grillo, R. (1985). *Ideologies and Institutions in Urban France: The Representation of Immigrants*. Cambridge: Cambridge University Press.

Gudykunst, W. (1983) 'Toward a Typology of Stranger-host Relationships', *International Journal of Intercultural Relations*, 7: 401–13.

Guillon, M. (1992) *Etrangers et immigrés en Ile-de-France*. Unpublished PhD dissertation, Université de Paris.

Hammar, T. (ed.) (1985) *European Immigration Policy: A Comparative Study*. London: Cambridge University Press.

Hargreaves, A. (1996) 'A Deviant Construction: The French Media and the "Banlieues"', *New Community*, 22 (4): 607–18.

Harvey, D. (1989) *The Condition of Postmodernity*. Oxford: Blackwell.

Haussermann, H. (1998) 'The Integration of Immigrant Populations in Berlin', in OECD, *Immigrants Integration and Cities: Exploring the Links*. Paris: OECD, pp. 137–60.

L'Histoire, 'Dossier Special: Les derniers jours de l'Algerie Française', April 1999. Paris: Societé d'editions scientifiques.

Hotline for Foreign Workers (2002) *'For You Were Strangers': Modern Slavery and Human Trafficking in Israel* (in Hebrew), Tel Aviv.

INSEE (*Institut Nationale de la Statistique et des Etudes Economiques*) (1999) *Recensement de la population de 1999*. Paris: INSEE, http://insee.fr.

Ireland, P. (1994) *The Policy Challenge of Diversity: Immigrant Politics in France and Switzerland*. Cambridge, MA: Harvard University Press.

Jackson, P. and Smith, S. (1984) *Exploring Social Geography*. London: Alan and Unwin.

Jacobs, J. (1961) *The Death and Life of Great American Cities*. New York: Random Press.

Kastoryano, R. and Crowley, J. (1999) *Paris City Template*, MPMC. http://unesco.org/most/p97.htm.

—— (2001) 'Citizenship in a Local Key: A View from Paris', in Rogers, A. and Tillie, J. (eds) (2001) *Multicultural Policies and Modes of Citizenship in European Cities*. Aldershot: Ashgate.

Keil, R. (1998) 'Globalization Makes States: Perspectives of Local Governance in the Age of the World City', *Review of International Political Economy*, 4 (4): 616–46.

Kemp, A. and Raijman, R. (2000) '"Aliens" in the Jewish state – the New Politics of Labour Migration in Israel' (in Hebrew), *Sociologia Israelit*, 3 (1): 79–110.

—— and Raijman, R. (2003) 'Foreign Workers in Israel' (in Hebrew), *Meida al Shivion*, 13: 1–30. http://adva.org.
——, Raijman, R., Resnik, J. and Gesser, S. (2000) 'Contesting the Limits of Political Participation: Latinos and Black African Migrant Workers in Israel', *Ethnic and Racial Studies*, 23 (1): 94–118.
Kesteloot, C. and Cortie, C. (1998) 'Housing Turks and Moroccans in Brussels and Amsterdam: The Difference between Private and Public Markets', *Urban Studies*, 35 (10): 1835–53.
Kloosterman, R. and Van der Leun, J. (1999) 'Just for Starters: Commercial Gentrification by Immigrant Entrepreneurs in Amsterdam and Rotterdam Neighbourhoods', *Housing Studies*, 14 (5): 659–77.
Knippenberg, H. (1992) *De religieuze kaart van Nederland*. Assen: Van Gorcum.
Korac, M. (2003) 'Integration and How We Facilitate It: A Comparative Study of the Settlement Experiences of Refugees in Italy and the Netherlands', *Sociology*, 37 (1): 51–68.
Koser, K. (1998) 'Out of the Frying Pan and into the Fire: A Case Study of Illegality amongst Asylum Seekers', in Koser, K. and Lutz, H. (eds) (1998) *The New Migration in Europe: Social Constructions and Social Realities*. London: Macmillan, pp.185–98.
Kraal, K. (2001). 'Amsterdam: From Group-specific to Problem-oriented Policy', in Rogers, A. and Tillie, J. (eds) *Multicultural Policies and Modes of Citizenship in European Cities*. Aldershot: Ashgate, pp. 15–39.
—— and Zorlu, A. (1998) *City Template Amsterdam*, MPMC, http://unesco.org/most/p97.htm.
Krupat, E. (1985) *People in Cities: The Urban Environment and its Effects*. Cambridge: Cambridge University Press.
Kymlicka, W. (1995) *Multicultural Citizenship*. Oxford: Clarendon Press.
Lacaze, J-P. (1994) *Paris, urbanisme d'Etat et destin d'une ville*. Paris: Flammarion.
Lahav, G. (1998) 'Immigration and the State: The Devolution and Privatisation of Immigration Control in the EU', *Journal of Ethnic and Migration Studies*, 24 (4): 675–94.
Landman, N. (1992) *Van mat tot minaret*. Amsterdam: VU Uitgeverij.
Laurence, J. (1999) '(Re)constructing Community in Berlin: of Jews, Turks and German Responsibility'. Berlin: Science Center for Social Research.
Le Quesne, N. (2002) 'Islam: France's Second Religion', *Time*, 12 June 2002, p. 62.
Levinas, E. (1961) *Totality and Infinity* (transl. Lingis, A. 1969). Pittsburg, PA: Duquesne University Press.
Levine, D. (1979) 'Simmel at a Distance', in Shack, W. and Skinner, E. (eds), *Strangers in African Societies*. Berkeley: University of California Press.
LIA (Local Integration/Partnership Action) (2000) *Paving the Way for Innovative Actions on Integration*. Maastricht: European Centre for Work and Society.

Lijphart, A. (1968) *The Politics of Accommodation: Pluralism and Democracy in the Netherlands*. Berkeley: University of California Press.

Lindo, F. (1999) *Heilige wijsheid in Amsterdam*. Amsterdam: Het Spinhuis.

Lipsky, M. (1980) *Street-level Bureaucracy: Dilemmas of the Individual in Public Services*. New York: Russel Sage Foundation.

Lofland, L. (1973) *A World of Strangers: Order and Action in Urban Public Space*. New York: Basic Books.

Lucan, J. (1992) 'Les points noirs des îlots insalubres', in Lucan, J. (ed.) *Eau et gaz a tous les étages: Paris 100 ans de logement*. Paris: Edition du Pavillion de l'Arsenal (Picard), pp. 76–91.

Lucassen, J. and Penninx, R. (1997) *Newcomers: Immigrants and their Descendents in the Netherlands 1550–1995*. Amsterdam: Het Spinhuis.

Mak, G. (1999) *Amsterdam – a Brief Life of the City*. London: Harvill Press.

Mamadouh, V. (2002) 'Immigration, Citizenship and the Ethnicization of Politics in the European Union: Contrasting Experiences from France and the Netherlands'. Paper prepared for the 25th Annual Applied Geography Conference, 23–26 October 2002, Binghamton, USA.

Mazzella, S. (1996) *L'enracinement urbain: intégration sociale et dynamiques urbaines*. Unpublished PhD dissertation, Ecole des Hautes Etudes en Sciences Sociales, Marseille.

McLemore, S. (1970) 'Simmel's "Stranger": A Critique of the Concept', *Pacific Sociological Review*, 13: 86–94.

Menahem, G. (1993) *Urban Economic and Spatial Restructuring and Absorption of Immigrants*. Paper presented at International workshop on immigrant absorption, Technion – Israel Institute of Technology, May 1993.

METROPOLIS, http://international.metropolis.net.

Meyer, J. (1950) 'The Stranger and the City', *American Journal of Sociology*, 56: 476–83.

Meyers, E. (2000) 'Theories of International Immigration Policy: A Comparative Analysis', *International Migration Review*, 34 (4): 1245–82.

Miles, R. (1993) *Racism after 'Race Relations'*. London: Routledge.

Ministry of Industry, Commerce and Employment, State of Israel (2004) *Interministerial Report on the Planning of the Employment System of Foreign Workers in Israel and Conditions for Permits*, August 2004, Jerusalem (in Hebrew).

Misiani, S. (1999) 'La risposta Romana all'immigrazione straniera: linee per una ricerca sulla politica capitolina (1989–1994)'. Unpublished draft.

Money, J. (1999) *Fences and Neighbors*. London: Cornell University Press.

Moore, D. (2001) *Ethnicité et Politique de la Ville en France et en Grande-Bretagne*. Paris: l'Harmattan.

MPMC (Multicultural Policies and Modes of Citizenship in European Cities). http://www.unesco.org/most/p97.htm.

Municipality of Amsterdam, Research and Statistics Bureau (1999) Department of Social, Economic and Cultural Development (Bestuursdienst MEC), General Affairs Division, *De Kracht van een Diverse Stad: Uitgangspunten*
—— (2003) *Jaarboek Amsterdam in cijfers 2002*. http://onstat.amsterdam.nl.
—— (2004) *Amsterdam leeftsamen*. Municipal brochure.
—— (2005) *Kerncijfers Amsterdam 2004*.
Municipality of Paris (1995) *Convention entre l' Etat et la Ville de Paris sur la Politique de la Ville*, 27 March 1995.
—— (2000) *Contrat de Ville*, Paris.
Municipality of Rome (2000) *Oltre l'accoglienza: il Comune di Roma per gli immigrati* (publicity brochure), Rome: Ufficio Speziale Immigrazione.
Municipality of Tel Aviv-Yafo (1999) *MESILA: Aid and Information Center for the Foreign Community in Tel Aviv-Yafo* (brochure).
—— (2000) *Principles and guiding lines for Israeli government policy on the subject of foreign workers* (in Hebrew), 25 October 2000.
—— (2001) *Strategic Plan for Florentin* (in Hebrew). Final Report, Planning Division, April 2001.
—— (2002a) *Profil Ha'ir.* Strategic Plan for Tel Aviv (in Hebrew).
—— (2002b) *Preparation for Integrated Strategic Plan for the Stations Area. Report Stage 2: Characterization and analysis of existing situation* (in Hebrew). Planning Division, March 2002.
—— (2004a) *Statistical Yearbook 2004* (in Hebrew).
—— (2004b) *Stations Area – Strategic Plan*, Planning Division/Tayar-Asif, June 2004 (in Hebrew).
Musterd, S. (2002a) 'Successful Immigration in the Netherlands?'. Paper presented at the annual meeting of the German Academy for City Planning, Frankfurt, 24–27 October 2002.
—— (2002b) 'Urban Segregation, Integration and the Welfare Regime'. Keynote lecture, Olof Palme conference, Malmö, Sweden.
—— and Deurloo, R. (2002) 'Unstable Immigrant Concentrations in Amsterdam: Spatial Segregation and Integration of Newcomers', *Housing Studies*, 17 (3): 487–503.
——, Ostendorf, W. and Breebaart, M. (1998) *Multi-Ethnic Metropolis: Patterns and Policies*. Amsterdam: Kluwer Academic Publishers.
Neymark, K. (1998) 'Immigrants, Integration and Cities: A Brief Review of the Recent Literature', in OECD, *Immigrants, Integration and Cities – Exploring the Links*. Paris: OECD, pp. 17–31.
Nijman, J. (2000) 'The Global Moment in Urban Evolution', in Deben L., Heinemeijer, W. and Van der Vaart, D. (eds) *Understanding Amsterdam*. Amsterdam: Het Spinhuis, pp. 19–58.
Nivet, P. (1992) *Le conseil municipal de Paris de 1944 a 1977*. Unpublished PhD dissertation, Université de Paris I.
—— (1994) *Le conseil municipal de Paris de 1944 a 1977*. Paris: Publications de la Sorbonne.

Palidda, S. (1998) 'The Integration of Immigrants in Changing Urban Environments: The Example of Italy', in OECD, *Immigrants, Integration and Cities: Exploring the Links*. Paris: OECD, pp. 117–34.

Park, R. and Burgess, E. (1921) *Introduction to the Science of Sociology*. Chicago: University of Chicago Press.

Penninx, R. (1979) *Ethnic Minorities: Report to the Government*. The Hague: Netherlands Scientific Council for Government Policy (WRR).

——, Kraal, K., Martiniello, M. and Vertovec, S. (eds), *Citizenship in European Cities: immigrants, Local Politics and integration Policies*. Aldershot: Ashgate.

Phalet, K. (2001) 'Minority Families and Educational Investment: Turkish Youth in Dutch Schools'. Paper presented at European Colloquium: Les jeunes issues de l'immigration turque, 25–26 October 2001, Paris.

Pinçon, M. and Pinçon-Charlot, M. (2001) *Paris Mosaïque*. Paris: Calmann-Levy.

—— (2005) 'L'embourgeoisment de Paris'. Paper presented at RC21 conference: Cities as Social Fabric, Paris, 30 June – 2 July 2005.

Pirschner, C. (2002) 'How to Approach Pluralist Societies? Usefulness and Risks of Diversity as Theoretical Concept and as Political Practice'. Final draft for MA thesis, University of Vienna, Faculty of Human and Social Sciences.

Pittau, F. (2001) 'Roma e Lazio: politiche per l'immigrazione' (draft). Archival material for *Immigrazione: Dossier Statistico 2001*. Rome: Caritas di Roma.

Poinsot, M. (2000) *CITNET (Citizens Organize Networks Against Discrimination) in Paris*. Berlin: Berliner Institut für Vergleichende Sozialforschung e.V., Edition Parabolis.

Quassoli, F. (2001) 'Neighbourhood Safety, Police Practices and Migrant Control'. Draft paper for RC21 conference, Amsterdam, 15–17 June 2001.

Racine, J.-B. and Mager, C. (1997) 'The foreigner and the city: from co-presence to interaction, in search of intercultural places in Lausanne (Switzerland)'. Paper presented to the IGU – Commission on Urban Development and Urban Life, University of Mexico, Mexico City, August 10–16, 1997.

Rath, J. (1999) 'The Netherlands: A Dutch Treat for Anti-social Families and Immigrant Ethnic Minorities', in Cole, M. and Dale, G. (eds) (1999) *The European Union and Migrant Labour*. Oxford: Berg, pp. 147–70.

—— (2000) 'A Game of Ethnic Musical Chairs? Immigrant Businesses and Niches in the Amsterdam Economy', in Body-Gendrot, S. and Martiniello, M. (eds) *Minorities in European Cities*. London: Macmillan Press.

——, Penninx, R,. Groenendijk, K. and Meyer, A. (2004) 'Making Space for Islam in the Netherlands', in Aluffi, R. and Zincone, G. (eds) *The Legal Treatment of Islamic Minorities in Europe*. Leuven: Peeters, pp. 159–78.

—— (2001) *Western Europe and its Islam*. Leiden: Brill.

Rex, J. and Samad, Y. (1996) 'Multiculturalism and Political Integration in Birmingham and Bradford', *Innovation*, 9 (1): 11–31.

Reyneri, E. (2001) 'Migrants' Involvement in Irregular Employment in the Mediterranean Countries of the European Union'. IMP Working Papers, International Labour Organization.

Rhein, C. (1998a) 'Globalisation, Social Change and Minorities in Metropolitan Paris: the Emergence of New Class Patterns', *Urban Studies*, 35 (3): 429–47.

—— (1998b) 'The Working Class, Minorities and Housing in Paris, the Rise of Fragmentations', *GeoJournal*, 46: 51–62.

Richards, C. (1995) *The New Italians*. London: Penguin.

Robinson, V., Andersson, R. and Musterd, S. (2003) *Spreading the 'Burden'? A Review of Policies to Disperse Asylum Seekers and Refugees*. Bristol: Policy Press.

Rogers, A. and Tillie, J. (eds) (2001) *Multicultural Policies and Modes of Citizenship in European Cities*. Aldershot: Ashgate.

Sartre, J. (1943) *Being and Nothingness*. New York: Washington Square Press (1966 edition).

Sassen, S. (1998) *Globalization and Its Discontents*. New York: The New Press.

Schama, S. (1997) *The Embarrassment of Riches*. New York: Random House.

Schnapper, D. (1994) *La communauté des citoyens: sur l'idée moderne de nation*. Paris: Gallimard.

Schnell, I. (1999) *Foreign Workers in Southern Tel Aviv-Yafo* (in Hebrew). Jerusalem: Florsheimer Institute for Policy Studies.

—— (2000) 'The Formation of a Migrant Workers Enclave in Tel Aviv' (in Hebrew). *Ofakim be-Geografia*, 52: 109–28.

—— (2001) *Guidelines to a Policy on the Foreign Workers in Israel* (in Hebrew). Jerusalem: Center for Social Policy Research in Israel.

—— and Alexander, M. (2002) *Municipal Policy toward Foreign Workers: Lessons from Tel Aviv-Yafo* (in Hebrew). Jerusalem: Florsheimer Institute for Policy Studies.

—— and Benjamini, Y. (2001) 'The Socio-spatial Isolation of Agents in Everyday Life Spaces as an Aspect of Segregation', *Annals of the Association of American Geographers*, 91 (4): 622–33.

Schuetz, A. (1944) 'The Stranger: An Essay in Social Psychology', *American Journal of Sociology*, 49: 499–507.

Sciortino, G. (1999) 'Planning in the Dark: The Evolution of Italian Immigration Control', in Brochmann, G. and Hammar, T. (eds) *Mechanisms of Immigration Control*, Oxford: Berg, pp. 233–60.

Sellier, L. (1937) *Rapports et documents au Conseil Municipal, 1937*, No.56 (relatif a l'amenagement des ilots insalubres), Municipality of Paris.

Short, J. (1999) 'Yuppies, Yuffies and the New Urban Order', *Transactions of the Institute of British Geographers*, 14: 173–88.

Shuval, J. and Leshem, E. (1998) 'The Sociology of Migration in Israel: A Critical View', in Leshem, E. and Shuval, J. (eds): *Studies of Israeli Society*, Vol. 8, London: Transaction Publishers.

Sibley, D. (1995) *Geographies of Exclusion: Society and Difference in the West.* London: Routledge.
Simmel, G. (1908) 'The Stranger', in Wolff, K. (transl. 1950) *The Sociology of Georg Simmel.* New York: Free Press.
Simon, P. (1994) *La société partagée: relations interethniques et interclasses dans un quartier en rénovation.* Unpublished PhD dissertation, Ecole des Hautes Etudes en Sciences Sociales, Paris.
—— (2000) 'The Mosaic Pattern: Cohabitation between Ethnic Groups in Belleville, Paris', in Body-Gendrot, S. and Martiniello, M. (eds) *Minorities in European Cities.* London: Macmillan, pp. 100–15.
Simon, P. (2002) 'When De-segregation Produces Stigmatisation: Ethnic Minorities and Urban Policies in France', in Martiniello M. and Piquart, B. (eds) *Diversity in the City.* Bilbao: University of Deusto, HumanitarianNet, pp. 61–94.
Smooha, S. (1990), 'Minority Status in an Ethnic Democracy: The Status of the Arab Minority in Israel', *Ethnic and Racial Studies,* 13: 389–413.
Soja, E. (1989) *Postmodern Geographies: The Reassertion of Space in Critical Theory.* London: Verso.
Soysal, Y. (1994) *Limits of Citizenship.* Chicago: University of Chicago Press.
Stonequist, E. (1937) *The Marginal Man.* New York: Scribner.
Tabboni, S. (1995) 'The Stranger and Modernity: From Equality of Rights to Recognition of Difference', *Thesis Eleven,* 43: 17–27.
Theunissen, M. (1984) *The Other: Studies in the Social Ontology of Husserl, Heidegger, Sartre and Buber.* Cambridge, MA: MIT Press.
Thranhardt, D. (1995) 'The Political Uses of Xenophobia in England, France and Germany', *Party Politics,* 1 (3): 323–45.
Toubon, J-C. and Messamah, K. (1990) *Centralité Immigrée: le quartier de la Goutte d'Or.* Paris: l'Harmattan.
Tribalat (1991) 'Combien sont les Français d'origine étrangere?', *Economie et Statistique,* 242: 17–29.
URBEX. www2.fmg.uva.nl/urbex/menureps.htm.
Van Amersfoort, H. (1998) 'An Analytical Framework for Migration Processes and Interventions', in Van Amersfoort, H. and Doomernik, J. (eds), *International Migrations: Processes and Interventions.* Amsterdam: Het Spuihuis, pp. 9–21.
Van Amersfoort, H. and de Klerk, L. (1984) 'The Dynamics of Immigrant Settlement: Surinamese, Turks and Moroccans in Amsterdam 1973–1983', in Glebe, G. and O'Loughlin, J. (eds) *Foreign Minorities in Continental European Cities.* Stuttgart: Franz Steiner Verlag Wiesbaden.
Van der Horst, H. (2001) *The Low Sky: Understanding the Dutch.* Schiedam: Scriptum/ Nuffic.
Van der Leun, J. (2003) *Looking for Loopholes: Processes of Incorporation of Illegal Immigrants in the Netherlands.* Amsterdam: Amsterdam University Press.

Van Heelsum, Anja (2002) 'The Relationship between Political Participation and Civic Community of Migrants in the Netherlands', *Journal of International Migration and Integration*, 3 (2): 179–99.
Vermeulen, F. (2002) 'Organisations and Community Structure: Migrant Organisations in Amsterdam 1960–1990'. Paper presented at 3rd workshop on contemporary European migration history, Erfurt, Germany, 7–9 November 2002.
Vermeulen, H. (ed.) (1997) *Immigrant Policy for a Multicultural Society*. Brussels: Migration Policy Group.
Vertovec, S. (1996) 'Berlin Multikulti: Germany, "Foreigners" and "World Openness"', *New Community*, 22 (3): 381–99.
Von Breitenstein, T. (1999) 'The Philippino Workers in Israel', in Nathanson, R. and Achdut, L. (eds) *The New Workers: Wage Earners from Foreign Countries in Israel* (in Hebrew). Tel Aviv: Hakibbutz Hameuchad.
Wagenaar, M. (1993) 'Monumental Metropolis, Airy Suburbs: Two Spatial Strategies to Solve Europe's Urban Crisis, 1850–1914', in Wagenaar, M., Cortie, C. and Dijkink, G. (eds) *Capital Cities in Europe: Vistas, Worries and Interrogations*. Amsterdam: Centrum voor Grootstedelijke Onderzoek, pp. 13–57.
—— (2001) 'Townscapes of Power', *GeoJournal*, 51: 3–13.
Waste, R. (1989) *The Ecology of City Policymaking*. Oxford: Oxford University Press.
Weil, P. (1991) *La France et ses étrangers: l'aventure d'une politique de l'immigration de 1938 à nos jours*. Paris: Gallimard.
Welz, G. (1993) 'Promoting Difference: A Case Study in Cultural Politics', *Journal of Folklore Research*, 30: 85–91.
White, P. (1993) 'Immigrants and the Social Geography of European Cities', in King, R. (ed.) *Mass Migrations in Europe*. London: Belhaven Press.
—— and Winchester, H. (1991) 'The Poor in the Inner City: Stability and Change in Two Parisian Neighborhoods', *Urban Geography*, 12 (1): 35–54.
Wihtol de Wenden, C. (1998) 'French Immigration Policy', in Van Amersfoort, H. and Doomernik, J. (eds) *International Migration*, Amsterdam: IMES, pp. 105–28.
Wintershoven (2001), *Demografisch eeuwboek Amsterdam*, Ontwikkelingen tussen 1900–2000. Amsterdam: DRO Amsterdam.
Wirth, L. (1938) 'Urbanism as a Way of Life', in Reiss, A. (ed.) *Louis Wirth on Cities and Social Life*. Chicago: University of Chicago Press.
Wolferstan, S. 'Rebirth of the Esquilino', *Wanted in Rome*, 3 October 2001, p. 11.
Wolff, K. (1950) (trans. and ed.) *The Sociology of Georg Simmel*. New York: Free Press.
Wolff, R. (1999) 'Minorities Policy in the City of Amsterdam and the Amsterdam Districts', in *Progress Report Amsterdam,* MPMC. Report presented at MPMC workshop, Liege, 30 October–2 November 1999, pp. 26–37.

Wood, M. (1934) *The Stranger: A Study in Social Relationships*. New York: Columbia University Press.

Workers Hotline, *Kav La'oved Newsletter*, Tel Aviv, May 2000 (in Hebrew).

Yiftachel, O. (1993) 'The "Ethnic Democracy" Model and Jewish-Arab Relations in Israel: Geographical, Historical and Political Angles' (in Hebrew), *Ofakim beGeografia*, 37–8: 51–9.

Zolberg. A. (2000) 'Preface', in Body-Gendrot, S. and Martiniello, M. (eds) *Minorities in European Cities*. London: Macmillan, pp. xiv–xvii.

Index

Note: bold page numbers indicate tables and figures; italic page numbers indicate boxes. Numbers in brackets preceded by *n* refer to footnotes.

advisory councils 5, 10, 10(*n*14), 48, 49, 49(*n*16), 103, 141, 163, 173, 178–9, 186, 188, 194, 201, 210
Algerian War 120, 134, 150
AMSTERDAM **3**, 15, 16(*n*19), 17, 20(*n*21), 23, 31, 153–95
   Bijlmermeer district 168–9, **170**, *171*
   'Civic integration'/'Diversity policy' *see under* policy phases
   civic organisations in 174, 175, 193 *see also under* migrants associations
   diversity in 153, 187, 208
   economy of 165, 168
   education in 106, 168, 177, 180–82, 189, *190*, 191–2, *192*, 210
   elections in 49, 173, 186, 187–8
   Far Right in 173, 173(*n*21), 182
   governance style 172–3
   host-stranger relations in 154–5, 165, *171*, 175, 181, 194, 202
   housing in 169, 174–6, 177, 184–5, *184*, 193
      policies 169, 174–6, 177
   labour market in 168, 180, 189, 191 *see also* labour market policies
   migrants in 26, 40, 165–95, **166**, *171*
      associations of 46, 50, 176–7, 179, 183–4, *184*, 188, 192–3
      distribution of 168–71, **170**
      ethnic minority councillors 173, 178–9, 188
      families of 165, 168, 175–6
      irregular/illegal 166, *171*
      Moroccan 166, **167**, 168(*n*19), 169, 176–7, 178, 179, 193–4
      numbers/composition 165–7, **166–7**
      second generation 166, 168
      Surinamese/Antillean 166, **167**, 168(*n*19), 169, 176–7, 178, 188, 193–4
      Turkish 166, **167**, 168(*n*19), 169, 174, 176–7, 178, 179, 187(*n*32), 193–4
   multiculturalism in 156–7, 163–4, 185
   municipality of 172–93
   Muslims in 31–2, 175, 182–4, 194
   pillarization in 174, 174(*n*23), 180–81, 207
   policy domains in
      Cultural-religious domain 182–4, 194
      Legal-political domain 178–9, 187–8, 194
      Socio-economic domain 179–82, 188–9, 194
      Spatial domain 184–5
   policy phases in 21, 21(*n*23), 153, 173–93, 201–3, 206, 207
      acceptance of permanence 175–8, 193–4
      'Civic Integration' policy 189–93, 194–5
      'Diversity Policy' 185–93, 194, 202, 211
      Guestworker policy **45**, 153, 174–5, 176, 193, 202, **212**, **213**
      Intercultural policy 181–2, 210, **211**, **212**
      'Minorities Policy' 40, 177–86, 194, 209
      Non-policy 173–4, 202
      Pluralist policy 17(*n*19), **43**, **44**, 153, 178–85, 194, 201, 202, 208, 209, **212**
   urban renewal in 51, 176, 184–5, **213**
   violence/protest in 21, 164, 182–3
   Welfare Division/welfare services in 179–80, 187, 188–9, 191(*n*34), 195
Antwerp **3**, 10, 16(*n*19), **44**, 47
Assimilationist response *see under* local migrant policy types/phases

asylum seekers 13(*n*18), 60, 74, 160
Athens **3**, 16(*n*19), 41, **43**, 83, 91, **211**

banlieues *see under* Paris
Barcelona 2, **3**, 16(*n*19), **43**, 47, 91, 210, **211**
Berlin **3**, **43**, **44**, **45**, 46, 47, 48(*n*12), **211**, **212**, **213**
Birmingham 2, **3**, 5, 10, 16(*n*19), **43**, **44**, 48, 51, 203, 210, **211–13**, 214
Bradford **3**, 10, **45**, **213**
Britain 2(*n*1), **3**, 6, 51
Brussels **3**, 16(*n*19), **43**, **45**, 47, 50, **211**, **213**

Caritas 60, 65, 67, 69, 71, 73
children 62, 67, 70, 76–7, 78, 82, 97, 101, 104–6, 168, **212**
see also education
Chirac, Jacques (Mayor) 130, 136–7, 139, 141, 147, 208 *see also under* Paris
cities
  development in *see* urban development/renewal
  significance of 1–2 *see also* local migrant policy, significance of
  migrant policies in *see* local migrant policy
  sociology of 26, 30–32
citizenship 8(*n*7), 9(*n*8), 49, 85, 103, 111, 141, 187–8, 201
  regimes model 8, 12, 13, 16
City Halls 20, **21**, *22*
civic rights *see* citizenship; voting rights
civic society *see* NGOs; associations (*under* migrants); civic organisations (*under* specific cities/countries)
Cologne **3**, 16(*n*19), **43**, **45**, **211**, **213**
communication/public awareness policy 6, **45**, 48, 51, 78, 82, 92, 95, 104–5, 108, 109, 136, 144, 148, 187, **213**
communitarianism 33–4, 48, 139(*n*29), 147, 163, 188, 207
cultural mediators 50, 56, 71, 75, **211**
Cultural-religious domain *see under* local migrant policy *and* specific cities

Delanoë, Bertrand (Mayor) 130, 141, 144–5, 146–8, 152, 201

deportation *see* repatriation

education 1, 4, **44**, 48, 50, 51, 70, 81, 76–7, 92, 97, 106, 141, 143, 156, 180–82, 191, **212**
  language education 9, 10(*n*14), **43**, 46, 50, 47, 74, 77, 107–8, 142, 143, 146, 151, 163, 164, 182, 190, *192*, 205, 210
elections 73, 130, 130(*n*16), 137(*n*26), 187–8, 204
  voting rights 49, 49(*n*15), 163
employers **42**, 88, 88(*nn*9, 10), 89, 98–9
ethnic
  advisory councils *see* advisory councils
  diversity 33–4, 153, 187, 208
  enclaves 5, 30, 31(*n*11), 36, **45**, 46, 51, 98, 108, 112, 138, 140, *140*, *171*, 207, **213**
  tension/violence 5, 6, 21–3, 23, 116, 118, 120, 129, 161, 162
ethnicity 1, **3–4**, 32
Europe 1
  history of labour migrants in 2, 39–40
  local migrant policies in 6, 16
  migration within **3**, 18
  national migrant policies in 7, 9
  see also specific countries
European Union 2, **4**, 49(*n*15)
exclusion 5, 28, 31, 33, 57, 119

families of migrants 2, 39, 56, 74, 91, 101
  reunification of 118, 126, 160, 162, 165
Fortuyn, Pim 163–4, 173, 182
France 2(*n*1), **3**, 116–21, 143, 146
  Algerians in 119–21, *120*
  assimilation in 17–18(*n*20), 116
  Far Right in 116, 118–19, 121, 128
  host-stranger relations in 116–18, 119, 121, 129, 139, 142
  immigration/integration policies 118–19, *120*, 139
  Politique de la ville 6, 119, 138–41, 150, 208
  protest/violence in 5, 23, 116, 118, 121
  Republicanism in 6, 116–17, 119, 139(*n*30), 147, 150
  see also Marseille; Paris
Frankfurt 2, **3**, **43**, **45**, 48(*n*12), **212**, **213**

Index

gateway cities 1, 59, 65, 116, 165, 199, 201
gentrification 127, 129, 136–8
Germany 49, 50
globalization 1, 7, 160
  of labour 20, 87
government
  local *see* local migrant policy
  national *see* national migrant policy
Greece **3**, 161(*n*14)
Guestworkers *see* labour migrants
Guestworker policy *see under* local migrant policy
Gypsies 25, 65, 70, 79, 162

Haussmann, Baron 131, 133, 151
headscarf debate 6, 121, 156
health insurance 88, 97(*n*17), 99, 104, 161
health services **43**, 46, 50, 97, 156
homelessness 65, 67, 69, 75, 97
  see also Pantanella crisis *under* Rome
host-stranger relations 1, 11–14, 15, 17, 23, 25–36, 197, 203
  hosts' attitudes in 27–32
  and local migrant policies *see under* local migrant policy
  and Otherness *see under* Otherness
  and power relations 4–5, 32, 33
  typology of 13–14, **14**, 21, 23, 25–7, 32–3, 34–5, **35**, 198
  see also under specific countries/cities
housing 1, 4, 57, 78–9, 88, 97, 161, **213**
  in policy phases/domains 46, 47, 48–9, 50, 51
  social 132–5, 156
  see also homelessness *and under* specific cities
Huldai, Ron (Mayor) 83, 96, 100–101, 103, 108–9, 110
human rights organizations 92, 95 *see also* NGOs; civic organisations (*under specific cities, countries*)
hygiene, *hygiénisme* 131–2, 133, 156

I-Other relations 23, 28–9
identity, national 8, 116 *see also in specific countries*
immigrants *see* migrants
immigration control 8(*n*7), 38

Intercultural response *see under* local migrant policy
Ireland, Patrick 1, 8–9
Irregular/illegal migrants **3** *see under specific cities, countries*
Islam *see* Muslims
Israel 20(*n*21), 83–9, 208
  Arab Israelis in 85(*n*), 86, **87**, 89
  dual labour market in 86–9, **87**
  as ethnocracy 84, 88
  Guestworker policy in 87–9, 98–9
  host-stranger relations in 84–6
  irregular/illegal migrants in 87, 89
    deportation of 86, 87(*n*8), 90–91, 92, 102, 103, 109
  Jewish migration to 84–5, 89(*n*11)
  NGOs/human rights groups in 92, 95, 107
  Palestinians in 83–4, 85–6, 85(*n*4), 87, **87**, 89
  see also Tel Aviv
Italy **3**, 49(*n*15), 208
  anti-immigration parties in 57, 72
  host-stranger relations in 56–8
  labour migrants in 56–9
  irregular/illegal 57–8
  legislation on migration 58–9, 58(*n*7), 65–6, 68(*n*19), 70
  amnesties/regularization 57(*n*4), 58, 58(*n*7), 59
  see also Rome

Jews 25, 26(*n*5), 56, 100, 132, 165

labour market 4, 11, 64, 76, 86–7, *87*, 90, 159, 168
  policies 11, **44**, 47–8, 50, 70, 74, 75–6, 80, 142 (*n*32), 163, 177, 180, 189, *191*, 194, **212**
labour migrants 2–4, **3**, 18–19, 39, 122
  irregular/illegal **43**, 46, 57–8
  local responses to 4–6, 12, 38–40
  in organizations **43**, 46, 49 *see also* migrants associations
  as Strangers 2–4, *see also* Otherness
  temporary status of 83–4, 85–6, 89, 95, 99, 103, 110–11, 204
  see also migrants

language education *see* education
Legal-political domain *see under* local migrant policy *and* specific cities
Leicester **44**, 50, **212**
Levinas, Emanuel 28, 29, 33, 112
Liege **3**, 10, 16(*n*19), **43**, **211**
Lille **3**, **43**, **44**, **211**, **212**
Lisbon (Oeiras) **3**, 16(*n*19), **43**, 50, 83, **211**
local government **19**, 20, *22*
  see also municipality *under specific cities*
local migrant policy 1, 5–7, 197–8, 203–9
  defined 37–8
  delegation/outsourcing of **43**, 49 (*n*17), 50, 55, 59, 65 (*n*14), 70–71, 73, 75, 81–2, 142, 146, 161, 179, 184, 188, 190, 194, 199, 208, **211**
  domains/issue areas **42–5**, 48–52, 49(*n*14), 205
    Cultural-religious 41, **42**, **44–5**, 48, 51, **212**
    Legal-political 41, **42**, **43**, 48, 49, **211**
    Socio-economic 41, **42**, **43–4**, 48, 50, **211–12**, 214
    Spatial 41, **42**, **45**, 48–9, 51–2, **213**
    see also under policy domains *in specific cities*
  future research on 214–16
    and host-stranger relations 12–13, 17, 27, 32–6, **35**, 37–53, 205–8
    and national policy 6–7, 15–16, 65–6, 208–9
  significance of 6–7
  studies of and criticism 7–8, 9–12, 14–23
  trajectories/transition 203–4
  types/phases of
    Assimilationist 13, 17, 23, 33, 35, **42–5**, 46–7, 51, 198, 203
    Guestworker 2, 13, 17, 39, **42–5**, 46, 53, 83, 198, 203
    Intercultural 210–14, 215–16
    Non-policy 13, 17, 20(*n*23), 38, 39–46, 41–6, **42–5**, 198, 203
    Pluralist 5, 13, 17, 21–3, 29, **42–5**, 47–8, 198, 203, 210, 214

  typology of 12–14, **14**, 15, 17–18, 21, 40–53, 41–8, **42–5**, 203, 204, 209–10, **211–13**
  potential/limitation of 52–3
  see also municipality *under specific cities*

Marseille **3**, 5, 10, 16(*n*19), 17–18(*n*19), 127
  migrant policies in **44**, **45**, 52(*n*23), 143, 144, **212**, **213**
media campaigns *see* communication policy
migrant policy *see* local migrant policy *and* national migrant policy
migrants 2(*n*1)
  associations **43**, 46, 49, 210, **211**
    see also under specific cities
  children *see* children
  councils *see* advisory councils
  economic *see* labour migrants
  enclaves *see* ethnic enclaves
  from Africa **3**, 18, **19**, 23, 61, 89, 91, 111, 122, **124**, 125(*n*12), 158, 166(*n*18)
  from Algeria 3, 19, 40, 118, 119–21, 122, 124
  from Balkans 2, 57, 60, 70(*n*22), 122, 156(*n*4), 161(*n*14)
  from Caribbean **3**, 157, 158, 159, 160, 166, **167**, 169, 171
  from China 3, 19, 60, 90, 122, 124
  from eastern Europe **3**, **19**, 57, 60–62, 70(*n*22), 90, 91, 98, 122
  from Egypt **3**, 59, 60, 89
  from European Union **3**, **19**, **61**, 166(*n*18)
  from Morocco **3**, **19**, 79, **124**, 158, 160, 161(*n*14), 162, 164, 169
  from Philippines **3**, **19**, 59, 59(*n*9), 60, 62, 90, 92
  from Russia/former Soviet Union 85, 91, **91**
  from South America **3**, 18, **19**, 60, **61**, 89, 107–8, 111
  from Southeast Asia 18, **19**, **91**, 122, 159
  from southern Europe (Italy, Portugal, Spain) 2, **3**, **19**, 118, 122, **124**, 159–60, 162, 165, **167**
  from Turkey 2, **3**, 90, 158, 160, 162, 164, 166, **167**, 169

geographical concentration of 2, 9, 30–32
postcolonial 39–40, 154, 157–9, 160–61
second generation 5, 18, 23
see also 'new migration' *and under specific cities/countries*
Milan **3**, 16(*n*19), 56, 59(*n*8)
Milo, Ron (Mayor) 96, 98–9, 100, 108
modernism/postmodernism 27–8, 27(*n*6), 30, 33–4, **35**, 151
Montreuil 7(*n*6), 143
mosques 31–2, **45**, 47, 144, 163, 183–4 *184*
multiculturalism 6, 34, 51, 59, 78, 81, 106, 156–7, 163–4
Muslims 64, 121, 144, 151, 157(*n*7)
  local policies toward 6, 10, 51(*n*21), 182–4, 210
  see also mosques; *and see under* Amsterdam
myth of return *see* return, myth of

national migrant policy
  defining immigration/immigrant policy 8(*n*7)
  and local policy 6–7, 15–16, 40, 65–6, 208–9
  theories of/problem with 7–9
Netherlands 2(*n*1), **3**, 50, 51, 208
  colonial legacy in 154, 157–9, 160–61
  education in 156–7, 163
  host-stranger relations in 153–8, 160–64
  immigration flows in 159–60, 163
  migrants in 154–65
    second generation 161, 162
    Surinamese and Antillean 158, 159, 160, 162
  'pillarization' in 153, 155, 163
  migrant policies in 155–64
  policy phases in
    Assimilationist 159, 164–5
    Guestworker 159–60, 161–2
    Pluralist, and reaction to 162–5
  political parties in 155, 155(*n*3), 164
  post-colonial migrant policies in 159–61
  racism in 158–9, 163
  refugees/asylum seekers in 160, 162
  religion in 154, 156, 158–9, 161
  violence/protest in 161, 162

  see also Amsterdam
'new immigration' cities 2, 39, 55, 60, 83, 91, 198, 210, 214
  see also Rome, Tel Aviv
'new migration' 39(*n*6), 160 *see also* 'new immigration' cities
NGOs **42**, 55, 90, 142–3 *see also* civic *and* migrant organisations *in specific cities*
Non-policy response *see under* local migrant policy

Oeiras *see* Lisbon
Otherness 1, 4, 12, 13, 46, 47, 106, 151, 157
  exploitation of 112, 136
  in host-stranger relations 25–7, 28–30, 31–2, 35–6, **45**, 85, 155–6
  positive potential of 47–8, 155

Palestinians 26, 60, 83–4, 85–6, 89, 107, 111
PARIS **3**, 15, 16(*n*19), 17, 50
  banlieues 115–16, 127, 139, 139(*n*30), 201, 207
  Belleville district 127, 129, 137, 138, 151
  Chirac/Tiberi administrations 136–41, 150 *see also* Chirac
  Citizenship Council 147–9, 151, 152
  civic organisations in 142–3
  class in 115, 117, 122, 125, 126, 131, 132–5, 149
  Delanoë administration *see* Delanoë
  'eastern crescent'/*croissant populaire* 125, **125,** 137–8, *138*, 151
  education in 143, 146, 151
  elections in 130, 130(*n*16), 137(*n*26)
  gentrification in 127, 129, 133, 136–8, 140–41, 149, 151, 207
  Goutte d'Or district 29, 125, 127, 139–40, *140*, 142, 151
  host-stranger relations in 127–9, 135–6, 151, 206
  housing in 126, 127, 131, 132–5, 137
    policies *see under* housing policies
  labour market policies *see under* labour market policies

migrants in 115–52
  Algerian 40, 119–21, *120*, **124**, 125, 129, 134, 207
  associations of 142, 143
  citizenship for 141, 147–9, 151–2, 201
  composition of 123–5, **124**
  distribution of 115–16, 125–7, **128**
  history of 121–9, **121**, **123**
  irregular/illegal 122, 136
  Muslims in 144, 151
  number of 122–3
  second-generation 123, 123(n11), 125, 129, 150, 151
  socio-economic categories of 126–7
municipality and central government 115, 119, 129–30, 208, 209
planning agency (APUR) 136, 145–6
policy domains in
  Cultural-religious domain 143–4, 149, 151
  Legal-political domain 141–2, 144, 147–9
  Socio-economic domain 142–3, 146–7
  Spatial domain 130–41, 149–51
policy phases in 21(n23), 130–41, 203–4
  Assimilationist **43**, **44**, **45**, 47, 115, 135–6, 139, 141, 142, 150, 151, 200–201, 207, **212**
  'Integration policy' 116, 144–9, 201
social services policy 146–7
urban development in 116, 131–8, **133**, 150, 200–201
violence/protests in 23, 116, 117–18, 120, 121, 128, 129, 150–51
welfare policy 142–3
see also Politique de la Ville
Pluralist response *see under* local migrant policy
police/policing 10, **44**, 50, 50(n20), 91(n13), 92, 118, *120*, 129, 129(n15), 136, 172, 193, **212**
Politique de la Ville (Pdlv) 6, 119, 138–41, 149, 152, 208
postmodernism *see* modernism/postmodernism

reception centres 73–5
refugees 13(n18), 39, 57, 74, 122, 160

religion 1, **44**, 51, 118, **212**
  in host-stranger relations 32, 48, 85, 86, 106–7, 108, 112, 214
repatriation/deportation 18, 33, 83, 86, 88, 88(n9)
return, myth of 2, 46, 83, 85–6, 89, 95, 99, 103, 110–11, 161–2
ROME 3, 6, 15, 16(n19), 17, 23, 55–82, 91
  asylum seekers/refugees in 74–5
  civic rights/status in 49, 71
  civic/religious organisations in 55, 59, 62, 64–5, 67–8, 71, 73, 75, 76–7, 80, 81–2, 198
  education 62, 68, 69–70, 76–7, 80
  Esquilino district 29, **63**, *64*, 78(n31)
  host-stranger relations in 63–5
  housing in 50, 63–4, 73, 78–9, 82, **213**
    see also Pantanella crisis
  Immigration Office (USI) 69–75, 81–2
  integration service 75–6
  mayors 66, 68, 69 *see also* Rutelli, Francesco *and* Veltroni, Walter
  migrants in 18, **19**, 55–6, 59–82, 206, 207
    associations of 71–2, 73, 76, 81
    children of 62, 76–7, 82
    composition of 59–62, **61**
    cultural integration of 77–8
    cultural mediators for 56, 71, 75
    distribution of 62, **63**
    irregular/transient 59–60, 80, 206
    labour 60–62, 65, 74
  municipality 65–6, 67–8, 72(n27), 81–2, 199, 208
  Pantanella crisis 6, 55, 57, 58, 62, 65, 68–9, 70, 71, 79, 80–81, 199
  policy domains in
    Cultural-religious 76–8, 82
    Legal-political 71–3, 81
    Socio-economic 68, 70, 73–6, 81–2
    Spatial 78–9, 82
  policy phases in 55–6, 67–82, 198–9, 203, 204
    Non-policy 17(n19), 20(nn22, 23), 41, **44**, **45**, 55, 67–8, 80, 198–9, **212**, **213**
    Pluralist ('Integration policy') **43**, 55, 76–8, 81, 82, 208, 209
  reception centres 73–5, 82

violence/protest in 63–4 *see also* Pantanella crisis
Rotterdam **3**, 10, **44**, 48, 164, 175
Rutelli, Francesco (Mayor) 1, 55, 66, 70, 71, 76, 80–81

St Denis 116(*n*2), 119
Sartre, Jean Paul 28, 29, 32
second generation *see under* migrants *and specific cities*
segregation 30–32 *see also* Spatial domain
Sheffield **3**, 48
Simmel, Georg 25, 26–7, 26(*n*5)
social services **43**, 50, 72, **211** *see also under specific cities*, Socio-economic domain
Socio-economic policies/domain *see under* local migrant policy *and* specific cities
Spatial policies/domain *see under* local migrant policy *and* specific cities
squatting 6, 55, 58, 62, 78–9, 79(*n*32) *see also* Pantanella crisis *under* Rome
Stockholm **3**, 16(*n*19), 49, 51
Strangers 25–36, 117, 206–7
  Otherness of 27, 28–30
  pervasiveness/spatial separation of 27, 30–32, 33, 35
  temporality of 27–8
  see also host-stranger relations
Stuttgart **3**, **43**, 50, 203, **211**, **212**, 214
Sweden 2(*n*1), **3**
Switzerland **3**, 9

TEL AVIV **3**, 7(*n*5), 13, 16, 17, 20(*n*21), 23, 50, 83–113, 199–200
  civic/human rights organisations in 95, 102, 105, 108, 112
  cultural policy 107–8
  education in 97, 104–6, 107–8
  health services in 97, 98, 103, 104
  host-stranger relations in 84, 95–6, 100, 108, 206
  housing in 95, 97
  Huldai administration *see* Huldai, Ron
  Jaffa 89, 92, 106–7
  labour migrants in **19**, 89–113, **90**
    associations of 46, 91–2, 103–4
    children of 92, 97, 101, 103, 104–6
    composition of 89–90, **91**, 111
    distribution of 92, *93*, **94**, 108–9
    history of 83–4, 89–92
    irregular/illegal 84, 89–91, 97, 102, 107, 200
    temporary status of 83–4, 85–6, 89, 95, 99, 103, 110–11, 206
    work permits for 87–8, 102
  Mesila (Aid and Information Center) 101–5, 107–8, 110, 111–12, 207
  Milo administration *see* Milo, Ron
  municipality 84, 98–106, 207–8
    and national policy 99, 102, 103, 107, 208–9
    Welfare Division 98–101
  Neve Sha'anan district 92, *93*, **94**, 95, 109
  policy domains in
    Cultural-religious 106–8, 112
    Legal-political 49, 102–4, 111
    Socio-economic 104–6, 111–12
    Spatial 108–9, 112
  policy phases in 84, 96–110, 204
    Guestworker 17(*n*19), **43**, **44**, **45**, 83–4, 98–109, 110, 111, 112, 199–200, 210, **211–13**
    Non-policy **44**, 96–8, 107, 110, 199, **212**
    Pluralist **43**, 112–13
  religious issues in 106–7, 108, 112
terrorism 21, 121, 182 *see also* violence *under* Paris, Amsterdam
trade unions 67, 75
Turin **3**, 16(*n*19), 18, **43**, 49(*n*15), 59(*n*8), 210, **212**

unemployment 6, 168, 180
urban development/renewal 4, 31, 39, **45**, 47, 48–9, 109, 112, 131–6, 206, **213**
Utrecht **3**, 10, **44**, **45**, 48(*n*13), **212**, **213**

Veltroni, Walter (Mayor) 66, 69, 70, 72, 81
'veteran immigration' cities 2, 18, 123, 198, 210, 214 *see also* Amsterdam; Paris
violence *see* ethnic tension/violence *and* violence/protest *under* specific cities/countries
voting rights 49, 49(*n*15), 163

welfare services/poverty relief 4, 12, **43**, 46, 50, 89, 156
'white flight' 5, 29, 32, 181
women 78, 143, 147, 184, 191
working class 115, 117, 122, **125**, **126**, 131, 132

xenophobia 5, 29, 32, *64*, 65, 96, 108

Yafo *see* Jaffa *under* Tel Aviv

Zurich **3**, 16(*n*19), **44**, **211**

For Product Safety Concerns and Information please contact our EU
representative GPSR@taylorandfrancis.com
Taylor & Francis Verlag GmbH, Kaufingerstraße 24, 80331 München, Germany

www.ingramcontent.com/pod-product-compliance
Lightning Source LLC
Chambersburg PA
CBHW071351290426
44108CB00014B/1500